THE VILLA D'ESTE AT TIVOLI

PRINCETON MONOGRAPHS

IN ART AND ARCHAEOLOGY

XXXIV

BARR FERREE FOUNDATION

PUBLISHED FOR THE

DEPARTMENT OF ART AND ARCHAEOLOGY

PRINCETON UNIVERSITY

THE VILLA D'ESTE
AT TIVOLI

BY DAVID R. COFFIN

PRINCETON, NEW JERSEY

PRINCETON UNIVERSITY PRESS

1960

PRINTED IN THE UNITED STATES OF AMERICA
BY PRINCETON UNIVERSITY PRESS AT PRINCETON, N.J.
OFFSET PLATES BY THE MERIDEN GRAVURE COMPANY,
MERIDEN, CONNECTICUT

TO MY MOTHER AND MY FATHER

PREFACE

DURING the middle of the sixteenth century one of the greatest private art patrons was Ippolito II d'Este, the Cardinal of Ferrara, but little except inventories and descriptions remains today to prove this patronage. His notable collections of art objects are scattered among the galleries of Europe or lost. Even his architectural possessions have been destroyed or drastically altered. His casino at Fontainebleau, a masterpiece of Serlio, is known only from prints. His villa in Rome on the Quirinal is completely transformed, and its gardens have disappeared. The same is true of the palace of Monte Giordano in Rome. Yet there is one impressive exception, the Cardinal's Villa and lavish gardens at Tivoli. Although there have been changes, the gardens remain in form and decoration much as the Cardinal created them, including the wonderful waterworks which amazed his contemporaries and intrigued later generations. The interior fresco decoration, despite repeated retouching, is preserved almost intact. Although the Tiburtine villa was merely his summer villa to be occupied only a month or two each year when he was in Rome, it is here that one can best see fulfilled the lavish patronage of the Cardinal.

There has never been a thorough study of the Villa d'Este from an art-historical point of view, but two very important studies contribute much to our knowledge of the Villa and gardens and have been of inestimable value to me. Seni's book (1902) contains many of the fundamental documents concerning the history of the building and gardens, but Seni knew primarily only the documents at the Archivio di Stato of Modena, which are filed under the building and gardening accounts of Tivoli. His work was also limited solely to a documentary history of the Villa with no analysis of it in terms of the history of art. The local Tiburtine historian Vincenzo Pacifici made the most significant contributions to our knowledge of the Cardinal's Villa in his biographies of Cardinal Ippolito II and Cardinal Luigi d'Este. Pacifici had been through the registers of Cardinal Ippolito II and presents a summary of them, but his interest is not completely in the Villa *per se* but, of course, in the lives of the Cardinals.

I am well aware that my own study is not definitive. At least two important aspects cannot be treated with certainty. First is the positive identification of the creator of the gardens and the source of their symbolism. This I suspect can never be surely ascertained. Second is the tantalizing problem of the fresco decoration. The archives preserve almost all the names of the artists, even to the *garzoni*, and most of the decoration is still well preserved, but at the moment it is very difficult to correlate the documents and the work. I have generally attempted only to identify the sections of the interior decoration in relation to the large workshops under the guidance of the various chief masters, such as Muziano, Federigo Zuccaro, Nebbia, and Agresti. It is obvious that in the frescoes created by each of these workshops there are many different hands at work, but I find it impossible at our present level of knowledge of mid-sixteenth century painting to attempt to identify the various hands in terms of the names in the documents. Except for the chief masters, who probably painted very little themselves at Tivoli, the other artists are now only names, some identifiable merely from other archival references, others completely unknown. As more knowledge of mid-sixteenth century Roman painting develops, this aspect of the Villa d'Este may be further clarified.

It was in a seminar on Renaissance art given at Princeton in the fall of 1945 by Dr. Erwin Panofsky of the Institute for Advanced Study that I became interested in the person and art of Pirro Ligorio, from which this study of the Villa d'Este derives. Dr. Panofsky has encouraged me ever since in my study of Ligorio, and it is obvious in this work that I am much indebted to his approach to the history of art. The principal impetus to my study of Ligorio, and consequently the Villa d'Este, was given by the award of a Fulbright grant for research in Italy for the academic year 1951-1952. During that time the Director of the American Academy at Rome, Mr. Laurence Roberts, his librarians, and other members of his staff were extremely kind in permitting me to use all the facilities of the Academy and in aiding my studies.

I have also been greatly aided by research grants from the Spears Fund of the Princeton Department of Art and Archaeology and from the University Research Fund of Princeton University. My colleagues in the Department of Art and Archaeology at Princeton were a constant source of encouragement and help, but, in particular, Professors Donald D. Egbert and Erik Sjöqvist were very generous in reading my manuscript and in making numerous useful suggestions regarding expression and organization, and Professor Robert A. Koch in calling to my attention the Ligorio manuscript in the Morgan Library, to which my fourth chapter is devoted. I am particularly indebted to Miss Harriet Anderson of the Princeton University Press for her care in editing my manuscript.

The noble purpose of the Fulbright grants to promote cultural interchange between Italy and the United States was certainly enhanced by the courtesy and helpfulness of all the Italian scholars with whom I came in contact during my Fulbright year in Italy or later. In particular, thanks are due to the directors and staffs of the following institutions: the Biblioteca Apostolica Vaticana in Vatican City; the Archivio di Stato and the Biblioteca Vittorio Emanuele in Rome; the Biblioteca Nazionale in Naples; the Archivio di Stato in Florence; the Archivio di Stato in Turin; and the Archivio di Stato and the Biblioteca Estense in Modena.

One Italian scholar, Dr. G. B. Pascucci, Director of the Archivio di Stato at Modena, was especially generous and kind in his assistance, which went far beyond the duties of his office.

I have received similar treatment and aid in other countries and at home: in the Bibliothèque Nationale and the Bibliothèque de l'Arsenal in Paris; the British Museum in London; and the Pierpont Morgan Library and the Department of Prints and Drawings of the Metropolitan Museum of Art in New York City.

Finally a great debt is owed my wife for both her moral and physical aid during the years devoted to this study. Anyone who has spent a winter in Italy walking and standing on the marble pavements of Italian archives and libraries will understand how loyal is the support of one who, with an intense dislike of the slightest cold, accompanied me through all my work.

Princeton, N.J.
August 17, 1959

CONTENTS

ILLUSTRATIONS

ILLUSTRATIONS

67-70. ROOM OF NOBILITY

67. Southwest Wall
68. Opposite Wall
69. Fresco of Personification of Nobility
70. Corner of Cove with Cardinal's *Impresa* (GFN C 5046)

71-75. ROOM OF GLORY

71. Detail Showing Illusionistic Painting
72. Ceiling and Cove (GFN C 5047)
73. Fresco of Allegory of Tempus
74. Fresco of Allegory of Fortuna
75. Fresco of Allegory of Religio

76-79. FIRST TIBURTINE ROOM

76. Fresco of Landing of Catillus (GFN E 28683)
77. Detail Showing Illusionistic Painting
78. Fresco of the Founding of Tivoli
79. Fresco of Hercules Saxanus

80-85. SECOND TIBURTINE ROOM

80. Fresco of Apollo the Sun-god
81. Northeast Wall Showing Illusionistic Painting
82. Fresco of the Madness of Athamas
83. Fresco of the Drowning of King Anio (GFN E 28684)
84. Fresco of Venus
85. Fresco of Worship of the Tiburtine Sibyl

86-89.

86. Room of Noah, Fresco of the Sacrifice of Noah
87. Room of Noah with Antique Landscape Frescoes
88. Room of Moses, Fresco of Landscape
89. Room of Moses, Fresco of Moses Striking the Rock

90-105. LIGORIO, MORGAN MS M.A. 542

90. Battle of the Greeks and Amazons
91. Marriage of Theseus and Hippolita
92. Birth of Hippolytus
93. Education of Hippolytus
94. Hippolytus the Horsetamer
95. Phaedra Spying on Hippolytus
96. Hippolytus Initiated into the Eleusinian Mysteries
97. The Attempted Seduction of Hippolytus
98. The Curse of Theseus
99. The Suicide of Phaedra

ILLUSTRATIONS

TEXT FIGURES

SOURCES OF ILLUSTRATIONS

Metropolitan Museum of Art (Whittlesey Fund), N.Y.: Figs. 1 and 135; Pierpont Morgan Library, N.Y.: Figs. 90-105; Wallace Collection, London: Fig. 137; Ashmolean Museum, Oxford: Figs. 107-110; Alinari, Florence: Fig. 22; Cav. U. Orlandini, Modena: Fig. 40; Comm. G. Albucci, Rome: Figs. 25, 32, 39, 58, 61-62, 64-65, 67-69, 71, 73-75, 77-82, 84-87, 89; and Gabinetto Fotografico Nazionale, Rome: Figs. 3-5, 7-13, 17, 19, 20, 26-28, 30, 31, 35-37, 41-57, 59-60, 63, 66, 70, 72, 76, 83, 106, 112, 114, 116, 134.

THE VILLA D'ESTE AT TIVOLI

ABBREVIATIONS

ASM = Archivio di Stato, Modena:
    Ambasciatori, Roma = Cancelleria Ducale, Estero:
        Ambasciatori, agenti e corrispondenti Estensi:
        Italia: Roma
    Fab. e Vill. = Camera Ducale: Fabbriche e Villegiature:
        Tivoli
    Registri = Camera Ducale: Casa Amministrazione:
        Registri del Cardinale Ippolito II d'Este
    Registri del Card. Alessandro d'Este = Camera Ducale:
        Casa Amministrazione: Registri del Cardinale
        Alessandro d'Este
    Registri del Card. Luigi d'Este = Camera Ducale: Casa
        Amministrazione: Registri del Cardinale
        Luigi d'Este
    Registri del Card. Rinaldo I d'Este = Camera Ducale:
        Casa Amministrazione: Registri del Cardinale
        Rinaldo I d'Este
ASR = Archivio di Stato, Rome:
    CF = Camerale I Fabbriche
AST = Archivio di Stato, Turin

Note: In the publication of documents many of the abbreviation signs have had to be omitted, but the spelling has been kept in a form as close to the original as possible.

CHAPTER I · EARLY HISTORY
OF THE VILLA

ON SEPTEMBER 9, 1550, the people of Tivoli greeted their new governor Ippolito II d'Este, the Cardinal of Ferrara, with a magnificent triumphal procession. A carefully selected cavalcade of one hundred gentlemen, serving as escort, met him about four miles from the city; and as he entered the Porta di Santa Croce to the thunder of artillery from the old citadel, one hundred boys bearing palms received him in front of a festive triumphal arch decorated with the coats of arms of the Pope, the Cardinal, and the community of Tivoli. From a pilaster erected for the occasion near the gateway a citizen clad in armor as Tiburtus, the legendary founder of Tivoli, recited verses in praise of the new governor. Within the city the Cardinal was welcomed not only by the local magistrate and bishop but by a triumphal chariot drawn by Moorish slaves.[1]

The Cardinal of Ferrara had received the governorship of Tivoli as a result of the recent papal conclave. This conclave, which had assembled on November 29, 1549, following the death of Pope Paul III, brought into open conflict the interests of three groups of cardinals: the Imperial party supporting Cardinal Pole, the French faction led by the Cardinal of Ferrara, and the Farnese appointees. The long and futile stalemate among the three factions was finally broken by the proposal of a compromise candidate, Giovan Maria Cardinal del Monte, who was immediately supported by the Cardinal of Ferrara. Within a month after his election the new Pope, Julius III, expressed his gratitude to the Cardinal of Ferrara, by appointing him governor for life of the nearby city of Tivoli, which had been a country retreat for inhabitants of the city of Rome since ancient times.

Because of the turbulent nature of the Tiburtines, the governorship of Tivoli was often an uncomfortable appointment. In fact, Alessandro Cardinal Farnese, nephew of Pope Paul III, had earlier renounced the honor for this very reason. The Cardinal of Ferrara, however, as revealed later in his somewhat highhanded treatment of the Tiburtines, was not a man to be easily daunted. Ippolito II d'Este (1509-1572) was the son of Alfonso I d'Este, the third Duke of Ferrara, and of Lucrezia Borgia, daughter of Pope Alexander VI. The Estes, who had been rulers of Ferrara since 1393, prided themselves on being one of Italy's oldest ruling families in direct descent—the Medici of Florence, who had received the title of duke as recently as 1532, were merely bourgeois upstarts in the eyes of the Ferrarese rulers. Not only were the Estes proud of their family prestige but of the city of Ferrara, which through their endeavors in the fifteenth and early sixteenth centuries had become one of the great centers of humanism and

---

[1] A sixteenth century account of the entry is preserved in *Annali e memorie di Tivoli di Giovanni Maria Zappi* (Studi e fonti per la storia della regione tiburtina, 1), ed. by V. Pacifici, Tivoli, 1920, pp. 31-32.

art in Italy. The alliance of such a family with the Borgias, two of whom had been elected pope during the fifteenth century, could scarcely have failed to produce an heir with the highest belief in his right to rule and to patronize. But as second son he was, of course, not destined to rule Ferrara. Like most of the second sons of the Este family his fortune was the Church and the Chair of Saint Peter his ultimate goal.

However, his obvious desire to be pope, together with his ostentation and pride, kept him from it. The ambassador to Rome of the rival family of the Medici at Florence observed: "The Cardinal of Ferrara is a very splendid and most noble lord, and for family, richness, and partisanship there is perhaps none his equal in this College. However, there are not lacking those who accuse him of wishing to show too much pride."[2] In the same vein later the Venetian ambassador reported: "He is esteemed the wisest and most experienced of all the cardinals; he is endowed with a patience so incredible in all things, that his like is unknown, but two things damage him, one is that he is born too great, the other is the excessive desire that he has shown at one time or another to be exalted to the pontificate, whereby men are easily persuaded to believe that he has too high designs in mind."[3] The Cardinal exerted all his efforts during five successive conclaves to be elected, using to the full his great resources of money, political power, and family prestige. During the first of these conclaves, which elected Julius III, he must have been full of confidence; for the Ferrarese ambassador reported to the Cardinal's brother that the palace of Monte Giordano, to which Ippolito returned with his party after the defeat, was newly decorated as if that "of a pope and not a cardinal."[4]

Although the Cardinal of Ferrara failed to achieve his goal he had at least the pleasure of trying to emulate pontifical splendor in his life and surroundings. Actually the Cardinal was born too late for complete success. Most of his active life was spent during the early phase of the Counter-Reformation when luxury, humanism, and even art were suspect at the papal court. If, as has been said, Julius III was the last of the Renaissance popes, then Ippolito II d'Este was the last of the Renaissance cardinals. Perhaps only Alessandro Cardinal Farnese could compete with him. This decline of worldly values is reflected in a letter written in 1568, reporting the complaints of a former Vatican architect and one time archaeologist to the Cardinal of Ferrara. The letter was written by a Ferrarese agent in behalf of Pirro Ligorio, who was interested at this time in obtaining the appointment as private archaeologist to the Cardinal's nephew, the Duke of Ferrara: "Now only those are esteemed and honored who under a pretext of continence and humility promote the greater part of their interests not only without spending but also without sponsoring persons of worth and intellect such as he [Ligorio]. Now that our Cardinal [i.e. the Cardinal of Ferrara] and the Farnese [Cardinal] are gone, one could see well that there was no one who had the means much

---

[2] V. Pacifici, *Ippolito II d'Este, Cardinale di Ferrara*, Tivoli, n.d., p. 120 n. 4.

[3] E. Albèri, *Le relazioni degli ambasciatori veneti al senato*, x, Florence, 1857, p. 143.

[4] V. Pacifici, *op.cit.*, p. 112 n. 3.

less the desire to spend money, so that this court [i.e. the papal court] has been reduced to such extremity that men of his kind must find their living and fortune elsewhere."[5]

The munificence of the Cardinal of Ferrara was particularly evident in his patronage of the arts. Benvenuto Cellini was his goldsmith, designing masterpieces for the Cardinal's own table and luxurious gifts for other princes and nobles; Girolamo da Carpi, Girolamo Muziano, Federigo Zuccaro, Livio Agresti, and Titian painted for him; Palestrina was the most famous musician he employed; the poets Ariosto and Tasso both dwelt at times in his household. He revealed his interest in the arts not only by his patronage of contemporary artists, but like most Renaissance princes he gathered together great collections of ancient Roman sculpture and other art objects, which were used to decorate his residences. During the excavations at Tivoli and Rome for ancient art and inscriptions, he employed as his private archaeologist one of the leading archaeologists of the time, Pirro Ligorio, mentioned above.

Wherever he lived the Cardinal had to have a proper residence for his splendid court. In his native town of Ferrara he owned the pleasure house of Belfiore, the Palazzo di San Francesco, and held part interest in the Palazzo del Paradiso. For his numerous visits to France, where he served as Papal Legate, Ippolito employed the Italian architect Sebastiano Serlio to build him at Fontainebleau a very charming small palace or casino. He likewise endowed new buildings at the Abbey of Chaalis in France, one of the numerous benefices that provided the wealth necessary for the Cardinal's luxurious life. As a prince of the Church, however, his greatest building efforts were expended on Rome and its neighborhood. Within the older part of the city he rented for life the Palazzo di Monte Giordano and drove the artists day and night to complete decorations of such lavishness that they amazed even the Romans. In the more salubrious region of the Quirinal Hill at Rome, he also rented for the remainder of his life a villa on Monte Cavallo near the ancient statues of the Dioscuri, from whose steeds the hill had received its name. The Cardinal immediately embellished the villa in his usual fashion, and later, from 1550 on, created the splendid garden that anticipated his triumphs at Tivoli. The Roman villa, almost completely rebuilt in the late sixteenth and seventeenth centuries, became the chief papal villa at Rome and is now the presidential palace.

After the pomp of his triumphal entry into Tivoli, it is not surprising that the Cardinal was dissatisfied with the official residence assigned to him as governor. It was a monastery, attached to the church of Santa Maria Maggiore,[6] which had been taken

---

[5] ASM, Ambasciatori, Roma, Busta 45, letter from Rome of Cavaliere Francesco Priorato to ducal secretary G. B. Pigna at Ferrara, dated June 12, 1568: ". . . essendo quelli, solo estimati et honoratj hora quali sotto ombra, de continenza, et humiltà, auanzano la magg.ʳ parte de le loro entrate, senza non solo spender' in cosa alcuna ma ne anco con intertener' le persone ualorose, et d'intelletto come lui, et che leuato il Car.ˡᵉ n'ro et di Farnese, poteua lui molto ben conoscere che no' è era alcuno ch'hauesse modo, ne meno uolesse spendere, di modo che questa corte era ridotta in tale estremità, che l'huomini pari suoi, doueuan procacciar' altr'onde il uitto, et la fortuna loro, . . ."

[6] F. S. Seni, *La Villa d'Este in Tivoli*, Rome, 1902, p. 44 n. 1, has a record of the apartments

away from the Benedictine Order in 1255 by Pope Alexander IV and given to the new Order of the Franciscans. Since they did not require the whole building, the Camera Apostolica eventually assigned the part not used by the Franciscans to those cardinals who were appointed governors of Tivoli.

The Cardinal of Ferrara remained at Tivoli until October 28, 1550, finding the climate very beneficial to his health, which had been weakened by the rigors of the conclave that elected Pope Julius III.[7] After being at Tivoli a month the Cardinal wrote to his brother, Duke Ercole II of Ferrara, that he found the air so good that he felt rejuvenated.[8] Since the monastery had such a salubrious setting, the Cardinal decided to rebuild it as a country palace or villa, and in a style befitting one of the wealthiest ecclesiastics of the sixteenth century and one of the most secular cardinals of the period of the Council of Trent. The decision was fortunate for our own times since the gardens of the Villa d'Este at Tivoli present perhaps the best preserved evidence of the sixteenth century garden of Central Italy. The Papal gardens of the Vatican are destroyed or transformed, the Farnese gardens on the Palatine are lost to archaeological excavation, the gardens of the Villa Madama at Rome are an imperfect fragment of their original plan, the sixteenth century nucleus of the Boboli gardens at Florence is overwhelmed by later additions and expansion. Only the gardens of the Villa Lante at Bagnaia or the Palazzo Farnese at Caprarola, and to some extent the Medici gardens of Castello and Petraia, remain true to their sixteenth century origins.

The old monastery, the nucleus of the new villa, was located in the quarter of Tivoli called Santa Croce and was attached to the right or northern side of the church of Santa Maria Maggiore, now called San Francesco (Fig. 3). The church and monastery were on the summit of a hill that sloped westward to the Valle Gaudente (Fig. 2). Both hill and valley were covered with gardens and vineyards, with here and there a few farms and churches. Santa Margherita was situated in the lower part of the valley, and a hospital with its church of Sant'Antonio di Vienna farther down near the Porta Romana. From this gate the principal road wound up to the church of San Filippo and a cluster of houses.

In addition to the benevolent climate, Tivoli had another attraction for the Cardinal. From youth he had been an avid collector of antiquities. Now as governor of Tivoli he had control of territory that included the ruins of the villas of such important ancient Romans as Hadrian, Quintilius Varro, and Maecenas. A letter of one of the Ferrarese agents, written on October 20, 1550, to Duke Ercole II, notes that the Cardinal was not only well but already undertaking excavations for antiquities.[9] Un-

---

being rented from June 10, 1550, by Francesco Novello in the name of the Cardinal of Ferrara.

[7] V. Pacifici, *op.cit.*, p. 110 n. 1. For the unhealthful conditions in the conclave see L. von Pastor, *The History of the Popes*, XIII, London, 1924, p. 29; and R. Brown, ed., *Calendar of State Papers and Manuscripts, Relating to English Affairs, Existing in the Archives and Collections of Venice*, v, London, 1873, pp. 300-301, no. 630 (letter of Venetian ambassador, Dandolo, dated January 22, 1550).

[8] V. Pacifici, *op.cit.*, p. 120 n. 2.

[9] *Idem.*

doubtedly the Cardinal's personal archaeologist, Pirro Ligorio, accompanied him on this initial trip to Tivoli. It may have been at this time that Ligorio began the excavations that resulted in the first attempt to recreate the plan of the nearby Villa of Hadrian.[10]

In October 1550, in preparation for the Villa gardens, the Cardinal through his Master of the House, Bishop Pietro Ghinuzzi, began to purchase a few of the gardens and vineyards in the valley lying below the old monastery.[11] During the next decade, however, little or no work was accomplished at the Villa. Except for the summer of 1555 the Cardinal did not visit Tivoli again until 1560.[12] In this year the Cardinal and his agents once more began to buy up property in the Valle Gaudente and these purchases of property continued for the next six years.[13] This activity eventually aroused the citizens of Tivoli, who found a large section of their town being shut off from them. One church, Santa Margherita, was destroyed to make way for the new gardens,

[10] Three statues at least were discovered in 1550 which the Cardinal's brother, Duke Ercole II of Ferrara, desired. See A. Venturi, "Ricerche di antichità per Monte Giordano, Monte Cavallo e Tivoli nel secolo XVI," *Archivio storico dell'arte*, III (1890), pp. 196-197, where documents regarding the purchase and repair of ancient statues are published.

[11] A record of sale dated October 22 and two dated October 24 are published in F. Seni, *op.cit.*, p. 52 n. 2, and two of October 27 are published in V. Pacifici, *op.cit.*, p. 163 n. 1.

[12] The periods of residence at Tivoli are given by V. Pacifici, in *Atti e memorie della società tiburtina di storia e d'arte*, I (1921), p. 60 n. 1: usually two or three summer months in the following years: 1550, 1555, 1560, 1564, 1565, 1567-1572. The political events affecting the Cardinal during these years may be summarized briefly: In 1552 the Cardinal was named lieutenant of the French king in Siena, which was under the control of French troops, and here he remained for two years. The election of Pope Paul IV in 1555 brought an enemy of the Cardinal into power, and on September 5, 1555, while he was at Tivoli, the Cardinal of Ferrara, under the accusation of simony during the conclave, was removed as governor of Tivoli and ordered to proceed directly to Lombardy without even returning to Rome (V. Pacifici, *Ipp. II d'Este*, p. 269). In the meantime the city of Tivoli was in an upheaval because of the war of Pope Paul IV with the Spaniards. In 1557 Paul IV sent his architect, Sallustio Peruzzi, to Tivoli to fortify the city. Peruzzi proposed to level the quarter of Santa Croce in order to erect fortifications,

but the protests of the Tiburtines to the Pope prevented this project. The election of a new Pope, Pius IV, in December 1559 released the Cardinal of Ferrara from his North Italian exile. Restored to the lifetime position of governor of Tivoli on May 28, 1560, the Cardinal could enjoy only the summer of 1560 at Tivoli before he was sent as Papal Legate to France, where he remained until 1563.

[13] Most of these documents are referred to in F. Seni, *op.cit.*, p. 52 n. 2 on pp. 53-56, but since much of Seni's information does not agree exactly with the documents, we note the essential material of these documents below. All are from ASM, Fab. e Vill., Tivoli, Busta 70, Pte. 1:

fasc. 3, f. 1v—Sept. 9, 1560, house of Bernardino Neri bought for 30 *scudi*.

f. 2r—Dec. 19, 1560, vineyard of Maestro Andrea Pariti for 18 *scudi* 50 *baiocchi*; Dec. 19, 1560, vineyard and garden of Madonna Tradita for 20 *scudi*; Dec. 19, 1560, small garden of Madonna Iuliana and son for 4 *scudi*.

f. 2v—April 10, 1561, vineyard of Madonna Saulina of Tivoli for 100 *scudi*; April 15, 1561, vineyard and garden of Paolo Zappi for 110 *scudi*.

fasc. 5, f. 1r—Oct. 19, 1564, garden of the church of Santo Stefano for 15 *scudi*.

fasc. 7, f. 1r—Feb. 23, 1565, garden of Giuseppi Caffi at Tivoli for 25 *scudi*.

fasc. 9, f. 1r—Sept. 21, 1565, third part of the walls of a farm of Guido and Ascanio Amici for 100 *scudi*.

fasc. 11, f. 1r—May 3, 1566, part of a garden of Angelo Salon for 18 *scudi*.

and three churches, San Pietro, Santa Maria in Colle Marii, and San Filippo, lost many of their parishioners. Some of the buildings of the Hospital of Sant'Antonio di Vienna were leveled. By 1568 a series of lawsuits against the Cardinal were undertaken by the Tiburtines,[14] and some of the complaints were undoubtedly legitimate. The complaints were principally leveled against Giovanni Alberto Galvani, the architect of the Cardinal, and Visdomino Visdomini, the Cardinal's superintendent and agent at Tivoli. The evidence produced in the lawsuits is concerned not only with the manner of expropriation and the remuneration offered, but with the highhanded seizure of antiquities from churches and the destruction of religious sanctuaries. It was charged that the Cardinal's archaeologist Ligorio showed no respect for private property, that he had owners imprisoned or banished when they opposed excavation on their property, and that he stripped the churches of antiquities.

One of the first problems in the creation of the gardens must have been that of filling in the hollow of the Valle Gaudente near the Porta Romana, which was to be the southwestern portion of the present garden. This hollow, when filled in and supported by great retaining walls, provided a flat area for the lower part of the gardens. The terrain was then made to slope evenly down from the Villa to one side of the new terrace. This adjustment of the terrain probably occurred between 1563 and 1565.[15]

[14] The basic study is E. Coccanari-Fornari, "Querele contro il Cardinale Ippolito II d'Este sporte dal comune e dai cittadini di Tivoli nel 1568," *Bollettino di studi storici ed archeologici di Tivoli*, I-II (1919-1920). The information here is from vol. II, fasc. 6 (April 1920, the only fascicule I was able to find), pp. 68-70, and from V. Pacifici, *op.cit.*, p. 163 n. 1.

[15] The lack of documentation for this work, which must have been considerable, is strangely disproportionate to the wealth of the total documentation preserved. It is probable that the work is hidden under the general payments specified only as for the "building of Tivoli" and paid to the Cardinal's agents, Visdomini, Baviera, Briganti, Santucci, and Sacco. The only specific references to such work are dated 1565 in ASM, Registri, Pacco 127, Spese per il Cardle di Ferrara 1563-1568, a series of loose leaves in a folder dated 1565 as follows:

A di 3 Aprile 1565
Misura della terra che acauato et Portata aristeo et Compagni i nela Piazza che acanto alauato della Peschiera del forro dala Parte disopra verso il Monte Misurata per mi Alberto galuani—▽ 66.

A di 14 Aprile 1565
Misura della terra che acauata et Portata cacca cuore et compagni in la costa da baso che tra la vigna del Illmo gardinal di ferrara e l'orto chera del Bernardelo misurata per mi Alberto di galuani da ferrara—▽ 20 b 69.

A di 23 Aprile 1565
Misura dela terra che aleuata spica calcica et compagni in la spiagia dela Parte di sopra del conduto in la vigna vechia sotto il Palazzo—▽ 16 b 14.

A di 22 Maggio 1565
Misura della terra che a cauata Pietro spoletino e compagni in la costa sotto il Palazzo—▽ 32 b 80.

A di 13 febraro 1565
Misura dela terra che aleuata et Portata aristeo et compagni in Piu luochi inel giardino dabaso sotto ale Peschiere e in la spiagia di S.to Pietro e drieto aluiali sopra il foro—▽ 52.75.

Since there was a great deal of land purchased in 1560 and 1561, and little evidence of work in 1562, this grading would appear to have occurred later. In combination with the documents above, the fact that the pergola and fish pools were in construction by 1565 suggests that the grading must in general have been completed by the spring of 1565.

Even before all the land was purchased for the new gardens, great effort was expended to furnish sufficient water for the fountains. The immediate concern for this problem foreshadowed the importance of the fountains and the water displays in the over-all plan of the gardens. Two great sources of water-supply were utilized. From the distant Monte Sant'Angelo water was brought by conduit to the Piazza di San Francesco and thence to the gardens. This work was under way in 1560 and probably completed by 1561.[16] When this supply proved insufficient for the numerous fountains planned in the gardens, the mason Tomaso da Como, began in 1564 to excavate an underground conduit, more than 585 feet long, from the famous Cascade of Tivoli in the river Anio (Fig. 2), where there was a masonry receptacle in which the water could be stored, to an outlet in the garden near the Oval Fountain.[17]

With the water supply established by 1565, work on the fountains and pools could begin. During the next seven years most of the fountains, pools, grottoes, and landscaping were completed. Also during this period the old monastery was transformed into a villa. The original cloister of the monastery was refurbished in 1566 by the stonecutter Raffaello of Florence with a classic travertine arcade on three sides to provide a central court for the Villa (Fig. 3).[18] This court was entered through a vaulted passageway that opened at the eastern corner of the Villa onto the Piazza di San Francesco (Fig. 7). The southeastern side of the court, the wall of the old church of San Francesco, was decorated with an ancient Roman marble statue of Venus reclining under a large arch flanked by pairs of Doric columns. A Roman sarcophagus below her forms the basin of a fountain (Fig. 4).[19]

On the garden side of the Villa, the building is divided into three stories with the principal rooms arranged in a long file on the first and second stories facing the

[16] F. Bulgarini, *Notizie di Tivoli*, Rome, 1848, p. 4, gives 1561 as date of work. A payment to Camillo Marzi on Dec. 19, 1560 (F. Seni, *op.cit.*, p. 52, note 2 on p. 54) indicates that the work was begun in the previous year and specifies that the total cost of the work was 1,250 *scudi*, of which the Cardinal arranged to pay only 400 *scudi*. The remainder was put up by the commune of Tivoli, which was also to benefit. That the water was used by other citizens is indicated in the concession by the Cardinal to Bernardino Sacchi, Prior of Tivoli, of water rights from the conduit (*ibid.*, p. 52, note 2 on pp. 55-56).

[17] G. M. Zappi, *op.cit.*, p. 55. The layout of this subterranean conduit is indicated on the map of Tivoli published by Daniel Stoopendal in 1622 (V. P[acifici], "La più antica pianta di Tivoli," *Atti e memorie della società tiburtina di storia e d'arte*, II, 1922, pp. 60-61, pl. II).

The document for the excavation of the conduit is as follows: ASM, Fab. e Vill., Tivoli, Busta 70, Pte. 3, f. 1r: "Misura del Conduto che a Cauato m.ro Tomaso Murator in Tiuoli nel anno 1564 e de lanno 1565 il detto Conduto la fatto Cauare lo Ill.mo Cardinal di ferrara Comenca dal fiume e uene per sina al suo giardino sotto terra Misurata per mi Alberto di galuani da ferrara lungo Canne n.o 140 a giulj 15 la canna mota ▽ 210" (partially published in F. Seni, *op.cit.*, p. 41 n. 1).

[18] ASM, Registri, Pacco 117, Libro di mandati 1566, section "Dan.ri a Tivoli per la Fabriche," Feb. 19, 1566, and ASM, Fab. e Vill., Tivoli, Busta 70, Pte. 1, fasc. 12, f. 47, estimate for work from 1566 through April 1567.

[19] V. Pacifici, *Ipp. II d'Este*, p. 179, suggests that this fountain dates probably from the time of Luigi Cardinal d'Este (i.e., after the death of Cardinal Ippolito II in 1572), but the description of the Villa by Foglietta in 1569 mentions this fountain (Foglietta's letter published in F. S. Seni, *op.cit.*, see p. 63).

gardens. Most of the masonry and stonecutting for the refurbishing of these apartments appears to have been done in 1566 and 1567, since evaluations of the stonecutting of window and door frames and five chimney pieces by Raffaello and Biasioto date from that time.[20] The architecture of the Villa d'Este is basically that of a Roman palace, a large simple mass of three superimposed stories marked merely by string moldings and tiers of windows. Only a very elegant two-story loggia, erected also by Raffaello and Biasioto in 1566 and 1567[21] at the center of the northwest side of the

[20] ASM, Fab. e Vill., Tivoli, Busta 70, Pte. 1, fasc. 12;

f. 47r: "Misura di m.ro Fello chi comenca delano 1566 et fenise per tuto Aprile delano 1567. Stima de li lauori di scarpello trauertino che a fatti m.ro Rafaelo scarpellino . . ."

f. 47v: "17. Item per auer fatto la finestra di trauertino in la Camera Picola del sig.re Caualiero con la sollia stipeti architrave sti.m ▽ 1 b 50.

. . . .

20. Item per auer fatti doi solie ale finestre dele Camere di Mon.re Arciuescuo . . . ▽ 2.

21. Item per auer fatto cinq Camini de trauertini uno ale stancie da baso sotto quele di Mon.re Arciuescuo e doi ale dite stancie di Mon.re e doi in le camere dil sig.re sipione insieme ▽ 7 b 50."

f. 49v: "63. . . . fatto una architraue di trauertino sopra ala Porta della Camera ultima del Cardinal che intra neli coritori . . . b 45.

64. . . . fatto doi giunte ali stigieti della finestra delutima camera del Cardinal da Este soto la loggia . . . b. 60."

f. 79r: "Misura et stima deli lauori di trauertino che a fatti m.ro Biasioto el sbrigola fratello . . . che comenca del mese d'agosto 1565 per il mese d'agosto del 67. . . .

5. . . . doi finestre di trauertino mese in opera ale stancie doue staua Mon.re dandino dala Parte di sopra. . . ." Also several doors are recorded as nos. 6-9 in above, and the architrave for a door as no. 12.

[21] ASM, Fab. e Vill., Tivoli, Busta 70, Pte. 1, fasc. 12:

f. 47r: "Misura di m.ro Fello chi comenca delano 1566 et fenise per tuto Aprile delano 1567. Stima de li lauori di scarpello trauertino che a fatti m.ro Rafaelo scarpellino . . ."

. . . .

2. . . . doi Cantonate di trauertino con le soi base et capitelli una fatta ala cantonata della loggia uerso la stancia del sig.re Caualiero elatra nel canton dela cantonata che va ala scalla che va da baso . . . ▽ 30.

3. . . . per una Cantonata Comencata da m.o gio Jacomo in el canton della loggia che [illegible word] finestra del Cameron del Cardinale . . . ▽ 8."

f. 47v: "12. . . . per auer fatto le doi nichie di trauertino in cappio ale loggie acanto ala camera del sig.re Caualiero . . . ▽ 7 b 50.

. . . .

16. Item per auer fatti li risati deli cimase che sopra ali Pilastreli del Parapeto della loggia di sopra stimati ▽ 5.

18. Item per auer fatto 14 Capiteli ali rinscontri deli Pilastri sotto lo Peduci dele volte della loggia stimati insieme ▽ 12."

f. 60r: "Misura et stima deli lauori di scarpello che a fatti m.ro Rafaelo fiorentino scarpelino a un sua Robba in la fabrica dela scalla . . . da di p.o Maggio 1567 peru.o 7bre 1568.

1. In Prima il scalino che core sotto li Piedi stalli della logeta e di qua dila dali doi scalle sotto li Cocoli el Primo scalino dele scalle e in le doi teste che risuolta . . . ▽ 18.

. . . .

9. Item per sei Piedistalli di trauertino sotto li 4.o Colloni doriche eli doi Pilastri deli Cantoni dela ditta logeta . . . ▽ 30.

10. Item per le 4.o Collone doriche doi fatte di tuta robba ele altre doi rimese epichiati eli doi Pilastri in suso li cantoni con le soi base e capitelli . . . ▽ 38.

. . . .

20. Item per la Porta di trauertino di dentro che in bocha ala Nichia della Leda con li stipeti el suo arco scornisato . . . ▽ 7 b 50."

f. 61r: Corinthian columns.

f. 62r: Total for work on loggia 1206 *scudi* 99 *baiocchi*.

f. 81r: Estimate of work of "m.ro Biasioto scarpelino . . . di P.o de setenbre 1566 per tuto il mese d'otobre 1568.

1. Item scalini fatti in le doi scalle del Palazzo che conpagnia la loggia di trauertino.

. . . .

3. Item scalini 64 mesi ale doi scalli che

Villa overlooking the gardens (Fig. 5), converts an urban residence into a less forbidding country house. This structure serves several purposes. The lower story of the loggia forms the small grotto of the Fountain of Leda. Two great stairs lead up to the ground floor salotto, the main entrance from the garden into the Villa. The top of the loggia, surrounded by a balustrade, is a balcony opening off the principal room of the Villa, the salone, and providing a wonderful vista that carries the eye from the gardens below across the gardens and the *campagna* to the distant blue mountains that encircle Tivoli.

Late in 1569 the same stonecutters constructed another great loggia at the west end of the main terrace (Fig. 6),[22] an outdoor dining room with access to the kitchens at the southern rear of the Villa. The loggia, projecting out upon the main terrace, serves as a terminus at the southwest end of the Villa. The three open sides command views through great arches over the gardens and *campagna*. These arches alternate with niches in the rather Vignolesque architecture, which once were adorned with both ancient and sixteenth century sculpture. An interior stairway leads up to a balustraded terrace from which these views are even more magnificent and which in addition permits an unobstructed view of the tennis court below, set between the loggia and the Villa. This tennis court was one of the last additions to the Villa during the lifetime of the Cardinal.[23]

It is interesting to note that the fresco in the lower salotto of the Villa, which was presumably executed in 1568, reveals no corner towers on the façade (Fig. 8). In the painting this garden façade consists merely of an elevation nine windows in width added to the block of the Villa, with reentrant angles where the façade joins the sides. In his description of the Villa in 1569 Foglietta specifically claims that "the façade does not preserve the same straight line, for the end sections rise on both sides in the

---

smonta dal Piano del Palazzo e smonta ala logeta del Cardinal."

ASM, Registri, Pacco 120, Giornale di le fabriche 1568, f. xxiiii: Aug. 13, 1568, "A spesa dj Tivoli ▽ diciotto m^ta Pag a m° batt. dal lago et m° giouanj dj Dom.^co fiorentino stucatorj . . . per Hauer' finitto la uoltta della fontana della Ledda in Tiuolj . . . ▽ 18."

ASM, Registri, Pacco 120, Registro de 1568, f. 31: Aug. 13, 1568, "a m° Batt. da lugnano et m° Giouanj dj Dom.^co fiorentino stucatorj," and f. xxxviiii: Dec. 14, 1568, "a Gio' matteo dj bruttj . . . per giornatte diecj ch lui alauoratto dj stucho alla fontana della Ledda a Tiuolj ▽ 80."

[22] ASM, Fab. e Vill., Tivoli, Busta 70, Pte. 1, fasc. 12:

f. 68r: Estimate of work of "m^ro Rafaelo scarpelino" for "la fabrica del cenacolo che in Capo al viale del Palazzo del Illmo Cardinale di Ferrara in Tiuoli e in diuersi lochi che co-

menca del mese di ottobre efenise per tuto di mese di xbre 1569."

f. 87r: "Misura et stima deli lauori di scarpelo e trauertino che a fatti m^ro biasioto scarpelino e l sbrigola suo fratello inel Cenacolo che in capo al viale del Palazzo del Illmo Cardinale di ferrara in Tiuoli e i altri lauori che comenca del mese Nouembre 1569 e fernise per tuto xbre 1569.

5. . . . la nicia grande uerso la cucina."

[23] V. Pacifici, "Luigi d'Este: Capitolo XI," *Atti è memorie della società tiburtina di storia e d'arte*, XXIV (1951), p. 38. During the mid-sixteenth century tennis had become one of the most popular games among the nobility in France and the Cardinal had undoubtedly become interested in the game during his residence there. In fact, he had much earlier built a tennis court at his palace at Fontainebleau. V. Pacifici, *Ipp. II d'Este*, p. 141, note 1 on p. 142.

form of towers, terminating and fortifying the sides of the building."[24] This is, of course, in precise agreement with Dupérac's engraving of 1573 (Fig. 1), but the present structure denies both Foglietta and Dupérac and there is no evidence that such towers were built and then lopped off at the roof level at a later date. As in other features of his engraving, Dupérac represented projected elements which were never accomplished. One may assume that Foglietta took the same liberties in his written account, and since the construction of the pavilions had probably been started in 1569 he may well have assumed that his description would shortly be verified.

The corners of the Villa d'Este no longer have the reentrant angles shown in the fresco but are filled out beyond the level of the façade and project slightly as end pavilions, yet do not rise above the main cornice level as in Dupérac's engraving (Fig. 1). Therefore the end pavilions were filled in at some time later than the 1568 fresco in the salotto. This is indicated by several other bits of evidence. The masonry on the exterior is not continuous between the main block of the Villa and the end pavilions; in fact, very few of the string courses running horizontally across the Villa and the end bays correspond in both level and form. Likewise on the interior, between the interior rooms of the main block of the building and the rooms in the corner pavilions, the walls are much thicker than the other interior walls, suggesting that at one time they were actually exterior walls as shown in the salotto fresco.[25] This would explain the fact that the two galleries at the southwestern end were not decorated during the 1568-1569 painting campaigns but much later.[26]

This has consequences for the large rooms that fill the interior of the northwestern pavilion at the other end of the Villa. These rooms originally must have been half their length, and the decoration of the Room of Noah on the ground floor is later than the original painting campaigns of 1568 and 1569. The surviving building documents do not furnish any decisive information as to when these end pavilions were added to the Villa, but information from various sources can be correlated to suggest that these additions were probably made in 1568 or 1569. The inventories made in 1573 and 1579 after the death of the Cardinal of Ferrara both note a "Sala Nuoua d'Este," which in the inventory of 1579 must correspond to the large room on the *piano nobile* within the northwestern pavilion.[27] There is also a record in April 1572 of the purchase of

---

[24] U. Foglietta, "Uberti Folietae, Patricii Genuensis, Tyburtinum Hippolyti Estii, Cardinalis Ferrariensis ad Flavium Ursinum, Card. Amplissimum," in J. G. Graevius, *Thesaurus Antiquitatum et Historiarum Italiae*, I, pt. 2, Leyden, 1704, col. 1223.

[25] The wall between the Room of Glory and the end gallery is about 123 cm thick, and the wall between the Second Tiburtine Room and the corner Room of Moses is about 173 cm thick, while the interior walls between the

other rooms range from about 58 to 82 cm in thickness.

[26] A. del Re, *op.cit.*, pp. 14 and 24, notes in 1611 that these galleries were not decorated at that time.

[27] ASM, Registri del Card. Luigi d'Este, Pacco 153, Libro dare e hauere delle Robe di Guarda Roba di Tiuoli . . . da di 20 Marzo 1573 p tt° di 13 Ag^to 1582, f. 5 under date 1573, and Pacco 162, Inuentario generale . . . dlla Guardarobba 1579, f. 159r.

brick "for the room of the Cardinal d'Este,"[28] presumably for some interior work on the *piano nobile*. These accounts suggest that the work was accomplished at least by the early 1570's, but more specific information may be gained from the documentation for the interior decoration. As discussed in a later chapter,[29] the decoration of the walls of the corner room on the ground floor, the Room of Noah, may date from 1570 and the vault from 1571. This suggests that the architecture of the corners of the Villa dates from late 1568 or 1569, when the loggia at the southwestern end of the Villa was built.

The addition of the southwestern pavilion raises the problem of the spiral stairway at the southwestern end of the Villa, which now ascends from the level of the tennis court to the gallery in front of the Cardinal's Chapel. As the gallery was added presumably in 1568-1569, the entrance of the spiral staircase into the gallery must have been made about this time, although the only mention in documents regarding the spiral stair is much later, when in 1578 and 1580 there were payments for the cutting of eleven travertine steps.[30]

In preparation for the visit of Pope Gregory XIII to the Villa in September 1572, which marked the climax of the Villa and its gardens under the Cardinal of Ferrara, one important fountain was built. This Fountain of the Dragon (Fig. 1, no. 23), supposedly completed the night before the arrival of the Pope, commemorated the dragon device on his coat of arms.

Two months later the Cardinal of Ferrara died in Rome and was buried at Tivoli in the church of San Francesco. The Cardinal had willed that the Villa d'Este should be owned by the senior cardinal in the Este family or, in default of one, by the Dean of the College of Cardinals;[31] thus, the Villa d'Este, as well as most of the other possessions of the Cardinal of Ferrara, were inherited by Luigi Cardinal d'Este. He did little of note to the Villa except to finish some incomplete details. When his death in 1586 left the Estes without a cardinal, Alessandro Cardinal Farnese, as Dean of the College took possession of the Villa.

---

[28] ASM, Registri, Pacco 123, Registro del 1572, f. 94v: April 23, 1572, ▽ 3.30 "per pag^re 1500 matoni comprati per mand^re a tiuli per matonare la camera del cardinale d'este."

[29] See below pp. 64-67.

[30] ASM, Registri del Card. Luigi d'Este, Pacco 165, Conto Generale, f. xliii: July 24, 1580, "▽ 6.50 a m^ro Giouanni sbrigola scarpelino per resto del ammontare d'ondice scalini di treuertino ch'esso ha fatto per seruitio della scalla lumaga nel Pallazzo di Tiuoli in rag^e de g^ll xv l'uno a Conto de quali gli fu pagato ▽ti diece per le mani di messer Bernard.^o Sacco sotto di vltimo febraro 1578 come in Zor^l ▽ 6.50."

[31] The will is published by F. Seni, *op.cit.*, pp. 237-244.

CHAPTER II · THE GARDENS
AND FOUNTAINS

THE GARDENS of the Villa d'Este cover two steep slopes, descending like the southeast and northeast tiers of an amphitheater to a flat terrace (Fig. 1). The principal promenade of the garden, flanked by two minor ones, follows a major axis starting at a gate near the Porta Romana and terminating in the entrance to the Villa's two-story portico. This lower entrance to the promenade gives the axis its principal direction since the view from here commands the southeast slope crowned with the Villa and reveals the entrances to the numerous grottoes recessed in the slope.

In the sixteenth century only one major fountain, that of the Dragon (Fig. 1, no. 23), was centered along these axes, and the important water displays were arranged on the two sides of the gardens. Several cross-axes, such as the so-called Hundred Fountains and the fish pools, serve to connect the major fountains. Since Bramante's project for the Belvedere Court, many sixteenth century gardens had been built on sloping sites, but in all of them the elements of major interest had been set along the central axis, and any flow of water would concur with the axis of the gardens.

Early Renaissance gardens, such as those of the Villa Medici at Careggi or of Poggio Reale at Naples had grown out of the mediaeval garden—a small walled plot for cultivating herbs or flowers—and the complexity of these Renaissance gardens was simply the result of combining several such gardens. Bramante in the Belvedere Court of the Vatican had introduced a simple unity into this scheme by arranging these several gardens on ascending terraced levels visible as a whole along a central axis from the windows of the Papal Apartments in the Vatican.[1] Raphael apparently intended this type of plan for the Villa Madama gardens at Rome, and Vignola designed the Villa Lante at Bagnaia and the Palazzo Farnese at Caprarola in this manner.[2] The

[1] J. S. Ackerman, *The Cortile del Belvedere* (Studi e documenti per la storia del Palazzo Apostolico Vaticano, III), Vatican City, 1954, pp. 122-124.

[2] H. Geymüller's attempt to reconstruct Raphael's original garden layout of the Villa Madama (*Raffaello studiato come architetto*, Milan, 1884, pp. 59-70) has been rightfully questioned by M. Bafile, *Il giardino di Villa Madama* (R. Instituto d'archeologia e storia dell'arte: Opere d'arte, XII), Rome, 1942. Bafile's reconstruction of the gardens on the slope along the central axis to the Villa Madama, while very satisfactory from an aesthetic point of view, does not quite concur with the only evidence we have of the garden project, that is, the plan by Raphael. In his figure 5 Bafile actually reconstructed the gardens to fit the

evidence of Raphael's plan, but he discarded this layout as the gardens would not then be centered on the Villa.

The Farnese Gardens by Vignola on the Palatine at Rome, although entered by a flight of stairs, were not designed particularly in relation to a sloping site, nor were the gardens of the Villa Giulia.

The gardens of the Palazzo Farnese at Caprarola and those of the Villa Lante at Bagnaia, both of which are built on slopes, are probably later than the Villa d'Este. Most of the garden architecture at Caprarola may have been done by Girolamo Rainaldi toward the end of the century (W. Lotz, *Vignola-Studien*, Würzburg, 1939, pp. 59-60). This is indicated by the fact that the land on which the Casino is built was only acquired in 1587 (M. L. Gothein, *A His-*

gardens at the Villa Giulia in Rome, on the other hand, return to the idea of three separate enclosed areas arranged on a single axis but without any visual unity.

The central axis at Tivoli preserves the feeling of visual unity, but, as the visitor begins to experience the gardens in his walk along this axis to the Villa, he is constantly diverted by cross-axes revealing the most interesting fountains of the gardens. It is only the continuity of the view of the Villa that keeps him on the central axis until he reaches the row of the Hundred Fountains. At that point, although the visual axis continues to the Villa, the physical access does not. Beyond the Hundred Fountains a network of diagonal paths spreads across the upper slope to the level of the Cardinal's Walk, the last crosswalk below the terrace of the Villa. However, to reach this terrace one has to leave the main axis again and mount either of the two stairs to the terrace, where the four stairs to the portico of the Villa finally lead back to the central axis under the loggia of the portico at the entrance to the ground floor of the Villa itself.

This constant deviation from the principal axis, whether forced or only suggested, means that the observer can never fully experience the gardens in a Renaissance manner from a fixed objective viewpoint. His experience of the gardens becomes a much more subjective one of continuous exploration and surprise, unified by the constantly varying sounds of water.

As the visitor entered the lower gate in the sixteenth century his first impression of the gardens at Tivoli must have been a serene one.[3] A wide wooden pergola led

---

tory of Garden Art, London and Toronto, 1928, I, p. 278) and the brevity of the description of the surroundings in Montaigne's description in 1581 (M. de Montaigne, *Journal de Voyage,* ed. by L. Lautroy, 2nd ed., Paris, 1909, pp. 457-460). For Bagnaia see A. Breschi, "Bagnaia," *Quaderni dell'Istituto di storia dell'architettura,* no. 17 (1956), p. 10.

[3] Although the gardens have undergone many changes since the sixteenth century, there is fairly good pictorial and literary evidence for their original condition. Most important is the engraving of the Villa and its gardens by Etienne Dupérac, dated April 8, 1573, which is usually included in Lafreri's *Speculum Romanae Magnificentiae* (Fig. 1). This engraving was made after a lost drawing of the gardens by Dupérac, which the Cardinal sent with a letter to the Emperor Maximilian II late in 1571. (H. von Voltelini, "Urkunden und Regesten aus dem K. u. K. Haus-, Hof- und Staats-Archiv in Wien," *Jahrbuch der kunsthistorischen Sammlungen des allerhöchsten Kaiserhauses,* XIII, 1892, p. LXI, no. 8906.) The inscription on the 1573 engraving records that it was taken from this drawing. The draw-

ing must have been based upon a projected design for the gardens, since the engraving shows certain elements that were never built, such as the Fountain of Neptune (Fig. 1, no. 29) at the lower end of the fish pools or the belvederes on the corners of the Villa. This is not unusual, as several of the other Lafreri engravings are made after projects and not the executed buildings, as in the Villa Giulia (J. Coolidge, "The Villa Giulia," *Art Bulletin,* XXV, 1943, pp. 224-225) and San Pietro in Vaticano (J. Coolidge, "Vignola, and the Little Domes of St. Peter's," *Marsyas,* II, 1942, pp. 112-119). Another pictorial representation of the gardens is the fresco in the ground floor Salotto of the Villa itself (Fig. 8). (V. Pacifici, "L'antico Quirinale in un affresco rinvenuto in Villa d'Este," *Atti e memorie della società tiburtina di storia e d'arte,* IX-X [1929-1930], pp. 385-387. Although the fresco was repainted in 1949 after its discovery under whitewash in the 1920's, it is useful for presenting corroborative evidence on the appearance of the gardens in the sixteenth century.) There is a wealth of literary evidence useful in correcting and analyzing the Dupérac engraving. In addition to

from the entrance gate to the wall enclosing the gardens. Centered on either side of the pergola rustic fountains by Curzio Maccarone quietly introduced the theme of running water which was so fully exploited in the gardens.[4] At the end of the pergola the visitor stepped out onto the wide terrace forming the lower part of the gardens. There a great wooden cross-pergola, begun probably in 1565,[5] divided this terrace into four large compartments containing herb gardens. At the center of the cross-pergola was an octagonal domed pavilion with four fountains made in the form of giant flowers. Eight silver-white eagles perched watchfully on the corners of the entablature of the octagon and a golden lily gleamed at the summit, two of the favorite devices of the Estes. The vaults of the pergolas were covered with shady vines, and espaliered fruit trees lined the sides. Fruit trees were also spaced about the four

---

the numerous archival records of contracts and payment for the work at the Villa, there are preserved three sixteenth century and one early seventeenth century description of importance. The earliest literary account is the description written in 1569 in a letter of Uberto Foglietta, a member of the Cardinal's entourage, addressed to Flavio Cardinal Orsini. (U. Foglietta, "Uberti Folietae, Patricii Genuensis, Tyburtinum Hippolyti Estii, Cardinalis Ferrariensis ad Flavium Ursinum, Card. Amplissimum," in J. G. Graevius, *Thesaurus Antiquitatum et Historiarum Italiae*, I, pt. 2, Leyden, 1704, cols. 1217-1224. With some omissions this was translated into Italian and published in F. Seni, *La Villa d'Este in Tivoli*, Rome, 1902, pp. 58-64.) More important is the anonymous description, written about 1571, which is preserved in two later manuscript copies at Paris and Vienna. (Paris, Bibl. Nat., cod. Ital. 1179, ff. 247r-267r and Vienna, Nationalbibliothek, cod. 6750, ff. 449r-461v. The text of the Parisian manuscript is given in Appendix A.) The importance of this account lies in the fact that it presents the original project for the gardens. The two preserved manuscripts are probably copies of the original manuscript descriptions which accompanied Dupérac's drawing to the courts of Paris and Vienna. These manuscripts claim to be a description of what exists, but this is impossible because they describe many things that were only planned and never executed, exactly as in Dupérac's engraving and undoubtedly also in his drawing. So four fish pools and the Fountain of Neptune are specified as existing, although they were never completed. The local Tiburtine chronicler Giovanni Maria Zappi included a long portrait of the Villa, dated 1576, among his descriptions

of several of the ancient Roman villas at Tivoli. (G. M. Zappi, *Annali e memorie di Tivoli di Giovanni Maria Zappi* [Studi e fonti per la storia della regione tiburtina, 1] ed. by V. Pacifici, Tivoli, 1920, pp. 55-65.) Antonio del Re, another local notary and historian, also devoted the majority of his attention to the Villa d'Este in his treatise on the ancient villas of Tivoli published in 1611. (*Dell'antichità tiburtine capitolo V*, Rome, 1611, pp. 1-71. Later translated into Latin and published in J. G. Graevius and P. Burmann, *Thesaurus Antiquitatum et Historiarum Italiae*, VIII, pt. 4, Leyden, 1723.)

[4] ASM, Fab. e Vill., Tivoli, Busta 70, Pte. 1, fasc. 12, f. 33r: Estimate of masonry work of Tomaso da Como "che comenca al Principio del mese di Nouembre 1568 e fenisi per tuto il mese d otbre 1569," and f. 37r: "46. Item per auer taliato il muro in le doi Nichie doue a fatto Curcio le doi fontane soto la Pergola dela intrata del giardino" and "53. Item per auer Cauato laterra dele doi fontane sotto la Pergola." Also f. 70r: Estimate of the masonry of Jacomo da Pratta from Jan. 1570 through Dec. 1570; f. 75r: "6. Muro di matoni deli 4° vasceti del Paualione da baso del giardino"; f. 76r: "2. Item per auer murato et cauato le buse di trauiceli n° 26 in torno ala Pergola del giardino da baso" and "15. Item per auer Cauato sei buse edricato sei arcarece et nuoate [?] per fare li tre Portoni in Capo ala Pergola dui in la intrata elatro verso la muralia che se ruinata"; and f. 76v: "22 . . . . 4° vaschete de Paualion."

[5] ASM, Registri, Pacco 116, Registro i Mand.ti 1565, f. 19v: March 28, 1565, 2.85 *scudi*, "A m.ro Mattheo et Jacomo falegnami . . . per sua mercede d'hauere fatta la parte delle dua pergole della sena misurata da messer Gio: Aberto."

potherb gardens. This section of the gardens is a direct descendant of the mediaeval walled garden which was planted with herbs and fruit trees, and in Italy, from at least the time of Boccaccio, would have had a cross-pergola as its central feature.

On each side of the cross-pergola two labyrinths were planned, each composed of different trees—oranges, marine cherries, pines, and spruce (Parisian MS, folios 249-250v). The use of labyrinths, like the cross-pergola, is also a mediaeval horticultural practice. However, apparently only the two labyrinths on the southwest side of the herb garden were planted, and it is unlikely that they date from the Cardinal's lifetime since they are not mentioned in the description of 1569 but are noted in Zappi's account of 1576.[6] The same is true of the elm trees that were planted according to Zappi along the southwest side of the gardens to protect them from the "sea air" and to afford shade during the summer months.

Beyond the cross-pergola is the first main cross-axis of the gardens formed by the fish pools and the Water Organ on the slope above them at the northeast side. At the other end of the pools a Fountain of Neptune (Fig. 1, no. 29) was planned but never executed. This fountain, which was to contain a statue of Neptune driving his chariot of four sea horses, was to "represent the Sea."[7] The Fountain of the Water Organ (Fig. 1, no. 24; Fig. 9) was begun in 1568 by the French fountain expert called by the Italians Lucha Clericho, perhaps in French Luc LeClerc, assisted for a while by Claude Venard.[8] It consists of a great frontispiece with a broken curved pediment. As archi-

---

[6] G. M. Zappi, *op.cit.*, p. 57.

[7] Paris, cod. Ital. 1179, f. 253v (see Appendix A, p. 145) and Dupérac's engraving (Fig. 1, no. 29).

[8] The Parisian MS, f. 254r (see Appendix A, p. 145) claims that the fountain "resta imperfetta per la morte dell'Artefice inuentore" [i.e. Luc LeClerc?]. If this refers to LeClerc then the Parisian manuscript must date after November 16, 1568, which is the last mention of LeClerc in documents, see below.

The documents for the work on the fountain are as follows: ASM, Registri, Pacco 120, Giornale di le fabriche 1568, f. iii: Jan. 31, 1568, 10 *scudi*, "m° Lucha francese fontanier" . . . a conto dj sua puisioni"; f. viii: Mar. 16, 1568, 10 *scudi*, "A m° Lucha Cliriche francese fontanier'"; f. 11: April, 19, 15 *scudi*; f. xii: April 26, 8.70 *scudi*; f. 17: June 14, "A m° Lucha Claricho francese ▽ ventj m^ta"; f. 24: Aug. 20, 20 *scudi*, "M. Lucha Clericho fontanier"; f. xxviiii: Oct. 15, 15 *scudi*; ASM, Registri, Pacco 120, a register of 1568 but its title illegible, f. 38: Nov. 12, 5 *scudi*, "amo luca francesi fontanier p lui a Claudio suo s^no . . . a buo' conto di sua puisione" and Nov. 16, 10 *scudi*, "a m° Luca fontanier' per luj a Claudio uenardo suo s^ri . . . a buo' coto dj sua puisione." ASM, Fab. e

Vill., Tivoli, Busta 70, Pte. 1, fasc. 12, f. 25r:

"1. Muro del fondamento della fontana di m. Lucha drieto à san Pietro.

2. Muro del fondamento et masiso sotto la grotto doue va la dea della Natura dentro in la nichia.

3. Muro del Masisco fatto sopra il fondamento doue Posa sopra li 4° termeni ele Nichie Picole della ditto fontana."

f.28r:

"4. Item Terra cauata del conduto che a fatto far m. Lucha che Porta laqua a la sua fontana che comenca dal Monte di Curcio per si ua ala muralia della giesia di san Pietro."

f. 81r: Estimate of the work of "m^ro Biasioto scarpellino . . . di P.° di setenbre 1566 per tuto il mese dotobre 1568.

. . . .

12. . . . doi cimase ali doi Piedi stalli ele doi baseti sotto tonde che fa li Cocoli.

13. . . . 4° Piedi di Trauertino ali 4° Termini che ala fontana del ditto."

f. 81v:

"14. . . . 8 bugne Rustiche che riciuete li 4° Termini.

. . . .

17. . . . doi fontispici rotti la cornice che fa le uolute tonde."

tectural supports there are four great herms with crossed arms, their travertine busts carved by Pirrino del Gagliardo.[9] In the large central niche stood a travertine statue of the many-breasted Diana of Ephesus (Fig. 10). Called in documents the Goddess of Nature or of Fortune, it was executed by the Fleming Gillis van den Vliete after an ancient statue formerly in the Farnese collection.[10] At the sides between the pairs

---

Records also continue on folio 82. ASM, Registri, Pacco 120, Registro del 1568, f. xvi: Mar. 15, 1568, 2.70 *scudi*, "a mᵒ franc.ᵒ uenditor' de cose maritime . . . per piu cose maritime date per la fontana dj Tiuolj che fa mᵒ Lucha" and 3.48 *scudi*, "a m. Vincᵒ stampa . . . per dodici pezzi dj marmoro nero et pezzi diecj dj marmoro rosso et uno pezzo dj colona dj porfido che seruino per la fontana che fa mᵒ Luca atiuolj."

[9] ASM, Registri, Pacco 120, Giornale di le fabriche 1568, f. 14: May 18, 1568, 11.60 *scudi*, "A mᵒ Pirino dj gagliardj scultore scudj diecj dᵒ inᵒ aluj . . . conto dj ▽ 30 simillj che luj douera Hauere quando hauer' fatto Quatro teste di Terminj co' il collo de grandezza de Palmj iiij½ di buona misura luna tutte dj Teuortino del suo atutte sul Spese"; f. xvi: June 2, 11.60 *scudi*, "A mᵒ Pirino dj gagliardj scultor' ▽ diecj dᵒ inᵒ . . . a buoncoto delli quatro statue dj Tiuertino . . . per la fontana dj Tiuolj che fa Il francese"; and f. 20: July 4, 10 *scudi* in gold as final payment of 30 *scudi* in gold.

[10] *Ibid.*, f. xviiii: June 25, 1568, 29 *scudi*, "A m. Gilio della Vliette fiamengho scultor' ▽ uenti cinque dᵒ inᵒ aluj . . . a coto di ▽ 50 simillj che luj douera Hauer quando Hauera fatto una statua dj Teuertino per la fontana del francese detta la Dea della fortuna di Altezza de palmi 18"; and f. 28: Oct. 12, 10 *scudi*, "a mᵒ Gillio scultore a contto della statua della dea della Natura"; ASM, Registri, Pacco 119, Registro del 1568, f. lxxxxvii: July 20, 1568, "Eadi ditto ▽ tredᵒ inᵒ . . . a m. Giulio della Vellita scultore per pagᵒ il fitto della sua Camera doue lui sta mentʳᵉ S. S. Ill stava in Tiuoli ▽iii b."; ASM, Registri, Pacco 120, another register of 1568 with illegible title, f. 40r: Dec. 30, 1568, part of 50 *scudi*; ASM, Registri, Pacco 120, Registro del 1569, f. cxiv: undated "a mʳᵒ Gilio della Vieletta et m.ᵒ Pietro della motta Fiaminghi, cpi scultori, per Fattura dell' Infe statue di Treuertino che loro hanno fatte in Tiuoli cioe una Dea della Nattura per scudi cinqᵗᵃ otto"; and f. clxiiii: Feb. 28, 20 *scudi* to both sculptors, and May 26, 19 *scudi* to Gillio for goddess of Nature; ASM, Registri, Pacco

120, Registro d'entrata e opere del 1569, f. 163v: Feb. 28, 20 *scudi* to both sculptors as above, and May 26, 19 *scudi*, "a mʳᵒ Gilio per resto de ▽ 58 simili per la statua della Dea della Natura di Treuertino"; ASM, Fab. e Vill., Tivoli, Busta 70, Pte. 1, fasc. 12, f. 68r: Estimate of work "che comenca del mese di ottobre efenise per tuto di mese di xbre 1569"; and f. 68v: "21. Item per auer Prestato la Corda à mʳᵒ Andreon che tirete la dea dela Natura dala giesia di san saluestro . . . ▽ 1." Likewise on f. 68v there is an enigmatic record referring to a goddess of Nature: "Item per auer Cauato un Pezzo dela dea dela Natura delorto del Capitano Nardo marcino . . . ▽ 1."

For the Tiburtine Diana see H. Thiersch, "Artemis Ephesia," *Abhandlungen der Gesellschaft der Wissenschaften zu Göttingen: Philologisch-Historische Klasse*, ser. 3, no 12, Berlin, 1935, p. 100. The Farnese Diana is now in the Museo Nazionale, Naples (no. 665). The Renaissance version at Tivoli is very close to the ancient one at Naples with the only important difference from the present condition of the antique example being the reduction of the rows of animals and insects on the lower part of the figure from six to five. However, Thiersch (*ibid.*, p. 17) points out that the Farnese Diana was restored in the eighteenth century and that old engravings and a drawing by Dosio (*ibid.*, p. 19) show that it originally had only five rows of figures like the Renaissance example.

The suggestion that the Renaissance version was based on the Ephesian Diana found in Hadrian's Villa at Tivoli, now in the Vatican (V. Pacifici, *Ipp. II d'Este*, p. 172) is not only doubtful in resemblance but impossible because that statue was not excavated until the late eighteenth century (P. Gusman, *La villa impériale de Tibur*, Paris, 1904, p. 43, H. Thiersch, *op.cit.*, pp. 22-23, and G. Lippold, *Die Skulpturen des Vaticanischen Museums*, III, 2, Berlin, 1956, pp. 167-169 and p. 540, no. 22).

The idea of the Ephesian Diana, as the Goddess of Nature, used as a fountain occurred earlier to the Florentine sculptor Tribolo in a

of herms were empty smaller niches intended, according to the Parisian description (folio 254r), to contain statues of Apollo and Diana, but from which jets of water spurted out into basins, while other jets rose from below with such a quantity of water that the fountain was often entitled the Deluge.[11] Behind the figure of Nature was the Water Organ itself developed by the Frenchman Claude Venard.[12] A sudden rush of water into an enclosed cavity forced air through the various organ pipes, while the water also by its flow activated the mechanical controls which opened and closed the different pipes, producing a harmony of music introduced by two trumpet calls.[13] Classical antiquity had invented a water organ which was known to the Renaissance from its description in Vitruvius (Book x, chap. viii) and Hero of Alexandria,[14] but the ancient organ had keys which were played by an organist, while the Tiburtine organ was the wonder of its period because the only human intervention necessary was to set the water going. So in September 1572 when Pope Gregory XIII visited the Villa he was so pleased with the Water Organ that he requested to have it play several times and then asked to speak to Venard, the inventor of the organ device.[15]

The frontispiece of the Organ was apparently not completed during the sixteenth century. In 1609 Alessandro Cardinal d'Este, following the original conception expressed in the Parisian manuscript (folio 254r), added the eagle perched on the Cardinal's *impresa* at the top within the break of the pediment. Soon after 1611 he removed the central statue of the Goddess of Nature, which is now in its own rustic fountain against the entrance wall at the northwest, and erected the *tempietto* in the central niche to protect the Organ (Fig. 13). The statues of Apollo (Fig. 11) and Orpheus (Fig. 12) must have been placed in the side niches at the same time.

Four fish pools were planned to form the main cross-axis and to carry the water from the Fountain of the Water Organ to the Fountain of Neptune, which as noted above

work sent to Francis I of France to decorate Fontainebleau (G. Vasari, *Vite*, VI, Florence, 1881, p. 61). Tribolo's piece is now in the Louvre ([P. Vitry], *Musée national du Louvre: Catalogue des sculptures du moyen âge, de la renaissance et des temps modernes: Partie 1, Moyen âge et renaissance*, Paris, 1922, p. 99, no. 813).

[11] Paris, cod. Ital. 1179, f. 254r (see Appendix A, p. 145); G. M. Zappi, *op.cit.*, p. 62; and A. del Re, *op.cit.*, p. 67.

[12] ASM, Registri, Pacco 121, Protetione di Francia 1570, f. xxi: July 22, 1570, 7 *scudi*, "a Claudio uenardo fontanier' puisione per tutto Decembre," and with the same date, 6 *scudi*, "per sua puisione dj Gen°"; ASM, Registri, Pacco 125, Salariati 1569, f. 121v: To Clodio Francese or Clodio di venerdi, May 15, 1569, 2 *scudi* for Dec. 1568; May 15, 6 *scudi* for Jan., Feb. and March 1569; Sept. 29, 10 *scudi* for 5 months finishing last of Aug.; Dec.

31, 1 *scudo* on account, owed 7 *scudi*; ASM, Registri, Pacco 125, Salariati 1570, f. 114v: July 22, 1570, 7 *scudi* for half of Sept. through Dec. 1569; July 22, 6 *scudi* for Jan. through March; Sept. 12, 6 *scudi* for April through June; Oct. 30, 4 *scudi* for July and Aug.; Dec. 6, 4 *scudi* for Sept. and Oct., owed 4 *scudi*.

[13] The mechanical functioning of this instrument is briefly described by M. de Montaigne, *op.cit.*, p. 269, and in more detail in S. de Caus, *Les raisons des forces mouuantes avec diuerses machines*, Frankfort, 1615, ff. 39v-43r.

[14] Hero of Alexandria, *Opera quae supersunt omnia, I. Pneumatica et automata*, ed. by W. Schmidt, Leipzig, 1899, pp. 192-203.

[15] G. M. Zappi, *op.cit.*, p. 62. V. Pacifici, "Luigi d'Este e la villa tiburtina," *Atti e memorie della società tiburtina di storia e d'arte*, XX-XXI (1940-1941), p. 126 n. 2, corrects Zappi's date of 1573 with respect to the Papal visit.

was never built (Fig. 14). Nor were the four pools ever fully carried out. In the estimate of masonry executed by Tomaso da Como by October 1565 much of the work was for these fish pools, but only two of the pools were completed at this time according to Foglietta.[16] Zappi in 1576, however, mentions three pools as finished, as they are today, and "there remains another fish pool commenced, but not finished, under the organ."[17] The engraving by Dupérac in 1573 (Fig. 1) shows four fish pools completed, but this is simply because the engraving is taken from the original project and not from the actual condition of the gardens. Around the edges of the two central pools, which contained many types of fishes and swans, were travertine columns from which jets of water shot up and joined one another like rainbows over the pools. Dupérac depicts in the center of each of the two middle pools (Fig. 1, no. 25) an imitation of the Meta Sudans, an ancient conical fountain at Rome which exuded water imperceptibly. He also shows a bridge and divisions in the side pools, none of which occurs in the written descriptions except in the Parisian manuscript, which, of course, like the engraving is based upon the original plan.

The year 1566, the year following the initiation of the fish pools, seems to mark the first great impetus to work in various parts of the gardens. Money was paid in the three months of May through July to several stonecutters for canals and conduits in the gardens.[18] Also at this time there begin to appear accounts for the purchase of trees, such as cedars from Corneto, oaks, laurels, firs, and elms, and plants used to landscape the gardens—accounts which, of course, continue until the Cardinal's death in 1572.[19]

[16] F. Seni, *op.cit.*, p. 58. Selections from the estimate of the masonry, dated October 10, 1565, from ASM, Fab. e Vill., Tivoli, Busta 70, Pte. 1, fasc. 10, ff. 5 and 8-10, read as follows:

"A di 10 Ottobre 1565
Misura et stima deli lauori di muro che a fatti m°ᵒ Tomaso da Como Murator in Tiuoli in el giardino da baso del Ill°ᵒ gardinal di Ferrara in le pescieri elovato in li conduduti Misurato p mi Alberto di Galuani da ferrara Presente m°ᵒ Tomaso e m. Visdomino in Primo (f. 5r).

. . . .

65. Muro del tramezo della Pesciera di sopra verso lorto chera del Bernardelo doue in Posta le doi volte (f. 8r).

. . . .

81. Muro del fondamento dele teste dele doi Pesciere in el uial di mezo doue se fatto le cascate delaqua" (f. 8v).

[17] G. M. Zappi, *op.cit.*, p. 57. Zappi gives their measurements as 40 *passi* (ca. 59.52 m) long, 22 *passi* (ca. 32.74 m) wide, and 30 *palmi* (ca. 6.70 m) deep.

[18] ASM, Registri, Pacco 117, Libro di mandati 1566, under the section indexed as "Dan°ⁱ a

Tiuoli per la Fabriche": May 25, 1566, 20 *scudi*, "M. Dante a buo' conto de li canali"; May 13, 5 *scudi*; May 17, 20 *scudi*; May 22, 6 *scudi*; June 4, "Dante fiorentino" 15 *scudi*; June 5, 6 *scudi*; June 13, 6 *scudi*, "a m°ᵒ Filipo Vasselaro p dar a bon coto de condotti"; June 17, "Dante scultore" 20 *scudi*; June 8, 10 *scudi*, "a Cesaro Uasselaro resto de ▽ 16 che sono il preccio de cendotti 200 mandati a Tiuli"; and July 9, Dante received 40 *scudi*.

[19] ASM, Registri, Pacco 117, Libro di mandati 1566, under the section indexed as "Dan°ⁱ a Tiuoli per la Fabriche"; May 25, 1566, 3 *scudi*, "a Siluestro de Calcinaia per hauer portate pianti de cedri da Corneto a Tiuli" and Feb. 4, 15.2½ *scudi*, "al Rosso da Cassia per suo resto de sc°ⁱ 23 b. 2+ che douea h're per piante date per Tiuli." ASM, Registri, Pacco 119, Registro del 1568, f. cxxii: Jan. 17, 1568, 3.8 *scudi* for transportation of "77 castagne per piantare"; Feb. 18, 4.74 *scudi* for "102 Castagni"; Mar. 13, 11.50 *scudi* "per il prezzo de 51 Abbetti" and 17.40 *scudi* "per prezzo d'olmi 70 a 7 b. luno, lauri 380 a 25 b. il c.ᵒ chelui ha datto per piantar a Tiuoli da di 24 9bre 1567 per tt°

The engraving of Dupérac also indicates that a grotto of the Sibyls (Fig. 1, no. 25) was planned for the terrace directly below the Water Organ, and a Fountain of Antinous (Fig. 1, no. 26) was to be below this grotto at the head of the pools. The Parisian description adds that the Grotto of the Sibyls, which was to honor particularly the Tiburtine Sibyl, was to have nine ancient statues of Sibyls, one in each grotto. None of this work was accomplished, and in 1611 parts of the giant statue of Neptune, whose fountain at the other end of the fish pools was never executed, were in the central niche at the head of the pools where they are to this day with the great cascade flowing over them.

The fish pools bordered one edge of the flat area of the gardens, beyond which the steep incline ascended to the terrace of the Villa. Three travertine stairs were planned to ascend the lower wooded slope, one stair continuing the main axis from the cross-pergola and the other two the secondary paths between the herb gardens and the labyrinths. Only the central and the southwest ones begun in 1567 were completed.[20] Again it is the northeast slope which is unfinished. These stairs, which are called the Stairs of the Bubbling Fountains (Scale dei bollori), have stepped balustrades (Fig. 15), on each step of which is a little jet or "flower" of water in a cup from which the water then flows into an elliptical basin on the next lower step thus creating a continuous stream of bubbling water down the balustrades.

Part way up the slope the central stairs are diverted into two oval flights around the Fountain of the Dragon (Figs. 16 and 17). According to sixteenth century chroniclers this fountain was built almost overnight in honor of the visit in 1572 of Pope Gregory XIII,[21] whose coat of arms was believed to contribute the dragon motif. However, a Fountain of the Dragon was intended at this location long before Gregory XIII was even elected Pope, since it is mentioned in the Parisian manuscript (folio

---

li xii Marzo 1568." ASM, Registri, Pacco 120, Registro d'entrata e opere del 1569, f. 126r: Dec. 7, 1569, 4.8 *scudi* "per prezzo di piu piante di Castagno et passoni"; Dec. 24, 35.40 *scudi* "per 110 piante"; and f. 126v: Dec. 3, 3.70 *scudi* "per piu piante." ASM, Registri, Pacco 123, Registro del 1572, f. 94v: March 3, 1572, 11.9 *scudi* "per tanti sp^si in piu Arbori comprati a marino per piant^re nel giard.^ino di Tiuli."

[20] ASM, Fab. e Vill., Tivoli, Busta 70, Pte. 1, fasc. 12, f. 47, estimate of the stonecutting of Rafaello which begins 1566 through April 1567, f. 48r:

"27. Item per auer fatto 22 vasceti di Trauertino ala scalla deli bolori di sopra doue casca laqua deli bolori . . . ▽ 26 b 4.

28. Item per auer fatto le Pietre dele vascete ouate ala deta scalla lungi insieme cane 44 . . . ▽ 30 b 88.

. . . .

30. Item per auer fatto 22 fiori per fare li bolori ala detta scalla . . . ▽ 28 b 60."
f. 49r:

"52. Item per auer fatto 22 vasceti ala scala da baso fatta a cordoni doue fa li bolori . . . ▽ 26 b 40.

53. Item per auer fatto le Pietre dele vasceti ouate . . . ▽ 42." ASM, Registri, Pacco 120, Giornale di le fabriche 1568, f. xxiii: July 23, 1568, 3 *scudi*, "A spesa di Tiuolj ▽trj m.^ta pag.^ti a Manilo [or Manuello in another record] scultor' . . . per una maschara dj Marmaro da getar aqua et una tazza dj tiuertino per balorj"; and f. 23: July 31, 6 *scudi*, "A m° federicho dj Venosa Vasari ▽ sei m.^ta . . . per resto di noui uasj alto quatro palmj l'uno che suino per li bolorj a Tiuolj."

[21] F. Seni, *op.cit.*, pp. 71-72 and V. Pacifici, *Ipp. II d'Este*, p. 352 n. 2.

255r). This fountain has a centerpiece consisting of four winged dragons which spit into the oval basin while a tall jet of water rises above them. The jet varied so that at times "it made explosions like a small mortar, or many arquebuses discharged together; and at times it grew larger like a pavilion representing a downpour of rain."[22] The stairs which lead up around each side of the oval basin have an outer handrail consisting of a channel with little steps down which water gently ripples.

The crosswalk at the foot of this fountain leads to the entrance of the Fountain of the Owl (Fig. 1, no. 21; Fig. 18) at the southwest edge of the gardens. The records of the commencement of work on this fountain by Giovanni del Duca do not seem to have been preserved. The first account of activity is in 1566 when Raffaello Sangallo took over after the death of Giovanni; the work then continued until 1568 when Ulisse Macciolini added the stucco figures of three fauns with a wineskin.[23] The fountain has a wall-enclosed rectangular area with entrances on the three sides and the fountain proper at the short end above the retaining wall at the southwest. In the enclosing wall is a series of niches for which Leonardo Sormanno in 1572 carved eight satyrs holding vases from which water poured.[24] The fountain had a great niche flanked by Ionic columns entwined with garlands of golden apples from the Cardinal's *impresa*. Above the niche in stucco and mosaic was the Cardinal's coat of arms supported by two angels, and over the columns stood two female statues. The top of the fountain was decorated also with elements of the Cardinal's coat of arms—a white eagle perched in the center flanked by two yellow mosaic lilies. In the niche were three stucco youths standing above a large vase and holding upended a wineskin from which water flowed into the vase and so down to the basin. On the artificial mount which supported the vase were little tree branches with bronze birds which sang with the play of water until suddenly an owl appeared whose cry, also created by the water, silenced them. This game between the birds and owl with all the sounds created by the flow of water was natu-

---

[22] A. del Re, *op.cit.*, p. 65.

[23] ASM, Registri, Pacco 117, Libro di mandati 1566, section entitled "Dan^ri a Tiuoli per la Fabriche": May 25, 1566, 15 *scudi*, "a Rafaello sangalle a bon conto de fenir la fontana che faceua mr'o gio: scultore"; May 13, 5 *scudi*; May 18, 15 *scudi*, "a mro Raffaelo a bon conto del fontana che haua comenciato mro Giouanni bo: me: a Tiuli"; June 4, 25 *scudi*; June 16, 10 *scudi*; July 9, 15 *scudi*; and June 26, 15 *scudi*. ASM, Registri, Pacco 118, Libro dei Depositarii 1566-1567, f. 23r: "E adi detto [Oct. 28, 1566] scudi diecii giulij al detto [Ulisce Macciolini] abuon Conto di fatte le Figure de stucco alla Font.^a di m° Gioanni a Tiuoli." ASM, Registri, Pacco 120, Giornale di le fabriche 1568, f. 3: Feb. 4, 1568, "m. Ulisse Macciolinj Pitor" 14 *scudi* as final payment of 33 *scudi* "per hauer fatto alla fontana in Tiuolj detta dj m° giouannj trj faunj trj satirj duj vassj uno utro co' li posam di faunj tutto dj stucho . . . ▽ 14.40."

[24] ASM, Registri, Pacco 123, Registro del 1572, f. 142v: July 1, 1572, 46.40 *scudi* to "m^ro Leonardo Sormano . . . a conto de otto figure de satiri di pipirino che lui ha preso ha far per tt° il mese di Agosto 1572" and ASM, Fab. e Vill., Tivoli, Busta 70, Pte. 2, f. 13 published in F. Seni, *op.cit.*, p. 37, note 3 on p. 38. At about the same time this fountain and the Fountain of Pandora must have required considerable repair as recorded in ASM, Registri, Pacco 123, Registro del 1572, f. 140v: March 22, 1572, 3 *scudi*, "m^ro Andrea Fontaniero deue dare A di 22 Marzo . . . a conto della restauratione della fontane della ciuette et della pandora"; April 8, 2 *scudi*; April 22, 2.50 *scudi*; last of May, 5 *scudi*; June 26, 5 *scudi*; and October 3, 2.66 *scudi*.

rally one of the great attractions of the gardens. In this case the water-driven automata were simply copied from the ancient Greek treatise on pneumatics written by Hero of Alexandria.[25] A seventeenth century print shows that at least by that time there were trick water spurts from the pavement to surprise visitors.

Next to the Fountain of the Owl was another enclosed fountain (Fig. 1, no. 20) with stairs on each side mounting to the upper level of the Fountain of Rome. This little enclosed fountain, now called the Fountain of Proserpina (Fig. 19), was intended to be an outdoor dining room called the Fountain of the Emperors from its statues of four Roman emperors who built villas in the Tiburtine territory.[26] The architectural grotto of the fountain, after the design of his architect Galvani, was completed in 1569 and 1570 during the lifetime of the Cardinal of Ferrara.[27] The frontispiece has four spiral composite columns entwined with vines. These were inspired by the Solomonic column preserved in St. Peter's, which Raphael made popular in sixteenth and seventeenth century art through his tapestry cartoons for the Sistine Chapel. There is a large deep niche in the center with two smaller niches between the pairs of spiral columns. The niches were intended to contain statues of the nymph Arethusa flanked by two other nymphs, as the Parisian description indicates (folio 256v), but these statues were never created.[28] In the seventeenth century a stucco group of Pluto carrying off Proserpina, from which the fountain now receives its name, was placed in the central niche.

Above the Fountain of the Emperors was one of the chief features of the gardens, the Fountain of Rome (Fig. 1, no. 19; Fig. 20). Although there is a brief mention of work on the fountain in 1567, serious work commenced only in September 1568 when the *fontaniere* Curzio Maccarone took charge.[29] Actually this fountain depicts both

[25] Hero of Alexandria, *Opera quae supersunt omnia*, pp. 90-97. The mechanics of this fountain, like that of the Water Organ, are explained in S. de Caus, *op.cit.*, ff. 29v-30v.

[26] Paris, cod. Ital. 1179, f. 256r (see Appendix A, p. 146) and the engraving of Dupérac of 1573 (Fig. 1).

[27] ASM, Fab. e Vill., Tivoli, Busta 70, Pte. 1, fasc. 12, f. 66r: "Misura et stima deli lauori di Trauertino che a fatti mro Rafaelo scarpelino a tuto sua robba in la fabrica del Palazzo e altri lochi del Illmo Cardinale di ferrara in Tiuoli che comenca del mese di ottobre 1568 per tuto il mese d otobre del '69 Misurate et stimati per mi Alberto di galuani da ferrara.

1. In Prima per scalini di Trauertino quali sono mesi in opera sotto li Piedi stalli della mia fontana deli Collone torti . . . ▽ 6 b."
f. 70r: Estimate of work of "mro Jacomo da Pratta Murator" from Jan. 1570 through Dec. 1570, evaluated by Galvani, records masonry "dun Pezzo di volta fatto in la scalla dela mia

fontana doue se fatto il Piano lunga."
f. 85r: Estimate of Biasioto's work from Nov. 1568 through Oct. 1569; and f. 85v:
"19. . . . le Pietre dele cimase dele Collone torte ala mia fontana di trauertino . . ."

[28] Dupérac's engraving shows a separate Fountain of Arethusa on the Cardinal's Walk (Fig. 1, no. 9).

[29] *Ibid.*, f. 49r: Estimate of work by the stonecutter Rafaello ending the last of April 1567:
"56. Item per 4° Pietre busate ala fontana della Roma in capo ali condutj per fare li saquatori di Pietre grande stimati 80 b."
ASM, Registri, Pacco 120, Giornale di 1568, f. 28: Oct. 6, 1568, "A spesa dj Tiuolj ▽ sei m.ta pag.li a mo Curcio fontanier' . . . per giornatte otto datto alauorar' alla roma finite per tutto dj xviii Settemb."; f. 29: October 16, 13.50 *scudi*, "Tivoli . . . a mo Curcio fontanier' . . . per giornate 18 che luj a datto allauorar' nel giardo della Roma a baj 75 la giornatta." ASM, Registri, Pacco 120, Registro del 1568, f. xxxvii:

Tivoli and Rome. The flow of water begins at the upper left near the Villa where a cascade plunges down into the fountain and gardens (Fig. 21). This, of course, represents the celebrated Cascade of the river Anio at Tivoli, since at the top of the cascade is a stucco river god holding the round Temple of the Sibyl which actually stands at Tivoli near the crest of the famous Cascade. Below the cascade of the fountain a stucco personification of the Apennines with arms upstretched supports the river Anio. The water then flows down to join the Tiber, which is depicted as an outstretched river god almost immersed in the falling water. His overturned vase augments the stream which flows down to the level of the little court in front of the fountain. The main part of the fountain is set upon a podium about seven feet high, with the Tiber flowing past the foot of the podium. In the center of the Tiber is a small stone boat with an obelisk as its mast (Fig. 22), depicting the present island of San Bartolomeo at Rome. At one end of the bark was a serpent spitting water, representing the Temple of Aesculapius on the island, which was originally dedicated to that deity; an eagle at the other end, symbolized the Temple of Jupiter also on the island. Beyond the boat a sloping bridge crosses the stream up to the podium.

On the podium the fountain was arranged as a theatrical set portraying the ancient city of Rome (Fig. 23). Unfortunately, in the middle of the nineteenth century most of the small buildings imitating the famous monuments of Rome were destroyed by the collapse of the sustaining wall, leaving only the brick remains of two of the Seven Hills at the southern corner (Fig. 24), now completely overgrown with shrubbery and vines. The most important pictorial source for the original appearance of the fountain is a seventeenth century engraving of Venturini (Fig. 23), and the building accounts for the masonry work of the fountain in 1570 help to identify some of the buildings.[30]

October 28, 1568, 9 *scudi*, "a Curcio fontanier' . . . per giornatte dodici datti alla roma et altri luochj."

[30] ASM, Fab. e Vill., Tivoli, Busta 70, Pte. 1, fasc. 12, ff. 70r-75v, estimate of the work of "mᵣᵒ Jacomo da Pratta Murator" from Jan. 1570 through Dec. 1570:

"16. Muro fatto sopra al dito fondamento che fa il Pilastro per andar a tor suso la volta della Roma. . . .

17. Muro del masisco fattonel vaso della Roma che a fatto Creser di Piu. . . .

18. Muro della volta fatto sopra il Corso dela qua doue se fatto la strada soto la Roma per andare il loliueto à canto ala vigna chera di messer Camillo. . . .

. . . .

22. Muro del masisco fatto direto la Riua del fiume della Roma . . .

23. Muro del masisco quale a fatto far Curcio per il leto del fiume quale si parte dela figura del fiume. . . .

. . . .

31. Muro dela faccata del Terco Monte verso la vigna chera di messer Camilo Marcio. . . .

. . . .

34. Muro dela volta del dito monte.

35. . . . quarto Monte

. . . .

38. . . . quinto Monte. . . .

. . . .

46. Muro dela faccato del Palazzo Magiore.

47. Muro del Masisco del Tempio dela dea vitoria.

48. Muro della scalla del dito tempio. . . .

49. . . . sesto mote.

50. Muro della faccata del fianco verso la roma.

. . . .

53. . . . alutimo Monte. . . .

54. Muro del masisco del tempio dela dea

The theatrical scenery of the fountain, for so it is labeled in the description of 1611,[31] was arranged in a semi-oval with seven elements, which projected toward the center of the oval, representing the Seven Hills of Rome. Each pair of hills was connected at the back by an arch "in imitation of the aqueducts of Claudius."[32] Two mediaeval gates closed the scenery at each end. In front of each projecting hill was a round or rectangular temple, while other temples, palaces, columns, arches, and towers were built up on the hills. The building accounts are rather meager in mention of specific monuments and too scant to identify the location of such monuments. The two monuments which can be identified by the accounts are the two end gates: the Flaminian Gate, nearest the Villa, and the Gate of St. Paul's. In the records the hills are numbered one to seven beginning at the south with the hill nearest the Villa. Accordingly, the round temple in front of Hill Seven, the Temple of the goddess Murcia, identifies the Aventine. The round temple in front of Hill Five, the Temple of Victory, identifies the Palatine. This identification is substantiated by the record of building there the "Façade of the Palazzo Maggiore," the name still used in the sixteenth century for the Palatine. For further identification the accounts are too vague. There is mentioned the building of a round temple before Hill One and a square temple before Hill Two, which are to be seen in Venturini's engraving. Also noted are the "Façade of the Palazzina on the Quirinal Hill toward Rome" and a "round temple before said hill," indicating that Hill Three must be the Quirinal, since the central hill must certainly be Capitoline. The name of the Capitoline also occurs in the accounts but with no specifications. There was also the Arch of Septimius

---

Murcia.

. . . .

15. Muro dun fundamenta dun Pilastro fatto in fra li doi Pilastri di fora ala roma in mezo ala volta grande che saueua da far Prima el vano se fatto piu stretto. . . .

16. Muro fatto sopra al dito fondamento che fa il Pilastro per andar ator suso la volta della Roma. . . .

17. Muro del masisco fattonel vaso della Roma che à fatto creser di Piu che non non nera Prima. . . .

. . . .

26. Muro duna volta fatta in Capo al dito masisco per seguitar il leto del fiume verso la Porta di san Pauolo. . . .

. . . .

58. Muro delatra facca del dito Monte doue ela Palacina. . . .

. . . .

67. Muro del Masisco fatto sopra il Monte del Campidoglio.

68. Muro del Tempio tondo doue sono le Collone dopie fatto sopra il monte.

. . . .

73. Muro delatra facea del fianco del dito Monte uerso la fontana deli oceli. . . .

. . . .

78. Muro dela faciata dela Palacina al Monte quirinale verso la roma.

. . . .

80. . . . Tempio tondo dinaci al dito Monte.

. . . .

102. Muro di una Palacina al Monte del Campidoglio dala banda uerso la cucina.

103. Muro dela faceata del monte che a fato ruina Curcio. . . .

. . . .

112. . . . Palacina nel fianco del terco monte.

113. . . . Palacina del secondo Monte.

. . . .

119. . . . tempio tondo dinaci al Primo monte che a canto ala Porta flaminia.

120. . . . tempio quadro dinaci al monte secondo uerso la dita Porta."

[31] A. del Re, *op.cit.*, p. 56: "in forma di Scena, ò Teatro semiouato."

[32] Paris, cod. Ital. 1179, f. 262v (see Appendix A, p. 148).

Severus apparently somewhere near the Temple of Murcia. The Parisian manuscript (folio 262v) lists among the buildings depicted, "the Amphitheater of Vespasian, the Pantheon of the Campidoglio, the Trajanic and Antonine Columns, the Naumachia, circuses, hippodromes, the corridor of Caligula, pyramids, the Mausoleum, the Mausoleum of Hadrian, and numerous other things." The description of Zappi in 1576 mentions in addition the three Arches of Septimius, Titus, and Constantine, and the Torre dei Conti.[33] Several of these monuments can be seen in the depictions of the fountain. For example, three columns are visible in Venturini's engraving. Between Hill Six, probably the Celian Hill, and the Aventine was a three-story amphitheater, most likely the Colosseum. A five-story tower at the far right is undoubtedly meant to be the Septizonium.[34] Certainly the temple with a portico standing in front of the central hill is intended to be the Pantheon, even if its portico is only hexastyle. This proves then that the central hill was the Capitoline as the Parisian account speaks of the "Pantheon of the Campidoglio" being depicted at the fountain.

In the center of the fountain in front of the Pantheon was seated the personification of Rome (Fig. 25), carved by the Fleming Pierre de la Motte. This was made after the design of the Cardinal's archaeologist, Pirro Ligorio, except, as is noted in the contract of 1568, "that in place of that statuette which said Rome has in her hand in accordance with the drawing, I mean to make a sword or lance as it will seem better to the Cardinal."[35] The statue of Rome, with lance grasped in her right hand and sheathed sword in her left, still sits on the podium of the fountain with two shields beneath her and another helmet under her left foot. Wearing a helmet, Rome is clad in a chiton with right breast bared and himation on her left arm and lap. According to

[33] G. M. Zappi, *op.cit.*, p. 59.

[34] The location of the Septizonium, not near the Palatine but near the Aventine, may seem out of place to us, but this is just where Ligorio locates it in his book on antiquities (*Libro di M. Pyrrho Ligori Napolitano delle antichità di Roma*, Venice, 1553, f. 36r). He claims that there were two Septizonia, an old one near the Palatine and that of Septimius Severus in the "Regione della Piscina publica," which is the twelfth region of Rome outside the walls between the Porta Ardeatina and the Porta Appia.

A discussion regarding Ligorio's opinion on this matter is in D. Métral, *Blaise de Vigenère*, Paris, 1939, p. 224, and Métral reproduces a woodcut after Ligorio's design of the Septizonium (pl. III), which resembles the tower in the engraving of the Rometta.

[35] ASM, Fab. e Vill., Tivoli, Busta 70, Pte. 4, f. 5, published in F. Seni, *op.cit.*, p. 66, note 1 on p. 69, but Seni's version is not an accurate transcription in minor points of the original contract.

The accounts for payment for the carving of the statue are as follows: ASM, Registri, Pacco 120, Giornale di 1568, f. xxviii: Sept. 30, 1568, 10 *scudi* to Pietro della Motta on account; f. 28: Oct. 12, 10 *scudi*; f. 29: Oct. 26, 15 *scudi*; ASM, Registri, Pacco 120, Registro di 1568, f. 40: Dec. 30, 1568, 50 *scudi*, "A m. Gillio Della Vulietti et m. pietro da Motta scultorj ... a buo' coto della Roma et altre statue." ASM, Registri, Pacco 120, Registro d'entrata e opere del 1569, f. 163v: May 26, 1569, 10 *scudi*, "am.ro Pietro per resto de ▽ 65 per fattura della statua di Treuertino detta la Roma."

Late in 1568 there was some slight work to prepare the base for the Roma, ASM, Fab. e Vill., Tivoli, Busta 70, Pte. 1, fasc. 12, f. 27: Estimate of work by Tomaso for the year ending October 1568:

"14. Per auer fatto un Pezzo di muro di matoni sotto la figura della roma per Poter Posar per la uorarla il scultor."

the contract, the statuette that Ligorio's figure carried in her hand was a small Victory, inspired no doubt by the personification of Rome carrying a statuette of Victory on Roman coins from the time of Hadrian and later.[36] De la Motte also carved the group of the wolf suckling the twins, Romulus and Remus (Fig. 26), and a large travertine Eagle.[37] At the time of the Inventory of 1572 these were under the Water Organ, probably in the grotto intended to contain the Sibyls. By at least 1611 the wolf group was placed in the Fountain of Rome on one side of the figure of Rome, while on the other side was the group of an horse attacked by a lion added in 1607 after the design of G. B. Albergati.[38] The latter group, according to the description of 1611, represented the struggle between Tivoli and Rome and the domination of the latter (the Lion) over Tivoli (the Horse).

Enough of the brick and stucco buildings on the podium can be identified as specific ancient monuments to prove that Ligorio designed the Fountain of Rome to be a reconstruction of the ancient city analogous to the maps which he had prepared in 1553 and 1561. Of course the arrangement of the Seven Hills in a semi-oval is not an accurate reconstruction of the topography of Rome, but Ligorio had to organize the representation as a background for the fountain. The disposition of the buildings at the back of a podium calls to mind a Renaissance theatrical set as seen in Serlio's Second Book (1545) or as still preserved in the Teatro Olimpico at Vicenza (ca. 1584). The question arises whether this fountain was also to serve as an outdoor theater or whether it was simply a fountain inspired and influenced by the contemporary theater. Del Re in the early seventeenth century pointed out that the fountain was "in the form of a Scene, or semi-oval Theater."[39] Certainly it seems made for theatrical performances. An architectural background is set on a raised podium with a small piazza in front as a sort of *cavea*. That this section of the garden had theatrical associations is also substantiated by the small stucco relief at the foot of the stairs near the entrance to the piazza in front of the fountain. This stucco relief shows the Este eagle flanked by two comic theatrical masks (Fig. 20). The theater was one of the Cardinal's favorite recreations, and several members of his entourage, especially the French humanist

[36] J. M. C. Toynbee, *The Hadrianic School*, Cambridge, 1934, pp. 135-137 and especially the coin of Septimius Severus (pl. XVIII, no. 22); also J. M. C. Toynbee, *Roman Medallions* (Numismatic Studies, No. 5), New York, 1944, p. 163 and especially the coins of Magnentius (pl. VI, no. 6) and Elagabalus (pl. XXVIII, no. 8).

[37] ASM, Registri, Pacco 120, Registro d'entrata e opere 1569, f. 163v: May 26, 1569, 7 *scudi*, "a m^{ro} Pietro della motto per resto di ▽ 90 per la statua del Fiume, d'vn'Aquila grande, et d'vna Lupa con Romolo et Remo, tutti di Treuertino."

[38] Both groups are described in their loca-

tion in the fountain in A. del Re, *op.cit.*, pp. 58-61, but Pighius (*Hercules Prodicius*, p. 531), who visited Tivoli in 1575 seems to have noted the statue of the Wolf and Twins near the river god Tiber in the Fountain of Rome. On the other hand Zappi in 1576 does not mention this group. Pighius is, of course, not too reliable as he worked in part from an engraving of the Villa, but in this case the engravings also do not depict the statue of the Wolf. The account for the group of the Horse and Lion by Albergati is published in F. S. Seni, *op.cit.*, p. 118 n. 2.

[39] A. del Re, *op.cit.*, p. 56.

Marc-Antoine Muret, wrote plays for his enjoyment. One would expect the Cardinal to have provided a theater for his summer visits to the Villa, just as he built a tennis court near the kitchens for the enjoyment of the other fashionable sixteenth century recreation.

However, it is unlikely that the Fountain of Rome was built to be used as a theater, since there are some obstacles to such an identification. The first and only strong objection is caused by the lack of any references to its use as a theater in contemporary or subsequent documents. The closest such reference is the description of Del Re, already noted. It does not seem possible that, if the fountain was used for dramatic performances, some references to this would not turn up in the many descriptions of the Villa or the letters written by the Cardinal or his friends. Also the use of water in relation to the area does not particularly suggest a theater. For example, Del Re in 1611[40] notes four water tricks against unsuspecting spectators in this section of the gardens. Thus, the seats that were arranged along two sides of the piazza for admiring the fountain were made with secret holes so that the weary beholder would soon find his buttocks wet. The stairs to the little flat green below the cascade were made with a surprise jet of water which "bathes from the navel down" whoever steps there. Two different jets of water were also contrived in relation to the iron gate which closed the middle of the bridge to the podium. Venturini's seventeenth century engraving (Fig. 23) of the fountain shows one of the jets on the bridge in action. Finally and most conclusively, the Parisian description, which is the most knowledgeable account, specifies only that the podium was to "serve as the dining room of the fountain" (folio 263r).

The Fountain of Rome stands at the end of one of the chief cross-axes of the garden, the so-called Lane of the Hundred Fountains (Fig. 1, no. 13), probably begun in 1569 (Fig. 27).[41] This axis continues across the gardens to the Oval Fountain. Along this lane were three channels terraced one above the other, the upper one having twenty-two small boats[42] from which spurt jets of water. Each boat was then separated

---

[40] *Ibid.*, pp. 57-58.

[41] ASM, Registri, Pacco 120, Registro d'entrate e opere del 1569, f. 125v: Aug. 18, 1569, 7 *scudi*, "a Luca Antonio da Figoli Fontaniero per il pᵐᵒ vano che lui ha fatto al gran condotto come d'un bollore all'altra computa vna nauicella et mezza per vano," and Sept. 3, "per il secondo vano"; f. 126r: Sept. 13, "terzo vano," Sept. 24, "per il quarto et quinto vano," Oct. 12, "sesto uano," and Oct. 21, "settimo vano." ASM, Registri, Pacco 121, Protetione di Francia 1570, f. 20: July 3, 1570, 10 *scudi*, "A Luca Ant.º figullj da Caglio . . . a Contto della sua puisione dj hauer a lauorar' a Tiuolj"; f. xxii: July 30, 6 *scudi*, "a mº Paullo figollj Scoltor' acoto delle barchette che fa nel gia cdtto"; f. xxiiii: Aug. 21, 5 *scudi*, "a Lucantº figollj acoto dj sua puisione di lauorar a Tiuollj" and

3 *scudi*, "a Paullo figollj acoto delle barchi"; f. xxv: Aug. 31, 2 *scudi*, "A Paullo figollj . . . a Contto delle barchette" and Sept. 8, 4.64 *scudi*, "Paullo figollj"; f. xxvi: Sept. 23, 4 *scudi*, "A Paolo Figoli . . . per resto de ▽ 19 e b. 64 che lui doueua hauere per hauer fatte il barchetto di Calce con li bollori al gran condotto"; f. 26: Oct. 10, 5 *scudi*, "A mº lucantonio Figoli da Cagli"; and f. 27: Nov. 7, 5 *scudi*, "mº Lucantonio Figoli da Cagli," ASM, Registri, Pacco 123, Registro del 1572, f. 141v: June 3, 1572, 10 *scudi*, "m.ʳᵒ Bassi Vasaro Bolognese . . . a conto delli settandui vasi che ha preso a far' per li condotti de Tivoli per ttº luglio."

[42] G. M. Zappi, *op.cit.*, p. 59, states that there were 25 such boats, while Del Re, *op.cit.*, p. 53, specifies 22, the number in existence today.

from the next by three vases. Below each boat and vase at the back of the middle channel of water were stucco reliefs of Ovid's *Metamorphoses* which are now almost completely worn away and are generally covered with Venus's-hair and moss (Fig. 28). Streams of water flowed from the upper canal between these stucco reliefs into the middle channel. Small heads of animals in the retaining wall then spit water down into the lowest channel which ran along the path. The charm of this lane was, and is, the innumerable varieties of jets, spurts, and streams of water which make a symphony of sound and light, but this Lane of the Hundred Fountains has been changed several times. Venturini's engraving of it in the late seventeenth century shows the change which occurred in 1622[43] when eagles and fleur-de-lis were substituted for some of the vases (Fig. 29). Since then the remaining vases have been replaced by obelisks and more fleur-de-lis, so that there are now actually ninety-one fountains of four types: fleur-de-lis, obelisks, boats, and eagles, the first three of which shoot up different types of water jets. The fleur-de-lis has a single tall jet; the obelisk a short, wide fan; and the boat a tall, fan spray.

At the northeast end of the Lane of the Hundred Fountains one steps into the enclosed area before the Fountain of Tivoli or the Oval Fountain (Fig. 1, no. 14; Fig. 30). This fountain was one of the earliest fountains undertaken in the gardens after the problems of leveling the terrain and supplying water were solved. In 1565 there was an evaluation of the excavation for the fountain, and another evaluation in the same year is concerned with the masonry completed by Tomaso da Como including work "to cut nine windows in the lime deposit (*tartaro*) in the Oval. . . ."[44] In August 1566 a contract was given to the *fontaniere* Curzio Maccarone to make the great Oval Fountain, on which he worked steadily through May 1567.[45] The masonry by Tomaso

[43] V. Pacifici, "Luigi d'Este e la villa tiburtina," *Atti e memorie della società tiburtina di storia e d'arte*, XX-XXI (1940-1941), p. 144 n. 1.

[44] ASM, Fab. e Vill., Tivoli, Busta 70, Pte. 3, f. 1r: "Misura del Conduto che à Cauato m^ro Tomaso Murator in Tiuoli nel anno 1564 e de lanno 1565 il detto Conduto la fatto Cauare lo Illmo Cardinal di ferrara Comenca dal fiume e uene per sina al suo giardino sotto terra Misurato per mi Alberto di galuani da ferrara lungo canne n.º 140 à giulj 15 la canna mota ▽ 210.

Item il detto M^ro Tomaso à cauato tartaro erena doue ela loggia delouato . . . ▽ 13 b. 44."

The masonry accounts are in *ibid.*, Pte. 1, fasc. 10, ff. 5r-8r and 10r, e.g.:

"A di 10 Ottobre 1565
Misura et stima deli lauori di muro che a fatti m^ro Tomaso da Como Murator in Tiuoli in el giardino da baso del Illmo gardinal di ferrara in le pescieri elouato in li conduduti Misurato p mi Alberto di Galuani da ferrara

Presente m^ro Tomaso e m. Visdomino in Primo.

. . . .

2. Muro del secondo Pilastro Pasato il fos'o verso lovato. . . .

3. Muro del archo che in Posta sopra ali dui Pilastri che trauersa il fosso . . ." (f. 5r).

"13. Muro del sesto Archo che finisce sotto la Piazza delouato. . . .

14. Muro che un archo Pasato il fosse verso la Muralia dela Terra. . . .

15. Muro delutimo Pilastro sotto al detto Archo che finisce. . . .

16. Muro del Masiso fatto sopra ali Archi grandi che comenca sotto la Piazza delouato . . ." (f. 5v).

"19. Muro del Primo Parapeto del conduto al Piano del uiale . . ." (f. 6r).

"Per auer fatto taliar noue finestre nel tartaro in louato. . . .

Colla di Matoni Pisti nele ditte finestre quadrate . . ." (f. 10r).

[45] The contract, dated August 22, 1566, in

da Como and stonecutting by Raffaello Fiorentino for the fountain continued through 1568 at which time the work was basically completed, since the great statues in the upper grottoes were then in place.[46] In 1570 the work had progressed far enough to

ASM, Fab. e Vill., Tivoli, Busta 70, Pte. 3, f. 3r, is partially published in F. Seni, *op.cit.*, p. 115 n. 2 on p. 121. Curzio's monthly salary of 11 *scudi* is recorded in ASM, Registri, Pacco 118, Libro dei Depositarii 1566-1567, f. 21r: August 22, 1566, 11 *scudi*; f. 22r: Sept. 12, 11 *scudi*; f. 25r: Dec. 2, 9 *scudi*, f. 25v: Dec. 16, 11 *scudi*; f. 26v: Jan. 21, 1567, 10 *scudi*; f. 27r: Feb. 5, 30 *scudi*; f. 29r: March 24, 11 *scudi*; f. 29v: April 3, 9 *scudi*; f. 30r: April 23, 10 *scudi*; f. 30v: April 15, 15 *scudi*; and f. 31v: May 5, 22 *scudi*, May 10, 15.70 *scudi*, and May 21, 16.94 *scudi*.

Curzio Maccarone was already an eminent *fontaniere* having set several fountains in the Vatican in 1551 under the direction of Girolamo da Carpi (J. S. Ackerman, *The Cortile del Belvedere*, p. 165, doc. 75).

[46] ASM, Fab. e Vill., Tivoli, Busta 70, Pte. 1, fasc. 12, f. 5v:
"Muro fatto di dentro della faccata doui' sono le nichi' grande della loggia delouato. Muro della volta della loggia del ouato. Muro del conduto fatto di Nouo che si Parte dalouato et seguita drieto la Tribuna di San Pietro."
f. 11r: "A di 28 Maggio 1567 questa misura e per ento il mese di setembre del dito anno 1567.
1. Muro del fondamento della volta che fecu' far messer Piro per far il monte la Prima volta dala banda verso il Monte.
. . . .
3. Muro della volta che fe cu' messer Pirro per far il P° Monte che a fatto Curcio.
. . . .
5. Muro del Primo Pilastro che a fatto far Curcio uerso il vial di San Pietro doue comenca il mote."
f. 11v:
"10. Muro del Masisco fatto soto la statua del fiume uerso le grotte.
11. Muro del Masisco fatto sotto la figura della donna."
12. Ditto other river.
f. 21r: Estimate of work "che Comenca à di primo ottobre 1567 e fenisi per per tuto il Mese d otobre 1568.
. . . .
8. Muro del fondamento che diuide la Piaz-za delouato el boscheto che drieto al uial di san Pietro."
f. 21v:
"20. Muro fatto sotto li scalini di trauertino dela scale chi monte sopra ala loggia delouato."
f. 33r: Estimate of work "che comenca al Principio del mese di Nouembre 1568 e fenisi per tuto il mese d otbre 1569."
f. 36v:
"37. Item per auer fatto taliare le doi fenestre à Canto al longo in la loggia delouato."
f. 47r: "Misura di m^ro Fello chi comenca delano 1566 et fenise per tuto Aprile delano 1567. Stima de li lauori di scarpello trauertino che a fatti m^ro Rafaelo scarpellino in el Palazzo del Illmo Cardinal di ferrara in Tiuoli misurati et stimati per mi Alberto di galuani da ferrara. . . ."
f. 48r:
"24. Item per auer fatto le solie dele Nichie soscornisate alouato doue sono le figure di Peperino che buta laqua in tuto n.° 10 e piu 10 Pietre di Trauertino busati che fa li laquatori [?] ▽ 10 b 50."
f. 49r:
"48. Item per auer tirato le Pietre dele statue deli fiumi di gioanino tolte ala strada della Porta del cole e condute a mote da cordo con messer visdomino 16 sc."
f. 6or: "Misura et stima deli lauori di scarpello che a fatti m^ro Rafaelo fiorentino scarpelino . . . alouato . . . stimata per mi Alberto di galuani da ferrara da di p° Maggio 1567 peru.° 7bre 1568."
f. 62v: "In Prima balaustri al Parapeto atorno alouato n.° 64 . . . ▽ 76 b 80.
f. 66r: "Misura et stima deli lauori di Trauertino che a fatti m^ro Rafaelo scarpelino . . . che comenca del mese di ottobre 1568 per tuto il mese d otobre del '69.
. . . .
2. Item per la manifatura dun vaso di tuffo quale meso in frali Piedistallini in sopra la loggia delouato . . . ▽ 3."
ASM, Registri, Pacco, 120, Giornale di 1568, f. 1or: April 6, 1568, "A m° Raffaello scarpelino scudi trenta m.^ta aluj per b/a coto del Parapetto di balaustrj che fa del ouatto nel giardo di Tiuolj . . . ▽ 30." This work may have begun as early as February 25, 1568, since Raf-

permit Paolo Calandrino to set the mosaic decoration "of the façade which he makes at the Oval," and for the stucco-worker Bartolommeo di Conti of Mantua to make the *bollori*.[47]

The Oval Fountain, which the Parisian description (folio 256v) calls "the principal one of all the fountains of this garden and perhaps of all Italy," consists of a great oval basin, the rim faced with majolica tiles, and the far half surrounded by a semi-oval arcade. In the niches between the arches were set ten statues of water nymphs holding vases from which water shot into the basin (Fig. 31). These statues were carved in 1567 of peperino covered with white stucco by Giovanni Battista della Porta after the designs of Pirro Ligorio.[48] At the center rear of the basin was a large crater or basin at the level of the top of the arcade. The water from above overflowed this crater on all sides forming a great cascade into the basin. In the center of the crater was a ball which shot up jets of water so as to form the outline of a fleur-de-lis, one of the devices of the Cardinal. The enclosed area before the oval basin was planted with shade trees, but the most appealing shade from the hot summer was that of the walk beneath the arcade. However, the unwary spectator who traversed this shady walk would not only be deafened by the noise, since the walk went directly under the cascade, but he would also be surprised by trick jets of water spurting from the walk activated by his step, like the tricks of the Fountain of Rome.[49]

Stairs at either end of the arcade lead to the upper level where there are three grottoes in the artificial porous stone hill. In the central grotto is seated the local Tiburtine Sibyl Albunea with her right hand resting on the back of a nude boy (Fig. 32), probably Melicertes, who stands beside her. He was the son of Ino, who was transformed into Leucothea, and she, in turn, is often assimilated with the Sibyl Albunea. The group was carved out of travertine probably in 1568 by the Fleming Gillis van den Vliete, undoubtedly after the design of Pirro Ligorio, although the contract for this sculpture, unlike that for the ten nymphs, is no longer preserved.[50]

---

faello received 10 *scudi* at that time for unspecified "tazzette et balaustrj" (ASM, Registri, Pacco 120, another journal of 1568 with illegible title, f. xiiij).

[47] ASM, Registri, Pacco 121, Protetione di Francia 1570, f. 21: July 23, 1570, 11 *scudi*, "A m° Paullo Calandrino . . . a Contto della facciatta che fa alouatto"; f. xxii: July 30, 2 *scudi*, "a m° bart° dj Contj mantoano stucator' acoto dellj bulorj del ouatto"; f. 23: August 21, 22 *scudi*, "A m° Paullo Calandrino fontanier' . . . a Conto della grotta della dianna et del musaicho del grande ouatto"; f. xxiiii: August 21, 1 *scudo*, "a Bart° dj Conttj a coto dellj bulorj del ouatto" and August 29, 5 *scudi*, "A m° bart° dj Contj mantoanno stuccator' . . . per resto dj ▽ 8 simillj per Haur bolorj co' Inuencione alouatto."

[48] The contract with Della Porta, signed July 4, 1567, is published in F. Seni, *op.cit.*, p. 66 n. 1. According to the contract, five of these statues were to be finished by the end of August, one was already made, and the four remaining were to be completed by the end of September. Della Porta had already been paid 10 *scudi* on May 2, 1567, "per Il pcio dj una statua porpocionatta a uno dellj nichj del ouatto del giard° dj Tiuolj secondo Il disegno dj messer pirro Ligorio" (ASM, Registri, Pacco 118, Giornale de 1567, f. liii).

[49] G. M. Zappi, *op.cit.*, p. 60.

[50] ASM, Registri, Pacco 120, Giornale di 1568, f. xxviii: Sept. 30, 1568, "Gillio della Valeti fiamingo ▽ trj . . . a buo' conto dj Hauer acomodatto la statua della Sibilla." ASM, Registri, Pacco 119, Registro del 1568, f. 111: October 12,

Albunea and the boy would seem to be inspired by the Roman statue of a matron and her son now in the Museo Capitolino at Rome. The ancient statue was presented to the Roman people in 1566 by Pope Pius V when he stripped the Belvedere Court in the Vatican of the great collection of sculpture that Pirro Ligorio had gathered together for Pope Pius IV.[51] The Tiburtine Sibyl is a reversal of the Roman sculpture. In addition to the composition of the group, the very small scale of the boy suggests a relationship between the Tiburtine group and the Capitoline statue, although there are differences in drapery, especially the boy Melicertes being nude in contrast to the Roman boy in his tunic and toga. That the Tiburtine Sibyl was done after Ligorio's design is not only suggested by the fact that the nymphs were designed by him but by the resemblance of the full classic face and the curly-headed boy with the similar group in Ligorio's fresco of the *Dance of Salome* in the Oratorio of San Giovanni Decollato, Rome.

In the grottoes at each side of the Sibyl are statues of the river gods of the two local rivers, the Erculaneo and the Anio, perhaps carved in 1566 by Giovanni Malanca.[52] These are very similar except that they are reversed and the left-hand figure, the Erculaneo (Fig. 33), holds a cornucopia of fruit. The statues are, of course, based on the general river god figure known in many Roman examples, but the Erculaneo seems to be quite close to the statuette of a reclining river god, now in the Museo Capitolino,[53] which, like the prototype for the Sibyl, was part of the collection formed

1568, "am° Gilio della Vellita fiamengo scultore per sua mercede d'hauer' acconcio la statue di Treuertino detta l'Albenia ch sta in mezo la font dl l'ouato ▽ v iij."

Gillis van den Vliete from Malines, usually known to the Italians as Egidio della Riviera, was an important sculptor at Rome toward the end of the sixteenth century (A. Bertolotti, *Artisti belgi ed olandesi a Roma nei secoli XVI e XVII*, Florence, 1880, pp. 194-205). I believe that this work at Tivoli is the earliest known sculpture of Van den Vliete.

[51] H. S. Jones, *The Sculptures of the Museo Capitolino*, Oxford, 1912, p. 131, as Galleria 56, illus. pl. 22. The statue, which was in the Belvedere Court of the Vatican, is no. 59 in the Boccapaduli Inventory (*ibid.*, p. 368) where it is noted that the child was at that time without a head.

[52] ASM, Registri, Pacco 117, Libro di mandati 1566, under section indexed as "Dan^ri a Tiuoli per la Fabriche"; May 26, 1566, "A m. Giouanni Malanca scultore per il prezzo de tre statue de treuertino agiacere de longhezza de pal 20 dal piede ala Testa che gettanto acqua." See also note 46 above for record of setting "le statue deli fiumi di gioanino." Pacifici suggests

(*Ipp. II d'Este*, p. 169 n. 1) that the statue of the Sibyl was executed for one of the grottoes under the Water Organ and that a third river god, now near the Rometta, was to be in the present location of the Sibyl. However, the river god near the Rometta is undoubtedly the one for which Della Motte was paid in 1569 (see note 37). The Parisian manuscript (f. 250r) also tends to support Pacifici's hypothesis in its claim that the Grottoes of the Sibyls were "per honorare massimamente la Sibilla tiburtina." This idea must have been almost immediately changed because the evaluation of 1567 (see note 46) remarks on foundations for two river gods and one "figura della donna."

[53] H. S. Jones, *op.cit.*, p. 119, as Galleria 46c, illus. pl. 24. It was either no. 70 or no. 72 in the Boccapaduli Inventory (*ibid.*, p. 368). The arrangement of the river god within a grotto with a basin below him is very like that of the sixteenth century setting of the Tigris in the Statue Court of the Belvedere in the Vatican (see *Die römischen Skizzenbücher von Marten van Heemskerck*, ed. by C. Hülsen and H. Egger, I, Berlin, 1913, pl. 63).

by Ligorio to decorate the Belvedere Court of the Vatican. At the top of the artificial mountain behind the Sibyl is poised a winged Pegasus (Fig. 34), perhaps based upon a coin of Hadrian,[54] about to leap from Mount Helicon where, according to Greek legend, a fountain appeared in his hoofprints.

The enclosed area in front of the Oval Fountain has a gateway toward the north leading by a path through trees to the Water Organ. On either side of the front entrance were wall fountains dedicated to Bacchus (Fig. 1, no. 16), which were prepared in 1569.[55] Made of brick covered with stucco, these fountains consisted of niches flanked by columns. Originally irregular rocks were set in the stucco to simulate a rustic effect, and the remains of these can still be seen in the ruins of the right fountain. Within each of the shallow niches stood a statue of the nude Bacchus with a vase under his arm from which water gushed down into a basin, and from behind his head water sprayed out to form a veil. The description of these figures in Del Re[56] as nude, except partially covered with a tiger's skin, and leaning on a tree trunk suggests the type of Praxiteles' Satyr, of which the best version, now in the Museo Capitolino, came from the Secret Garden here at the Villa d'Este.[57] This comparison is further supported by the fragmentary remains of the figure still in the niche of the left fountain (Fig. 35), which seems to be nude except for a skin over the left shoulder. The strong reverse S-curve of the figure is simply a reversal of the Praxitelean statue. On the other hand the statue in the right fountain shows no resemblance to Del Re's description. The figure is completely clothed in chiton and cloak with calf-high boots decorated with masks and without an ivy crown (Fig. 36). In fact, this statue in its similarity to the statue of Orpheus (Fig. 12), added to the Water Organ in the seventeenth century, suggests a later substitution for the sixteenth century Bacchus.

The southeast wall of the fountain area has four windows and an entrance into three rooms set in the slope of the hill, originally known as the Grotto of Venus (Fig. 1, no. 17).[58] Now stripped of everything except the water rushing into a basin,

[54] H. Mattingly, *Coins of the Roman Empire in the British Museum*, III, London, 1936, pl. 82. Actually closer to the Tiburtine Pegasus, although less likely the inspiration, since it is not an ancient object, is the image of Pegasus on the reverse of a medal of Pietro Bembo (*Renaissance Bronzes from the Kress Collection*, Washington, 1951, no. A 1159.422A, illus. p. 120).

[55] ASM, Fab. e Vill., Tivoli, Busta 70, Pte. 1, fasc. 12, f. 85r, which is an evaluation of the stonecutter Biasioto's work "del mese di Nouembre 1568 per tuto il mese di otobre 1569. . . . 9. Item per le Pietre di trauertino che fa ilbro ali vasi dele fontane deli bacci ala Piazza delouato . . ." and f. 86r: "40. Item per doi vascete di trauertino uno mesa sopra ala nicia doue va lesculapio elatra alafontana del bacho

che a fatto Curcio in la Piazza delouato. . . ."

[56] A. del Re, *op.cit.*, p. 53.

[57] T. Ashby, "The Villa d'Este at Tivoli and the Collection of Classical Sculpture which it contained," *Archeologia*, LXI, pt. 1 (1908), pp. 248 and 249; the sculpture is now in the Museo Capitolino, Rome: Stanza del Gladiatore, no. 10 (H. S. Jones, *op.cit.*, pp. 350-351, illus. pl. 87).

[58] ASM, Fab. e Vill., Tivoli, Busta 70, Pte. 1, fasc. 12, f. 81r: Estimate of work of "m^{ro} Biasioto scarpelino . . . di P.° de setenbre 1566 per tuto il mese d otobre 1568."
f. 81v:
"28. . . . doi Pezzi di guida che si sone mese sotto li Piedi dela venere in la grotta delouato ala fontana. . . ."
f. 85r: Estimate of Biasioto's work "del mese di

the main fountain in this grotto had an ancient statue of Venus of the Capitoline Venus type shown stepping from her bath. Nearby were statues of two nude *putti*, one astride a goose, the other holding a goose about its neck. On the edge of the basin around Venus stood four more nude boys with vases on their shoulders from which the water spurted. Before 1611[59] the two statues of the boys with the geese were moved to the so-called Fountain of the Swans (Fig. 37), built sometime after the Cardinal's death in the lower part of the garden. Presumably at the same time the Venus was removed and a Bacchus substituted, as can be seen in Venturini's engraving of the grotto (Fig. 38). The other two rooms of the grotto were never completed because of the Cardinal's death, as Del Re indicates. The inventory of the statues taken immediately after the death of the Cardinal[60] lists some other ancient and modern statues in these side rooms, including two ancient figures of Hercules which were later placed in the gardens above the Fountain of the Dragon and four sixteenth century statues of the Seasons intended for the large dining hall. This suggests that the two side rooms were used as temporary storage for sculpture.

On the slope above the Alley of the Hundred Fountains, diagonal paths led upward through thick woods. At the ends and intersections of these paths were small grottoes built into the slope. Many of these grottoes were never completed. Only the architecture and flowing water were created for the grottoes called the Fountain of Pomona and the Fountain of Flora in Dupérac's view (Fig. 1, nos. 11 and 12). Running along the top of this wooded slope below the terrace of the Villa was a crosswalk which extended the full width of the gardens. This path was called the Cardinal's Walk, even in the building accounts of 1569,[61] since the Cardinal was accustomed to stroll here with his humanist friend Marc-Antoine Muret, discussing philosophy or reading his breviary. At the northeastern end of this walk there was cut into the wall supporting the stairs to the upper terrace a grotto dedicated to Aesculapius (Fig. 1, no. 8). The statue is now in the Louvre.[62] In the other corner of the angle set below the terrace itself (Fig. 1, no. 8) was the grotto of Aesculapius's daughter, Hygeia. The statue has been removed to the Vatican.[63]

Nouembre 1568 per tuto il mese di otobre 1569."
f. 85v:

"31. Item per auer fatto la cimasa sopra il Parapeto dela fontana dela venere in la stancia delouato. . . ."

[59] The inventory of 1572, published by T. Ashby, *op.cit.*, p. 242, lists in the grotto the Venus with two *putti* on geese ("ducks" in the inventory) and four *putti* with vases. A. del Re, *op.cit.*, p. 71, in 1611 locates the two *putti* on geese at the Fountain of the Swans.

[60] T. Ashby, *op.cit.*, p. 244.

[61] ASM, Fab. e Vill., Tivoli, Busta 70, Pte. 1, fasc. 12, f. 43r: Estimate of work of Tomaso da

Como "comenca del Principio di Nouembre efenisi per tuto il mese xbre 1569," including work "al vial del Cardinale"; and f. 44r; "4. Muro di matoni del parapeto deli doi Nichi in capo il viale del Cardinale doue se meso lesculapio."

[62] T. Ashby, *op.cit.*, pp. 244 and 245. As the above and following accounts indicate, the preparations for setting up the statue of Aesculapius and the transportation of the statue from Rome date at the end of 1569: ASM, Registri, Pacco 120, Registro d'entrata e opere del 1569, f. 111v: Dec. 31, 1569, 4 *scudi* "per hauer condotto . . . da Roma a Tiuoli l'esculapio."

[63] T. Ashby, *op.cit.*, pp. 244 and 245.

On the main axis of the gardens a loggia completed in 1570,[64] called the Fountain of Pandora (Fig. 1, no. 10), was built out over the Cardinal's Walk. At the back of this loggia, which also sheltered the entrance to two of the stairs to the upper terrace, were three niches which contained antique statues. In the center was the Pandora now in the Museo Capitolino at Rome, at her right a Minerva, and at the left a female figure, also called Minerva in the Parisian manuscript (folio 265v), which Zappi in 1576 and the inventory of 1572 list as nameless. It is also preserved in the Museo Capitolino.[65]

At the western end of the Cardinal's Walk is the most elaborate grotto of all, cruciform in plan, the Grotto of Diana (Dupérac [Fig. 1, no. 18] by mistake indicates this grotto on the piazza of the Fountain of Rome). The floor was covered with rich majolica tiles depicting "lilies, golden apples, and white eagles arranged according to the emblem of the house of Este, . . . similar to the pavement which Pope Leo X made in the loggia of the palace of the Pope in the city of Rome."[66] At the corners of the central square are stucco relief statues of women in classic costume (Fig. 39), carrying on their heads baskets of golden apples. From the baskets branches grow up over the vault of the grotto, which is covered, as the pavement once was with white eagles, lilies, golden apples, and roses. The walls have stucco reliefs with the stories of Perseus and Andromeda, Diana and Actaeon, Apollo and Daphne, Pan and Syrinx, and Diana and Callisto. Rich, colorful mosaics by Paolo Calandrino cover some of the reliefs and the wall.[67]

Accenting the walls of the grotto were ancient statues, which are now in the Museo Capitolino at Rome.[68] On each side of the entrance arm was an Amazon, one of which the Parisian manuscript (folio 265r) calls Penthesileia, Queen of the Amazons, and the other the Roman heroine Lucretia. At the rear was Diana with her bow, accom-

---

[64] ASM, Fab. e Vill., Tivoli, Busta 70, Pte. 1, fasc. 12, f. 70r: Estimate of the work of "Jacomo da Pratta Murator" for the year 1570, and f. 76v: "33. Item per auer dato m⁽ᵒ⁾ Jacomo la Calza à luca Antoni e al fratello per fare le barchette e lauorar ala Pandora eala grota dela diana, e à m⁽ᵒ⁾ Pauolo da bologna per fare il musacho ala dita grota e a fare li Animali solo alercho le che in la nichia sopra ali conduti e per fare li fioroni che fa li 4⁰ fioroni soto che fa la 4⁰ fontane e piu la Calza à m⁽ᵒ⁾ Pietro per fare le fontane che sono nel giardineto e piu la calza à m⁽ᵒ⁾ girolamo per fare il stucho ala volta dela Pandora e la Pocolana per fare la calza moto."

In 1572 this grotto, like the Fountain of the Owl, required restoration and repair, see note 24.

[65] T. Ashby, *op.cit.*, pp. 244 and 245. H. S. Jones, *op.cit.*, pp. 345-346, illus. pl. 86 (the so-called Pandora) and pp. 125-126, illus. pl. 21.

[66] G. M. Zappi, *op.cit.*, p. 63.

[67] See note 64, and ASM, Registri, Pacco 123, Registro del 1572, f. 94v: March 7, 1572, 3.80 *scudi*, "a m⁽ᵒ⁾ Barthol⁽ᵒ⁾ sturelli per paternostri datti per le fabriche di Tiuli" and 3 *scudi* "per paternostri di vetro pau.⁰ et turchini per le fontane di Tiuli"; f. 95r: June 16, 10 *scudi* "am Michele caualcat⁽ʳᵉ⁾ per tanti che ha speso in terra de piu colori, e paternostri di vetro et altre robbe portati a Tiuli per la grotta de Diana"; and f. 95v: Aug. 5, 10.45 *scudi*, "per pretio. de colori smalti, paternostri et altre robbe." One of the tiles in the Grotto of Diana is actually dated 1572, see V. Pacifici, *op.cit.*, p. 174 n. 3.

[68] T. Ashby, *op.cit.*, pp. 244 and 245. See H. S. Jones, *op.cit.*; Amazon no. 29 on pp. 342-344, Stanza del Gladiatore 4, illus. pl. 85; Amazon no. 30, pp. 286-287, Salone 19, illus. pl. 69; Diana, pp. 44-45, Atrio 52, illus. pl. 6; and Minerva, p. 299, Salone 36, illus. pl. 73.

panied by a dog. The end of the left arm was dominated by an armed Minerva, while the right arm opens into a loggia overlooking the countryside. This arrangement does not entirely agree with the original conception presented by the Parisian account which mentions a fountain of the chaste Hippolytus in place of Minerva.

Above the Grotto of Diana is the large open-air dining room (Fig. 6). According to Zappi's description of 1576, the four niches, now empty, overlooking the garden were decorated with the sixteenth century peperino statues of the Four Seasons, which at the time of the Cardinal's death in 1572 were still stored in one of the side rooms of the Grotto of Venus. The Parisian manuscript notes that these statues were intended for the dining loggia. Ancient statues of Mars, now in the Ince Hall collection in England, and Bacchus[69] were on the entrance façade toward the terrace.

Attached to the center of the Villa is a two-story loggia, the lower story of which (Fig. 5) has three niches forming the Fountain of Leda (Fig. 1, no. 6). The central niche contained a statue of Leda and the Swan, now in the Borghese collection at Rome, with a statue of Helena at her right and Clytemnestra at her left.[70] Figures of the brothers Castor and Pollux stood just outside the fountain.[71] In front of the loggia was the Fountain of the Sea Horses on a small balustraded terrace projecting over the Fountain of Pandora. It consisted of a tripod antique basin containing three sea horses which supported a smaller basin.[72]

A large fountain dedicated to Thetis (Fig. 1, no. 7), shown reclining with her left arm over the shoulders of a bull,[73] adorned the eastern end of the terrace and served to balance the dining loggia at the western end.

On the eastern side of the Villa the Secret Garden was a sort of pendant to the tennis court on the western side. Many sixteenth century Italian gardens, for example the Vatican and the Villa Giulia, had a secret garden, a small walled garden of mediaeval descent. Dupérac's engraving (Fig. 1, no. 2) shows a spacious rectangular walled garden planted with trees and a large Janus-arched pavilion in the center. The work on the decoration of this garden began in 1565 when conduits were prepared to bring water from the Piazza di San Francesco to the pavilion in the garden.[74] In 1566 pay-

[69] T. Ashby, *op.cit.*, pp. 246 and 247. See B. Ashmole, *A Catalogue of the Ancient Marbles at Ince Blundell Hall*, Oxford, 1929, pp. 24-26, no. 43, illus. pls. 16 and 17.

[70] T. Ashby, *op.cit.*, pp. 246 and 247. Ashby suggests that the so-called Helena may be the figure of Juno in the Ince Hall Collection; see B. Ashmole, *op.cit.*, p. 4, no. 3, illus. pl. 37.

[71] G. M. Zappi, *op.cit.*, p. 64.

[72] Illustrated in G. A. Boeckler, *Architectura curiosa nova*, Nuremburg [1664], fig. 67. The present fountain is a modern copy of the original now in the Louvre but only of the lower part (V. Pacifici, in *Atti e memorie della società tiburtina di storia e d'arte*, XXII-XXIII [1942-1943], p. 66, n. 1 on p. 67). The upper

part of the sea horses is at present in the Vatican (Sala dei Busti, 312; see T. Ashby, *op.cit.*, pp. 250 and 251).

[73] The Parisian description does not mention this fountain, but the Inventory of 1572 (T. Ashby, *op.cit.*, p. 244) and Zappi (*op.cit.*, p. 64) give evidence of it. A. del Re (*op.cit.*, p. 35) objects to this nomenclature in the Dupérac engraving and calls it Europa and the Bull.

[74] ASM, Registri, Pacco 127, Spese per il Card.le di Ferrara 1563-1568, loose leaves:
"A di 3 setembre 1565
Misura deli muri et conduti che afatti m.ro Jacomo d'Alessio et compagnj Muratori inla Conserua che suso la Piazza di s:to francesco per Receuer laqua che ui ua dala fontana di

ments were made to Maestro Antonio Francesco Fiorentino and Maestro Giulio dalle Fontane for the "pavement under the pavilion and small fountain of the little garden," and work on this garden continued until 1570.[75] Remnants of the mosaic pavement have been discovered about sixteen inches below the present garden.[76] The decoration of this pavement consisted of the Cardinal's eagles and lilies with fountains in the four corners of the mosaic. The description on Dupérac's view (Fig. 1, no. 4) says that there was a "pavilion with four fountains which spout water in the form of a mirror." In the southern corner of the Garden near the Villa, the Fountain of the Unicorn (Fig. 1, no. 3) was set into the back wall, which served as a retaining wall for the piazza of San Francesco. The inventory of 1572 lists a standing nude Venus and Cupid accompanied by a dolphin[77] in this Secret Garden, in addition to the marble unicorn. In 1611 Del Re saw the Venus in a niche in the center of the back wall, but there is no trace of it today.[78] The inventory also mentions two nude Fauns in niches at the end of the garden.[79]

The Secret Garden was entered from a room on the eastern side of the ground floor of the Villa. This room actually served as a grotto for the small garden and was

S:ta Croce per il conduto laqual da laqua al Paualione del giardin Picolo al Piano del Palazzo Misurata per mi alberto di galuani da ferrara—▽ 69 b 43."

[75] ASM, Registri, Pacco 117, Libro di mandati 1566, under the section indexed as "Danri a Tiuoli per la Fabriche": June 17, 1566, 1.10 *scudi*, "per tanti smalti . . . del giardinetto"; June 21, 1 *scudo*, "a mro antº francº fiorentino a bonconto del cottimo del pauimto del padiglion del fontana ch'e nel giardº"; July 4, 9.16 *scudi*, "a mro Anton Francº fiorentino et mro Giulio dalle Fontane cpi a buo Conto del pauimento sotto il padiglione et Fontanina del Giardtº"; and July 8, 10.33 *scudi* "per tanti coragli cochiglie et malre [?] . . . per la Fontanina." ASM, Registri, Pacco 118, Libro dei Depositarii, 1566-1567, f. 20r: Aug. 11, 1566, 10 *scudi*, "a Iacº Tiuolino a buon co' delli Pauimenti che fa nello Giardº secreto di SS. Ill. a Tiuoli"; f. 21r: Sept. 2, 3 *scudi*, "a mº Iacº da Tiuli abuo Conto del Pauimento del Giardinetto segretto in Tiuoli"; and f. 21v: Sept. 12, 1.20 *scudi*, "à Gio: Iacº alias Il Tiuolino acconto del Cottimo difarne il musaico nel Giardº secreto de SS. Ill.ª in Tiuoli." ASM, Registri, Pacco 120, Giornale di le fabriche 1568, f. 2: Jan. 31, 1568, 3 *scudi*, "A mº Melchior basaro [or in another account book "Michello Vasaro"] . . . a Conto dj quatro aquille che vano allj frontispicij del padiglione di Tiuolj et dj dodicj giglj dj Terra che a

pmesso far apar mto; f. xxiii: July 24, 6 *scudi*, "A mº Filippo Galuano uascharo . . . a Contto dj Aquille che fa"; and f. 23: July 31, 2.32 *scudi*, "a mº Giouannj francese . . . per hauer cotto tre aquille co' un gilio grande in maggio dj altezza dj palmj quatro che suino per il pauaglione del giardino secreto." ASM, Registri, Pacco 121, Protetione di Francia 1570, f. 23: Aug. 12, 1570, 2 *scudi*, "a Antonio longarino da Pauia qtº per tre aquille dj terra cotta datta per Il Padeglione del giardº dj S.S. Ill.mo"; and f. 26; Oct. 21, 0.70 *scudo*, "a mº Francº indoratore per poluere di marmo, et per hauer fatto macinare Colori per l'acquile che uanno al Padiglione del Giardinetto." ASM, Fab. e Vill., Tivoli, Busta 70, Pte. 1, fasc. 12, f. 70r: Estimate of work of "Jacomo da Pratta Murator" for the year 1570, and f. 76v: "33. Item per auer dato mro Jacomo . . . la Calza à mro Pietro per fare le fontane che sono nel giardineto. . . ."

[76] V. Pacifici, "Residui di mosaico in Villa d'Este," *Atti e memorie della società tiburtina di storia e d'arte*, ix-x (1929-1930), p. 387, and pl. xxii. There is nothing left of the original garden, especially since this area suffered the most destruction during the past war.

[77] T. Ashby, *op.cit.*, pp. 248 and 249.

[78] A. del Re, *op.cit.*, p. 26.

[79] One Faun is preserved in the Museo Capitolino, Rome. See H. S. Jones, *op.cit.*, pp. 350-351, Stanza del Gladiatore 10, illus. pl. 87.

adorned with a rustic fountain containing a figure of a sleeping Venus with two cupids and a marble hare. Flanking the basin of the fountain were two antique statues of women holding vases from which water flowed.[80]

The two main features of the Villa d'Este and its gardens were the great collection of ancient statues, bought in Rome or excavated at Tivoli, and the innumerable fountains with their lavish supply of water. As early as 1568 the Imperial agent, Niccolò Cusano, described the incomplete Villa to his master the Emperor Maximilian II as "a royal palace filled with endless pleasures and with the rarest fountains, which costs him [the Cardinal] more than one hundred thousand ducats and certainly I have seen no other such in all of Christianity."[81] This enthusiasm aroused interest in the Emperor for whom Dupérac made a drawing of the Villa and gardens reproduced in the engraving of 1573.

It is the quantity of water at Tivoli that has charmed visitors of all periods. This abundance of water furnished the *fontanieri* a rare opportunity to create numerous effects. They treated the water as a sculptor might clay, molding it into a variety of forms. Tall, thin jets vied with transparent veils or heavy cascades of water. In the center of the Oval Fountain jets of water formed the lily of the Este coat of arms, matching the lilies and eagles created of terra cotta by the sculptors. The two-dimensional rectangles of the central fish pools were vaulted over by streams of water. In most cases it was not the movement of the water that was being exploited as much as its malleability, so that the water assumed an architectonic or sculptural quality.

Italian sixteenth century gardens were simply to decorate architecture.[82] In the tradition of ancient Roman gardening, all the elements of nature—water, stone, and verdure—were meant to reveal man's dominance. So at Tivoli the entrance under a long wooden pergola flanked by high walls proclaimed the control of man. As one stepped out upon the lower plain of the garden the steep slope up to the foot of the Villa was awesome not in the Romantic mode of nature's grandeur but in the power of man to shape nature to his will. On the plain the central cross-pergola defined the quadratic pattern of the lower garden which was carried out in the rectilinear mazes and herb gardens visible in Dupérac's engraving (Fig. 1) of the original project. The four rectangular fish pools beyond the plain marked the break in terrain where the slope mounted rapidly to the terrace of the Villa, but the incline on the left side of the garden was ignored in a classic manner. A maze was set on the hillside as if the

[80] T. Ashby, *op.cit.*, pp. 248 and 249. One Cupid is in the Museo Capitolino (H. S. Jones, *op.cit.*, pp. 87-88, Galleria 5, illus. pl. 18), and one of the feminine statues is in the Ince Hall Collection (B. Ashmole, *op.cit.*, p. 21, no. 37, illus. pl. 23).

[81] L. von Pastor, *The History of the Popes*, XVII, London, 1929, p. 406, doc. no. 52.

[82] Serlio in his fourth book, first published in 1537, asserts: "Li giardini sono ancor loro parte dell'ornamento della fabrica" (*Tutte l'opere d'architettura*, Venice, 1600, f. 197v). He illustrates this by including the plans or patterns for four garden parterres and two labyrinths with his drawings of carved wooden ceilings. The forms are analogous so that the planted patterns at one's feet outside the architecture harmonize with the carved wooden ceilings of the interior.

ground were a flat continuation of the plain. The principal slope of the garden was planted with trees, widely spaced on the lower slope, on the upper slope massed. There was, therefore, a gradual intensification of the verdure from the specimen planting of the herb gardens to the dark green mass of the upper slope, as there was an accompanying intensification of the water displays. Finally, above the wall of massed trees rose the stone walls of the Villa.

The axes and cross-axes of the rectilinear garden plan set up vistas but never the long unbroken vistas of the Baroque garden. The large cross-pergola of the lower garden formed small, intimate herb gardens. The passage through the cross-pergola was a long alley confined by the architectural elements. At the end of the cross-pergola the continuing vista did not recede, but, because of the steep slope, the Villa and the Fountain of the Dragon loomed above the spectator. It is only along the cross-axes that there is a sense of recessive depth, and one is conscious always that this is counter to the axis of the garden. From the Villa itself there is naturally a magnificent vista out over the countryside, but in this vista the garden plays a minor role. It lies below one as a controlled parterre intermediate between man's habitation and uncontrolled nature.

Following a long tradition advocated in the early fourteenth century by Pietro de' Crescenzi, most Italian gardens, particularly those of villas, are situated on a hillside. The building either stands below the hill with gardens mounting the hill behind—as at Castello, Caprarola, the Boboli gardens at Florence, and many of the gardens of Frascati—or it stands toward the summit of the hill with the gardens leading up to it. This latter type was developed at Rome in the circle of Bramante and Raphael, as seen in the Belvedere Court of the Vatican or the Villa Madama, and then later appeared at Bagnaia or the Tuscan gardens of Petraia and Pratolino. Except for Pratolino, the Tuscan gardens tend to be symmetrical around a central point, usually stressed by a free-standing sculptural fountain.[83] The gardens of Rome and its environs, including Caprarola and Bagnaia, emphasize an axis through the gardens. The Villa d'Este is unique in combining important cross-axes with the central axis, creating deviation and variety which was not exploited in other sixteenth century gardens but which appeared in a modified form in Baroque garden architecture.

The gardens and fountains of the Villa d'Este are intended for aural as well as visual delight. Not only is the water used mechanically to produce artificial sounds such as the music from the Water Organ, the artillery of the Fountain of the Dragon, or the birds in the Fountain of the Owl, but a wide variety of natural water sounds is exploited. The pergola at the entrance with its two small rustic fountains prepared the visitor for the principal motif of the gardens. The wide fish pools must have been rather serene with only the fall of the spray from the surrounding pillars to agitate

[83] A very succinct and clear definition of the differences between the Tuscan and Roman gardens, and their relative use of sculpture and water, is to be found in B. H. Wiles, *The Fountains of Florentine Sculptors*, Cambridge, Mass., 1933, pp. 17-21.

the pools, but as one mounted the stairs up the slope to the Villa the element of water became more apparent as it seethed and gurgled down the sides of the stairs. The Hundred Fountains set up both a visual and aural wall across the gardens which accompanied every step of the visitor until he burst with momentary relief into the enclosed area of the Oval Fountain only to be overwhelmed by the great roar of the cascade within those four walls. To walk beneath the arcade of the Oval Fountain increased this roar to a deafening, almost insane, pitch, as the cascade poured over one. Even the ground floor of the Villa itself continued this theme of water with its several rustic fountains, and only the main floor apartments remained quiet with simply the distant background of the murmur of water. During the deadly hot Roman summers the gardens of the Villa d'Este were to bathe all one's senses, visual, aural, and tactile, with the refreshment of water.

CHAPTER III · THE INTERIOR DECORATION
OF THE VILLA

THE ARCHITECTURE of the Villa d'Este is of minor interest, but the public rooms of the Villa were sumptuously decorated with frescoes. Most of this interior decoration is still preserved, although it has undergone constant restoration and retouching. However, there is lacking today the rich decoration supplied by the Cardinal's collection of antique sculpture, almost all of which is scattered throughout Europe in numerous museums.[1] There is no basic unity in the fresco decoration of the interior, either in subject matter or in artistic style. The rooms were painted in groups of two or three from 1565 to 1572 by several workshops of painters and stucco-workers headed by Girolamo Muziano, Federigo Zuccaro, Livio Agresti, and Cesare Nebbia. Each group of rooms was concerned with a different subject matter and symbolism. The unity of symbolism is, therefore, not apparent as a program for the interior decoration but must be considered in relation to the symbolism of the exterior decoration formed by the gardens and the fountains. Each room of the interior of the Villa is related to some aspect of the garden symbolism to form a final integrated unity.

The fresco decoration is confined to the first two floors of the Villa. The *piano nobile*, which on the interior is at the level of the main courtyard, has four decorated rooms which comprise the Cardinal's apartment, including a salon, an antechamber, bedchamber, and chapel. The salon is located at the center of the *piano nobile* facing onto the gardens below, while the other rooms of the Cardinal's apartment (Text Fig. A, nos. 1-6) range in a file toward the southwest. On the other side of the salon toward the northwest were several apartments which received no painted decoration of importance during the sixteenth century.[2] On the ground floor below the *piano nobile* (Text Fig. B) almost all the rooms were painted in the sixteenth century.

[1] A very thorough account of the ancient sculpture at the Villa is in T. Ashby, "The Villa d'Este at Tivoli and the Collection of Classical Sculptures which it contained," *Archaeologia*, LXI, pt. 1 (1908), pp. 219-256.

[2] On July 22, 1567, an agreement was signed to furnish by August 10 three sets of leather wall coverings embossed in silver and gold for three undecorated rooms of the *piano nobile* (rooms labeled D, G, and N on the plan of 1687, Fig. 40). ASM, Registri del Card. Luigi d'Este, Pacco 81, loose unnumbered sheets: Agreement dated July 22, 1567, at Tivoli with "Mro Bartholomeo rascone orpelaio nel pellegrino in Roma . . . di far tre stanze di Curame d'oro et argento per seruitio del palazzo de Tiuoli cioe la quarta Camra dell' appartamento di sopra di S. S. Illma et la terza camera

del Cardinal da Este et la p.ma del Arciuescouo di Siena."

Some of the furnishings of the Villa were made in 1565. The noted French woodcarver Flaminio Boulanger made two walnut four-posted bedsteads, and Girolamo Muziano prepared cartoons illustrating the fable of Vulcan for the embroidered hangings of one of the bedsteads. ASM, Registri, Pacco 116, Conti dele ent.a de Ferrara 1565 D, f. 17: Aug. 20, 1565, 15 *scudi* "A mo flaminio francese Intagliator' . . . a buon conto dj Hauere afar' due Letier' dj noce con otto colone e otto stagu' cioè una per una Trabacha e una per uno pauagliano per seruicio de Tiuolj"; Aug. 20, 7.20 *scudi* "A mo Pieroanto Sediar' . . . per ualutta de sej sedie dj noce guarniette dj Curamo rosso ordo seruirno per forastierj a Tiuolj"; Aug. 20,

THE CARDINAL'S APARTMENT

In the spring and summer of 1568 some thirty-five painters and stucco-workers were active at various intervals in the Villa, apparently all, or almost all, under the direction of the painter Livio Agresti of Forli. Certainly it is at this time that Agresti and his assistants decorated with personifications of Virtues at least two of the chief rooms of the Cardinal's apartment (Text Fig. A, nos. 1, 2), that is, the central salon and the adjoining room toward the southwest. The Cardinal's bedroom on this floor (Text

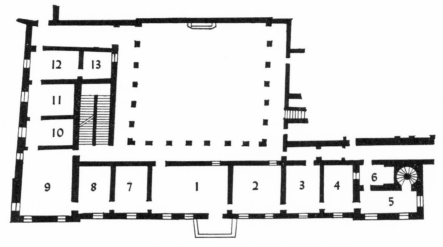

A. Plan of the *Piano Nobile* of the Villa d'Este

Fig. A, no. 3) was also decorated with a similar frieze of Virtues, but it would seem doubtful that this frieze was executed in 1568 as the accounts definitely indicate that the carved wooden ceiling in this room was created only in March and April 1569, and, although the style of painting is quite similar to the other two rooms, the colors of this frieze are stronger than in the other rooms.

The salon in the center of the *piano nobile* has its present decoration restricted to a coved ceiling and frieze (Fig. 41). Running around the top of the walls is a wide frieze composed of oval stucco frames flanked by frescoed personifications of Virtues. The areas encompassed by the oval frames are blank, and Del Re in 1611 claimed that "within them should be depicted portraits of men of the highest worth corresponding

---

16.40 *scudi* "A messer Aluigj Alfonsj . . . per ualuta de libre 4 di 4½ sedda Turchina torta a Julj 38 libra datta per far' fragia a una trabacha dj Dam^co Turchino"; f. xviiii: Oct. 8, 3 *scudi* "A messer Hier^o Muzano . . . per tantj che luj a spesj in duj cartonj dellj recamj della trabacha fatta alla fabulla dj Valehano come apar' m^to de dj 20 Agosto 65" and ASM, Registri, Pacco 116, Reg^tro i Mand^ti 1565, f. 36v: June 15, 15 *scudi* to Flaminio Francese "a buon conto delle due lettiere da trabacca chei' ha

tolto afar'"; f. 55r: Aug. 31, 15 *scudi* to Flaminio on account of "2 lettiere di noce et otto staggie"; Aug. 31, 7.20 *scudi* to Pietro Antonio sediaro for "6 sedie di noce"; Aug. 31, 16.40 *scudi* to Aloisi Alfonsi; f. 63v: Nov. 2, 3 *scudi* "amesser Girolamo Muzzano . . . per tanti che lui ha spesi per fare doi cartoni delli recami del cortinaggio fatto sopra la fabula di Vulcano cioe per fare il disegno delle bandinelle che mancano a detto cortinaggio."

to the grotesques, arabesques, and other sorts of painting, . . . if the death of said Cardinal of Ferrara had not happened and made them remain unfinished."[3] On each of the side walls are six seated female Virtues (Fig. 42) and on each of the end walls four, or a total of twenty personifications, executed in yellow, pale green, violet, and a soft brick red.[4] Above each Virtue a winged genius holds a symbol, such as a palm, a trumpet, olive branches, a lamp, a cross, a cardinal's hat or bishop's miter, probably to identify the Virtue as belonging to the owner, the Cardinal of Ferrara. Within the broken pediments above the horizontal oval frames are pairs of music-making *putti* or angels. Finally the corners of the frieze are masked by stucco coats of arms of the Cardinal.

In the center of each large cove a rectangular or square stucco frame again sets off a void, which was presumably intended to be painted (Fig. 41). Flanking each of these frames are large semi-nude atlantes. On the end walls grotesque decoration on a white background and small ovals with personifications of the Four Seasons fill the triangles formed by the coves (Fig. 43). In the longer side walls rectangular landscape scenes complete the coves.

The four landscapes, which are depicted in a very romantic fashion,[5] are probably meant to portray the Tiburtine region, since one has the ruins of a classic round temple set above a small waterfall like the so-called Temple of the Sibyl at Tivoli (Fig. 44) and another has a ruined circular temple within which is a statue of Hercules, the patron deity of Tivoli (Fig. 45). Painted in neutral greens and browns, the landscapes recede toward a horizon which is almost white, and the distant architecture is sketched in light brown. The painter has undoubtedly been influenced by ancient Roman landscape painting; this is particularly apparent in two of the landscapes having in the middle distance small bridges on which little men and animals are depicted with a few brushstrokes.

Livio Agresti, who was in charge of the decoration of the Cardinal's apartment except for the Chapel, was assisted by two groups of artists.[6] Most of the time six

---

[3] A. del Re, *Dell'antichità tiburtine capitolo V*, Rome, 1611, p. 12.

[4] For a description of the Virtues in the three rooms of the Cardinal's Apartment see Appendix C.

The source of most of these personifications is to be found in ancient Roman coins. In a letter of Annibal Caro to Fulvio Orsini, dated Sept. 15, 1562, Caro describes some personifications found in his collection of ancient coins (A. Caro, *Lettere del commendatore Annibal Caro*, ed. by A. F. Seghezzi, Milan, 1807, III, pp. 149-156, no. 76). Many of these personifications, such as Hilaritas, Laetitia, Pax, Justitia, and Aequitas, resemble the same personifications at Tivoli.

[5] These landscapes have undoubtedly been repainted many times. They have a crispness of touch and clarity of detail which could only be due to repainting, but in composition and representation they probably depict the originals quite well.

[6] Agresti apparently received a rather slight monthly salary of 10 golden *scudi*, but added to that is the fact that his room rent was paid by the Cardinal (ASM, Registri, Pacco 119, Registro del 1568, f. lxxxxvii: June 7, 1568, 6 *scudi* "am Cesaro Gentille per affitto d'una sua Camera doue alloggia messer liuio Agresto"). That Agresti is the chief painter is suggested not only by the listing of his salary in the accounts as an item separate from the usual long lists of artists but by the record in at least one case of the payment being made to Agresti on

painters composed one group. The highest paid painter was Giovanni dal Borgo,[7] who was undoubtedly Giovanni de' Vecchi from Borgo San Sepulcro, who entered the Accademia di San Luca at Rome in 1570 and worked with Taddeo Zuccaro at Caprarola for the Cardinal Farnese.[8] Next was Giovanni Paolo di Severi da Pesaro, who worked in the Vatican in 1586 and assisted Domenico di Michele, a pupil of Federigo Zuccaro, to decorate the Villa of the Cardinal of Montalto.[9] The artist Guidonio Gualffi, also listed as Gelffo or Lidonio dal Borgo, was probably Galeazzo Ghidoni or Guidoni,[10] an assistant later of Matteo Perez da Lecce, who was also soon to be active at Tivoli. The painter Bernardo da Chiaravalle or Bernardo da Melia is unidentifiable.[11] The last two painters of this atelier were Flemings, "Cornelio fiamingo"[12] and "Dionisio fiamingo," who is very possibly the later important Bolognese master, Denis Calvaert.[13]

---

behalf of six of the stucco-workers (ASM, Registri, Pacco 120, Giornale di le fabriche 1568, f. 6: Mar. 5, 1568, "A spesa dj Tivolj ▽ cinquantatrj m.ta pagtl amesser liuio agresta pitor' qst per pagar' lj sotto scrittj sette stutatorj che lauorararo a Tiuolj per sua puisione dj uno mese principiando qto dj v dettj apar mto ▽ 53, Jac stucator' ▽ 10, Tiuolino ▽ 9, Oratio ▽ 8, Bramante ▽ 7, Jac gargione ▽ 5, Cesaro milanese ▽ 8, Domco macinator' ▽ 6"). The accounts for Agresti's work are in *ibid.*, f. iii: Feb. 1, 1568, 21.77½ *scudi* "a messer Liuio Agresto pitor' qst p pagar' colorj cparj per suicio dj Tiuoli"; f. 6: Mar. 5, 23.20 *scudi* or 20 golden *scudi* as salary; f. xi: April 12, 6 *scudi* "amesser Liuio agresto qto . . . per suo salario per suiz atiuolj per uno mese ch finisca adj 5 maggio"; f. 13: May 10, 11.60 *scudi* or 10 golden *scudi* "a Conto dj sua puisioni apar' mto dì dj 4 maggio"; f. xviiii: June 25, 11.60 *scudi* "per sua puisione dj uno mese."

[7] ASM, Registri, Pacco 120, Giornale di le fabriche 1568, f. ix: Mar. 27, 1568, 15 *scudi* for month finishing April 28. V. Pacifici, *Ippolito II d'Este*, Tivoli, [1920], p. 391 identifies this artist as Jan van der Straet of Bruges, but this seems unlikely as Straet was working about this time in Florence and was a close assistant of Vasari, so that it would be extremely unlikely to find him employed by an Este for whom Pirro Ligorio was an adviser.

[8] G. Baglione, *Le vite de' pittori, scultori et architetti*, Rome, 1642, pp. 127-129 and *Thieme-Becker Künstler Lexikon*, XXXIV, Leipzig, 1940, p. 152, s. v. Vecchi, Giovanni de.

[9] A. Bertolotti, "Federico Zuccari," *Giornale di erudizione artistica*, V (1876), pp. 131 and 151. At Tivoli Giovanni Paolo received a

monthly salary of 12 *scudi*; ASM, Registri, Pacco 120, Giornale di le fabriche 1568, f. ix (Mar. 27, 1568 for a month commencing that date); f. xv (May 19 for month ending May 28); f. xviii (June 18 for month ending June 28); f. xxii: July 20, 4 *scudi* "p il loro salario pro dj 7 luglio"; and f. xxiii: July 20, 4.40 *scudi* "per piu giornatti."

[10] *Thieme-Becker Künstler Lexikon*, XIII, Leipzig, 1920, p. 547, s. v. Ghidoni. He received 10 *scudi* monthly on the same dates as Giovanni Paolo di Severi, see note 9 above.

[11] The payments are identical as to time and amount with those of Ghidoni, see note 10 above.

[12] An attempt to identify the "Cornelio Fiamingo" in this workshop at Tivoli is practically impossible. Perhaps he is the painter Cornelis Leysens of Antwerp who was *camerlingo* of the Archiconfraternità di Campo Santo from 1559 to 1561 and who died at Rome in 1570, see G. J. Hoogewerff, *Bescheiden in Italië omtrent nederlandsche Kunstenaars en Geleerden*, pt. II (Rijks Geschiedkundige Publicatiën, Kleine Serie no. 12), The Hague, 1913, especially pp. 305-307.

However, there were several other Flemings, named Cornelis, active as painters in Rome in the late sixteenth century. In 1556 and 1557 one "Cornelio Fiammingo" was a member of the Accademia di San Luca and, as the notice in *Thieme-Becker* (VII, p. 425, s. v. Cornelio Fiammingo) indicates, this is probably not the famous engraver Cornelis Cort as he does not seem to have been in Rome at that time. There was also a Cornelius Bogarde "pittore fiamengo," perhaps the Cornelis of the Accademia, who died in Rome in 1581, see G. J. Hooge-

At the same time that this group of six painters was working at Tivoli a workshop of seven stucco-workers was engaged probably in making the stucco frames, masks, coat of arms, and *imprese* of the Cardinal which are combined with the painted Virtues of the friezes executed by Agresti and his assistants.[14]

werff, "Nederlandsche Kunstenaars te Rome, 1600-1725," *Mededeelingen van het Neder-landsch Historisch Instituut te Rome*, ser. 2, VIII (1938), p. 116 and n. 2.

"Cornelio Fiamingo" was not active at Tivoli as long as the other members of this work-shop: ASM, Registri, Pacco 120, Giornale di le fabriche 1568, f. ix: Mar. 27, 1568, 12 *scudi* for a month commencing that date; f. xv: May 19, 12 *scudi* for month ending May 28; f. xviii: June 18, 12 *scudi* for month ending June 28.

[13] ASM, Registri, Pacco 120, Giornale di le fabriche 1568, f. ix: Mar. 27, 1568, 12 *scudi* for a month commencing that date; f. xv: May 19, 12 *scudi* for month ending May 28; f. xviii: June 18, 12 *scudi* for month ending June 28; f. xxii: July 20, 4 *scudi* "p il loro salario pr° dj 7 luglio"; and f. 22: July 20, 1.20 *scudi* "per piu giornatte."

The name "Dionisio fiamingo" occurs, as far as I can ascertain, only in relation to one artist in Italy in the second half of the six-teenth century and that is, of course, Denis Cal-vaert of Antwerp. For example, G. J. Hooge-werff, who published many documents regard-ing artists from the Lowlands active in Rome at this time (*Nederlandsche Schilders in Italië in de XVIe Eeuw*, Utrecht, 1912, and in *Mede-deelingen van het Nederlandsch Historisch In-stituut te Rome*, ser. 2, II, 1932, pp. 159-173; III, 1933, pp. 197-219; and VIII, 1938, pp. 49-125) and A. Bertolotti (*Artisti belgi ed olandesi a Roma nei secoli XVI e XVII*, Florence, 1880) do not include any other "Dionisio." The date of activity in Tivoli from March to July 1568 would fit in with our limited knowledge re-garding the early life of Denis Calvaert but would radically change our interpretation of his career in one respect.

On the basis of the life of Calvaert written by C. C. Malvasia (*Felsina pittrice*, Bologna, 1678, I, pp. 249-262) it has been assumed that sometime, probably in the early 1560's, Cal-vaert left Antwerp to go to Rome, but on his way through Bologna he was so well received by the prominent local family of the Bolognini that he remained there studying with Prospero Fontana and Lorenzo Sabbatini until 1572,

when he accompanied Sabbatini to Rome to assist in the decoration of the Vatican Palace. He then returned to Bologna about 1575 where he trained Domenichino and influenced Guido Reni, Albani, and Guercino.

Contemporary scholarship (S. Bergmans, "Denis Calvart," *Memoires: Académie royale de Belgique, Classe des beaux-arts, Collection in-4°*, ser. 2, IV, fasc. 2, 1934, pp. 25-36) has worked out his career in Bologna before going to Rome in 1572 on the basis of two works. One is the painting of *Vigilance* in the Pinaco-teca, Bologna, which the early nineteenth cen-tury writer Bolognini-Amorini (*Vite dei pit-tori ed artefici bolognesi*, part III, Bologna, 1843, p. 127, note 1 on p. 129) claimed was signed and dated 1568, but which Miss Berg-mans (*op.cit.*, p. 25) admitted could not be read. The more recent catalogue of the Pina-coteca (E. Mauceri, *La regia pinacoteca di Bo-logna*, Rome, 1935, p. 79) says that the date is 1662 and apocryphal. Even if the date 1568 were sure, this picture would not preclude Calvaert's activity at Tivoli, which was com-pleted by July 1568 and would, therefore, leave some five months to work in Bologna.

This suggestion that "Dionisio fiamingo" may be Denis Calvaert is, of course, conjectural but must be considered as a possibility in any analysis of the early career of Calvaert. Our knowledge of Calvaert's later activity at Rome with Sabbatini may strengthen this supposi-tion. For example, according to Malvasia (*op.-cit.*, I, p. 252) the Cardinal d'Este, who would be Luigi Cardinal d'Este, the nephew of the Cardinal of Ferrara, showed particular interest in Calvaert's work at this time, and thus we find Calvaert in contact with the Estes. Also Calvert's pay in 1573 of 12 *scudi* a month for assisting Sabbatini in the Sala Regia is pre-cisely the same pay that "Dionisio fiamingo" received five years previously at Tivoli. For the salary of Calvaert in the Sala Regia see S. Bergmans, *op.cit.*, p. 8.

[14] The names of these stucco-workers and their monthly salaries as they occur in the records are Jacomo (10 *scudi*), Tivolino (9 *scudi*), Orazio (8 *scudi*), Cesaro Milanese (8 *scudi*), Bramante (7 *scudi*), Domenico Macina-

These painters and stucco-workers were joined later in the spring or summer of 1568 by many more artists, some of whom worked for an extended period, others briefly. There is no certainty that these men were working with Livio Agresti in the Cardinal's apartment, since decorative work was also proceeding at this time in other rooms of the Villa. For example, some of these artists may have been working with Matteo Neroni in two rooms of the ground floor.[15] Two men who received a good salary but were not employed very long were Gaspare Gasparini,[16] Sermoneta's pupil from Macerata, whose work until now has only been known as limited to the Marches, and Francesco Gioli, otherwise unknown.[17] Among the numerous other artists,[18] at least four are known in the history of art for sculpture or stucco-work done elsewhere. Cecchino da Pietrasanta was a Florentine sculptor who was active later in Rome under the architect Domenico Fontana.[19] Giovanni di Domenico Fiorentino was another Florentine sculptor who had been active in 1559 at Perugia with Lodovico Scalza.[20]

---

tor or Masina (6 *scudi*), and Jacomo "garzone" (5 *scudi*). ASM, Registri, Pacco 120, Giornale di le fabriche 1568, f. 6: Mar. 5, 1568, 53 *scudi* "A spesa di Tivolj ▽ cinquantatrj m.^ta pag^ti amesser liuio agresta pitor' qst per pagar' lj sotto scrittj sette stutatorj che lauorarano a Tivolj per sua puision dj uno mese principiando q^to dj v dettj apar m^to"; f. 10: April 5, 40 *scudi* to Jacomo, Tivolino, Oratio, Cesaro, and Jacomo "garzone"; f. xiiii: May 13, 46 *scudi* to Jacomo, Tivolino, Oratio, Cesaro, Bramante, and Jacomo "garzone" from May 5 through June 5; f. 18: June 18, 38 *scudi* to Jacomo, Tivolino, Oratio, Cesaro, and Jacomo "garzone"; f. 22: July 20, 1.56 *scudi* to Oratio "p piu giornatte"; f. xxiii: July 20, 4.66½ *scudi* to Jacomo, 2.97 *scudi* to Domenico, 3.30 *scudi* to Cesaro, and 2.33½ *scudi* to the *garzone* "p piu giornatti"; and ASM, Registri, Pacco 120, Registro di 1568, f. 18: April 12, 1568, 6 *scudi* "a m° Dom^ro dorator p lui amesser Liuio agresta . . . per il suo salario dj uno mese che finira adj 5 Maggio"; f. 29: July 20, 1.56 *scudi* "a Oratio p giornate trj"; f. 31: Aug. 15, 8 *scudi* "a Dom.^ro masina dor' per hauer suitto mesj uno giornj diecj finittj adj 14 agosto a Tiuolj."

[15] See below pp. 52 and 55.

[16] ASM, Registri, Pacco 120, Giornale di le fabriche 1568, f. 16: June 2, 1568, 10 *scudi* "a Conto della sua puisione di dipinger' a Tiuolj"; f. xviii: June 18, 5 *scudi* "p resto de ▽ 15 per uno mese che finera adj 3 Luglio."

[17] *Ibid.*, f. xviii: June 18, 1568, 15 *scudi* for month ending June 11; f. xxii: July 20, 13 *scudi* "p il loro salario pr° dj 7 luglio"; f. 22: July 20, 1.50 *scudi* specified in ASM, Registri,

Pacco 120, Registro di 1568, f. 29 as from July 8 through July 10.

[18] Of these remaining artists we shall note only their names, monthly salaries, and date of employment. Their accounts are to be found in ASM, Registri, Pacco 120, Giornale di le fabriche 1568 and Registro di 1568: Pompeo da Pesaro (10 *scudi*, May 10, 1568, to July 20), Benedetto fiorentino, a stucco-worker (12 *scudi*, June 11 to July 11), Andrea da Reggio (12 *scudi*, June 14 to July 14), Antonio da Pesaro (11 *scudi*, June and a few days in July), Giovanni Paolo da Fermo (7 *scudi*, June 3 to July 3), Paolo Cervia (12 *scudi*, April 26 until about July 17), Giovanni Antonio Martinelli (2.50 *scudi*, for about two weeks beginning July 7), Lorenzo Bochetto francese (12.20 *scudi*, beginning July 7), Giovanni Battista da Lungano, stucco-worker (5.65 *scudi*, beginning July 7), Giacomo Catani da Pesaro (4 *scudi*, beginning July 7), Pace da Bologna (7.50 *scudi*, beginning July 7), Cesano Dominici and Pompeo da Alberti working together (4.20 *scudi*). It is to be noted that a few of these artists may not be concerned with the decoration of the Villa but with work on the grottoes.

[19] See I. A. F. Orbaan, "Dai conti di Domenico Fontana," *Bollettino d'arte*, VIII (1914), p. 65. Cecchino is listed as a painter at Tivoli for one month from April 26 at 9 *scudi* (ASM, Registri, Pacco 120, Registro di 1568, f. xx).

[20] A. Rossi, "Documenti per la storia della scoltura ornamentale in pietra," *Giornale di erudizione artistica*, III (1874), pp. 234-235. Giovanni di Domenico is listed as a stucco-worker from June 21; ASM, Registri, Pacco 120, Registro di 1568, f. xxviiii: July 20, 1568, 4

Filippo Gamberasi, or Gambazzazzo in the Tiburtine accounts, had served as *stucca-tore* in 1563 on the decoration of the Casino of Pius IV in the Vatican.[21] The most interesting name is that of Domenico da Melli, perhaps Domenico Fontana from Melide in North Italy who became famous later as the architect of Pope Sixtus V.[22] Finally the painter who is recorded variously as Mattheo Martus da Lechio or Matteo da Lacco or Lago must be Matteo da Lecce who had a wide-flung career, even working in the New World of South America.[23]

In the antechamber to the southwest of the salon (Text Fig. A, no. 2; Fig. 47), the system of decoration is similar to that of the salon. A large frieze is centered on each wall in a horizontal oval flanked by vertical ovals all surrounded by rather complex, Manneristic stucco frames. These areas are blank as in the salon. Female personifica-tions of Virtues (Fig. 46) stand as supporters between these frames. The colors are all very light with white predominant and are the unusual colors Mannerism favored: pink, pale green, violet, peach, sometimes combined as a *changeant*. At each corner of the frieze is the stuccoed *impresa* of the Cardinal, a crowned white eagle carrying a branch of golden apples. The large coves leading up to the flat ceiling are filled with grotesque decoration on a white ground. Set within the grotesque decoration are two small landscapes painted within a Greek cross frame. In the center of the flat ceiling two youths supported the Cardinal's coat of arms, but by 1952 a large section of the plaster had fallen revealing the cane backing to which the plaster had been attached for these decorated ceilings.

Beyond this antechamber is the Cardinal's Bedroom (Text Fig. A, no. 3), which varies the decorative system with a flat wooden ceiling (Fig. 49). Another deep frieze with blank frames runs along the top of the walls. The oval panels in the corners are flanked below by seated personifications of Virtues and above by pairs of winged

scudi "a mº Giouannj fiorentino a Contto dj sua puisione che principio adj 21 Giugº"; July 20, 2.80 *scudi*; and ASM, Registri, Pacco 120, Giornale di le fabriche 1568, f. xxii: July 20, 2.80 *scudi* "p il loro salario prº dj 7 luglio."

[21] W. Friedländer, *Das Kasino Pius des Vier-ten*, Leipzig, 1912, p. 132 and note 1. ASM, Reg-istri, Pacco 120, Registro di 1568, f. xxiiii: June 8, 1568, "A spesa di pitorj . . . a mº filippo gambazzazzo stucator' . . . par sua puisione di duj mesj che finirano adj 9 Luglio."

[22] Domenico da Melli was employed for the month ending July 9, 1568 at 10 *scudi*; ASM, Registri, Pacco 120, Giornale di le fabriche 1568, f. xviii, June 18. G. Baglione (*Le vite*, p. 84) says of Fontana that "Fu da Mili, luogo del lago di Lugano, il Caualier Domenico Fon-tana. Venne in età giouanile a Roma, & esser-citossi a lauorare di stucci, e ne diuenne buon Maestro." He came to Rome in 1563 as a youth

of twenty (A. Muñoz, *Domenico Fontana ar-chitetto 1543-1607*, Rome and Bellinzona, 1944, p. 13). All of this would accord well with the Domenico from Melide or Melli who was briefly employed at Tivoli, although at Tivoli Domenico is listed with a group of painters, but there is great laxity regarding the differ-entiation between painters and stucco-workers in these accounts, as, for example, the stucco-worker, Orazio, is grouped for one payment with seven other artists as "8 painters"; ASM, Registri, Pacco 120, Giornale di le fabriche 1568, f. 22, July 20, 1568.

[23] ASM, Registri, Pacco 120, Giornale di le fabriche 1568, f. xviii (June 18, 1568, 11 *scudi*), f. xxii (July 20, 9.90 *scudi*), and f. 22 (July 20, 1.8 *scudi*). For Matteo da Leccio see *Thieme-Becker Künstler Lexikon*, XXVI, Leipzig, 1932, pp. 409-410, s. v. Perez de Alesio, Mateo.

putti with garlands of fruit (Fig. 48). The colors are similar to the preceding rooms except that on occasion they are slightly stronger, a full green or a crimson red. The coved wooden ceiling is the most notable feature of this room. Carved, at least in part, by Giovanni da Tivoli early in 1569, it was painted and gilded by Leandro Romano and Giovanni Battista Veneziano in March and April.[24] This wooden ceiling is carved in three bands with six hexagonal coffers forming the outer bands and three octagonal coffers the central band. The middle octagonal coffer is decorated with the Cardinal's coat of arms and the other two octagons have his *impresa* of the Este eagle with the motto: *Ab insomni non custodita dracone.*

Beyond the Cardinal's Bedroom is another chamber (Text Fig. A, no. 4) which was not decorated until the twentieth century when a frieze of modern labors was added in a system analogous to the decorative system of the Bedroom. This room leads into a narrower room (Text Fig. A, no. 5) at the corner of the building, which is called the Gallery in old inventories, and which was not decorated in the sixteenth century.

THE CHAPEL

Behind the Gallery is the Cardinal's private Chapel (Text Fig. A, no. 6; Fig. 50) with a door from the Gallery and a window opening into the previous room (Text Fig. A, no. 4) decorated with modern labors. In his description of the Villa in 1611 Antonio del Re claims that both the Gallery and the Chapel were not yet decorated, except for the image of the Madonna di Reggio on the altar.[25] However, Del Re must be in error about the decoration of the Chapel, as he probably was with the Room of Moses,[26] for the building accounts record a fair sum of money spent for the decoration of the Chapel. In 1566 there was some brief work there by the painter and sculptor Ulisse Macciolini.[27] Then from late February through June 1572 over two hundred *scudi* was paid out to several painters and stucco-workers for decoration in the Chapel. The artists were furnished by Federigo Zuccaro, but he himself did not work in the Chapel. In the documents of 1572 none of the artists is specified by name, but in 1573 three of the painters, Giovanni, Ventura, and Cesaro, are noted as receiving an unpaid balance of wages for this decoration.[28]

[24] ASM, Registri, Pacco 120, Registro d'entrata e opere del 1569, f. 124r: April 13, 1569, 2.60 *scudi*, "Gioanni da Tiuoli per hauer intagliato li rosoni della sofitta." Although this date for carving is after some of the payments for painting of the ceiling, it is probably due to a delay in payment.

The payments for painting are in ASM, Registri, Pacco 120, Registro del 1569, f. clxvi: "M.ro Leandro et M.ro Gio: batt'a venetiano compagni Pittori 23 Marzo ▽ 5 a Conto della sofitta che hanno tolta a indorare," and on Mar. 28, 6 *scudi* for final payment, and f. 166: Mar. 28, 11 *scudi* "d'hauer indorato et dipinto il solar della camera del Cardinal in Tiuoli,"

and ASM, Registri, Pacco 120, Registro d' entrata e opere del 1569, f. cxxiiii: Mar. 4, "Leandro romanesco indoratore" and "Batt'a venetiano indoratore" 5 *scudi* each for 15 days until Mar. 20, and f. 124r: April 13, 5 *scudi* for "m.ro Batt'a dorattore per giorni quindici finiti adi 9 Aprile."

[25] A. del Re, *op.cit.*, p. 14.

[26] See below pp. 66-67.

[27] ASM, Registri, Pacco 118, Libro dei Depositarii 1566-1567, f. 23r: Oct. 28, 1566, 14 *scudi* "am° Ulisce Macciolini Pittore per rso de △ 15 che douea lui per la Capp.la de Tiuoli."

[28] The accounts of payment to Zuccaro do not specify the work as in the Chapel, but he

The walls of the Chapel are lined with painted, brownish-yellow Ionic pilasters against a simulated violet marble revetment. Between the pilasters in front of small rectangular niches are painted two Prophets (Fig. 51) on each of the side walls and two Sibyls on the end wall opposite the sanctuary (Fig. 52). The niches are too small for the large figures, which seem even more ample because of their abundant draperies, so that the figures stand precariously on the front edge of the niche, arms and garments thrust boldly out into the real space of the Chapel. Above each of the figures is a yellow monochrome panel with a scene presumably appropriate to each. Over the small window into the nearby room is a larger monochrome panel of the Presentation of the Virgin in the Temple. The barrel vault over the Chapel has a large central panel of the Coronation of the Virgin by God the Father and the Son surrounded by a glory of angels. Flanking this large fresco are two smaller panels, the Birth of the Virgin toward the southeast wall and the Marriage of the Virgin toward the northwest. The smaller barrel vault over the sanctuary (Fig. 50) has a very sumptuous stucco relief decoration in the center of which is a fresco of God the Father in glory with music-making angels. The Death of the Virgin is painted at the back of the niche on the right of the altar corresponding to the window at the left into the corridor. The rear wall over the altar is filled with a copy of the famous Madonna di Reggio surrounded by a heavy stucco garland of fruit. Although this painting was extant by the time of Del Re's description in 1611, it must date later than the rest of the decoration, for the original painting of the Madonna di Reggio was executed only in 1573

---

is recorded as paying painters working at Tivoli at about the same time that the other accounts specify painters occupied in the Chapel. Likewise, the description in Vasari (*Le vite de' più eccellenti pittori, scultori ed architettori*, G. Milanesi, ed., VII, Florence, 1881, p. 102) of the decoration in a chapel of the now destroyed Jesuit church of San Mauro at Rome, which Federigo Zuccaro executed just after his completion of the Salotto at Tivoli and before the decoration of the chapel at Tivoli, suggests a close resemblance in organization and iconography between the Jesuit chapel and that at Tivoli.

ASM, Registri, Pacco 123, Registro del 1572, f. 139v: Feb. 26, 1572, 25 *scudi* to "messer Fedricho Zuccari Pittore per pag.re homini che andarono a lauorar ativli"; f. 94v: Feb. 27, 6.59 *scudi* "per piu colori datti a messer Federico Zuccaro per depingiere a Tivoli," and Mar. 30, 49 *scudi* "adiuersi pittori et stucatori che lauorano a Tiuli per loi salario de uno mese"; f. 95r: April 8, 14 *scudi* "a 3 pittori che han'o lauorato a Tiuli nella cappella"; April 10, 42.50 *scudi* "a diuersi pittori et stucatori che lauorano a Tiuli"; April 25, 14.6 *scudi* for colors; May 13, 19.25 *scudi* "a diuersi stuca-

tori che hanno lauorato a Tiuli nella capella"; May 23, 62 *scudi* "a diuersi pittori che hanno lauor.to a Tiuli nella capella"; f. 95v: July 1, 36.30 *scudi* for "mordenti per la capella de SS. Ill.ma"; and ASM, Registri del Card. Luigi d'Este, Pacco 152, Giornale di Scarlatj 1573-1574, f. 30v: 1573, "Adj x dettj [March] ▽ uentotto m.ta bach quaranta pag.ti allj sotto scrittj trj pitorj che anno depintj nella Capella dj Tiuollj della f. M. di Mons.re Ill.mo et R.mo dj ferrara com' ne apar' Mandatto di dj 24 luglio 72 ▽ 28.40, m.o Giouanj pitore fu pag.to per tt.o dj 23 maggio et p tt.o dj 20 Giugno che hanno da Tiuollj fenitta la Capella auere per sua prouisioni in ragione dj ▽ 12 il mese ▽ 10.80, m.o Ventura pitore fu pagatto per tt.o dj 23 maggio et per tt.o dj 20 Giug.o auer' per sua puisioni a ▽ 11 il mese ▽ 9.60, m.o Cesaro pitore fu pag.to per tt.o dj 20 maggio che uno mese intier che alauoratto auaza ▽ 8." It is possible that the following account in the same account book may be concerned with this work in the Chapel, f. 42r: "Adj dettj [Mar. 28] ▽ sei m.ta pag.ti amesser Jac.o Squillj Pitore fiorentino per resto di lauorj fatto a Tiuollj per seruicio della f. M. dj Mons.re Ill.mo et R.mo dj Ferrara."

by Giovanni Bianchi after the design of Lelio Orsi.[29] In fact, the Tiburtine copy probably dates from the first decade of the seventeenth century during Cardinal Alessandro d'Este's occupancy, as the miracle-making fame of the original painting at Reggio Emilia dates from 1596. The lunette at the top of the rear wall has in its center the Visitation (Fig. 52), while in the two quadrant panels which fill out the lunette the kneeling Virgin and Angel Gabriel form the Annunciation.

SALOTTO OR THE ROOM OF THE FOUNTAIN OF TIVOLI

In the building accounts of the spring of 1565 six painters are recorded as working under the direction of Girolamo Muziano in "the large room and the Salotto below." These two rooms must be the salon in the center of the ground floor (Text Fig. B, no. 1), which is listed in other accounts as the Room of the Small Fountain (Sala della Fontanina), and the contiguous large Room of Hercules. The style of this workshop

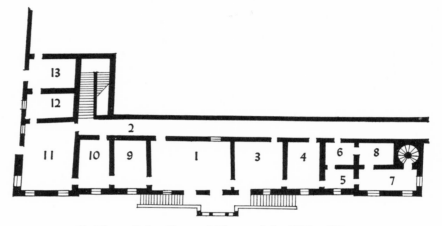

B. Plan of the Ground Floor of the Villa d'Este

is visible in the large painted coves of the Salotto (Fig. 53). At the corners of these coves stuccoes of the Cardinal's *impresa* are supported by pairs of seated pagan deities: a semi-nude Jupiter with his eagle and thunderbolt and Juno with a peacock and flaming torch (Fig. 54), Mercury and an armed Minerva (Fig. 55), Mars and Venus (Fig. 56) and a Bacchus and Ceres (Fig. 57). The Mercury has been noted as a self-portrait of Muziano,[30] which is possible, but more important it indicates Muziano's style, as the facial type is reminiscent of his Christ in the *Ascension* of Santa Maria in Vallicella at Rome.[31]

[29] G. B. Toschi, "Lelio Orsi da Novellara," *L'Arte*, III (1900), pp. 6-7, for recent bibliography on the painting and Lelio Orsi's drawing dated 1569 see R. Salvini and A. M. Chiodi, *Mostra di Lelio Orsi: Catalogo*, Reggio Emilia, 1950, pp. 136-137, no. 29.

[30] V. Pacifici, *Ippolito II d'Este, Cardinale di Ferrara*, Tivoli, n.d., p. 190; and U. da Como, *Girolamo Muziano*, Bergamo, 1930, p. 77.

[31] U. da Como, *op.cit.*, p. 143, incorrectly entitled *The Transfiguration*.

The wide areas of the coves are filled with a very delicate grotesque decoration (Fig. 59) of deftly painted little figures, animals, and bits of floral ornament and garlands against a white background. In the center of the coves are rectangular paintings with rich stucco frames. The center of each of these paintings is dominated by a large mask set on a pedestal as groups of girls or men worship at the statues of the pagan deities, Diana, Apollo, Ceres, and Bacchus. Filling out the coves at the ends are little panels with personifications of the Four Seasons.

According to the agreement with Muziano the decoration of these two lower rooms was to be completed by June 24, 1565.[32] However, during March and April 1566 Muziano had some painters back at work at Tivoli in "the rooms below."[33] Muziano's name then disappears from the Tiburtine records except for a single minor payment in 1571. In 1567 a group of artists headed by Federigo Zuccaro appears in the building accounts, probably working in these rooms.[34] The style of Zuccaro is found in the great rectangular panel covering the center of the vault of the Salotto. This painting is surrounded by a colonnade painted in *di sotto in sù* perspective (Fig. 53). Raphael had used a similar device in the corners of some of his vaults in the Loggia at the

[32] ASM, Registri, Pacco 116, Conti dele ent.ª de Ferrara 1565 D, ff. xii through xx contain the monthly salary of eleven *scudi* to Muziano from Feb. through Sept. 1565, but this is his general salary and includes work elsewhere than at Tivoli for the Cardinal.

ASM, Registri, Pacco 116, Reg[tro] i Mand[ti] 1565, f. 23v: April 11, 1565, "alli sei pittori quali hanno preso a cottimo la sala grande et il salotto d'abasso al Picano [piano?] del coritore del palazzo di S.S. Ill[ma] in Tiuoli per il prezzo de △ 350 m.ta dico scudi trecento cinquanta a finire detto lavoro per tt.° gli 24 Giugno pross.° 1565 con le conuentione che si contengono nel scritto di detto accordo, et per lidetti a messer Girolamo Muzzano depositario scudi cinquanta et questi sono per capara et abuon conto di detta cottimo ▽ 50"; f. 28v: May 6, "Alli sei Pittori che hanno preso il cottimo di tiuoli . . . ▽ 50"; f. 30v: May 18, "Alli Sei Pittori che pingono a Tiuoli et per loro amesser Girolamo Muzzano . . . a buon conto del suo cottimo che hanno a Tiuoli ▽ 50"; f. 34v: June 4, ▽ 50 to the 6 painters "a buon conto del loro cottimo fu adi 3"; June 4, ▽ 50 "a bon conto di detto suo lavoro p.mo di Giug.° qual mandato annulla un altro simile dato sotto di"; f. 36v: June 15, "Alli sei pittori che lauorano a Tiuoli . . . et per loro amesser Girol.ª Muzzano et sono per suo resto de scudi trecento cinq[ta] m[ta] che imp[ta] il cottimo che hanno del camerone et sala che pingono nel palazzo de Tiuoli ▽ 50."

[33] ASM, Registri, Pacco 117, Libro di mandati 1566, section indexed as "Dan[ri] a Tiuoli per la Fabriche": March 30, 1566, "a messer Gerol.° Muzzano per comprare piu colori per lauorari a Tiuli ▽ 13.62"; April 8, "un mandato a messer Gerol° Muzzano per pagar lauoranti pittori che depingono le cam.re da basso del allogiam.to de Tiuli ▽ 10.70"; April 13, ▽ 15.25.

[34] ASM, Registri, Pacco 118, Libro dei Depositarii 1566-1567, f. 30v, April 15, 1567, 25 *scudi* to Zuccaro and 15.80 *scudi* for colors; f. 31r, April 22, 1.50 *scudi* for horse transportation for Zuccaro; f. 31v, May 5, 27 *scudi*.

ASM, Registri, Pacco 118, Registro del 1567, f. lxxxxv, May 2, 1567, 12.50 *scudi* to two Flemings: Giulio and Stella; May 18, 45.15 *scudi* to Zuccaro for eight painters; May 29, 12 *scudi* for colors.

The Giulio Fiamingo is perhaps the Northern painter who is listed in accounts elsewhere as "Giulio della Croce fiammingo pittore" but whose Flemish name is unknown. Giulio della Croce was active in Rome just at this time having become a member of the Accademia di San Luca in 1563 and having executed work in Santa Maria dell'Anima at Rome in 1569. See G. J. H[oogewerff] in *Thieme-Becker Künstler Lexikon*, VIII, Leipzig, 1913, s. v. Croce, Giulio della.

ASM, Registri, Pacco 118, Libro de minuti piaceri 1567, f. 24r, June 21, 1567, gift of 50 *scudi* to Zuccaro.

Vatican. Above the colonnade is a painting of the Feast of the Gods (Fig. 58) which is based very closely upon Raphael's *Wedding Feast of Cupid and Psyche* in the Villa Farnesina at Rome, except that Zuccaro has reversed the composition and made it more compact. Instead of the long frieze of Raphael, Zuccaro has three groups of figures with the Graces and Hours forming garlands of arms over the seated deities.

The chief ornament of this room is the rustic fountain (Fig. 60) at the northeast end where is represented in relief the Tiburtine Temple of the Sibyl set up on imitation rocks beside a small cascade of water. The contract for this novel adornment was signed on May 18, 1568, by Paolo Calandrino of Bologna, who was later to decorate with mosaic the Grotto of Diana in the gardens, and who here agreed to complete the fountain within two months.[35] Both the contract and some of the records of payment indicate that this decoration had been begun earlier by the *fontaniere* Curzio Maccarone, who worked on the Oval Fountain and the Fountain of Rome in the gardens. According to the contract, Calandrino was to finish the fountain "from the cornice down." The final payment was on August 13, 1568.[36] The little fountain is surrounded by a stucco frame with herm supports. Draped along the top of the lintel of the frame are branches of the Cardinal's favorite Tiburtine symbol of golden apples with the white Este eagle perched in the center.

The walls of the rooms are painted illusionistically with pairs of gold-capped, white spiral columns between which landscapes are visible (Fig. 53). These landscapes were probably executed about the time of the work on the small fountain in 1568. At this time Matteo Neroni of Siena, who had already painted small landscape frescoes of the Seasons in the Sala Ducale of the Vatican, was active at Tivoli.[37] As he is principally a landscape painter, it is possible that he painted the walls of the room.[38]

---

[35] See Appendix D, no. 1.

[36] ASM, Registri, Pacco 120, Giornale di le fabriche 1568, f. xiiii: May 15, 1568, 8 *scudi* "A m° Paulo Calandrino da bologna fontanier' scudj otto m.^ta aluj per b'a conto dj 60 scudi d° in° che douera Hauer quando Hauera finitto la fontanine che Principio Curcio nella gra' salla da bassa dj Tiuolj"; f. xvi: May 31, 8 *scudi*; f. 17: June 13, 8 *scudi*; f. 18: June 21, 8 *scudi*; f. 19: June 28, 8 *scudi*; f. 22: July 20, 8 *scudi*; f. xxiii: July 22, 4 *scudi*; f. 23: July 29, 8 *scudi*; f. xxiiii: Aug. 13, 2 *scudi* "per Hauer' finitto la fontanina della salla del Palazzo dj Tiuolj." Payments for materials are accounted for in another journal: ASM, Registri, Pacco 120, Registro di 1568, f. 23: May 26, 1568, 3.17 *scudi* "per piu smaltj di piu Colorj et altri cose per la fontanina della salla dj Tiuollj"; f. xxiiii: June 5, 4 *scudi* for "smaltj"; f. xxv: June 13, 4 *scudi* for "smaltj"; f. xxvi: June 21, 8.44 *scudi* "per il prezzo di smaltj uerge batoncellj"; f. xxviii: July 6, 14.63½ *scudi* "per piu

smalti"; and f. 30: July 22, 5.50 *scudi* for "smalti."

[37] G. Baglione, *op.cit.*, p. 44; A. Mayer, *Das Leben und die Werke der Brüder Matthäus und Paul Brill* (Kunstgeschichtliche Monographien, XIV), Leipzig, 1910, p. 10 and pls. VI-VIII; and H. Voss, *Die Malerei der Spätrenaissance in Rom und Florenz*, Berlin, 1920, II, p. 533. The accounts at Tivoli are apparently the first ones to specify Matteo's family name as Neroni.

ASM, Registri, Pacco 120, Registro di 1568, f. 19: April 16, 1568, 12 *scudi* "A spesa di pitorj . . . a Matteo dl Geronnj pitore . . . p sua puisione dj una mese dj Hauer adipinger' a Tiuolj che finira adj 21 maggio"; f. xxviiii: July 20, 6.40 *scudi* "a Matteo di Heronnj pitore"; f. 29: July 20, 1.20 *scudi* "A Matteo da Sienna giorni trj."

Ibid., Giornale di le fabriche 1568, f. xvii: June 8, 1568, 12 *scudi* "A Matteo Heronnj da Sienna pitor' ▽ dodicj m.^ta alui . . . per sua

Some of the landscapes are antique in subject matter, but others are sixteenth century topographical views of the possessions of the Cardinal of Ferrara. On the end wall (Fig. 62) flanking the small fountain is a door at the left into the First Tiburtine Room, and on the right a complementary entrance created illusionistically in paint with a young page standing in a half open door. Between the doors and the fountain are slight glimpses of ancient landscapes, one of ruins above a bay of water, the other with a round temple. On the long rear wall (Fig. 53) is centered a painted window with a landscape visible through it, at left a door into the rear corridor and at right an actual window into the corridor. Between these real and illusionistic openings are more landscapes, the two at the left being particularly connected with the Cardinal, as one in the left corner depicts the Oval Fountain at the Villa itself, and the landscape on the right of the door represents the Cardinal's Villa and gardens of Monte Cavallo in Rome. The southwest end wall has a large view of the Villa d'Este and its gardens (Figs. 8 and 53) painted between another simulated door and the actual door into the Room of Hercules. The false door is painted as if partially open within which stands a man in red hose and brown tunic holding on a chain a hunting cat. On the garden wall are four slight landscapes. One must have been painted or repainted after the mid seventeenth century as there is seen the Fountain of the Water Organ with the Tempietto in its center and the great cascade down to the level of the fish ponds as it was revised under Cardinal Rinaldo I. At the far right, however, is a quick sketch of the same Water Organ (Fig. 61) contemporary with the decoration of the room, for it does not have the great eagle at the top added by Cardinal Alessandro in 1609 or the snake-limbed caryatids of the attic and the statues of Apollo and

---

puisione dj uno mese dj depinger atiuolj che finira adj xvi giugno"; f. xxii: July 20, 6.40 *scudi* "per il loro salario dj 7 luglio . . . a Matteo de Heronnj"; f. 22: July 20, 1.20 *scudi* "p piu giornatti . . . a maestro Matteo da Sienna."

These frescoes were later covered with whitewash and were only uncovered in the 1920's. First mention of their discovery was made by V. Pacifici, "L'Antico Quirinale in un affresco rinvenuto in Villa d'Este," *Atti e memorie della società tiburtina di storia e d'arte*, IX-X (1929-1930), pp. 385-387. Because of their worn condition these landscapes were restored in 1949, according to Sig. Giordano, the Assistente at Tivoli.

[38] Sometime before the middle of 1570 an accident must have damaged the decoration of the Salotto. The rustic fountain had to be repaired, and at about the same time Matteo Neroni was paid to restore the fresco of the vault.

ASM, Registri, Pacco 121, Protetione di

Francia 1570, f. xviii: June 10, 1570, 11.80 *scudi* "A m⁰ franc⁰ da uolterra . . . per far' il parapetto dj legno dj pero per la fontanina della Salla in Tiuollj"; f. 18: June 11, 2 *scudi* "A Gio' iac.⁰ dettj Il Tiuolino . . . a conto dj raconciar' la fontanina della Salla dj Tiuollj"; f. 22: Aug. 5, 6 *scudi* "A m⁰ franc⁰ da Volterra . . . per resto dj 17.80 scudi per hauer fatto Il parapetto alla fontanina dj Tiuollj"; and opposite f. 28: Dec. 27, 5 *scudi* "a messer Vincenzo Stampa per il prezzo de piu smalti, et Coralli che ha comprati per la Fontana de Tiuoli della sala et consigniati a m⁰ Tiuolino come dice sino lug.⁰ et Agosto app.ᵉ m.ᵗᵒ de di ult.⁰ Ag.ᵗᵒ sig.ᵗᵒ."

Ibid., f. 22: Aug. 1, 1570, 12 *scudi* "a m⁰ Matteo neronj . . . p hauer ritochatto la Istoria del quadro dj meggio ['mezzo' in the bound register of 1570, f. 94r] della salla della fontanina in Tiuollj"; f. xxiii: Aug. 12, 9 *scudi* "a otto pitorj e Indorattorj e stucatorj p piu giornatte datte in finire la salla della fontanina di Tiuollj."

Orpheus in the side niches. As this Fountain was being created in 1568 the fresco cannot date earlier than that year; on the other hand, in the central niche of the Fountain is depicted in the fresco a circular screen open at the center which was probably replaced late in 1569 by the statue of Nature. Therefore, the date of the fresco would seem to be limited either to 1568 or 1569.[39]

The layout of the decoration of this Salotto shows a marked similarity to the decorative scheme of the Sala dell'Ercole in the Palazzo Farnese at Caprarola. Both rooms have at one end an interior rustic fountain with a local topographical view, that at Caprarola depicting the Farnese city of Parma. The vaults of both rooms are painted with mythological scenes or ancient deities, while the side walls have landscapes, some representing specific locations controlled by the two great families, the Estes and the Farnese. In both rooms the rustic fountain is flanked by doors of which the left one opens into a contiguous room, whereas the right one has an actual architectural frame but within the frame an illusionistic painting of a man stepping into the room. This illusionistic false door had been used as an element in an earlier Farnese program of decoration, that is, in the Sala Paolina or the Sala del Consiglio painted for Pope Paul III in the Castel Sant' Angelo.[40] The temporal relationship between the Caprarola and the Tiburtine rooms cannot be absolutely determined except to note that they are approximately contemporary. The dates for the Tiburtine decoration are fairly closely fixed, as has been related. The painted vault of the Salotto at Tivoli was begun in 1565 and completed 1567, while the side walls were probably executed in 1568 by Matteo da Siena. The contract with Calandrino for the rustic fountain is dated 1568, but this contract notes that the fountain had already been begun by Curzio Maccarone, who was working on the great Oval Fountain in the gardens in 1566 and 1567. On the other hand the decoration of the Sala dell'Ercole at Caprarola is dated sometime between 1567 and 1569.[41] In addition to the formal resemblance between these two rooms, there is the fact that the painter, Federigo Zuccaro, was engaged at least in part with both of these programs. It is possible that Caprarola is the source of these ideas, since the general program for the overall decoration of Caprarola had been worked out in 1559 or 1560. However, at that time the program may have been developed only in very general terms, so that one cannot determine surely the origin of specific elements of decoration.

THE CORRIDOR

On the ground floor behind all the principal rooms is a dark corridor (Text Fig. B, no. 2) leading from the stairs at the northeast end of the Villa through the length of the building to the service quarters at the southwest. In 1565 the northeast end of

[39] The fountain in the fresco differs from the actual fountain in that the central arch is smaller and does not rise up into the attic story.

[40] E. Rodocanachi, *Le château Saint-Ange*, Paris, 1909, p. 144, pl. 20.

[41] F. Baumgart, "La Caprarola di Ameto Orti," *Studj romanzi*, xxv (1935), pp. 174 and 178.

this corridor was painted by assistants of Girolamo Muziano headed by a Maestro Andrea and by the Fleming Luigi Karcher.[42] The vault of the corridor was decorated as if it were a green arbor filled with birds. Then in 1569 two small rustic fountains were added to the unbroken rear wall of the corridor, one fountain by Andrea Romano and the other by Ludovico di Negri.[43] The pleasant murmur of these rustic fountains and the one in the Salotto as heard from the nearby Salotto was the principal admiration of Foglietta in his letter of 1569 to Cardinal Orsini.[44]

THE ROOM OF HERCULES

To the southwest of the ground floor Salotto is a large room (Text Fig. B, no. 3) the decoration of which was commenced by Muziano in 1565 when the vault of the Salotto was painted.[45] The style of Muziano and his workshop is visible in the twelve feats of Hercules painted on the coves of the vault. Very elegant gold Corinthian pilasters are painted around the walls of the room (Fig. 64). In the corners are actual or illusionistically frescoed doors and windows, the latter of which contain landscape views. In the center of the walls are framed landscapes probably executed by Matteo Neroni of Siena in 1568 when he was active in the Salotto.[46] Above the doors are feigned small hangings with the Cardinal's *impresa* of the white eagle with a wreath of golden apples.

The coved vault which covers the room is comparted by vertical bands of stucco and fresco decoration in the angles of the coves (Fig. 63). At the base of these decorative

[42] ASM, Registri, Pacco 116, Reg[tro] i Mand[ti] 1565, f. 28r: May 5, 1565, 23.50 *scudi* "a messer Girolamo Muzzano . . . per pagare opere vi½ de pittori che hanno lauorato nel coritore del piano del palazzo de Tiuoli per tt.° q.° di et per colori et altre cose"; f. 31r: May 21, 26.95 *scudi* "per tt.° gli 16 Maggio"; f. 34r: June 2, 20 *scudi* "am[ro] Andrea Pittore et compagni . . . a buon conto del cottimo che hanno a dipingere la parte da bassa del coritore del Palazzo di Tiuoli"; f. 37r: June 15, 20 *scudi* "am[ro] andrea et compagni Pittori . . . per resto del cottimo che hanno di pingere il coritore d'abasso quale essi hanno tolto a fare per d.[to] pretio de scudi 60 m[ta] et fu sino a di 6 pn'te"; f. 40v: June 23, 15 *scudi* "a m[ro] luigi carchiera et comp[i] pittori . . . a buon conto de scudi trentacinque m.[ta] che tanti importa il cottimo chessi hanno tolto a fare cioe dipingere il coritore colli duo lati sino in terra et al principio di detto corritore farli due arme con ador-mem[ti] nel palazzo di Tiuoli"; f. 42r: July 4, 10 *scudi* "a m.[ro] luigi carchiera et compi Pittori . . . inpingere la uoltacina in capo il coritore a Tiuoli"; f. 43v: July 15, 10 *scudi* to ditto "per resto di scudi 35 simili che tanti im-portaua il cottimo tolto afare de dipinge la

uoltacina sino in terra che e in capo il coritore" and July 15, 13 *scudi* to ditto "per hauere fatto il bassam.[to] del coritore et acconccatola stanza che sta acanto la sala che è uerso il giardi-netto."

For Karcher see G. Gruyer, *L'Art ferrarais à l'époque des Princes d'Este*, Paris, 1897, II, p. 479. Beginning in 1579 Karcher took over the tapestry atelier of his father at Ferrara for Duke Alfonso II d'Este.

[43] ASM, Registri, Pacco 120, Registro del 1569, f. 125v: Aug. 18, 1569, 40 *scudi* "a m[ro] Andrea romano fontaniero, per la fontanina ch'egli ha fatto in mezzo al Corittore da basso in Tiuoli"; this account is then broken down on f. 169v: April 28, 3 *scudi*; May 9, 8 *scudi*; July 3, 4 *scudi*; and Aug. 18, 25 *scudi* "per resto." *Ibid.*, f. 167v: Mar. 31, 1569, 3 *scudi*, "M.[ro] Ludouico di negri fratello del Tiuolino deue dare adi 31 Marzo . . . a Conto della fon-tana che lui s'è obligato di fare nel Corittore da basso in Tiuoli per prezzo di scudi 10 simi-li"; and April 25, 7 *scudi* "per resto."

[44] F. S. Seni, *La Villa d'Este in Tivoli*, Rome, 1902, pp. 62-63.

[45] See above note 32.

[46] See above note 37.

strips are the coat of arms of the Cardinal in stucco supported by pairs of winged *putti*. Above these stuccoes are small vertical frescoes with female personifications of the four Cardinal Virtues. In the center of each of the four coves is a large stucco framed section containing an oval cartouche with one of the feats of Hercules (Fig. 65), while above is a cartouche with the three lilies of the Este family. The remainder of each cove has a delicate grotesque decoration against a white background while at the base, on either side of the oval cartouche, Hercules performs one of his various feats. Twelve, therefore, are depicted, three on each cove. Not all of these twelve scenes are the classic ones given by Apollodorus, but all but the madness of Hercules are found in Boccaccio's list.[47] This scene at Tivoli is analogous to the depiction of the insanity of Athamas in the Second Tiburtine Room (Fig. 82),[48] with which the story of Ino, resuscitated as the Tiburtine Sibyl, begins. The cove on the garden side of the Room of Hercules depicts three of the Deeds: with Cerberus, with Antaeus, and with a Centaur. The northeast wall depicts his struggle with the Nemean Lion, the Cattle of Geryon, and the Lernaean Hydra, shown as a seven-headed Hydra suggestive of the *impresa* of Duke Ercole I in the Second Tiburtine Room.[49] On the rear wall Hercules wrestles with the Cretan Bull, kills the centaur Nessus as he makes off with Dejanira, and slays a Stymphalian Bird. Finally at the southwest he is depicted with the two Columns of Gades, insane as he murders one of his sons, and supporting the globe of Atlas.

At the center of the vault over the room Federigo Zuccaro painted the Council of the Gods (Fig. 66),[50] presumably in 1567 when he created the central panel of the Salotto. As with his Banquet of the Gods in the Salotto, the Council of the Gods is taken from Raphael's similar composition in the Villa Farnesina at Rome, omitting the left-hand group of Psyche and Mercury as inappropriate to the story of Hercules and compressing Raphael's frieze-like tapestry into a more compact square. The figure of Venus toward the center has been extensively changed by Zuccaro, who has, however, modeled her almost exactly on Raphael's Galatea in the Farnesina in reverse image. This scene of the Council of the Gods is really an Apotheosis of Hercules resulting from his Deeds depicted below, since Hercules now sits at the left among the Olympian deities, his pose taken from the Belvedere Torso.

THE ROOM OF NOBILITY

Vasari in his lives of the artists relates that "the Cardinal of Ferrara, having employed many painters and stucco-workers to decorate the very beautiful villa which he has at Tigoli [i.e. Tivoli], finally sent Federigo [Zuccaro] there to paint two rooms, one of which is dedicated to Nobility and the other to Glory [Text Fig. B, nos. 4 and 5 respectively]; in which Federigo performed very well and created some beautiful and

---

[47] G. Boccaccio, *Della geneologia de gli dei*, Venice, 1606, ff. 210v-212r.
[48] See below p. 63.

[49] See below p. 64.
[50] See above note 34.

charming inventions."[51] As Federigo Zuccaro was active at Tivoli both in 1566 and 1567 and as Vasari in 1568 specifies only the two rooms dedicated to Nobility and Glory, the decoration of these rooms probably dates from the earlier campaign of 1566.[52] Even without Vasari's statement a comparison of details of the decoration of these two rooms with the later frescoes by Federigo Zuccaro in his own house at Rome prove his authorship,[53] although in actual execution probably only the central ceiling panels were created by Federigo Zuccaro personally. The rest of the decoration was painted by assistants under his guidance.

In the Room of Nobility (Fig. 67) painted Ionic columns divide each wall into a wide central field, containing personifications, flanked by smaller areas. In the upper part of each of the smaller fields are painted portraits of ancient philosophers and lawgivers in imitation of classic busts. Commencing with Plato at the right of the window wall and proceeding clockwise, the portraits are labeled: Pythagoras, Bias, an unidentified figure, Solon, Diogenes, Socrates, and Periander. The long side walls are painted in the manner of ancient Roman frescoes with female personifications set against a Pompeian red background. These personifications are in part difficult to identify, especially as a coherent group, since they seem to be both Virtues and Liberal Arts. On the north wall (Fig. 68) the first group consists of three nude Graces accompanied by two *putti*. This group may symbolize Friendship (Amicitia) as noted later by Cesare Ripa.[54] In the next field a regally enthroned woman may be Temperance. On the blue wall toward the corridor the standing female figure with a large mirror and wand is probably Prudence. The other long wall also (Fig. 67) has two female personifications on the Pompeian red background. The one, seated on a globe and holding a compass, right angle, and a paper with geometric figures, is presumably Geometry. The other, with books at her feet and an open book in her hands, is probably one of the other Liberal Arts.

In the four corners of the coves (Fig. 70) of the ceiling are the Cardinal's coat of arms or his *impresa* of the white eagle with two branches of golden apples and the

[51] G. Vasari, *Le vite*, VII, p. 102.

[52] ASM, Registri, Pacco 117, Libro di mandati 1566, section indexed as "Dan^ri a Tiuoli per la Fabriche": May 25, 1566, "un mandato amaestro Federico Zuccaro per pagare gli pittori che uanno a lauorare a Tiuoli arendere conto ▽ 20"; May 26, ▽ 8.

ASM, Registri, Pacco 116, Conto Generale 1566, f. LXXXXV: July 9, 1566, "E adi detto ▽ trenta m.^te Datti a maestro Federico Pittore."

ASM, Registri, Pacco 118, Libro dei Depositarii 1566-1567, f. 19r: July 15, 1566, "E adi 15 scudi trentatre b nonanta qti àm° Federico pitt^re per pagare 14 Pittori che hanno lauorati a Tiuoli app^rl m.^to ▽ 33.90"; *idem*, 8.60 *scudi* for colors; July 23, 22.20 *scudi* for painters; July 23, 12.10 *scudi* for colors; July 31, 1.57

scudi for colors; July 31, 16 *scudi* for painters; f. 20v: Aug. 18, 3.30 *scudi* "à maestro Federico per pag^re colori per finir' de Diping^re le stantie de Tiuoli"; Aug. 18, 35.30 *scudi*, "al detto maestro Federico per vli° pagam.^to delli huomini che hanno depinto à tiuoli le stantie del Palazzo."

[53] W. Körte, *Der Palazzo Zuccari in Rom* (Römische Forschungen der Bibliotheca Hertziana, XII), Leipzig, 1935, plates. For example, compare the personification of Glory at Tivoli with the Transfiguration of the Artist in the Sala Terrena at Rome (pl. 19) or the feminine types in the personification of Nobility at Tivoli with the same Roman fresco or the Allegory of Design at Rome (pl. 33).

[54] C. Ripa, *Iconologia*, Siena, 1613, p. 25.

customary motto: *Ab insomni non custodita dracone.* On the coves are four inscribed personifications: Honor, three men kneeling in respect before an older seated man; Rerum Natura, which is the Ephesian Diana; and two female figures labeled Opulentia and Immortalitas.[55] In the center of the flat ceiling is a rectangular panel with a personification of Nobilitas flanked by Liberalitas and Generositas (Fig. 69).

THE ROOM OF GLORY

As has been said above, the very small, charming Room of Glory (Text Fig. B, no. 5), was decorated likewise in 1566 by the same workshop headed by Federigo Zuccaro that frescoed the Room of Nobility. Marble cupboards counterfeited in paint balance the actual doors. The curtain of the imitation cupboard on the northeast wall conceals its contents, but the two in the southern corner have their curtains partially looped back to reveal the objects within them (Fig. 71). The one on the southeast or rear wall contains a candlestick, an open book, and some cushions. The bishop's miter and cardinal's hat in the other cupboard refer, of course, to the owner of the Villa. These illusionistic cupboards are an interesting survival—or, perhaps better, revival—of such decorations as the intarsia work from the *studiolo* in the Ducal Palace at Gubbio, now at the Metropolitan Museum of Art in New York, or the small sacristy frescoed by Mantegna which was formerly in the Belvedere Villa of the Vatican.[56]

In the areas between these painted cupboards and the actual doors and window are traditional female personifications of the four Cardinal Virtues. On the rear wall Temperance is identified by the bridle she holds; while on the southwest wall the woman leaning against a column is, of course, Fortitude. Flanking the window are Justice with sword and scales and a doublefaced Prudence who looks at a mirror in her right hand and has a snake entwined about her left arm.

A rather elaborate coved ceiling (Fig. 72) depicts personifications of the Seasons in vertical panels upon the corner struts. The octagonal panel over the rear wall, which is inscribed Magnanimitas, has a crowned woman with a scepter, accompanied by a lion, and enthroned before a street of noble Renaissance palaces and temples. At her feet are two *putti*, one with a balance and the other a bag of money. A medallion inscribed "Tempus" (Fig. 73) depicts a winged Father Time seated on the band of the Zodiac, his hands outstretched to touch large mirrors held on each side of him by *putti*. Below Father Time two more *putti*, one crowned with the sun, the other the moon, are writing in a large book. Over the window Fortuna (Fig. 74), seated upon the back of an ostrich with large eagle wings, brandishes a club with three iron balls attached to it. From a small cloud which hides Fortune's eyes there fall into her lap, coins, rings, and other signs of earthly fortune such as a papal tiara, a cardinal's hat, and a crown and scepter. Around Fortune is a group of *putti*, some of whom are struck

---

[55] The figure now entitled Immortalitas, according to A. del Re, *op.cit.*, p. 24, was labeled Caritas in the early seventeenth century.

[56] A. Taja, *Descrizione del palazzo apostolico vaticano*, Rome, 1750, p. 402.

down by Fortune's club as they attempt to gather up the symbols of good fortune which fall from her lap. Finally, Religio (Fig. 75), represented as a young woman clad in the sacerdotal cope, bears in one hand the two keys presented through Peter to the Church and in the other a rod. She is flanked by two *putti*, one holding the Tablets of the Laws, the other presumably the New Testament.

In the center of the ceiling a nude young girl represents Gloria (Fig. 72), supported on her left by a clothed girl wearing the moon as a crown and on her right by a semi-nude youth with a sun-halo about his head. Unfortunately in 1955 all this central panel was destroyed except the feet of the left-hand figure.

The iconography of many of these personifications is rather striking and new. Actually the source of most of the personifications is to be found in one book published a short while before the execution of the frescoes. The source is Antonfrancesco Doni's *Le pitture del Doni trattato primo* which appeared at Padua in 1564. With hardly any changes the five personifications of the ceiling of the Room of Glory and the central panel of the ceiling of the Room of Nobility are described in Doni's book.[57] What is more interesting, Doni mentions the painter Federigo Zuccaro in regard to his personification of Time. In a letter to the Archbishop of Florence Doni adds: "I send to your Most Reverend Sir the copy of the painting of Time, which is at the head of the room [in Doni's imaginary frescoed villa]. It is painted by the hand of a youth, in design so elevated and of such profound valor that today there are few his equal. This is one Messer Federigo from Urbino, who will be another Raphael."[58] This suggests either that the artist Zuccaro controlled the iconography from a source well-known to him, after the Cardinal had chosen the general subject matter, or, more likely, Zuccaro was chosen as the artist because the iconography of these personifications pleased the Cardinal or his advisers.

Behind the Room of Glory is another small room (Text Fig. B, no. 6) with later decoration on three walls and the ceiling. The walls have grotesque decoration arranged in vertical strips like wall paper. A small landscape is painted over the door into the Room of Glory, and the vault has in its center a tent of heaven. The small window (Fig. 67) which now opens between this room and the corner of the Room of Nobility is a later addition, probably made at the time of the decoration of the smaller room. This is indicated by the replastering and retouching of the Zuccaresque decoration around the window on the wall of the Room of Nobility. Beyond the Room of

[57] A. F. Doni, *Le pitture del Doni trattato primo*, Padua, 1564, p. 8r (Nobility), p. 8v (Glory), pp. 14r and v (Fortune), pp. 21v and 22r (Time), p. 25r (Magnanimity), and pp. 30v and 31r (Religion).

The two principal differences between the written descriptions and the frescoes are in the personifications of Nobility and Religion. In Doni's description of Nobility (p. 8r), one of the accompanying figures is Courtesy instead of Liberality as Zuccaro labels her, although the two personifications bear the same symbols. Religion according to Doni (p. 31r) carries the rod of Aaron in her left hand and the keys of the Church in her right. Zuccaro's reversal of these symbols is wrong for then the rod of Aaron is on the side of the *putto* with the New Testament, and the keys of the Church are toward the *putto* with the Tablets of the Laws.

[58] A. F. Doni, *op.cit.*, p. 22r.

Glory is another Gallery (Text Fig. B, no. 7) the walls of which are decorated with later hunting scenes.

FIRST TIBURTINE ROOM

The decoration of the two rooms contiguous to the Salotto toward the northeast is devoted to mythologies centering around Tivoli. The chief painter of these two rooms was probably an assistant of Girolamo Muziano, Cesare Nebbia, whose name appears in the accounts as Nebula. Nebbia's activity is revealed here in a comparison of the figure of Athamas in the scene of his insanity in the second of these Tiburtine rooms (Text Fig. B, no. 10; Fig. 82) with the left-hand executioner in his fresco of the *Martyrdom of St. Lawrence* at Santa Susanna in Rome. The decoration of the Tiburtine rooms must have occurred from late February through June 1569 when Nebbia's name appears in the building accounts.

The walls of the first Tiburtine room (Text Fig. B, no. 9) are covered with a richly illusionistic decoration (Fig. 77). Various effects are achieved in paint in a Mannerist fashion with a constant element of surprise and novelty in the illusionism. From a painted imitation marble inlay dado rise simulated violet composite columns topped by gold capitals. In the center of three of the walls—the fourth has the window out upon the gardens—are painted figured hangings with edges furled under somewhat like the large frescoes on the walls of the Hall of Constantine in the Vatican. On the northeast wall the tapestry hangs above the fireplace so that the lower scalloped edge is counterfeited in stucco over the top of the fireplace molding. Doorways on the garden end of the two longer walls are balanced toward the inner wall by two painted doorways with very complex broken pediments. Through one of these doors a dog tries to escape by pulling on a tassel attached to the door handle.

The ceiling of this room has in its center a rectangular scene (Fig. 76) showing the embattled landing at Latium of the three Greek brothers, Catillus, Coras, and Tiburtus, legendary founders of Tivoli. The four coves leading up to the central panel have representations of the founding and building of the city of Tivoli. On the cove above the rear wall the three brothers, present at the sacrifice under the holm oak, see the augury of the thunderbolt in the sky. Next is the scene of the sacrifices made at the founding of the city (Fig. 78) as Tiburtus in the background guides the ox-drawn plough which outlines the area of the city. The remaining two cove paintings depict the building of the ancient city and its houses.

Flanking the feigned tapestries and the window, are painted niches within which are images of the ancient gods in natural color (Fig. 77). These deities are grouped in pairs on each wall: Vulcan and Venus with Cupid, Jupiter and Juno, Apollo and Diana, and on the garden side, Ceres and Bacchus. Finally small landscapes in painted frames above the doors imitate easel paintings, and others above the images of the gods imitate tapestries hanging free from the walls. The one at the left of the window shows the Oval Fountain unfinished when the mountains with the river gods were being built above the basin. Since, according to the accounts, the Oval Fountain was receiving its finishing touches in 1568 and 1569, this landscape confirms that the frescoes in these two rooms were painted in the spring of 1569.

Like the central ceiling painting the three feigned tapestries with large scenes in the center of the walls are concerned with the legendary founding of the ancient town of Tivoli. Over the fireplace at the northeast a battle scene, now in damaged condition, shows the three Greek brothers driving the Sicani from Siculetum, later named Tibur or Tivoli after the brother Tiburtus. On the opposite wall sacrifices of a ram and an ox are presented after the victory. In the center of the rear wall is the story of Hercules Saxanus (Fig. 79), who, when returning with the cattle of Geryon, was forced to do battle for the cattle against the brothers Albio and Bergio and when driven to his knees was aided by Jupiter, who threw stones down upon the soldiers. Hercules, with the additional titles of Saxanus or Invictus, then became the chief deity of ancient Tivoli, as well as the legendary ancestor of the Cardinal's family, the Estes.

The workshop that executed these frescoes was headed by Cesare Nebbia, although his salary of eleven *scudi* a month was less than that received by some of the other artists. He was active for the whole period of work from late February through June 1569 and was reimbursed for various expenses "for the painters."[59] Only a few of the artists who had worked at Tivoli during the previous year of 1568 were back at work with Nebbia in 1569, among them Gaspare Gasparini,[60] Matteo Martus de Lechio or Lecco,[61] and Paolo Cervia.[62] In addition to Gasparini, the two painters who received the high salary of fifteen *scudi* a month were Giovanni Battista Fiorini, who had painted one of the small frescoes in the Sala Regia of the Vatican in 1565,[63] and

---

[59] ASM, Registri, Pacco 120, Registro d'entrata e opere del 1569, f. 123v: Feb. 25, 1569, 11 *scudi* "per sua prou.ne d'un mese principiato adi 25 ditto"; Mar. 21, 1.63½ *scudi* "a maestro Cesare nebula Pittore per tanti spesi per li pittori"; and Mar. 28, 11 *scudi* "per sua prouisione d'un mese che finira a di 25 Aprile"; f. 124r: April 13, 0.56 *scudo* "per tanti per lui spesi"; f. 124v: May 6, 11 *scudi* until May 25; and f. 125v: June 29, 13.20 *scudi* "per sua prou.ne dadi 25 maggio per tutto ult.mo Giugno."

For the most recent account of Nebbia's career and bibliography see A. Venturi, *Storia dell'arte italiana*, IX, pt. 5, Milan, 1932, pp. 908-912.

[60] ASM, Registri, Pacco 120, Registro del 1569, f. cxxv: May 10, 1569, 10.80 *scudi* from May 10 through end of May at 15 *scudi* a month; and f. 125: June 8, 7.50 *scudi* for June 1 through 15.

[61] ASM, Registri, Pacco 120, Registro d'entrata e opere del 1569, f. 124r: April 14, 1569, 6 *scudi* for 15 days beginning April 14; f. 124v:

May 6, 6.40 *scudi* to May 15; and May 15, 6 *scudi* to end of May; and f. 125r: June 8, 6 *scudi* to June 15; and June 28, 3.20 *scudi* for last half of June "ribattendoui giorni sette che e stato malato."

[62] *Ibid.*, f. 124r: April 14, 1569, 6 *scudi* for 15 days beginning April 14; f. 124v: May 6, 6.40 *scudi* until May 15; and May 15, 6 *scudi* to end of May; and f. 125r: June 8, 6 *scudi* to June 15; and June 28, 6 *scudi* to end of June.

Three other men who were active previously are: Lorenzo Bochetto francese (11 *scudi* per month from April 20 to the end of June) and the two stucco-workers, Filippo Gamberasi (11 *scudi* per month from May 4 to July 1) and Giovanni di Domenico fiorentino (12 *scudi* per month from March 4 to the end of June).

[63] *Ibid.*, f. 124r: April 14, 1569, 7.50 *scudi* for 15 days beginning April 14; f. 124v: May 15, 15.50 *scudi* "da di 30 Aprile per tutto maggio a scudi 15 il mese"; and f. 125r: June 8, 7.50 *scudi* until June 15; and June 28, 7.50 *scudi* to the end of June.

A. Bertolotti, *Artisti bolognesi, ferraresi ed*

Giovanni Gapei or Giovanni da Cherso,[64] who had worked with Federigo Zuccaro on part of the decoration of the Casino of Pius IV in the Vatican. Only a few of the other men are known to the history of art for work elsewhere: The stucco-worker and sculptor Alessandro Scalza at times worked with his more famous brother, the architect Ippolito Scalza.[65] Among the painters, Giulio da Urbino[66] was active in Siena, and Ferdinando d'Orvieto[67] was a pupil of Cesare Nebbia. The artist who is listed as Giacomo Palma is very likely the Venetian painter Jacopo Palma il Giovane, who was certainly in Rome in 1568.[68] The artist referred to simply as Giovanni Battista da Modena may be the G. B. Ingoni, whom Vasari mentions as the rival of Niccolo dell'Abbate.[69]

As in the previous year, some of the artists were from Northern Europe—Flanders and France—and several from the province of the Marches in Italy.[70] The Marches

---

alcuni altri del già stato pontificio in Roma nei secoli XV, XVI e XVII, n.p., n.d., p. 44.

[64] Giovanni appears in these Tiburtine accounts always as "Giovanni Gapei veneziano" but that this painter is the same one who appears in the Vatican records as "Giovanni da Cherso" is indicated by one reference to him in the Vatican records as "Giovanni Capei" (W. Friedländer, *Das Kasino Pius des Vierten*, Leipzig, 1912, p. 129 n. 2).

ASM, Registri, Pacco 120, Registro d'entrata e opere del 1569, f. cxxiiii: Feb. 25, 1569, 7.50 *scudi* for half a month beginning Feb. 25; and Mar. 21, 7.50 *scudi* until Mar. 25; and Mar. 28, 7.50 *scudi* for half a month beginning Mar. 28; and f. 124r: April 14, 7.50 *scudi* until April 25.

[65] *Ibid.*, f. 124r: April 14, 1569, 12 *scudi* to "Ales.ro da oruietto per un mese che principio ad 27 Marzo"; f. 124v: May 6, 7.20 *scudi* from April 28 to May 15; and May 15, 6 *scudi* to the end of May; and f. 125r: June 8, 6 *scudi* to "Alessandro scalazza" until June 15; and June 28, 6 *scudi* to "Alessandro scalza" to the end of June.

[66] *Ibid.*, f. 123v: Mar. 4, 1569, 5 *scudi* for 15 days until Mar. 20; and f. 124r: Mar. 28, 5 *scudi* until April 5; and April 13, 1.5 *scudi* for 3 days finishing April 9.

[67] *Ibid.*, f. 123v: Feb. 25, 1569, 3 *scudi* for half a month beginning Feb. 25; Mar. 21, 3 *scudi* to Mar. 25; and Mar. 28, 3 *scudi* for half a month beginning Mar. 25; f. 124v: May 6, 4 *scudi* from April 25 to May 15; and May 15, 3 *scudi* to the end of May; f. 125r: June 8, 3 *scudi* to June 15; and f. 125v: June 28, 3 *scudi* to the end of June.

[68] *Ibid.*, f. 124r: April 14, 1569, 5 *scudi* for 15 days beginning April 14; f. 124v: May 6, 5.33 *scudi* to May 15; and May 15, 5 *scudi* to the end of May; and f. 125r: June 8, 5 *scudi* to June 15.

W. Arslan, in *Thieme-Becker Künstler Lexikon*, XXVI, Leipzig, 1932, p. 176, s. v. Palma, Jacopo.

[69] ASM, Registri, Pacco 120, Registro d'entrata e opere del 1569, f. 125r: June 8, 1569, 9.40 *scudi* to "Gio: batta da Modena da di 21 maggio, per tutto mezzo Giugno"; and June 28, 5.50 *scudi* to the end of June.

G. Vasari, *Le vite*, VI, Florence, 1881, p. 482. It would seem so much more reasonable to identify this Modenese painter with Cesare Nebbia's later associate, Giovanni Guerra from Modena, since Nebbia is the leader of this workshop at Tivoli, but this identification seems impossible as Guerra is referred to in later documents only as Giovanni Guerra, never Giovanni Battista. For other documents regarding this Modenese painter see A. Bertolotti, *Artisti modenesi, parmensi e della Lunigiana in Roma nei secoli XV, XVI e XVII*, n.p., [1883], pp. 95-120.

[70] Of the remaining artists in 1569 we shall again note only their names, monthly salaries, and date of employment. Their accounts are to be found in ASM, Registri, Pacco 120, Registro d'entrata e opere del 1569: Cristiano fiamingo (12 *scudi*, Mar. 15 to June 30), Lazzaro francese (6 *scudi*, Mar. 4 to April 9), Luca Antonio da Cagli (12 *scudi*, Mar. 4 to June 15), Paolo da Cagli (10 *scudi*, Mar. 4 to May 31), Antonio da Cagli (6 *scudi*, Mar. 4 to April 9), Ferrante fiorentino (12 *scudi*, April 13 to June 30), Valerio Bocca romano (8 *scudi*, Feb. 25 to May 31), Cosimo del Borgo (10 *scudi*,

seem to have specialized in painters of the grotesque style of decoration. In the accounts of 1568 three artists came from Pesaro, one from Fermo, and Gasparini, who is active both years, came from Macerata. In 1569, besides Gasparini, at least three painters are from Cagli and one from Urbino.

SECOND TIBURTINE ROOM

The next room to the northeast was decorated by the same workshop undoubtedly at the same time, but the decorative system of this room is less complex (Text Fig. B, no. 10; Fig. 81). False and real doors follow the arrangement of the previous room with the addition of a real door at the right rear of the room into the corridor behind. Most of the walls behind the green columns are painted in imitation of rich marble inlay with inset paintings.

In the center panel of the ceiling Apollo the sun-god (Fig. 80), holding his lyre in the Renaissance interpretation of a bowed instrument, stands in his quadriga of two white and two piebald horses, each guided by a genius. In the center of each cove over the short end walls an oval painting deals with Tiburtine mythology. Over the window toward the garden Athamas (Fig. 82), husband of Ino, driven insane by the snake-locked, firebearing Fury at the right, murders his son Clearchus by smashing his head on a rock. In the left middle distance Ino flees with their other son Melicertes toward the cliff from which she will plunge into the sea, where mother and child are metamorphosed into the water deities Leucothea and Palaemon. In the opposite oval King Anio (Fig. 83), pursuing his daughter Cloris carried away by Mercury to Cethegus, is drowned in the Tiburtine river which, therefore, bears his name.

In each of the coves over the two longer side walls a rectangular mythological painting is flanked by small vertical ovals in which music and drama are personified by female figures holding musical instruments—such as a pair of long trumpets or a triangle of bells—an open music book, or a mask. The rectangular panel on the northeast depicts Ino, transformed into Mater Matuta or Albunea, the Tiburtine Sibyl. She is sitting with her child at the mouth of the Tiber, indicated by the river god, and surrounded by the goats identified with her because she dwelt in the mountains they frequented and dressed in their skins. The opposite cove has the three river gods associated with Tivoli, the Tiber, the Anio, and the Erculaneo, surrounded by goats and rabbits.

On the end wall a simulated tapestry (Fig. 84), hanging from the cornice as if in front of the columns, depicts Venus on her shell drawn by a dolphin as she comes to request from Neptune at the left that he save the drowned mother and child, Ino and Melicertes. At the right are the mother and child transformed into the water deities Leucothea and Palaemon. The Romans also knew Leucothea as Mater Matuta or

Mar. 4 to June 15), Bernardino del Borgo (4 *scudi*, for last half of June), Matteo da Genoa (5 *scudi*, Mar. 4 to June 30), and Giovanni (3.80 *scudi*, May 18 to June 15).

Albunea, the Tiburtine Sibyl. On the northeast wall the large painting shows the Tiburtines offering the sacrifice of a ram as they bring in the golden statue of Mater Matuta and her son (Fig. 81). On the opposite wall is the same golden statue of the mother and child before which the Tiburtines kneel in adoration (Fig. 85), priests with tablets standing at the left with the round Temple of the Sibyl in the background.

Over the four doors on the long walls of the room are pairs of *putti* as supporters for the Este *impresa* of the many-headed Hydra (Fig. 81), which was especially the mark of the Cardinal's grandfather Duke Ercole I.[71] The shorter end walls have small landscapes toward the corners, except in the space already filled by the door into the corridor. Over the landscapes and door are four chiaroscuro panels relating the myth of Ceres' search for her daughter Proserpina. On the garden wall at the right is the Rape of Proserpina by Pluto and on the left Ceres in her chariot drawn by dragons, probably searching for her daughter. On the end wall the story continues at the left with Ceres kneeling beside the pool as the nymph Cyane shows her the girdle of Proserpina as evidence of her disappearance. Over the corridor door Ceres is finally seen kneeling as suppliant before Pluto and Proserpina. Flanking the two principal wall paintings on the longer side walls are small figures of the Cardinal Virtues.

THE ROOM OF NOAH

Beyond the Tiburtine Rooms at the northeastern corner of the Villa is a large room (Text Fig. B, no. 11) with the story of Noah depicted in the center of the vault. The decoration of this room, and, in fact, the room itself can only date after 1568, as the fresco in the Salotto of that date depicting the Villa d'Este (Fig. 8) reveals that only the rear half of this room was in existence at that time and that a reentrant angle was at the corner of the building.[72] The walls of the room are painted with simulated tapestries containing large landscapes (Fig. 87). The illusionism of these simulated tapestries is not as complete as those in the Tiburtine Rooms, which appear to cast shadows and show folds. In this room the tapestries are only suggested by the continuous ornamental border with the Este fleur-de-lis and are plastered flat on the wall rather in the nature of wallpaper. These landscapes were probably executed by Matteo Neroni da Siena in 1570.[73] The landscapes have both contemporary and

---

[71] Rome, Biblioteca Apostolica Vaticana, Chigi MS I.I.14, f. 5r lists some "Imprese di Casa d'Este." Number ten is "una Idra con sette tette col foco di sotto appicuato in legni del duca Hercole primo." The Hydra in the Second Tiburtine Room at Tivoli varies as to the number of heads from eight to eleven.

[72] See pp. 11-13.

[73] ASM, Registri, Pacco 121, Protetione di Francia 1570, f. xvi: May 19, 1570, 15 *scudi* "a m.º Matteo Nerronnj Pitor' . . . a boncoto del comitto ch luj a preso adepinger' la Salla da baso dj Tiuolj"; f. xviii: June 10, 15 *scudi*

"A m.º Matteo Nerronj Senese Pitore . . . sino adj 28 maggio acoto del cotimo atolto adipinger' a Tiuolj"; f.. 18: June 10, 20 *scudi*; f. xviiii: June 18, 20 *scudi*; f. 21: July 23, 20 *scudi*.

These frescoes have been attributed to Girolamo Muziano or his pupils, see M. Vaes, "Appunti di Karel Van Mander su diversi pittori italiani conosciuti da lui a Roma, dal 1573 al 1577," *Atti del II congresso nazionale di studi romani*, II, Rome, 1931, pp. 509-519 and M. Vaes, "Appunti di Carel Van Mander su vari pittori italiani suoi contemporanei," *Roma*,

ancient views with high horizons, enlivened by small figures on the ground and birds in the sky.

The vault is covered with grotesque decoration. In the corners of the coves pairs of trumpet-blowing *putti* support the Cardinal's coat of arms with the Cardinal's *impresa* of the Este eagle and the Apples of the Hesperides painted above. Set within the grotesque decoration are six small panels of personifications and at the center of the vault a large fresco of God the Father appearing to Noah after the Flood. Four of the personifications represent the Seasons: Spring as a young girl seated in a flowering tree holding a bowl of flowers; Summer, a seated woman crowned with grain, holding a torch and sickle and surrounded by wheat; Fall, a young man crowned with leaves and seated on a vine holding a cup; and Winter as an old man warming himself by a fire. On the long axis of the room near to the central panel are the two female personifications of Prudence and Temperance.

The decoration of the vault of this room and the contiguous Room of Moses was begun July 1571 by a workshop headed by Durante Alberti.[74] In the center of the

---

IX (1931), p. 348 n. 5. However, the view of the Villa in the Salotto presumably dated 1568 would seem to deny any activity of Muziano in this room, as Muziano ceases to work at Tivoli after 1566. The Dutch painter Van Mander, *Het Schilder Boeck*, Haarlem, 1604, f. 192v, asserts that there were landscapes at Tivoli by Muziano and that "there were many more very lovely ones, but it is to be regretted that as a result of the change of the owner's taste the rooms were transformed where they were and those works of art, so exquisite, were destroyed." In July and August 1563 Muziano apparently did some painting at Tivoli, see U. da Como, *op.cit.*, pp. 173 and 175. It is possible that at that time Muziano did some landscape painting in the original small room at the northeast corner which had to be destroyed when the room was enlarged as the Room of Noah.

74 ASM, Registri, Pacco 122, Protetione di Francia 1571, f. 17r: July 10, 1571, 20.55 *scudi* "a maestro Durante, e Compagni pittore per il loro salario, et opere da di 5 per tutto li 14 luglio per depingere la sala, et Cam.^{a} da basso"; f. 17v: July 16, 28.55 *scudi* "a m.^{ro} Franc.^{o} e Compagni pittori per il loro sal.^{rio} et giornate che hanno date à depingere in Tiuoli da di 16 per tutto li 21 lug.^{o}"; July 23, 36.25 *scudi* to "m.^{ro} Franc^{o} e Comp.^{i} pittori per la loro prouis.^{ne} et opere che danno à depingere per tutto li 28 lug.^{o}"; f. 18r: July 30, 13.50 *scudi* "a maestro Durante Pittore, et Compagni per la loro prouisione"; Aug. 3, 16.50 *scudi* "à maestro Durante Pittore, e compagni, per opere che danno a depingere, le quale finiranno alli 4 del pn'te mese di Agosto"; Aug. 4, 7.12½ *scudi* "à messer Marc' Antonio Cambio per tanti che lui ha spesi in colori, et mandati, a Tiuoli"; Aug. 8, 13 *scudi* "a m.^{ro} Francesco et compagni, et per loro à m.^{ro} Durante per il loro salario per hauer depinto in Tiuoli"; Aug. 8, 16.50 *scudi* "a m.^{ro} Horatio, et compagni Pittori, et per loro a m.^{ro} Durante per opere che loro hanno dato a depingere da di 6 per tutto li xi Ag.^{to}"; f. 18v: Aug. 16, 10 *scudi* "a m^{ro} Franc^{o} e Compagni pittori, et per loro à m^{ro} Durante, per il loro salario per depingere in Tiuoli"; Aug. 16, 16.20 *scudi* "a m.^{ro} Horatio, e compagni pittori et per loro à m^{ro} Durante, per giornate che loro hanno date a depingere da di 13 per tutto li 18 Ag.^{to} in Tiuoli"; Aug. 24, 16.50 *scudi* "a Horatio, et Compagni Pittori, et per loro à m.^{ro} Durante, per opere che daranno à depingere da di 20 per tutto li 24 Agosto"; Aug. 24, 10 *scudi*, "a m.^{ro} Franc.^{o} et Compagni pittori, et per loro à maestro Durante per loro prouisione d'una settimana"; f. 19v: Sept. 2, 7.50 *scudi* "a maestro Durante, et maestro Camillo pittori per il loro salario di una settimana de depingere"; Sept. 2, 9.90 *scudi* "a maestro Horatio, et Compagni et per loro a maestro Durante, per tante giornate date a depingere da di 27 Ag.^{to} per tutto il di p.^{o} 7bre"; Sept. 6, 7.80 *scudi* "à maestro Horatio, et compagni Pittori, per giornate date à depingere in Tiuoli"; f. 23v: Nov. 20, 4.35½

vault, perhaps painted by Durante himself, is the scene of God the Father appearing to Noah and his family (Fig. 86) as they offer a sacrifice after the Flood. In the background is perched the Ark high on Mount Ararat, and in the right foreground, prominent among the animals from the Ark, is a white eagle, the symbol of the Estes. Behind the eagle an ox and ass gaze at the altar, foreshadowing the ox and ass that will stand guard over the manger of the Infant Jesus.

THE ROOM OF MOSES

On the northeastern side of the Villa next to the Room of Noah is a small chamber (Text Fig. B, no. 12) dedicated to Moses. The lower part of the walls is covered by marble revetment simulated in paint, and the upper part by landscapes (Fig. 88) flanked by gold caryatids supporting the cornice. Vertical tapestry-like panels at each end of the southwest wall, with personifications of the Virtues Justice and Fortitude in oval frames, match the doors in the northeast wall. Over these personifications and over the two doors are *sopra-porte* of the story of Moses in yellow chiaroscuro, Moses in the Bullrushes, Moses and the Burning Bush, Moses and Aaron in the Wilderness (Exodus 4:27)—and finally Moses before Pharaoh. The climax of the story is in the center of the vault where Moses strikes the rock, bringing water to the Israelites (Fig. 89).

The artist of the center of the vault was Durante Alberti, who painted the fresco of the Sacrifice of Noah in the vault of the nearby room and who supervised a workshop in the two rooms in 1571.[75] The decoration of the walls is less sure. Del Re in his book on the Villa as late as 1611 noted only the vault fresco of Moses striking the Rock and claimed that "the rest is not painted."[76] This does not seem possible on several accounts. The style of the frescoes of the walls agrees in date with the decoration of the Room of Noah, which Del Re described as completely frescoed; more important, the iconography of the walls of the Moses Room complements the vault of the Room of Noah. In the vault of the latter, as noted above, only the two Cardinal Virtues Prudence and Temperance were depicted, but on the walls of the Moses Room are the two missing Virtues Justice and Fortitude, suggesting that the two rooms were painted at the same time. Finally, a brief reference in the documents of 1565 indicates that in July Luigi Karcher, while painting in the nearby corridor, received a small sum for "having decorated the chamber [*stanza*] which is beside the room [*sala*] toward the little garden."[77]

The vaults of these two rooms are unusual iconographically in the total decorative program of the Villa in that, except for the Chapel, these are the only examples of

---

scudi "a messer Marc Ant.º Cambio per tanti che ha spesi in Colori, et consig.ti a maestro Durante Alberti Pittore per fornire de depingere la Cam.ra sala, et quadri della fazzata nel Cortile di Tiuoli, app.e mto de di ult.º

8bre."

[75] See above note 74.
[76] A. del Re, *op.cit.*, p. 25.
[77] See above note 42.

religious subject matter in the whole Villa and do not belong to the coherent icono-graphical program of both the interior and exterior decoration to be discussed later. This is not surprising if, as seems probable from the discussion above, they were later additions to the major decoration, which was created from 1565 to 1569.

CONCLUSION

The finest interior decoration of the Villa is in the Chapel and in the four rooms on the ground floor frescoed by Muziano and Federigo Zuccaro. The Cardinal's Apart-ment on the *piano nobile* presents a rather monotonous impression with its large frieze of stucco-framed panels and countless female personifications, although the heaviness of this frieze might have been partially offset in its original conception by wall hangings below. At first glance the Tiburtine Rooms of the ground floor are rather charming as decorative schemes, but a close examination of the individual scenes leaves one aware only of the inferiority of pictorial execution.

The four ground floor rooms at Tivoli are comparable to the interior decoration by Baroccio, Federigo Zuccaro, and Santi di Tito in the Casino of Pius IV (1561-1563) at the Vatican and to those rooms in the palazzo Farnese at Caprarola painted by the Zuccaro brothers (1561-1569). For example, the vault system of the Salotto at Tivoli is similar to that by Federigo Baroccio in the First Room of the Casino of Pius IV,[78] except that the Vatican room has a small frieze at the base incorporated into the system. In both, the corners of the coves are masked by ornate stucco shields flanked by large figures of personifications or classical deities, with winged *putti* gamboling above them. The coves are then filled out with grotesque decoration on a white ground into which are set larger panels of scenes, and the center of the vault is dominated by a large rectangle with the chief painting. While the Vatican vault tends to break up into rectangular compartments, the total vault at Tivoli is more unified in its organiza-tion. In fact, most of the rooms of the Villa d'Este, save for the Cardinal's Apartment by Agresti, are more unified in their decoration in the sense that the walls are frescoed in relation to the vaults, while the interior decoration of the Casino of Pius IV is primarily confined to the vaults. The walls of the Tiburtine Salotto on the other hand, as noted before, are similar in their conception to the Sala dell'Ercole at Caprarola, but again the Salotto is more unified in having the architectural features simulated in paint, slightly reminiscent of Peruzzi's Sala delle Prospettive in the Villa Farnesina at Rome or the Sala Grande of the Villa Imperiale at Pesaro. In the Sala d'Ercole at Caprarola the pilasters are not counterfeit. The rooms at Tivoli are smaller than the comparable ones at Caprarola, and the Tiburtine decoration tends to preserve the intimacy of size. Tivoli relies for its effect more upon the element of illusionism, the element of surprise and novelty engendered by the simulation of varied material surfaces.

[78] W. Friedländer, *Das Kasino Pius des Vierten*, Leipzig, 1912, pp. 54-72.

The age of Mannerism, particularly during the second half of the sixteenth century, is dominated by intellectual decoration, that is, extensive decorative schemes formulated by humanist advisers. Such programs are not to be judged aesthetically in their individual parts. They are not like most fourteenth and fifteenth century cycles of decoration in which the individual scenes are the dominant expressive elements. The appeal of the Mannerist programs is twofold, first as intellectual compendia and even enigmas conveying, often in a hidden fashion, ideas and morals, and secondly, in an almost contradictory fashion, as pure decoration. To achieve the latter, stucco-work was given an importance almost equal to painting, and a greater unity in the decorative schemes, as seen at Tivoli, had to be developed in which the individual paintings play a less dominant role.

CHAPTER IV · TAPESTRY DESIGNS
BY PIRRO LIGORIO

IN NOVEMBER 1569 the Cardinal's former archaeologist, Pirro Ligorio, completed a set of sixteen drawings illustrating the life of the Greek hero Hippolytus, accompanied by a textual commentary. In the introduction to the commentary Ligorio apologizes to the Cardinal for his delay in preparing the drawings, which were probably promised before his departure for Ferrara, presumably in the spring of 1569. The drawings and commentary, which are now preserved as a manuscript in the Morgan Library at New York (MS M.A. 542), bear a later title: *Life of Virbius, Otherwise Called Hippolytus, Son of Theseus, Described and Drawn in Imitation of the Antique in Sixteen Episodes by Pirro Ligorio, Famous Antiquarian, by His Own Hand for the Service of the Elder Cardinal d'Este, Who Wished to Have Made from Them a Series of Tapestries.*[1] Ligorio himself gives no indication in the manuscript that the drawings are necessarily for tapestries, he simply states that the manuscript is a "sketch of the life of Hippolytus." However, the arrangement of the manuscript suggests that the drawings are more than mere illustrations to a text since there is first an extensive introduction, which outlines the life of Hippolytus, followed by the sixteen pictures accompanied by explanatory comments. The emphasis is, therefore, on the drawings as items in themselves. If the drawings were for tapestries as the later title-page claims, it is very probable that the tapestries would be for the Villa d'Este. Their date in 1569, with the explanation that they were promised earlier, possibly in 1567 or 1568, agrees exactly with Ligorio's last involvement with the Villa d'Este and with the major decorative campaigns at the Villa. The Cardinal's other two building and decorative programs at Monte Cavallo and Monte Giordano in Rome were finished by 1566 with much of the work done during the early fifties. When they were completed the artistic activity was transferred to Tivoli. There is no evidence that Pirro Ligorio was ever concerned with the interior decoration of the Villa at Monte Cavallo, and his only activity at Monte Giordano was as early as 1549, when he painted the frieze of the large hall.

Many of the rooms of the Villa d'Este at Tivoli, particularly the northeastern apartments on the *piano nobile*, were undecorated or had merely embossed leather wall coverings,[2] where tapestries could be hung when the Cardinal was in residence but could also be moved with him if desired to his other residences. Likewise, the walls of the Cardinal's Apartment on the *piano nobile* were decorated only along the upper part by Agresti's frieze which begs for pictorial decoration of some sort on the bare walls below to match the rooms of the lower floor with their simulated tapestries. As will be discussed later, the principal personages of the tapestry story, Hippolytus,

[1] For the text and history of the Morgan manuscript see Appendix B.

[2] See Chapter Three, note 2.

Hercules, Aesculapius, and Diana, all play an important role in the garden decoration of the Villa d'Este. Even if the drawings were not for tapestries for the Villa, the manuscript helps extensively to explain the involved meaning of the decoration and gardens of the Villa, since it was produced by one of the chief artistic creators of the Villa for its owner.

The subject of the drawings, the life of Hippolytus and his Latin reincarnation as Virbius, was, of course, chosen in honor of the Cardinal's proper name Ippolito. In fact, the Cardinal's painter Girolamo Muziano had earlier painted canvases with scenes from the life of Hippolytus.[3] The story of Hippolytus-Virbius was composed from many sources as Ligorio himself notes (folio 2r), mentioning particularly Pausanias, Ovid, and Seneca. This compilation and selection was created in order to make the legend of the ancient hero parallel to some extent the life of his Renaissance namesake, the Cardinal of Ferrara.

The series of drawings begins with the battle of the Amazons and Greeks under the leadership of the Amazon Queen, Hippolita, and the Greek hero, Theseus, before the city of Athens (Fig. 90). The composition is undoubtedly derived from ancient sarcophagi decorated with the Amazonomachy. The picture is not at all a copy of the sarcophagus reliefs, but there are several motifs which resemble elements in two almost identical sarcophagi which Ligorio records in his Neapolitan manuscripts as having seen in the church of SS. Cosmas and Damian and in the Belvedere Court of the Vatican.[4] For example, the fallen Amazon with a shield at the center of Ligorio's drawing occurs at the left of the sarcophagus, and the Greek holding a shield and standing with his back to the spectator is at the right in both tapestry design and sarcophagus. Ligorio has then added to the upper rear of the combat a distant view of the city of Athens, before which the battle took place.

As a result of the Greek victory, Hercules, who took part in the battle according to Pausanias (v, xi, 4), captured the Amazon Queen and her girdle, which was one of his labors in service to Eurystheus. The next illustration depicts the marriage of Hippolita to Theseus (Fig. 91). Some of the ancient sources denied a legitimate marriage of Hippolita to Theseus, for example, the letter of Phaedra to Hippolytus created by Ovid in his *Heroides* (IV, 121-122). This apparently worried Ligorio who was, of course, trying to parallel as closely as possible the life of the ancient hero with that of the Renaissance Cardinal. As a result Pirro adds a small digression in his commentary to the illustration in which he discusses the ancient law promulgated by Dionysius that any wife taken by force, as was Hippolita, was legally married if the oath of marriage was taken in the presence of the *aegis* of Minerva. Ligorio then adds that "by this marriage is indicated the valor of Hippolita, her shapeliness, beauty, and

[3] V. Pacifici, *Ippolito II d'Este: Cardinale di Ferrara*, Tivoli [1920], p. 389.

[4] C. Robert, *Die Antiken Sarkophag-Reliefs*, II, Berlin, 1890, pp. 96-99, no. 79 and pp. 99-101, no. 80, pls. XXXIII-XXXV.

70

nobility as an unconquerable woman" (folio 4r), which description is quite fitting for the mother of the Cardinal of Ferrara, the lovely Lucrezia Borgia.

The marriage drawing (Fig. 91) has in its center a priest holding the *aegis* of Minerva on which the bride and groom take their marriage oath, while below the *aegis* is the young god, Hymeneus, holding two lighted torches, as Ligorio says "one for the husband, the other for the wife" (folio 4r). Theseus is accompanied by two older friends, the paunchy one with a large club and lionskin being, of course, Hercules who fostered the marriage by giving Hippolita to Theseus. Hippolita in turn has two feminine companions, presumably Amazons, one holding an Amazonian shield, the other a double-axe, which may be the weapons of Hippolita. The girl next to Hippolita has a rather prominent position, but Ligorio in his commentary gives no evidence for her identification. However, in his Neapolitan manuscript (Naples, Bibl. Naz., MS XIII.B.7, p. 195), Ligorio writes that Hercules "took among others, Menalippe and Hippolita, sister of Antiope, their Queen, but Hercules by whom Menalippe was struck down, received from the Queen her arms, restored [Menalippe], and so Theseus kept Hippolita." This story is not the same as that which Ligorio gives in his commentary to these drawings, since in these Hippolita is Queen of the Amazons, but it is possible that the second prominent Amazon is meant to be Menalippe.[5]

The third drawing of the series represents the birth of Hippolytus (Fig. 92). The mother reclines on a couch in the right background and the goddess Diana in her function as the goddess of childbirth, Lucina, tends her. In the foreground two maidservants bathe the child in a metal basin, while a third maidservant warms a garment at a brazier within the fireplace at the left. For a Renaissance man this depiction of a birth must have immediately brought to mind Christian scenes of nativity and, in particular, the Birth of the Virgin, in which the domestic activities of the maidservants are identical with those in Ligorio's nativity of a classic hero. For example, the fresco of the *Birth of the Virgin* executed in 1549 by Sermoneta in Santa Maria dell'Anima at Rome has several maidservants holding the child, who has just been bathed in a metal basin, while another servant heats a cloth at the left; or Sermoneta's later fresco (1565) of the same scene in San Tommaso dei Cenci, Rome, has three servants preparing the bath for the child in a metal basin.[6] However, Ligorio's rear group of the mother and attendant with a curtain behind them is very close also to the *Birth of Dionysus* in the Golden House of Nero at Rome,[7] suggesting that he may have taken the nucleus from a classic source and added elements from the Christian scene. In his commentary

[5] The second Amazon might also be Emilia, the sister of Hippolita, who was present at the marriage according not to ancient sources, but to the Italian Boccaccio who described the Amazonomachy and the marriage of both Hippolita and Emilia in his *Teseida* (G. Boccaccio, *La Theseida di Messer Giovanni Boccaccio da Messer Tizzone Gaetano di Pofi diligentemente rivista* [Venice, 1528], Book I,

136, describes Emilia's presence at the marriage). Boccaccio also relates (Book I, 134) that at the marriage the aid of Hymeneus was invoked, which Ligorio depicts.

[6] A. Venturi, *Storia dell'arte italiana,* IX, pt. 5, Milan, 1932, pp. 575 and 585.

[7] G. Carletti e L. Mirri, *Le antiche camere delle terme di Tito,* Rome, 1776, pl. XVII.

Ligorio relates that it is from this moment that the goddess Diana takes Hippolytus under her tutelage (folio 5r).

According to Pausanias (I, xxii, 2), the inhabitants of Troezen had a legend that "when Theseus was about to marry Phaedra, not wishing if any children should be born that they should rule Hippolytus nor that he should be king in their place, he sent Hippolytus to Pittheus to be reared and to be the future ruler of Troezen." Therefore, the fourth scene (Fig. 93) shows the young Hippolytus holding his school tablets, while the old King Pittheus seated at the right points to two statues of the virginal goddesses, Minerva and Diana, and instructs the boy to follow faithfully these deities. "At a later time," Pausanias continues, "Pallas and his sons arose against Theseus. Having slain them he went to Troezen for the sake of purification, and Phaedra first saw Hippolytus there."

The following scene, accordingly, shows Phaedra in a window at the upper left watching her young stepson as he exercises two horses accompanied by a centaur and a groom (Fig. 94). Since the account by Pausanias makes no mention at this time of Hippolytus' interest in horses, this scene may again be another attempt to bring together the lives of the ancient Greek youth and the Renaissance Cardinal, for Cato recalls later in his funeral oration for the Cardinal that Ippolito, when he was a youth at Ferrara, was accustomed to alternate with his study of the classics the practice of arms and equitation, in which he excelled.[8] The introduction of a centaur into the scene has no source in ancient literature that I have found, but Ligorio remarks in his introduction to the manuscript that Hippolytus "was fond of mastering horses as were the Lapiths, centaurs of Thessaly, whence he acquired the name of Hippolytus, that is, master of coursers" (folio 2r). To one with Ligorio's knowledge of antiquity this association of youth and centaur is probably also a reference to one of the greatest traditional scenes in antiquity of the instruction of a Greek hero, that is, the education of Achilles by the centaur Chiron.

In another passage in Pausanias (II, xxxii, 3), the ancient writer recalls seeing in the precinct at Troezen a temple of Aphrodite Spy overlooking the race course of Hippolytus. The temple was erected at the location where Phaedra was accustomed to observe Hippolytus as he exercised on the race track. So in the next design (Fig. 95) the young Hippolytus races another youth in chariots, while Phaedra watches him from an edifice at the right.

The seventh drawing is of key importance in paralleling the lives of the Greek hero and the Cardinal of Ferrara. In the composition (Fig. 96) Hippolytus and two other youths are kneeling before a statue of Ceres as two priests introduce them into the Eleusinian mysteries by crowning them with vitex. Two other young initiates behind the priests assist them, while Phaedra and two of her servants watch the ceremony

[8] E. Cato, *Oratione fatta dal Cavaliere Hercole Cato nelle essequie dell'Illustriss. et Reuerendiss. Sig. D. Hippolito d'Este Card. di* *Ferrara, celebrate nella città di Tiuoli,* Ferrara, 1587, p. 3.

from the rear. At the upper left a choir of three boys sing and play musical instruments. According to Ligorio's explanation Hippolytus is "clad in white." The classic inspiration for this incident is certainly Ovid in his *Heroides* (IV, 67-74) in which Phaedra writes that she went to Eleusis where she saw Hippolytus in "shining white . . . raiment, his hair bound round with flowers." It is obvious that Ligorio went to a rather unusual source for this episode in the life of Hippolytus so that it would correspond to the very significant moment in Ippolito d'Este's life when he was admitted to the priesthood before he was eleven years old. Even the presence of the choir and the two assisting boys suggests a Mass of Ordination. Ligorio adds (folio 9r) that it was ancient belief that "whoever was initiated into this order, could not die. Also they relate that one could go alive into Hell and return glorious among living men. This signifies allegorically the immortal fame of good works."

The story of Hippolytus then continues with the better known episodes based most probably on Seneca's tragedy *Hippolytus*. The attempted seduction of Hippolytus by Phaedra (Fig. 97) shows her rising from a classic couch, which is completely draped by curtains, and grasping with her right hand the garment of unwilling Hippolytus, who turns away to leave her. That this scene is taken from Seneca's tragedy is proved not only by Ligorio's introduction to the story, where he notes Seneca as one of his chief sources, but because Phaedra holds a sword in her left hand, since Hippolytus in the Latin play (lines 713-714) remarks, as he leaves Phaedra, "let this sword, polluted by your touch, quit my chaste side." In the commentary (folio 10r), however, Ligorio claims that the sword is that of Theseus. Ligorio's representation of the incident is again based upon a Christian prototype, that is, the repulse of Potiphar's wife by Joseph. In fact there is a slight resemblance to one of the most famous Renaissance depictions of the scene—the one painted in the Loggia at the Vatican, which was decorated under the direction of Raphael.[9] This was certainly well known to Ligorio as a result of his numerous years as papal architect for the Vatican Palace and because, as his writings indicate, he considered Raphael the greatest of all Renaissance artists. The general composition of both versions is quite similar in the way in which the hero turns away as the woman in a half-seated position snatches at his garment, except that Ligorio's design is more compact and has less movement.

Phaedra then accused her stepson of her own sin, whereupon Theseus rushed to Troezen to take revenge. The following drawing (Fig. 98) has Hippolytus in a chariot fleeing from the gate of the city as Theseus chases him with drawn sword. In this case the source of the picture seems to be Ovid's *Metamorphoses* (XV, 504-505) rather than Seneca, since Ovid has Hippolytus relate: "My father drove me from the city and, as I went, called down upon my head a deadly curse." The following scene of the discovery by Theseus of his wife's suicide and treachery is again from Seneca (lines 1159-1200). In the next drawing (Fig. 99) Phaedra lies dying with the suicide dagger

[9] A. Rosenberg, *Raffael* (Klassiker der Kunst), Stuttgart and Leipzig, 1906, p. 111 or Anderson photo 4316.

(a sword in Seneca) in her right hand and a letter in her left, in which according to Ligorio she wrote "her deceitful excuses." Theseus with outstretched arms is apparently being informed of his wife's false accusation by Diana, whom Ligorio has introduced into the suicide scene.

The death of Hippolytus (Fig. 100) shows the hero falling headlong from the chariot which is upset by the rearing horses, frightened by the sea-monster which appears as a result of the curse of Theseus. A horrified Diana watches the death scene from a cloud in the upper right.

The remaining five drawings are devoted to the less well-known continuation of the Hippolytus myth—the hero's reincarnation as Virbius. According to Ovid's *Metamorphoses* (XV, 533-534) and the Servius commentary to Vergil's *Aeneid* (VII, 761), Aesculapius at the request of Diana brought Hippolytus back to life by means of his healing powers. So in the tapestry design (Fig. 101) the lifeless body of Hippolytus is partially supported by Diana as Aesculapius kneels in front of the body, leaning on his snake-entwined club, and holding with his left hand the arm of Hippolytus. Ovid continues (XV, 537-542) with the Latin version of the myth in which Diana, having concealed Hippolytus from Jupiter in a thick cloud, debates whether to send him to Crete or Delos. She finally decides against both and chooses Ariccia in Italy as his hideaway. Ligorio in his account claims that Hippolytus went first to Crete and then to Sicily building temples to Diana on both islands before he went to Italy (folio 15r). The thirteenth illustration (Fig. 102), therefore, presents two galleys, one under the command of Hippolytus, who is seated in the poop, presumably on the way to Italy. Diana in the upper left is casting a cloud behind the ships to veil them from the gods. The galleys are drawn with a great deal of detail, as is natural for an archaeologist, but they are rather fantastic, festive ships with high curving sterns, one of which supports a large lamp.

After landing in Italy Hippolytus-Virbius proceeded to found the city of Ariccia. In the picture entitled "Aricia Condita" (Fig. 103) the hero is guiding the ox-drawn plough, which, in the Latin custom, he is using to outline the limits of his new city. The scene is undoubtedly taken from one of the several ancient Roman coins in which a Roman, veiled and laurel-wreathed, drives a yoke of two oxen attached to a plow.[10] Hippolytus in this depiction as the resurrected Virbius is now much older, with beard, rather prominent pointed nose, and laurel wreath about his head. In fact he shows

[10] For example, a denarius of Augustus (H. Mattingly, *Coins of the Roman Empire in the British Museum*, I, London, 1923, p. 104, no. 638, and pl. 15, no. 17). The French archaeologist Blaise de Vigenère illustrates the annotations to his translation of Livy with a picture of this type "tiré d'vn reuers d'Auguste, où vous pouuez voir la representation d'vne Colonie" (B. de Vigenère, *Les decades qvi se trovvent de Tite-Live, mises en langve fran-* çoise, . . . *par B: de Vigenere*, Paris, 1606, col. 1018). Since Vigenère knew Ligorio personally and received information and illustrations for his work from Ligorio, it is possible that the illustration from the coin of Augustus also came from Ligorio (for the relations of Vigenère with Ligorio see D. Métral, *Blaise de Vigenère, Archéologue et critique d'art, 1523-1596*, Paris, 1939, especially pp. 14 n. 8, 15 n. 2, and 196-200).

a resemblance, undoubtedly intended, to portraits of the Cardinal of Ferrara.[11] The aging appearance and change in name to Virbius is mentioned in Ovid's *Metamorphoses* (xv, 538-544) as Diana's means of hiding Hippolytus from the wrath of Jupiter, who was angered at Aesculapius resurrecting the dead. Behind Hippolytus is a group of men building the new city. The part of the myth telling of the exile of Hippolytus by his father may be a reference to the exile of the Cardinal under the accusation of simony in 1555 by his spiritual father, Pope Paul IV, and the resurrection of Virbius to the rehabilitation of the Cardinal under Pope Pius IV. In fact, Pius IV came from the Medici family in Milan, which in typical Renaissance style would suggest an allusion to the Italian word for doctor (*medico*) which Ligorio applies to Aesculapius (folio 16r: *suo medico che l'hauea data la uita*). Perhaps the building activity of Virbius then refers to that of the Cardinal at Tivoli and Monte Cavallo in Rome.

The following drawing (Fig. 104) is a depiction of the sanctuary of Diana which Hippolytus erected near Ariccia on Lake Nemi. In his text Ligorio remarks: "They say that in the Temple of Diana there was the image of Hippolytus Virbius and about this temple a restricted enclosure so that horses and other animals could not enter. This temple was above the lake, which today is called Nemo" (folio 17v). The picture has in the foreground Lake Nemi, called the Speculum Dianae in accordance with the Servius commentary on Vergil's Aeneid (vii, 515-516), as a small oval basin on each side of which are sacrificers. At the left, accompanied by a girl playing flutes, are two young women casting locks of their hair into the fire on an altar, for as Ligorio relates: "girls crowned with virginal vitex in devotion to Hippolytus, defender of virginity, offered to his chastity a part of their hair before they came to the act of matrimony" (folio 17v). On the right side an old priest with boy assistant and two girls holding lilies offers the sacrifice from a patera at another burning altar. In the center, directly behind the sacrifice, is the six-column façade of the Temple of Hippolytus Virbius with his statue set in the middle intercolumniation and a statue of Diana holding her bow at the right of the temple. This temple is then set into the high wall which surrounds the sanctuary of Diana. Behind the wall is the great circular Temple of Diana Nemorense modeled on the ancient Pantheon at Rome.[12] Flanking the central temple are two identical square or rectangular temples which are topped by peculiar three-story clerestories presumably of an octagonal shape. These temples are, according to their labels, dedicated to Vesta and Aesculapius. Ligorio explains that Vesta is another aspect of the goddess Diana while Hippolytus built a temple to Aesculapius "in memory of his doctor who had given him life" (folio 16r). The artistic inspiration of this picture may be an ancient Roman coin inscribed "Vesta Mater" which presents six female figures grouped three on each side of a central altar

---

[11] For example, note the portraits illustrated in V. Pacifici, *op.cit.*, pls. I and II, particularly the medallion by Pastorino, pl. I, no. 2.

[12] Perhaps inspired by Vitruvius (IV, viii, 4) mentioning the Temple of Diana Nemorensis in his chapter on circular temples.

at which they are sacrificing from a patera. They stand in front of a round temple of Vesta which has her statue in the central intercolumniation.[13]

The final scene (Fig. 105) for the set of tapestries illustrates the very unusual custom, mentioned by Pausanias (II, xxviii, 4) among others, that at the sanctuary of Virbius runaway slaves contested against one another in single combat, the victor receiving as prize the priesthood of the goddess. The loser, according to Ligorio, then had to return to his master in slavery. The drawing has two wrestling slaves, stripped to their loincloths, as four aged priests watch the combat, one holding the wreath of victory which will mean freedom and priesthood. The contest takes place before the same Temple of Hippolytus Virbius depicted in the previous drawing, except that Ligorio has now apparently omitted the stepped podium of the temple.

The style of these tapestry drawings is quite typical of Ligorio's draftsmanship. With some notable exceptions his drawing tends to be quite crude, but this crudity is often compensated for by a certain vigor, especially in their conception. Obviously the main interest for Ligorio in any of his drawings was the idea that he was trying to convey or interpret and not the style, in the sense of artistic quality. His figures usually tend to be heavy, especially around the hips and thighs. In part as a result of this, Ligorio is rarely able to impart a sense of movement to his figures or compositions. Probably the most striking aspect of his drawing is the handling of space. He is either not interested in depth or not able to depict it. For example, in the drawing of Phaedra first viewing the young Hippolytus as he exercises horses (Fig. 94), it is very difficult to associate correctly the front and rear halves of the two horses. In this same scene, the figure of Phaedra in a window of the palace at the background is as large as the groom so that Phaedra tends to push forward. In such pictures as the founding of Ariccia (Fig. 103) or the view of the sanctuary at Lake Nemi (Fig. 104), the ground plane does not run back level to the horizon. Instead the background architecture is pushed upward to ride almost as a second band or frieze above the principal incident of the foreground.

The most characteristic trait of Ligorio's draftsmanship, whether in hasty sketches or in his most finished drawings, is his invariable refusal to use one of the Renaissance's most particular contributions to art, a consistent system of one- or two-point linear perspective. So in the drawing of the sanctuary of Diana (Fig. 104) the lateral temples of Vesta and Aesculapius are drawn in an isometric projection in which the side elevations of the temple show no diminution in size as they recede into depth. This is also apparent in the drawing of the chariot race (Fig. 95) in which the temple at the upper left has both its side and façade depicted as if in the same plane. The lines of the stylobate and of the entablature are drawn parallel to one another and continuous for both elevations. Only the shading on the façade indicates a difference in plane.

It is impossible to believe that any Italian artist of the mid-sixteenth century, active at the papal court of Rome and later at the ducal court of Ferrara, would not be able to draw in linear perspective if he wished to do so. Indeed, Ligorio himself later

---

[13] H. Mattingly, *op.cit.*, v, London, 1950, p.169, no. 97 (Aureus of Julia Domna).

remarks in his notebooks at Turin that he learned mathematics and drawing, "not in order to make myself proficient in the art of painting, but in order to be able to express antique objects or buildings in perspective and in profile."[14] The explanation for this rejection of Renaissance perspective is, I believe, Ligorio's desire to recreate as closely as possible ancient Roman culture and art. The ancient monuments which he knew,[15] whenever architecture is represented, do not follow linear perspective but use a sort of oblique perspective with the side elevations skewed around toward the frontal plane. Therefore, Ligorio attempts to imitate this antique method of spatial delineation in his drawings. A similar philosophy of Ligorio in respect to the restoration of ancient statues has been revealed on the basis of his drawings of ancient sculpture in his Neapolitan notebooks.[16]

Ligorio's drawings combine a very sketchy, quick penstroke with a great interest in detail. These apparently incompatible traits are, I feel, rather characteristic of Central Italian Mannerism in such men as Ligorio's great rival, Giorgio Vasari, who takes pride in the speed of the execution of his paintings, yet in terms of representation lavishes great attention upon material detail. This combination of facets may be a result of the type of society and patronage for which the Mannerists worked. Court artists as they were, they had to be able to execute large commissions very quickly, for their impatient patrons forced them in their drawings and even finished work to develop a rapid technique. At the same time their art had to express the contemporary interest in the material splendor that their patrons exhibited as a means of glorifying their social position. This frequently caused the Mannerist artist to load his art with detail. In addition, Ligorio, being an archaeologist before he was painter or architect, was fond of presenting his archaeological knowledge in terms of extraneous detail.

Ligorio's art is characteristic of Mannerism as practiced in Central Italy during the mid-sixteenth century. Like some of the other painters and architects active in Rome at this time or a little earlier—as for example, Perino del Vaga, Peruzzi, or Livio Agresti—Ligorio's Mannerism has nothing to do with the Florentine school of art but is an outgrowth of the painting and architecture of Raphael and his followers.

These tapestry designs of Ligorio for the Villa d'Este are, as we shall soon see, very important for the comprehension of the symbolism of the gardens and decoration of the Villa at Tivoli, although the drawings were apparently never translated into tapestries.[17]

[14] D. R. Coffin, "Pirro Ligorio and Decoration of the Late Sixteenth Century at Ferrara," *Art Bulletin*, xxxvii (1955), p. 185 .n. 113.

[15] For example, the Column of Trajan, the relief of the Appearance of Dionysus to a Poet in the Museo Nazionale, Naples, the relief of Marcus Aurelius in triumph, now in the Palazzo dei Conservatori, Rome (see contemporary illustrations of latter two in C. Hülsen, *Das Skizzenbuch des Giovannantonio Dosio*, Berlin, 1933, pl. xxxviii, no. 69 and pl. lviii, no. 105), and especially ancient coins, which were always of particular interest to Ligorio.

[16] E. Mandowsky, "Some Observations on Pyrrho Ligorio's Drawings of Roman Monuments in Cod. B. xiii. 7 at Naples," *Rendiconti della pontificia accademia romana di archeologia*, xxvii (1952-1954), pp. 335-358.

[17] A note, probably in a nineteenth century Italian hand, attached to the rear flyleaf of the Morgan manuscript suggests that the tapestries may be those at that time in the Palace of Prince Barberini (Palazzo Sacchetti) at Rome, but I have been unable to find verification of this.

CHAPTER V · THE VILLA'S SYMBOLISM
AND PIRRO LIGORIO

THE SYMBOLISM

FOR A SIXTEENTH CENTURY VISITOR the Villa d'Este at Tivoli offered the charm of colorful frescoes, associations with ancient Rome in its collection of statues, and refreshment from the water of the numerous fountains. Except for the ancient sculpture, the Villa has the same delights for the modern visitor, but there was more than visual and aural delight for an educated sixteenth century man. The interior decoration of the Villa and the fountains of the gardens were organized to present a symbolic meaning, to which the Cardinal's companion Marc-Antoine Muret furnished a hint in several of the Latin poems he wrote celebrating the Villa at Tivoli. Two short poems are dedicatory works.

> Work did not crush Hercules, nor did seductive pleasure
> Ever soften the soul of chaste Hippolytus.
> Kindled with love of both these virtues,
> To Hercules and to Hippolytus, Hippolytus dedicates these gardens.[1]

So Muret specifies that the gardens are dedicated to the two Greek heroes whose names had such particular meaning for the Cardinal: Hippolytus, after whom he was named, and Hercules, the patron deity of Tivoli and of the Este family. The second poem of Muret is associated with the decoration both of the fountains and of the interior walls of the Villa.

> The golden apples which Hercules seized
> From the sleeping Dragon, these Hippolytus now holds.
> He, mindful of the accepted gift,
> Has wished to be sacred to the donor the gardens which he has planted here.[2]

This dedication explains the Cardinal's *impresa* and motto depicted in the rooms of the Villa. The painted ceilings in several rooms, particularly the ground floor Salotto, have the Cardinal's personal *impresa* of a white Este eagle clutching a wreath adorned with several golden apples. The wooden ceiling of the Cardinal's Bedroom has carved in two of its coffers the eagle and wreath of golden apples with the Latin

---

[1]   Dedicatio hortorum Tiburtinorum
Nec labor Alciden fregit, nec blanda voluptas
  Unquam animum casti molliti Hippolyti.
Ambarum hos hortos virtutum accensus amore,
  Herculi & Hippolyto dedicat Hippolytus.
M. A. Muret, *Orationes, epistolae & poemata*, Leipzig, 1672, "Poemata varia duobis libris distincta," Book I, p. 47, no. 52 (the *poemata*

are paginated separately within the *Opera omnia*).
[2]   Dedicatio hortorum Tiburtinorum
Aurea sopito rapuit quae mala Dracone
  Alcides, eadem nunc tenet Hippolytus.
Qui memor accepti, quos hic conseverat hortos,
  Auctori voluit muneris esse sacros.
M. A. Muret, *op.cit.*, p. 47, no. 53.

motto from Ovid: *"Ab insomni non custodita dracone."*[3] The motto probably means: "[The apples] no longer guarded by the sleepless dragon" but by the Este eagle. This device and motto also occur on the coves of the ground floor room dedicated to the Allegory of Nobility (Fig. 70). Festoons of golden apples hang over the stucco fountain in the Salotto, and similar garlands were originally entwined about the columns of the Fountain of the Owl, while the Grotto of Diana is covered with such garlands growing out of the baskets held by the caryatid-like figures in the corners of the Grotto.

The golden apples are, of course, the apples from the Garden of the Hesperides, which Hercules obtained as one of his labors for Eurystheus. The educated man of the sixteenth century would have understood quite readily the symbolism of the Golden Apples of the Hesperides. The Ferrarese mythographer Lelio Gregorio Giraldi specifies in his life of Hercules, written at Rome in 1514 and later dedicated to Duke Ercole II d'Este, brother of the Cardinal of Ferrara, that the three apples carried by the ancient bronze statue of Hercules on the Capitol signified the three virtues of Hercules: that he was "not irascible" (*non iracundus*), "not avaricious" (*non avarus*), and "not pleasure-loving" (*non voluptuosus*).[4] In 1556 the writer Valeriano in his commentary on hieroglyphs, which was a handbook for scholars, explains that the three virtues are "moderation of anger" (*excandescentiae moderatio*), "moderation of avarice" (*avaritiae temperamentum*), and "noble contempt of pleasures" (*generosus voluptatum contemptus*).[5] The three virtues, of course, are most appropriate to a wealthy cardinal of a powerful Italian family.

To analyze further the original meaning of the gardens we must rely to a great extent upon the Parisian manuscript description which preserves the original layout. By the time of the death of the Cardinal of Ferrara in December 1572, the gardens were basically arranged and planted, but a few of the statues and fountains were not in place. After his death, his nephew Luigi Cardinal d'Este, and much later Alessandro Cardinal d'Este, did complete some features of the original plan, but they also incorporated some changes.

The dedication of the gardens to Hercules, whom Muret eulogizes, was not apparent in the gardens at the time of the Cardinal's death, but two statues of Hercules were temporarily stored in a side room of the Grotto of Venus. These statues were intended to form two of the chief elements in the garden, according to the Parisian manuscript.

---

[3] Ovid, *Metamorphoses*, IX, 190.

[4] L. G. Giraldi, *Opera omnia*, Leyden, 1696, I, col. 581. The source of this symbolism of the three apples is found in the lexicon of Suidas, who describes the statue of Hercules: "Herculis simulacrum gestat sinistra manu tria mala, quod secundum tres animi partes ornatus erat. Hercules filius Pici sive Iovis, philosophus optimus, qui pingi solet pelle leonina amictus, clavam ferens, ac tria poma tenens, quae abstulisse eum ferunt, cum draconem

clava occidisset: id est, cum cupidinis affectum vicisset, exuviis leonis indutus, quae significant animi generositatem, et sic consecutus esset tria poma, id est, tres virtutes, non irasci, pecuniae non inhiare, voluptatibus non esse deditum" (*Suidae Lexicon Graece et Latine*, Halle, 1843, I, pt. 2, cols. 875-876).

[5] G. P. Valeriano Bolzani, *Hieroglyphica, sive de sacris Aegyptiorum literis commentarii*, Basel, 1556, f. 396 (as 386).

In the original plan there were to be three statues of Hercules set one above another on the central axis above the Fountain of the Dragon. In the niche at the rear of the Fountain of the Dragon was meant to be a standing "Hercules of colossal form with his club in hand" (Parisian MS, folio 255r). Above the Fountain of the Dragon behind the Lane of the Hundred Fountains was another "large niche corresponding to the Fountain of the Dragon below, in which is placed a reclining Hercules of old age" (folio 263v), the niche to be painted with the labors of Hercules. Over this niche, the Parisian description (folios 264r and v) specifies a "large pedestal above which was located a colossal ancient statue of marble, which represents the same Hercules who had a child in his arms wrapped up in the lionskin and a doe near his feet, because it is sometimes related that the child nourished by the milk of a doe was Achilles. This action of having been wrapped in the lionskin, in conjunction with the two first statues, the deed in which he killed the dragon and his repose lying above his spoils, then represents immortality because of which he was adored by men as God." Apparently at some time during the four years following the Cardinal's death the statue of Hercules with the child and the reclining statue of the aged Hercules were set up in their dominating locations in the gardens, as they are to be seen much later in Venturini's seventeenth century engraving (Fig. 16).[6] It is interesting to note that all the sixteenth century documents identify the statue of Hercules holding a child as Hercules with the young Achilles, although the child is obviously Telephus the son of Hercules.[7]

This setting of the heroic Hercules, tired but victorious, directly above the Fountain of the Dragon points up the meaning of the gardens. This is specifically indicated in the Parisian manuscript, which relates that the fountain is the "Fountain of the Dragon so called because it represents the famous Dragon which guarded the Garden of the Hesperides" and that Hercules is the "protector of the Eagle which killed the Dragon, alluding thus to the *impresa* of the Cardinal which is an Eagle with a branch of apples of the Hesperides and his motto [which] says: *Ab insomni non custodita dracone*" (folios 254v-255r). So the popular legend that the fountain was created

[6] G. M. Zappi (*Annali e memorie di Tivoli di Giovanni Maria Zappi*, ed. by V. Pacifici, Tivoli, 1920, p. 65) in his account of 1576 describes the two statues. Dupérac's engraving (Fig. 1) of 1573 seems to show these two statues in their location above the Fountain of the Dragon, but the engraving is dependent upon Dupérac's drawing executed in 1571 before the Cardinal's death, and many elements in the engraving only indicate what was intended and not what was actually in place. Also the fresco of the gardens in the ground floor Salotto of the Villa (Fig. 8) has a hint of the statue of the heroic Hercules in the niche directly behind the fountain. The original of this painting was executed before the fountain was built during the Papal visit in 1572 and is, therefore, also based in part upon the original project for the gardens.

[7] The inventory of 1572 (T. Ashby, in *Archaeologia*, LXI, pt. 1, 1908, p. 244), Zappi in 1576 (*op.cit.*, p. 65), and the Parisian manuscript (f. 264v) all identify the child as Achilles. This is true also in the account of payment in October 1570 for the repair of the statue (A. Venturi, in *Archivio storico dell'arte*, III, 1890, p. 204). The statue is now in the Louvre, Paris; see F. de Clarac, *Musée de sculpture*, V, Paris, 1851, pp. 27-28, no. 2002, illus. III, pl. 302.

overnight in honor of the visit of Pope Gregory XIII, whose device was a dragon, hides a deeper intent than that which was exploited at his visit in 1572. Valeriano, who identified the three apples of the Hesperides as three virtues, also specifies that the dragon stands for the "softness of voluptuous desire" (*voluptuosam libidinis mollitudinem*) which is conquered by Hercules.[8]

Therefore, the central section of the garden is concerned with the theme of virtue and vice. Two other fountains on the central axis carry the theme further. Above the statues of Hercules in the loggia constructed across the Cardinal's Walk was the Grotto of Pandora with an "ancient statue of a Pandora, larger than life and very beautiful, which is placed above a rock and holds in her hand a vase from which issues a lovely *bicchiere* of water; under the rock is a dragon which shoots forth water from its mouth into a large vase and forms a very beautiful veil" (folio 265r). Pandora was, of course, the ancient Greek prototype of Eve, the first mortal woman, whose foolishness unloosed upon mankind all the evils of mortal man, such as vice, old age, sickness[9]—the evils which Hercules conquered by moderation and immortality. Pandora was flanked by two statues of the immortal Minerva, goddess of wisdom. As we have seen in Ligorio's tapestry designs, she was one of the two patron goddesses whom the young Hippolytus was encouraged to worship by his tutor, King Pittheus.

Above the Fountain of Pandora, in turn, is the great two-story loggia attached to the façade of the Villa containing on its second story the principal entrance to the building. In the lower story of this loggia was the Fountain of Leda with the Swan. The statue of Leda was intended to be accompanied by "four other statues in four niches, two within and two outside, the first are Helen and Clytemnestra, the second Castor and Pollux, all four children of Jupiter and of Leda" (folios 265v-266r). The late antique mythographer Fulgentius, whose writings directly or indirectly were influential in the sixteenth century,[10] interprets the relation of Leda with Jupiter as the combination of injustice with power which is the "nursery of scandal and discord" as represented in their children.[11] Even if the iconographer of the gardens of the Villa d'Este was not aware of Fulgentius' specific explanation of the myth of Leda and the Swan, he was a man learned in classic mythology who would realize that the lustful union of Jupiter and Leda had brought only discord and evil to the Greeks. The Trojan War and destruction of Troy was caused by the love of Helen inspired in Paris by Venus as a reward for the golden apple of Discord which Paris gave her in the beauty contest of Juno, Minerva, and Venus. The tragedy of the great house of Atreus was provoked by the infidelity of Clytemnestra, who with her lover Aegisthus

[8] G. P. Valeriano Bolzani, *loc.cit.*

[9] Hesiod, *Works and Days*, 59-105 and Hesiod, *Theogony*, 565-612.

[10] J. Seznec, *The Survival of the Pagan Gods* (Bollingen Series, XXXVIII), trans. by B. F. Sessions, New York, 1953, especially pp. 234ff. For example, the Cardinal's archaeologist,

Pirro Ligorio, in his archaeological notebooks at Turin refers to Fulgentius and Suidas for some of his knowledge regarding antiquity (AST, J. a. III. 10, f. 155v).

[11] A. Van Staveren, *Auctores mythographi Latini*, Leyden and Amsterdam, 1742, pp. 694-696; quoted by J. Seznec, *op.cit.*, p. 89.

murdered her husband Agamemnon. Even the Dioscuri, Castor and Pollux, created trouble by seizing the daughters of Leucippus, who had been betrothed to Idas and Lynceus, the twin cousins of the Dioscuri. The basic theme of all these myths is the evil and discord produced by lustful love.

The Parisian manuscript then claims (folio 266r) that at the foot of the two stairs which mounted above the Fountain of Leda and the Swan were to be two large statues of Hercules and Achilles "which serve as the guard of the Palace." This may explain why all the sixteenth century writers identify as Achilles the child held by Hercules in the statue above the Fountain of the Dragon. The Villa is guarded by the two most powerful heroes of Greek mythology, Hercules, who achieved immortality, and Achilles, who failed immortality only by his mortal heel, for the attainment of immortality is obviously an important theme in the decoration of the Villa d'Este.

The theme of Virtue and Vice, however, is further exploited in other sections of the Villa, and it is again the manuscript description at Paris which makes this explicit. Facing upon the piazza in front of the Oval Fountain is the Grotto of Venus, which "is dedicated to voluptuous pleasure, and is adorned together with the two contiguous rooms, in addition to the fountain which is mentioned in its proper place, with many ancient statues, paintings, and marble tables made of various sorts of stone, with some summer outdoor beds for repose during the day" (folios 251r and v). In the Grotto was an ancient statue of Venus stepping from her bath surrounded by cupids and water nymphs. In contrast to the Grotto of Venus or Voluptuous Pleasure is the Grotto of Diana situated high on the slope of the gardens underneath the summer dining loggia attached to the west end of the Villa. The Parisian account specifies that as the Grotto of Venus "is dedicated to appetite and to voluptuous pleasure, thus this grotto [of Diana] is dedicated to virtuous pleasure (*piacer honesto*) and to chastity" (folio 252r). The Grotto of Diana was meant to contain "two fountains, one dedicated to Diana, goddess of chastity, the other to the youthful chaste Hippolytus, who preferred to suffer death rather than to succumb to the lust of his stepmother Phaedra; in the space which remains between the two niches at the sides of the entrances are two other statues on pedestals, one of Penthesileia, Queen of the Amazons, the other of the Roman Lucretia" (folios 264v-265r).

The location of these contrasting grottoes must be considered in relation to the statues of Hercules. The Greek hero stood in the center of the gardens at the head of the long straight axis which ran across the lower gardens and up the lower slope from the entrance to the garden. On the other hand, the Grottoes of Voluptuous Pleasure and of Chastity were on either side of Hercules toward the edge of the garden. This suggests that the gardens also present the theme of the choice of Hercules between Voluptas, represented by the Grotto of Venus, and Virtue, exemplified by the Grotto of Diana.[12] It is possible that even the general layout of the gardens may have been

---

[12] The iconography of the Choice of Hercules is studied fully in E. Panofsky, *Hercules am Scheidewege* (Studien der Bibliothek Warburg, XVIII), Leipzig and Berlin, 1930, on

conditioned by this subject. The Choice of Hercules was symbolized by the Pythagorean Y, since, after pursuing a straight uneventful path of life, a youth when he came of age had to choose between the diverging paths of Virtue or Vice as Hercules did. So in the Tiburtine garden the visitor followed a straight path through charming but quiet surroundings until the statue of Hercules was attained. At that moment the course splits into two diverging paths which continue up the slope. The Grotto of Venus or Voluptas is at the eastern end of the Lane of the Hundred Fountains about at the level at which Hercules stood. The Grotto is in the very luxurious and attractive setting of the Oval Fountain, and, as the Parisian description relates, it was meant by its furniture and decoration to convey the feeling of sensuous, relaxed enjoyment. In contrast the Grotto of Diana or Chastity is situated in isolation at the summit of the right-hand divergent path which climbs up the slope below the Villa. There was little of interest along this way or even around the Grotto until one finally entered it. Pictorial representations of the Choice of Hercules often have the personifications of Voluptas and Virtue pointing out to the young Hercules two contrasting ways.[13] Voluptas in a very alluring and charming costume offers Hercules an easy path leading to sensuous enjoyment. Virtue, on the other hand, of a plain and undesirable appearance, can only present an unattractive and difficult way up the hill of Virtue.

The interior fresco decoration of the Villa is organized to reflect or supplement the symbolism of the garden, for there is not, as we have seen, one general encompassing iconography for all the interior painting. Instead, single rooms or apartments are related to the different levels of symbolism that can be discovered in the gardens. To the theme of Virtue and Vice is devoted the greatest number of rooms, but only in terms of Virtue. The three principal chambers on the courtyard level, the Salone and the personal apartment of the Cardinal, have painted friezes composed of female personifications chiefly of virtues, such as Patience, Wisdom, Charity, and Humanity. Likewise, the two rooms on the ground floor decorated by the workshop of Federigo Zuccaro have the virtues as their subject. The vault of the first of these rooms has in its center the three virtues, Liberality, Nobility, and Generosity. The second room has on its walls personifications of the four Cardinal Virtues, Temperance, Fortitude, Justice, and Providence, crowned in the center of the vault by Glory. The walls of the first room have painted busts of such Greek philosophers and wise men as Socrates, Solon, Diogenes, and Periander. Even they were to appear in the original project of the gardens as related by the Parisian manuscript. Soon after describing the reclining statue of aged Hercules, the manuscript notes "three great niches without a façade containing three ancient statues, larger than life and very beautiful, two of which are of black stone, the other of the whitest marble. All three are seated with the dignity suitable to such figures, one, that is the one in the middle, being the very wise philosopher Socrates, another Solon, and the third Lycurgus, two very great lawmakers"

---

which I have relied heavily for my analysis of this subject at Tivoli.

[13] E. Panofsky, *op.cit.*, especially figs. 57, 60, and 65.

(folio 264r). These statues were apparently never set in place and the Parisian description is too vague to help identify surely the specific location for which they were intended.[14] The relationship between these statues and the interior painted figures is indicated by the existence of two of the sages, Socrates and Solon, in both groups. The association of the philosophers with the virtues is obvious, since they teach or legislate with the purpose of achieving the virtues. However, Hercules, too, belongs to this group, for the commentary of Servius to Vergil's *Aeneid* (I, 745), which like the writings of Fulgentius was influential in the sixteenth century, calls Hercules a philosopher who was taught the secrets of the universe by Atlas.[15] Therefore, the three figures of the ancient Greek wise men were presumably to be situated near the statues of Hercules, so that he would be associated with the philosophers.

This symbolism, presenting the virtues which should be the guides of life and the Choice of Hercules between Virtue and Voluptas, is naturally a personal symbolism praising the Cardinal of Ferrara for following the example of Hercules. In this same section of the gardens there was another symbolic image of a personal nature. One of the favorite recreations of the Cardinal of Ferrara at Tivoli was to stroll on the long path directly under the terrace of the Villa, which was always known as the Cardinal's Walk, and here he might be seen in earnest conversation with his humanist friends. At the ends of this path were fountains with very personal references. The southwestern terminus of this walk was dominated by the Grotto of Diana. As the description from the Parisian manuscript previously quoted indicates, this Grotto was to contain ancient statues which refer not only to the Cardinal's virtue of chastity but to his own personality. Originally one of the statues was to be that of the Greek youth Hippolytus whose name Ippolito II d'Este bore. The other principal figure was Diana, the goddess of chastity and the patron goddess of the ancient Hippolytus, as the tapestry designs of Ligorio show. The statue of Hippolytus was never set up, but in its place was put the goddess Minerva, another virginal goddess, who is also depicted in the tapestry drawings as a patron goddess of the Greek youth. There was even an ancient statue of the Amazon Queen Penthesilea, sister of the mother of Hippolytus. So the Grotto of Diana or Chastity is also the grotto of Hippolytus, the eponymic hero of the Cardinal.

At the opposite or northeastern end of the Cardinal's Walk were the Fountains of the Greek god of medicine Aesculapius and his daughter Hygieia. Ligorio's tapestry designs explain the existence of the Fountain of Aesculapius, since it was he who

---

[14] V. Pacifici (*Atti e memorie della società tiburtina di storia e d'arte*, xx-xxi, 1940-1941, p. 148, note 3 on p. 149) identifies the site as that of the present *Bicchierone* just above the statues of Hercules, but that site does not seem to agree with the Parisian reference to "Nicchi senza frontespitio" (f. 264r). Perhaps they were to be in the three simple grottoes at the same level which have only rusticated façades.

[15] P. Virgilius Maro, *Opera cum integris commentariis Servii, Philargyrii, Pierii*, Leovardia, 1717, I, p. 410. Seznec (*op.cit.*, p. 18) points out that "Brunetto Latini places Hercules side by side with Moses, Solon, Lycurgus, Numa Pompilius, and the Greek king Phoroneus as among the first legislators." So Suidas likewise labels Hercules "philosophus optimus." See above note 4.

resurrected the mortally injured Hippolytus as the Latin god Virbius. Even the ever-present image of Hercules belongs to this myth. It was Hercules who captured the Amazon queen Hippolita whom Theseus received as his spoils after the victory of the Greeks over the Amazons. This inspired Ligorio to depict Hercules as a rather prominent figure in the scene of the marriage of Theseus and Hippolita (Fig. 91), whose union resulted in the birth of Hippolytus.

The symbolism in the garden and decoration which centers around the person of Hercules is, however, more than just a personal symbolism for the Cardinal. It is also a family symbolism, for by at least the sixteenth century Hercules had become the mythical ancestor and patron of the Este family of Ferrara. In 1544 the Ducal secretary of Ercole II d'Este, Cinzio Giraldi, claimed to find the origin of the Este family in the marriage of Hercules to Galata, daughter of the King of the Celts.[16] In addition to the sculpture of the gardens, one room of the Villa at Tivoli was decorated with frescoes depicting the Labors of Hercules, that is, those deeds of hard work by which Hercules purified himself of the sin of murdering his sons during his insanity and thus achieved the immortality pictured in the center of the vault in the form of the Council of the Olympian Gods with Hercules present.

A third system of symbolism in the Villa and its gardens is of a geographical nature, and it is again the Parisian manuscript which makes this most evident. The dramatic Oval Fountain in the eastern corner of the garden is identified in the Parisian description as the "Fountain of Tivoli . . . so called because it represents the mountain and rivers of the countryside of Tivoli" (folio 256v). In the grottoes of the mountain are the statues "which represent the three rivers of the Tiburtine territory, that is, the Anio, called today the Tiber, the Albuneo, and the Erculaneo; the Albuneo, which is thought to be the Sibyl of Tivoli, being seated in the middle and the other two reclining at her side" (folio 257v). The great cascade of water that flows down from the river gods into the oval basin is then, of course, a controlled and artistically refined depiction of the famous Cascade in the Anio river at Tivoli.

The decoration of three of the ground floor rooms of the Villa complement and expand this geographical symbolism. The small wall fountain in the Salotto (Fig. 60) is a stucco representation of the rocky crags at Tivoli on whose summit is the ancient round Temple of the Sibyl from which water gushed in imitation of the Cascade. On the walls are frescoes portraying parts of Tivoli and Rome; for example, the Villa d'Este itself at Tivoli and the Cardinal's Villa of Monte Cavallo in Rome. Rome, as

---

[16] G. B. Giraldi Cintio, "De Ferraria et Atestinis principibus commentariolum," in J. G. Graevius and P. Burmann, *Thesaurus antiquitatum et historiarum Italiae*, VII, pt. 1, Leyden, 1722, cols. 4-5. See also D. R. Coffin, "Pirro Ligorio and Decoration of the Late Sixteenth Century at Ferrara," *Art Bulletin*, XXXVII (1955), pp. 171-172. This family symbolism continues into the seventeenth century; for example, in 1605 Michelangelo Buonarroti the Younger, grandnephew of the great artist, dedicated his play *Il natal d'Ercole* to "Don Alfonso da Este, principe di Modana," while the seventeenth century Este palace at Modena still contains a statue of Hercules on its façade as protective guardian of the palace just as the Villa at Tivoli was to have Hercules and Achilles as its custodians.

we shall see later, comes into the geographical symbolism. There are also pictures of the Oval Fountain (the Fountain of Tivoli) and the Water Organ.

The two neighboring rooms toward the northeast are devoted to the mythology of Tivoli. On the wall of the first room next to the Salotto is the scene of the Battle of Hercules Saxanus against Belgio and Albio in Italy as he returned with the cattle of Geryon and the golden apples of the Hesperides. The Cardinal's archaeologist, Pirro Ligorio, relates the story of the battle under the discussion of ancient inscriptions at Tivoli in his manuscript on antiquities at Naples,[17] and associates Hercules Saxanus with the worship of Hercules at Tivoli. On the other walls are depicted the battle of the brothers Tiburtus and Catillus with the natives of the region of Tivoli, the sacrifice of a ram and ox after the victory of the brothers, and a small landscape with the Oval Fountain being built. In the center of the vault is another view of the battle of the two brothers with the Latins as they land in Italy. Around this picture are views of the building of the city of Tivoli or Tibur, which was named after Tiburtus, and the sacrifices accompanying the founding of the city.

The other room decorated with local myths has on its vault Apollo as the sun-god surrounded by scenes of the drowning of King Anio, after whom the local river was named; three river gods, which are obviously the three rivers of Tivoli depicted in the Oval Fountain; the madness of King Athamas as his wife Ino, who becomes Leucothea and thence the Tiburtine Sibyl Albunea, flees with their son Melicertes, and a pastoral scene of a river god and a woman with a child (probably Ino and Melicertes as Mater Matuta and Portunus as they land at the foot of the Tiber). On the walls are Venus in her dolphin-drawn chariot, since she is instrumental in saving Ino by having Neptune change her into the water nymph Leucothea, and two sacrificial scenes centering around the golden statuette of a mother and child, presumably Ino and Melicertes as the gods Mater Matuta and Portunus (Ovid, *Fasti*, VI, 473-568).

To return to the garden, around the Oval Fountain or Fountain of Tivoli are other elements which are related to it. The Grotto of Venus or Voluptas opens upon the piazza in front of the fountain and there is probably a reference in this symbolism to the intercession of Venus on behalf of Ino as depicted within the Villa, since Ino as the Tiburtine Sibyl sits above in the center of the Oval Fountain.

Within the walls of the Oval Fountain on either side of the entrance is a statue of Bacchus. The Cardinal's humanist Muret speaks of these two statues in his poetry. In a long poem describing Tivoli, after mentioning the statues of the ten water nymphs of the Oval Fountain Muret writes that "Jacchus [i.e. Bacchus] stands near his nurses, mindful of his mother's death and his father's flames, he enjoys the waters and joyfully he mingles his gifts [i.e. wine] with them."[18] Therefore, Bacchus is associated with the

---

[17] Naples, Biblioteca Nazionale, MS XIII. B. 7, p. 185.
[18] M. A. Muret, *op.cit.*, p. 45. This poem was written in 1571, see *ibid.*, *Epistolae* Book III, pp. 656-657, no. XX. There are also two small poems of Muret dedicated solely to the statues of Bacchus, *ibid.*, *Poemata*, Book I, p. 47, nos. 54 and 55.

Fountain of Tivoli because, after his mother's destruction by the thunderbolt of Jupiter, he was raised by the water nymphs, who were sisters of his mother, and in particular by Ino who is, as we have seen, the Tiburtine Sibyl. That there were two statues of Bacchus, one on each side of the entrance, was inspired, I believe, by more than a pursuit of symmetry. Ovid in his *Metamorphoses* (III, 317; and IV, 12) calls Bacchus "twice born," since Bacchus was still in his mother's womb when she was destroyed by Jupiter's lightning, and the unborn child was torn from her womb and sewn up in the thigh of Jupiter until the time of birth. The idea of carving two identical statues of Bacchus may be a device to convey the concept of the "twice born" Bacchus, as the idea of death and rebirth is a fundamental one in the iconography of the Villa. The story of Hippolytus in the tapestry designs of Ligorio is concerned with the same significance.

At the summit of the hill of Tivoli prances the winged horse Pegasus about to leap into the air. Ancient Greek mythology recounts that the Fountain of Hippocrene, beloved by the Muses, sprang up from the hooves of Pegasus as he flew from Mount Helicon or Mount Parnassus.[19] So apparently the mountain of Tivoli is to be equated with Mount Parnassus, the home of the Muses; for as the Muses through their patronage of the arts and science made Mount Parnassus famous, so the Cardinal of Ferrara by his patronage has made Mount Tivoli a great center of the arts. Pirro Ligorio, the Cardinal's archaeologist, points out that the Fountain of the Muses, which was so created, signifies the Fountain of Virtue and of Memory,[20] thereby tying this iconography into the theme of Virtue which dominated the rest of the garden.

The Oval Fountain or Fountain of Tivoli stands at one end of the long axis of the Hundred Fountains which leads across the garden to the Fountain of Rome. Beside the Lane of the Hundred Fountains run three channels which, as the Parisian manuscript explains (folio 260v), make the waterway from Tivoli to Rome; that is, the three rivers of the Anio, the Albuneo, and the Erculaneo—the three rivers represented by the statues in the Fountain of Tivoli—which unite to become the Tiber as it comes to Rome. The little boat fountains along the upper channel of course identify the channel as a river. At the far end of the Lane of the Hundred Fountains is naturally the Fountain of Rome depicting the city in its physical form, not merely symbolically as the Fountain of Tivoli does. The geographical symbolism was intended to continue with the Fountain of Neptune, which was never created. Situated below the Fountain of Rome, the Fountain of Neptune was to receive the water of the Tiber flowing past Rome, since, as the Parisian description notes, it "represents the sea" (folio 253v) into which the Tiber empties. Even the Fountain of the Emperors located between Rome and the Fountain of Neptune belongs to this geographical symbolism as again

---

[19] The ancient myth varies as to whether the location is Mount Helicon or Mount Parnassus. Zappi (*op.cit.*, p. 62) in his description of the Villa in 1576 considers it to be Par-nassus: "[Pegasus] posandose a piedi al monte Parnaso ove fermò il piede, nacque una fonte."

[20] AST, MS J. a. II. 16, vol. XXIX of Ligorio MSS, f. 7v.

the Parisian manuscript proves, for it was to contain statues of the four Roman emperors "each of whom built splendid villas in the Tiburtine territory as appear from the remains which are preserved until today" (folio 256r).

The geographical symbolism is, of course, in honor of the Cardinal of Ferrara, since it depicts the cities of Tivoli and Rome, the centers of his greatest accomplishments in the patronage of the arts and, therefore, of his ennoblement. However, this system of symbolism also revolves about the image of Hercules that stood in the center of the gardens, for Hercules was the patron deity of Tivoli during antiquity. The Cardinal's archaeologist Ligorio in his description of the Villa of Hadrian points out that the statue of Hercules that was worshiped at Tivoli was of a special type: "They depict him differently than others do. In order to show that he was that Hercules who had overcome the Amazons, their shield was placed under his feet with other arms. And because he was the best guide and captain in warlike affairs, there were placed under him the breastplate and helmet, and scenes of his valor were depicted on his seat. He held his club in one hand, and in the other the Apples of the Hesperides."[21] As a result the statue of Hercules ties together all the systems of symbolism at Tivoli. Not only is Hercules the patron deity of the region of Tivoli and the mythical ancestor of the Este family, but the figure of Hercules at ancient Tivoli as described by Ligorio also combines the two Labors of Hercules that are emphasized in the decoration of the Villa d'Este as personal references to the Cardinal of Ferrara. The statue had the typical shield of the Amazons, signifying the Greek victory with the aid of Hercules over the Amazons from which evolved the marriage of Hippolita and Theseus, the parents of the Cardinal's eponymic hero, Hippolytus. The Tiburtine statue, moreover, held the Golden Apples of the Hesperides which symbolize the Choice of Hercules between Virtue and Voluptas. Therefore, as the dedicatory poems of Muret indicate, it is to the hero Hercules that the Villa and its garden are dedicated, and his statue appropriately dominated the garden. In fact, the garden of the Villa d'Este is the Garden of the Hesperides.

All the symbolism of the gardens and most of that of the interior decoration of the Villa is expressed in terms of classic mythology with no Christian subject matter. Within the Villa, only the Cardinal's private Chapel and the Rooms of Moses and of Noah facing the Secret Garden, are decorated with Christian stories. However, there exists the strong possibility that this pagan symbolism also has Christian overtones. Such a suggestion is only hypothetical for none of the writings describing the Villa presents any explicit evidence of this, yet there are a few hints and intimations. The decoration of the Villa and its gardens was executed during the early moments of the Counter-Reformation when the Christian interpretation of pagan mythology was severely frowned upon, although unsuccessfully, by the Church,[22] and Ippolito II

[21] P. Ligorio, "Descrittione della superba & magnificentissima Villa Tiburtina Hadriana," col. 1, in J. G. Graevius and P. Burmann, *Thesaurus antiquitatum et historiarum Italiae*, Leyden, 1723, VIII, pt. 4.

[22] J. Seznec, *op.cit.*, especially pp. 263-277,

d'Este was, of course, one of the Princes of the Church. On the other hand, although he was a Cardinal of the Church, Ippolito of all the cardinals was probably the least influenced by the Counter-Reformation. His instincts and attitude were those of the Renaissance, and he was usually detested or feared by the more stringent or even fanatical Popes of the Counter-Reformation, such as Paul IV and Pius V.

Ligorio's tapestry designs have definitely Christian overtones, as has been noted. Not only are the birth and seduction scenes derived from Christian iconography, but the depiction of the Eleusinian mysteries obviously is meant to parallel the Christian mass. In the Parisian description quoted earlier (folio 264v), the statue of Hercules with the infant Achilles "represents immortality because of which [Hercules] was adored by men as God." The statue of Hercules, standing triumphantly above the dragon of the central fountain, must have suggested to a Christian observer the well-known image of Christ trampling on the dragon. In fact the moralized Ovid at one moment calls Hercules Christ.[23] Contemporary with the decoration of the Villa d'Este (1560) the French poet Ronsard had composed a hymn entitled "The Christian Hercules," in which he parallels the lives of Christ and of Hercules,[24] and it is precisely at this time that the Cardinal of Ferrara was in France as Papal Legate (1561-1563), where he must have known the works of the French court poet. It is possible then that the Hercules at Tivoli is meant to be a prefiguration of Christ.

Other fountains in the Villa d'Este also may have Christian references. The Tiburtine Sibyl, who dominates the Oval Fountain was credited with having revealed to the Emperor Augustus the birth of Christ.[25] However, the statue of the Tiburtine Sibyl with the nude child likewise suggests a Christian Madonna and Child. This is even more true of the depictions of the worship of her golden statue as Mater Matuta on the walls of the Second Tiburtine Room (Figs. 81 and 85). In the same way the figure of Pandora in the Fountain above Hercules was an obvious parallel to Eve, since in Greek mythology she was the first mortal woman and brought evil to man.[26]

---

describes the struggle between the Church on one side generally and the artists and patrons on the other.

[23] Thomas Walkensis, *Metamorphosis Ouidiana moraliter*, n.p. [1515], f. 86v. The Vatican mythographer III while not explicit implies this equation. Following Fulgentius, he attempts to interpret philologically the Apples of the Hesperides as sheep, "nam *oves μῆλα* dicuntur" (G. H. Bode, *Scriptores rerum mythicarum Latini tres Romae nuper reperti*, Cellis, 1834, I, p. 248). As a result he calls Hercules "pastor ovium," which calls to mind the image of Christ as the Good Shepherd.

[24] P. de Ronsard, *Oeuvres complètes de P. de Ronsard*, ed. by P. Blanchemain, Paris, 1866, v, pp. 168-177. See also F. Yates, *The French Academies of the Sixteenth Century* (Studies of the Warburg Institute 15), London, 1947, pp. 191-192.

[25] The importance of the Sibyls for Christian art is discussed in E. Mâle, *L'Art religieux de la fin du moyen âge en France*, 3rd ed., Paris, 1925, pp. 253-279. The Sibyls with Christian associations were especially popular in Italy from the late fifteenth century.

[26] For example, in France there is the painting now in the Louvre attributed to Jean Cousin the Elder in which the figure of Eve has the inscription "Eva Prima Pandora," for a complete analysis of the iconography of Pandora see D. and E. Panofsky, *Pandora's Box*, New York, 1956.

Dupérac's engraving of the Villa gardens includes in the Secret Garden a Fountain of the Unicorn (Fig. 1, no. 3) set into the rear wall next to the Villa. Although not mentioned in the original project represented in the Parisian manuscript, this fountain was in existence by 1572.[27] Located in the enclosed Secret Garden, the Fountain of the Unicorn is a descendant of the mediaeval Christian legend, ultimately of classic origin, that the unicorn could only be killed with the aid of a virgin. In mediaeval Christian interpretation this is an allegory of the Incarnation with the virgin being the Virgin Mary and the unicorn Christ. This is particularly appropriate to the Secret Garden, since the Virgin was also often symbolized by an enclosed garden (*hortus inclusus*). However, the figure of a unicorn is equally appropriate as the decoration of a fountain, for according to mediaeval legend the unicorn by dipping its horn into a stream or fountain cleared the water of any poison. Therefore, it is very likely that in the original fountain at Tivoli the unicorn was represented with his horn in the water.[28] Thus again the iconography is centered about the theme of chastity and immortality as elsewhere in the gardens and decoration of the Villa.

Certainly the dominant theme penetrating all the iconography of both the garden fountains and the fresco decoration is that of immortality. Like the ancient Hercules the Cardinal of Ferrara was to achieve immortality through his virtuous life of chastity, temperance, and prudence (the three Apples of the Hesperides) and through his good works and munificent patronage of the arts at Tivoli and Rome.

In this analysis of the symbolism of the gardens several important fountains have played no role. The most significant of these fountains are the Water Organ[29] and the Fountain of the Owl. The main figure in the decoration of the Water Organ was the statue of the Diana of Ephesus, which is labeled the Goddess of Nature in all the old documents.[30] Hence, the Water Organ is actually the Fountain of Mother Nature appropriate to any garden. The same is true of the two small fountains dedicated, according to Dupérac's engraving (Fig. 1, nos. 11 and 12), to the horticultural deities Pomona and Flora. These two fountains, which were never completed, are not part of the original conception, at least as it is presented in the Parisian description. The Water Organ and the Fountain of the Owl have other than symbolic interest—that of

[27] T. Ashby, *op.cit.*, p. 248, the Inventory of 1572, no. 60.

[28] The statue of the unicorn no longer exists and Cardinal von Hohenlohe filled the niche of the fountain with a statue of St. Sebastian, see V. Pacifici, in *Atti e memorie della società tiburtina di storia e d'arte*, XXII-XXIII (1942-1943), p. 76.

[29] It is true that the so-called Water Organ or Fountain of Nature might belong in an indirect fashion to the system of iconography centered around the battle of the Amazons and Greeks. Pausanias (VII, ii, 6-7) relates that the original statue of Diana at Ephesus, a copy

of which was the centerpiece of the Water Organ, was, according to one legend, dedicated by the Amazons during their war against Athens and Theseus. However, that this is the reason for the selection of the Ephesian Diana is extremely unlikely. It has already been noted (see above p. 58) that here at Tivoli Federigo Zuccaro used the same image with the inscription Rerum Natura in the Room of Nobility to symbolize Mother Nature.

[30] For example, the Parisian manuscript, f. 254r or the archival accounts published in Chapter Two, notes 8 and 10.

being hydraulic curiosities in which the *fontanieri* express not the symbolic meaning of the gardens and fountains but rather the amusing devices that they can create.[31]

The idea that the decoration of a villa and its gardens should be unified in an iconographical program is consistent with sixteenth century Italian Mannerism in which all cultural phenomena had many levels of meaning.[32] The Villa d'Este, however, seems unusual in that both the garden decoration and the interior fresco decoration are correlated iconographically, but this unique quality may only be due to our lack of knowledge regarding other gardens. Since gardens and garden decoration tend to be ephemeral, it is very difficult to determine accurately their iconographical program. The symbolism of one other garden layout of this period is fortunately preserved and explained in Vasari's description of the gardens of the Villa Medici at Castello as it was developed by the humanist Benedetto Varchi and executed by the sculptor Tribolo in honor of the Medici.[33] In addition to personifications of the Four Seasons located appropriately in the garden, there were to be figures depicting the mountains Asinaio and Falterona, the city of Fiesole, and the rivers Mugnone and Arno, all geographical personifications to indicate the political holdings of the Medici. There were also to be statues portraying various members of the Medici family as personifications of the virtues and the accomplishments of the Medici in the arts, laws, and sciences.

Approximately contemporary with the Villa d'Este the interior decoration of the Palazzo Farnese at Caprarola illustrates how completely organized an iconographical program of decoration can be formulated by humanistic advisers, in this case, Annibal Caro, Onofrio Panvinio, and Fulvio Orsini.[34] The decoration of the two apartments which comprise most of the *piano nobile* are dedicated, one to the Active Life in terms of the deeds of the Farnese family or mythological stories, the other to the Contemplative Life depicted in the contemplation of the Cosmos, the activities of Angels, and Christian scenes of judgment and penance. The great front hall, the Sala d'Ercole, which served as a dining room like the Salotto at Tivoli, tells the myth of the creation of nearby Lake Vico by Hercules and combines with the topographical views on the walls of the Farnese possessions to develop a geographical symbolism analogous to the Tiburtine Rooms and the Salotto of the Villa d'Este.

---

[31] Such elements as the labyrinths and the cross-pergola are also purely horticultural features. Although it might be claimed that the labyrinths have an association with the Hippolytus myth, since it was into the Labyrinth that Theseus, the father of Hippolytus, went to kill the Minotaur, the combination of the labyrinths with the cross-pergola indicate that no symbolism is involved, but that they are merely heritages from an old Italian horticultural tradition.

[32] J. Seznec, *op.cit.*, pp. 279-323.

[33] G. Vasari, *Le vite*, VI, Florence, 1881, pp. 72-85 and B. H. Wiles, *The Fountains of Florentine Sculptors*, Cambridge, Mass., 1933, especially pp. 33-35.

[34] F. Baumgart, "La Caprarola di Ameto Orti," *Studj romanzi*, XXV (1935), pp. 77-179 and G. Balducci, *Il Palazzo Farnese in Caprarola*, Rome, 1910. For a later program by Fulvio Orsini with some similarities to that of Tivoli see J. R. Martin, "Immagini della Virtù: The Paintings of the Camerino Farnese," *Art Bulletin*, XXXVIII (1956), pp. 91-112.

The importance of the Villa d'Este is that it combines a garden iconography like that of the Villa Medici at Castello with a fresco program suggestive of Caprarola. However, neither the garden nor the fresco symbolism at Tivoli is a complete unit in itself, but each requires integration with the other to make the meaning explicit.

THE CREATOR

It has generally been assumed that Pirro Ligorio, the Cardinal's archaeologist, was the designer of the Villa d'Este gardens, yet no records fully substantiate this. Ligorio was in the service of the Cardinal of Ferrara from 1549 to about 1555,[35] when the idea of preparing a new Villa and gardens arose and the first acquisition of land took place, but it must be remembered that Ligorio's salary during this time was paid to him as "Antiquarian" of the Cardinal. Soon thereafter he entered Papal service as Vatican architect, where he remained until June 1567. It was about this time that Ligorio's name began to reappear in the building accounts of Tivoli. The earliest reference is an evaluation by Galvani for stonecutting, from January 1566 through April 1567, in which Ligorio is specified as ordering the cutting of a block of tufa.[36] On May 2, 1567, G. B. della Porta was paid to cut for the Oval Fountain a statue of a nymph "after the drawing of Messer Pirro Ligorio."[37] Another evaluation by Galvani for masonry completed from May 28, 1567, through September 1567 lists work executed by Curzio Maccarone under the direction of Ligorio for the Oval Fountain.[38] On July 4, 1567, G. B. della Porta signed the contract for the ten nymphs of the Oval Fountain, of which one was already completed, five to be finished by the end of August and four others by the end of September, all the statues "after the drawing of Messer Pirro."[39] Then on August 17, 1568, Pierre de la Motte signed his contract to carve for the Fountain of Rome a statue of Rome "in accordance with the drawing of Messer Pirro Ligorio which is, at present, in the hands of Messer Vincenzo Stampa."[40]

The account books of the Cardinal for 1567 and 1568 show no evidence of Ligorio receiving a salary during these years. However, he received recompense for his work in 1567 in the form of monetary gifts from the Cardinal, as the record of two of these gifts in the Cardinal's "Libro de minuti piaceri" for 1567 reveals.[41] During the next

[35] ASM, Registri, Pacco 106, Giornale: Libro di messer Benedetto 1549, ff. 67v-69r: Oct. 31, 1549, "Spesa de sallariati et per la detta cti alli mti sallariati di SS.R^ma li mti danari per la loro Prouisione de ottobre app Police' . . . messer Piero antiquario ▽ 4.0" and Pacco 110, Giornale di entrata e uscita 1555, f. 43v: Oct. 4, 1555, 7.63 *scudi* "A m Piro Antiquario per il mese passato."

[36] ASM, Fab. e Vill., Tivoli, Busta 70, Pte. 1, fasc. 12, f. 49r: "57. Item p auer fatto una Pietra di tuffo che fecu' far messer Pirro per meter sopra londe con scartoci e auer cauato

la Pietra ala Piazza di san Paulo stimata ▽ 2."

[37] See Chapter Two, note 48.

[38] See Chapter Two, note 46.

[39] F. S. Seni, *La Villa d'Este in Tivoli*, Rome, 1902, p. 66 n. 1.

[40] *Idem.*

[41] ASM, Registri, Pacco 118, Libro de minuti piaceri 1567 segnato M, f. 24r: June 23, 1567, "E adi detto à messer Pyrro ligurgo ▽ cinquanta che li dona S.S. Illma" and f. 25r: Sept. 9, "E adi 9 detto amesser Pyrro ligurgo ▽ uentitre et b 20 che li dona S.S. Illma."

Actually at least part of these gifts may have

year there is an account on September 4, 1568, for rent paid by the Cardinal for the "rooms where Messer Pirro Ligorio and his family lodge."[42] Finally in 1569 there is record of three reimbursements to Ligorio for unidentified expenses.[43] The first payment on February 5 specifies Ligorio simply as "Antiquarian," while that on April 4 calls him "Antiquarian of our Excellency the Lord Duke," since Ligorio was in the pay of the Cardinal's nephew, Duke Alfonso II of Ferrara, from December 1568. Therefore, the accounts for Tivoli show only that Ligorio was employed by the Cardinal as Antiquarian from 1550 to 1555 and that from 1567 to 1569 he was concerned with the Oval Fountain and the Fountain of Rome as well as with archaeology.

The question then arises whether there is any evidence in the building accounts to credit the creation of the gardens at Tivoli to someone else. There are perhaps two other candidates: Girolamo Muziano and Giovanni Alberto Galvani. The Tiburtine accounts indicate that the Cardinal's favorite painter, Girolamo Muziano, was active at Tivoli at least in 1563, 1565, and 1566. Muziano was in part responsible for the gardens of the Cardinal's Villa at Monte Cavallo in Rome as the accounts of 1563 reveal.[44] However, it is very unlikely that Muziano was involved with the gardens of the Villa d'Este as the records mention Muziano solely in respect to the interior pictorial decoration of the Villa.

From 1560 throughout the rest of the life of the Cardinal, Galvani from Ferrara was employed at Tivoli with the title of "Architect" at a monthly salary of six *scudi*.[45]

---

been meant as pay for archaeological excavations under the direction of Ligorio in the neighborhood of Tivoli, as the same Libro de minuti piaceri contains amounts for such work. Some of these accounts are published by A. Venturi, "Nuovi documenti: Ricerche di antichità per Monte Giordano, Monte Cavallo e Tivoli nel secolo XVI," *Archivio storico dell'arte*, III (1890), p. 201; to which should be added the following accounts from the same account book: f. 21v, Oct. 1, 1567, 32 *baiocchi*; Oct. 3, 30 *baiocchi*, "Eadi 3 detto soldi trenta donati armo uignarolo alli Villa di Adriano doue SS Illᵐᵃ estatta"; Oct. 5, 50 *baiocchi*; f. 22r, Oct. 6, 1 *scudo*, "Eadi 6 di Otteᵉ scuto uno d.º in oro donato alpatio della cartara doue S.S. Ill.ᵐᵃ e stata auedere lauorare"; f. 22v, Oct. 11, 7 *scudi* 20 *baiocchi*, "per tante opere che hanno cauato nelle anticaglie alla Villa di Adriano doue S.S. Illᵐᵃ fa cauare p la settimana presente cominciando alli otto per tutto hogi"; and f. 23r, Oct. 14, 5 *scudi* 55 *baiocchi*, "per trentassette opere che hanno lauorate heri et hogi alle caue alla Villa di Adriano"; Oct. 15, 3 *scudi* 15 *baiocchi*.

[42] ASM, Registri, Pacco 119, Registro del 1568, f. lxxxxviii: Sept. 4, 1568, "E adi iiij Sette'bre scudi otto m.ᵗ et per S.S. Ill ctj amesser Menico Gentile per il fitto delle stantie doue alloggia messer Pirro Ligurio et sua famiglia."

[43] ASM, Registri, Pacco 119, Registro del 1569, f. 20r: Feb. 5, 1569, "Adi 5 Febraro lire cent'una l'otto m.ᵗᵉ sono la valuta de ▽ᵗⁱ ventisei dº indº a Pietro Liguri Antiquario peraltro tanti che detto ha fatti pagare in Roma à S.S. Ill.ᵐᵃ app lese di Comess.ⁿᵉ del Caualleᵉ Priorato et in Zorleᵉ ▽ Cj l viij"; April 4, "A messer Pietro Ligurio Antiquario dell' Eccᵐᵒ S. Duca nr'o lire trentatre e sei dor sono la valuta de ▽ᵗⁱ dieci di m.ᵗᵃ per la medesima som'a che il Caualleᵉ priorato ha fatto scuodere à nome suo a roma app Zorle ▽ xxxiij l vj dº"; and f. 48r: July 23, "Adi 23 detto lire cent'una e quindeci mᵗᵉ amesser Pirio Ligurio per tanti ch' esso ha fatti pagare in Roma nelle mani di messer Marco Antº Cambio Tess.ʳᵒ app lero di Comiss.ᵉ del S.ʳ Cauallʳᵒ Priorato all Comess.ʳᵒ reg.ᵗᵃ in Registro secondo a 113 app in Zerle ▽ Cj l xv dº."

[44] ASM, Registri, Pacco 113, Entrata et uscita della Protett.ⁿᵉ 1563, *passim*. See also U. da Como, *Girolamo Muziano 1528-1592*, Bergamo, 1930, pp. 72 and 175.

[45] V. Pacifici, *Ipp. II d'Este*, p. 399. As an

It has also been noted that Galvani records in the accounts that one fountain, the Fountain of the Emperors, was his creation ("la mia fontana deli Collone torte").[46] However, there are numerous objections to giving credit for the whole layout to Galvani. In fact, the point that he specifically claims the Fountain of the Emperors to be his suggests that it alone is his design. There is the additional fact that Galvani just before coming to Tivoli was paid from March to August 1560 for his services as a "mason" in Rome on work at Santa Maria d'Aracoeli and on the corridors which went from there to the Palazzo Venezia. This work was executed for the Papacy and subscribed by the Papal Architect, who was at that time Pirro Ligorio.[47] Although the relation between architect and mason is still somewhat vague at this period, the documents suggest that Galvani was probably a building contractor who had worked up from being a chief mason. He would, therefore, have had sufficient architectural and building knowledge to superintend the rather minor architectural revision of the monastery into the Villa d'Este and to evaluate the work for the Villa, but not the classical knowledge and artistic creativity to plan the gardens at Tivoli.

The gardens of the Villa d'Este as a whole, even more than a single fountain like the Fountain of Rome, reveal on the part of the creator an erudite knowledge of classical mythology and antiquity. There is the intricate symbolism revolving around Hercules, Hippolytus, ancient Tivoli, and Rome. The Hundred Fountains were decorated with innumerable depictions from Ovid's *Metamorphoses*. The Fountain of the Owl is based on the writings of the ancient Greek, Hero of Alexandria, whose ideas were preserved at the time of the creation of the Tiburtine fountain in a few Greek and Latin manuscripts, which would be known primarily to a classical scholar and his circle.

There had been in the employ of the Cardinal at various times one man who combined a profound knowledge of classical antiquity with the artistic ability and imagination that were necessary for the creation of the gardens of the Villa d'Este at Tivoli. This was Pirro Ligorio, who was employed as the Cardinal's antiquarian during the first years when it was decided to create the Villa and its gardens and when the general plan for the gardens may have been developed. Soon the Cardinal's future architect, Galvani, was working on Papal projects under Ligorio's ideas. This does not mean that Ligorio was responsible for every detail in the gardens. The general theme behind the gardens may have been suggested by one of the humanists in the entourage of the Cardinal, such as Marc-Antoine Muret, who wrote the Latin dedica-

example of such pay: ASM, Registri, Pacco 116, Conti dele ent.ª de Ferrara 1565, f. xii: June 8, 1565, 12 *scudi*, "A messer Gio Alberto dj Galuanj . . . per sua puisione dil mese dj Nouembre et Decembre '64."

[46] See Chapter Two, note 27.

[47] ASR, CF 1520, f. 9: Payments to Maestro Alberto Galvani of Ferrara "muratore" from March 22 to August 31, 1560, "a conto della Fabbrica che ha da fare in Araceli et delli tre corridori che vanno a San Marco." The final payment on August 31 is "per resto del pagamento dell'opera di muro fatta in Araceli et nel corridore come per una lista de x del passato sottoscritta dal Prep.º e Architetti."

tions to the gardens, or Francesco Bandini Piccolomini, the Archbishop of Siena. Muret and Bandini, with other members of the Cardinal's court, such as Foglietta and Lelio Calcagnini, formed later in 1571 the Accademia degli Agevoli at Tivoli, which was particularly concerned with the history of ancient Tivoli.[48] However, their interest in the antiquities and ancient culture of Tivoli probably depended upon the investigations and knowledge of the Cardinal's archaeologist, Pirro Ligorio. Certainly Ligorio designed the two principal fountains dedicated to Tivoli (the Oval Fountain) and to Rome. It is probably Ligorio who contributed ideas for some of the other fountains, such as the hydraulic device of the Fountain of the Owl adopted from Hero of Alexandria's writings. That Hero's works were known to Ligorio is proven by the reference in his manuscripts at Turin to the fact that it is a mistake that "those who wish to make waterdrawn machines have not studied what power the water has with automatic machines which are moved by the striking of wheels, as those of Hero and of Philostratus."[49] Indeed, almost all the iconographic details of the garden decoration and the interior frescoes can be identified in Ligorio's archaeological notebooks at Turin and Naples. This is no proof that Ligorio was the creator of the Villa d'Este, for his archaeological notebooks at Turin form the largest encyclopedia dealing with antique culture as it was known at that time, including a fantastic command of classic sources and writings, but these notebooks prove that Ligorio had the knowledge that the creator of the decoration of the Este Villa must have had. For example, in his entry entitled the Golden Apple, Ligorio, citing Suidas, equates the three Golden Apples of the Hesperides possessed by Hercules with the "three passions of the soul, which overcome the three that trouble the soul and being acquired create quietude, tranquillity, and joy as their effects."[50] He then goes on to quote the phrase from Ovid ("Pomaque abinsomni non custodita dracone") which the Cardinal of Ferrara used as the motto of his *impresa*.[51] In his consideration of Pegasus, Ligorio remarks that the winged horse on Mount Helicon signifies Fame, a theme appropriate to the iconography of the Villa d'Este.[52]

Ligorio's two great fountains of Tivoli and Rome may have been suggested by his archaeological work for the Cardinal, that is, the investigation of the Villa of Hadrian

[48] M. Maylender, *Storia delle accademie d'-Italia*, I, Bologna, n.d., pp. 91-93.

[49] AST, MS J. a. II. 16, vol. XXIX of the Ligorio MSS, f. 21v: ". . . quelli che uogliono fare delli istrumenti da tirate acqua non hanno studiato che forza ha l'acqua con le machine Automate, che per accidenza di ruote si muouono; come le cose di Herone, et di Philostrato, . . ." I expect at a later time to study this unpublished manuscript of Ligorio, which is a treatise on the fine arts. In the manuscript Ligorio analyzes in terms of their faults several designs for fountains. The subject of many of these fountains suggests that they were rejected designs for fountains in the Villa d'Este.

[50] AST, MS J. a. III. 13, s.v. Malo Aureo: ". . . tre affetti dell'animo, che superano i tre che perturbano l'anima et acquistati suonano quiete et tranquillita et laetiatia i quali tre effetti, . . ."

[51] Ercole Cato in his funeral oration for the Cardinal asserts that the Cardinal chose the *impresa* of the Golden Apples of the Hesperides with the Ovidian motto at the time of his elevation to the Cardinalate in 1538 (*Oratione fatta dal Cavaliere Hercole Cato nelle essequie dell'Illustriss. et Reuerendiss. Sig. D. Hippolito d'Este*, Ferrara, 1587, p. 4).

[52] AST, MS J. a. III. 15, s.v. Pegasus.

near Tivoli. It was at this time that Ligorio prepared the first plan of the Hadrianic Villa that had ever been made. No longer extant, this plan is preserved in a seventeenth century version published in the eighteenth century.[53] Even more important than the plan of the ancient Villa was Ligorio's description of it in which he attempted to identify the various parts of the Villa. He followed the ancient description of Spartianus who points out that the many sections of Hadrian's Villa were created to represent famous geographical parts of the Roman Empire: the Painted Stoa and the Academy of Athens, the Canopus near Alexandria, the Valley of Tempe in Thessaly, and Hades.[54]

The great quantity of water and fountains which Ligorio encountered in the Villa of Hadrian must have influenced him to utilize water and water effects in the Villa d'Este as never before in the garden of an Italian Renaissance villa, but it is also probable that the description by Spartianus of the ancient Roman villa inspired the geographical symbolism in the Renaissance garden, with its depictions of the cities of Tivoli and Rome.[55] To Ligorio the Renaissance Cardinal of Ferrara with his love

---

[53] The most readily available version of this plan is P. Ligorio, *Ichnographia villae Tiburtinae Hadriani Caesaris*, rev. by F. Contini, Rome, 1751. The history of this plan is found in the Windsor codex VII, 36, where, according to R. Lanciani, *Storia degli scavi di Roma*, II, Rome, 1903, p. 113, it is stated that one M. D'Autreville bought the drawings of the Villa in Ferrara and brought them to France.

Although Ligorio's plan of the whole Villa is apparently no longer preserved, there is among the drawings in the Turin manuscripts (Archivio di Stato, MS J. a. II. 7, vol. XX, f. 91r) a rough sketch of a section of the Villa of Hadrian, probably that part with the so-called Torre di Roccabruna.

[54] Published in J. G. Graevius and P. Burmann, *Thesaurus antiquitatum et historiarum Italiae*, Leyden, 1723, VIII, pt. 4. There are preserved three different versions of Ligorio's description. Two of these, which are dedicated to the Cardinal of Ferrara, are only known in many later manuscript copies. One version entitled "Descrittione" is published in Graevius; the other carries the title "Trattato." The third version dedicated to the Trinity is contained in volume XX of Ligorio's manuscripts at Turin. Ligorio mentions on f. 3r that he has already written two versions of the description of Tivoli, one dedicated to the Cardinal of Ferrara, the other to Alessandro Cardinal Farnese. Of this latter version with a dedication to the Farnese Cardinal there is, as far as I can discover, no preserved evidence.

The ancient description of Spartianus of the Villa of Hadrian is published in H. Peter, ed., *Scriptores historiae Augustae*, I, Leipzig, 1884, p. 28: A. Spartianus, "De vita Hadriani," 26, line 5.

[55] It is undoubtedly true that the parts of Hadrian's Villa which are named after locations in the Roman Empire are not reproductions of those famous localities, see H. Kähler, *Hadrian und seine Villa bei Tivoli*, Berlin, 1950, p. 27. So P. Grimal (*Les jardins romains*, Paris, 1943, p. 280 n. 5) is correct in asserting that there is a different aesthetic involved in the naming of parts of Hadrian's Villa and the attempt at literal reconstruction in Ligorio's Fountain of Rome, but this judgment is based on modern archaeological knowledge, whereas the Renaissance and Ligorio may have considered the sections of Hadrian's Villa more in the nature of reproductions.

Tribolo's incomplete project for the gardens at Castello devised by Varchi contained a geographical symbolism and personifications of the Medicean virtues which might have influenced the iconography of the Tiburtine gardens (G. Vasari, *Le vite*, VI, 1881, pp. 72-84). However, it seems rather unlikely that a member of the Este family, which detested the Medici, created his gardens in the pattern of the Tuscan gardens, when near his Villa, within his own territory, and first explored fully by his own archaeologist, was an ancient villa which could be the source of influence.

of ancient culture was undoubtedly parallel to the Roman Emperor Hadrian who held dear the art and philosophy of ancient Greece. The letter of Foglietta in 1569 describing what was accomplished at that time in the Villa d'Este identifies, at least in part, Ligorio's contribution to this symbolism:

Thence from the [Oval] fountain is a triple canal which, cutting across the hill, goes with its water to the other fountain, which has the form of the location and of the city of Rome and of the Tiber. And from there it plunges down to a lower lake, to which has been given the name of the sea. And the statues are not only well arranged for decoration of the site and for the pleasant view, but there is a hidden theme, not wanting in gentility, to personify subtly the nature of the Tiburtine ground. Inventor of this was that most famous architect of our time and my very dear friend, Pirro Ligorio, a man as much of diverse erudition, as of admirable knowledge of antiquity.[56]

[56] F. S. Seni, *op.cit.*, pp. 61-62.

CHAPTER VI · THE LATER HISTORY OF THE VILLA AND ITS GARDENS

A T THE DEATH of the Cardinal of Ferrara on December 2, 1572, Luigi Cardinal d'Este, in accordance with the will of his uncle, inherited the Villa d'Este at Tivoli. This will was to torment the Este family and its ministers for at least the next fifty years since it provided that the Villa was to be the possession of any member of the Este family who held a cardinal's hat, but that in default of a qualified Este the Dean of the Sacred College was to be its proprietor. Within a year of the death of Cardinal Ippolito II a petition was addressed to Pope Gregory XIII requesting the revocation of the grievous provision and a substitution in favor of the Este Dukes and their descendants, whenever an Este Cardinal was lacking.[1] This request apparently was of no avail.

The new patron of the Villa, known as the Cardinal d'Este, was appointed lifetime governor of Tivoli in succession to his uncle and visited the Villa frequently both in summer and winter. He made, however, only minor additions or changes to the Villa and its gardens, although the death of his uncle had left a great deal of the original project unfinished. The registers of the Cardinal d'Este as they are preserved in the Archives at Modena reveal numerous payments to artists and workmen during the early part of 1573 and then a gradual diminution of payments until there is almost none during 1574. Actually the majority of these accounts are delayed reimbursements for work completed during the lifetime of the Cardinal of Ferrara, such as the Fountain of the Dragon, which is listed as the "Fountain of Tivoli of Our Lord Pope Gregory XIII."[2] There are also two payments to Giovanni Ferdinando Portoghese for several trips to Tivoli in 1573 to tune the Water Organ,[3] and the architect Francesco da Volterra (Francesco Capriani) received twenty *scudi* for earlier designs of fountains and other work at Tivoli and Monte Cavallo.[4] It is possible, therefore, that Francesco da Volterra was the designer of the Fountain of the Dragon.

One of the features of the original project for the gardens was completed by the Cardinal d'Este. The Parisian manuscript specified that a large statue of Hercules was to stand in the niche of the Fountain of the Dragon as the centerpiece both visually and symbolically of the gardens.[5] When the Cardinal of Ferrara died in 1572 the inventory of statues listed two statues of Hercules in a room off the Grotto of Venus next to the Oval Fountain, presumably in storage.[6] In Zappi's description of the Villa

---

[1] ASM, Fab. e Vill., Busta 70, Pte. 6, fasc. 1, dated Sept. 27, 1573.

[2] ASM, Registri del Card. Luigi d'Este, Pacco 152, Journal of Scarlati, 1573-1574.

[3] *Ibid.*, f. 41r: Mar. 23, 1573, 8 *scudi*; f. 69v: Nov. 27, 2 *scudi*.

[4] *Ibid.*, f. 46v: "A dj dettj [April 16, 1573]

▽ uentj mᵗᵃ pagᵗⁱ amesser francº da Volterra architetto per hauer' seruitto la f. M. dj Mons.ʳⁱ Illᵐº dj ferrara a Tiuollj et montecauallo infare più designj et far' acomodar' piu fontante et altri cose."

[5] Appendix A, p. 145.

[6] T. Ashby, "The Villa d'Este at Tivoli and

in 1576 these two statues are recorded as in place in the gardens; one was an aged, reclining Hercules in the niche above the Fountain of the Dragon and the other a vigorous Hercules holding the infant Telephus (called Achilles in Zappi) standing above the same niche.[7]

Commencing in 1577 there is record of work on a chapel and tomb for the Cardinal of Ferrara in the nearby church of San Francesco, the designs being furnished by the architects Annibale Lippi and Francesco da Volterra and the sculptor Silla Longhi.[8] This was in accordance with the Cardinal's will which specified four thousand *scudi* for such a chapel.[9] The work continued until at least 1580 with more than two thousand *scudi* expended on it through the agency of Count Ercole Tassone.[10] When Luigi Cardinal d'Este made his will in 1585, twenty-two months before his death, he assigned another two thousand *scudi* "for completing the building" of the chapel where he was to be buried with his uncle.[11] The two tombs were to stand in niches in the walls of the sanctuary flanking the chief altar, but, despite the money expended for the work, the chapel and tombs were never finished. In the late seventeenth century there were traces of the construction, but later restorations destroyed this evidence, and the two Cardinals remain humbly buried before the altar.[12]

In the gardens of the Villa certain repairs, especially of the woodwork, had to be undertaken. So in 1582 wooden joists were purchased for the supports of the labyrinths and espaliers, and in 1586 wood for the pergola of the Secret Garden.[13] The 1582 repairs were very possibly occasioned not by natural decay but by wanton human destruction, since during one night in May of that year someone smashed several of the fountains in the garden, especially the Water Organ and the Fountain of the Owl. The accounts of the damage mention only that the pipes and ducts of the fountains

---

the Collection of Classical Sculptures which it contained," *Archaeologia*, LXI, pt. 1 (1908), p. 244.

[7] G. M. Zappi, *Annali e memorie di Tivoli* (Studi e fonti per la storia della regione tiburtina, no. 1), ed. by V. Pacifici, Tivoli, 1920, p. 65.

[8] ASM, Registri del Card. Luigi d'Este, Pacco 158, Registro de Mandati 1577, f. 172r (entitled "Spesa di Tiuoli"): "Adi detto [Aug. 11, 1577] Ag° un m.to al mag.co Balbo, che paghi à messer Bernard.o sachi △ti trenta di m.ta per pagarli à messer Visdomo uisdomi per altri tanti che hà pagati di comiss.e de S.S. Ill.ma cioe à m.ro Anibale figlio de m.ro Nani Architetto △ti dodeci et à m.ro sila scultore △ti di deci, et à m.ro Franc.o Volterra △ti sei per pareri et dissegni che deueno fare per la capella et sepoltura che pigliandone quitanza ueserano nenati buoni nè 1200 conti △ 30."

[9] F. S. Seni, *La Villa d'Este in Tivoli*, Rome, 1902, pp. 240-241.

[10] ASM, Registri del Card. Luigi d'Este, Pacco 159, Conto generale 1577 -A-, f. cxiii: Aug. 13, 1577, 30 *scudi*, "à due scarpelini uenuti da Roma a Tiuoli per dar principio alla Capella et sepultura della f. M. del sig.re Cardinale di Ferrara"; Dec. 31, 580 *scudi*; Pacco 161, Registro de mandati x 1578, f. 137v: Nov. 14, 1578, 500 *scudi*; Pacco 163, Libro di Conti generale 1579, f. cxxviiii: Aug. 11, 1579, 150 *scudi*; Pacco 165, Conto Generale, f. xxxxii: Mar. 23, 1580, 50 *scudi* and between July 28 and Aug. 26, 1000 *scudi*.

[11] F. S. Seni, *op.cit.*, p. 245.

[12] *Ibid.*, pp. 94-101.

[13] ASM, Registri del Card. Luigi d'Este, Pacco 173, Conto generale di Tiuoli dell'anno 1582, f. 46: June 8, 1582, 4.50 *scudi* "per ualuta di trenta trauicelli per seruitio delli laberinti, et spalliere d'esso Giardino"; Pacco 183, Registro de mandati 1587, f. 41r: Jan. 17, 1587, 7.68 *scudi* "per sedici Arcarezzoli condotti à Tiuoli et seruite alla Pergola del Giard.o secreto.

were broken,[14] but it is very likely that other minor parts of the garden decoration, such as the wooden trellises, were destroyed at this time, for the wood for the new labyrinth and espalier trellises was bought early the next month.

A certain amount of utilitarian work at Tivoli was carried out during Cardinal Luigi's ownership. In the gardens a *pozzo dal vento* was built and a stonemason cut eleven steps for the spiral staircase in the Villa.[15] In 1583 a small room was added in the Villa "near the rooms of Monsignor Tolomeo."[16] From 1584 to 1586 new kitchen quarters were erected within the Villa.[17] However, the major building at Tivoli accomplished by the Cardinal was not properly at the Villa, but in the so-called Parco or Barcho.

There were two such parks at Tivoli which the Cardinal of Ferrara appropriated as Governor of Tivoli and then developed—a small one, the Barchetto, was in the city near the Rocca; the larger one, the Barcho, was outside of the city near the Ponte Lucano. The latter had been walled about in 1564, after the design of the Cardinal's architect Galvani,[18] to serve as a hunting park like those attached to the *delizie* or

[14] E. Rossi, "Roma ignorata," *Roma*, IX (1931), p. 133.

[15] For the *pozzo dal vento* see ASM, Registri del Card. Luigi d'Este, Pacco 163, Libro di Conti generale 1579, f. lxv: June 17, 1579, 10.37 *scudi* "a m^ro Matturino Muratore per sua pena di h're fatto il Condotto per il pozzo dal uento"; Pacco 165, Conto Generale, f. xxxxii: March 16, 1580, 10 *scudi* "a m^ro Matturino Muratore in Tiuoli, a buon conto d'un muro ch'egli ha fatto nel condotto che mena l'acqua, al Pozzo del uento"; f. xliii: July 27, 12.52 *scudi* "a m^ro Matturino Muratore per sua mercede di hauere fatto un Condotto che conduce l'acqua alla spiaggia del giardino nel Pozzo del vento."

The documents for the spiral stairs are in ASM, Registri del Card. Luigi d'Este, Pacco 164, Libro Registri di Mandati 1579, f. 81: Jan. 3, 1579, 16.50 *scudi* "à m^ro Giouanni sbrigola scarpelino per hauere fatto ondice scalini di Treuertino per la scalla a lumaga nel Pallazzo di quella in Tiuoli"; Pacco 165, Conto Generale, f. xliii, on July 24, 1580 he was paid 6.50 *scudi* as remainder of above, 10 *scudi* having been paid on the last of Feb. 1578.

[16] ASM, Registri del Card. Luigi d'Este, Pacco 173, Conto generale di Tiuoli dell'anno 1582, f. 73: Jan. 30, 1583, 1.20 *scudi*, "à mad.^a Lelia fornaciara per ualuta di matoni 600 per la fabrica fatta nel palazzo appresso le Camere di Monsr Tolomeo"; 1.50 *scudi*, "per ualuta di pianelle n.° 300 per metterle nel piccolo camerino che si fabrica appresso le Camere di Monsr Tolomeo."

[17] ASM, Registri del Card. Luigi d'Este, Pacco 179, Conto generale di Tivoli 1583-1586, f. 111: Feb. 3, 1584, 1.95 *scudi* for 180 *some* of pozzolana "per una Cucina secreta"; Feb. 26, 5.31 *scudi* for 295 *some*; f. 112: Mar. 28, 4.14 *scudi* "per l'ammontare di some 230 di Pozzolana per seruire alla Cucina secreta"; Pacco 182, Registro de Mandati 1585, f. 40v: Feb. 1, 1585, 1.95 *scudi* for 108 *some* of pozzolana; Feb. 26, 5.31 *scudi* for 295 *some*; f. 41r: Feb. 26, 7 *scudi* "a m^ro Mattia muratore" for work; f. 42r: Mar. 27, 4.14 *scudi* for 230 *some* of pozzolana; f. 43r: April 18, 1.90 *scudi* for 110 *some*; f. 45v: Aug. 31, 12 *scudi* "a m^ro Bertolino muratore . . . à bonconto della Cucina secreta che si fa nel Pal.° di Tiuoli"; Sept. 1, 6.36 *scudi* for 318 *some* of pozzolana; f. 48v: Dec. 31, 33.40 *scudi* "a m.^ro Alberto et m^ro maturino muratori, et compagni"; Pacco 183, Registro de mandati 1587, f. 42v: April 4, 1586, 5.97 *scudi* "per il prezzo di trecento trentatre some di Pocillana condotte p seruir' alla fabrica delli Credenzieri"; f. 44r: July 14, 7.56 *scudi* for 420 *some* of pozzolana; f. 44v: July 16, 10 *scudi* "a m^ro Bertolino muratore da Castello . . . a buon conto della manifatura d lauori di muro ch'esso fa per la Credenza, bottig^ria nel Pal° di Tiuoli"; July 26, 10 *scudi* for ditto; f. 45v: July 19, 20 *scudi*, "à m^ro Alberto muratore" for ditto; f. 45v: Nov. 28, 6 *scudi* "per il prezzo di cinqta tauole Albuzzo . . . per far' Porte, et finestre per la Credenza, et Bottiglieria."

[18] ASM, Fab. e Vill., Busta 70, Pte. 2, fasc. 1, contract of Oct. 10, 1564, with the masons Simeone da Venego di Lombardia and Salva-

pleasure villas in his native Ferrara. The question of the unlawful possession of both the parks appeared in 1568 as one of the accusations leveled against the Cardinal by some of the citizens of Tivoli, but in October 1569 the situation was clarified when the commune of Tivoli ceded the Barcho to the Cardinal.[19] It was only under Cardinal Luigi d'Este that extensive building activity occurred in the Barcho. This work, however, was completely of a utilitarian nature. The minor work accomplished in 1583 and 1584 was directed, and presumably designed, by the Cardinal of Ferrara's old architect Giovanni Alberto Galvani,[20] but in May 1585 a new architect, Flaminio Ponzio, appeared, anticipating Galvani's death, which occurred on August 11, 1586.[21] Ponzio was to become one of the leading architects in Rome during the early seventeenth century, particularly under the patronage of the Borghese family and Pope Paul V Borghese, but his career was cut short by his premature death. These accounts at Tivoli are apparently the first record of Ponzio's architectural activity since the earliest previously published account of his work dates 1596.[22] Among the buildings evaluated by Ponzio, and presumably designed by him, are a house for the Cardinal's huntsmen (*casciari?*), a large hayloft above the cowstalls, and an aqueduct.[23] It is in

---

tore Nicolini da Carrara; the contents of the contract are given in F. S. Seni, *op.cit.*, p. 103 n. 1.

[19] G. Presutti, "Altri documenti circa la questione delle acque tra gli Estensi e i Tiburtini," *Atti e memorie della società tiburtina di storia e d'arte*, II (1922), pp. 44-49.

[20] ASM, Registri del Card. Luigi d'Este, Pacco 169, Misure e stime p lauori fatti a Tivoli 1583-1587, f. 1: June 1, 1583, evaluation subscribed by Galvani for work on the "fenile del Barcho"; f. 3r: Mar. 14, 1584, evaluation by Galvani for work on the "Torrone di Ponte Luccano"; f. 5r: June 7, ditto for "Muro di terra fatto in el Barcho"; f. 7r: June 8, ditto for work in "diversi lochi al Barcho."

[21] *Ibid.*, Pacco 182, Registro de mandati 1585 (second part of register, but not so labeled), f. 14v; 1585, "A di 12 Agosto ▽ quindici moneta à Flaminio Pongia Architetto di SS. Illma per suo sallario da p.^{mo} Maggio passato p tutto vltimo luglio pass.^{o}"; f. 15r: Oct. 22, 15 *scudi* for Aug. through Oct.; f. 15v: Dec. 11, 10 *scudi* for Nov. and Dec. *Ibid.*, Pacco 184, Bolletta de Salariati 1586, f. 86r: Galvani "deue hauere per suo sallario da di p^{mo} Gennaro per tutto di xi Agosto che passo di questa, a miglior uita, in ragione de ▽ sei m' il mese ▽44."

[22] L. Crema, "Flaminio Ponzio architetto milanese a Roma," *Atti del IV convegno nazionale di storia dell'architettura*, Milan, 1939, p. 281.

[23] ASM, Registri del Card. Luigi d'Este, Pacco

169, Misure e stime per lauori fatti a Tivoli 1583-1587, ff. 9r-11v: Dated Mar. 21, 1585, but subscribed by Ponzio on Jan. 29, 1587, "Mesura de lauori di Muro di Manifatura fatti da m^{ro} Alberto da Caselano et m^{ro} Maturino da Castello Compagni mur^{ri} alla Fabricha della Casa noua per li casari nel Barcho"; ff. 15r-17r: Sept. 16, 1585, ditto "per li Casciari"; ff. 18r-18v: Sept. 17, 1585, ditto for the "fabricha del fenile grande sopra alle stalle delle uache et uitelle per il prochoio nell Barcho a Ponte Lucano"; ff. 21r-23r: Sept. 18, 1585, ditto for the "Casalazzo ó Caproroccia nell Barco"; ff. 24r-25r: Sept. 20, 1585, ditto for work "in diuersi lochi per seruitio dell Barcho a Ponte Lucano"; ff. 26r-27r: Oct. 14, 1585, ditto for work "alla Gionta dell Fenile grande ouero Portico fatto uerso l'Ara nell Barcho a Ponte Lucano"; ff. 29r-33r: Oct. 16, 1586, ditto for the "fabricha della Casa Nuoua per li Casciari nell' Barcho a Ponte Lucano"; ff. 34r-35r: "Adi 19 Ottobre 1586 sino adi 2 Gennaro 1587 in Tiuoli," ditto for "fabrica dell'Acquidotto cominciato uicino al Casalazzo nell Parcho a Ponte Lucano"; ff. 37r-39r: Oct. 18, 1586 to Jan. 2, 1587, ditto for work "in diuersi lochi per seruitio dell Barco a Ponte Lucano." The total expense for this work subscribed by Ponzio was 3,039.70 *scudi*.

On f. 12r is a measured drawing for the "Casa noua per li casari" evaluated on ff. 9r-11v.

this Barcho that the Cardinal d'Este kept fifty Turkish slaves as laborers. Twice in 1584 some of the slaves managed to escape, once murdering one of their guards and throwing the other guards into a well. As a result of these rebellions, in August 1584 the Cardinal sold to the court at Naples thirty-six of the Turks who were the most difficult to handle.[24]

On December 30, 1586, Cardinal Luigi d'Este died at Rome and was buried with his uncle in San Francesco at Tivoli. In his will the Cardinal chose his brother Alfonso II, the Duke of Ferrara, to inherit his property,[25] but this immediately precipitated the old question of the inheritance of the Villa at Tivoli caused by the Cardinal of Ferrara's will, since there was no longer an Este cardinal. The court of Ferrara claimed that the clause in the will of the Cardinal of Ferrara was superseded by the Cardinal d'Este's will. By January 10, 1587, Pope Sixtus V had sequestered the Villa until the inheritance was decided, but in the meantime the Ferrarese agents removed all the movable decoration and furniture, including all the statues that were not fastened in niches. Late in February Alessandro Cardinal Farnese, as Dean of the Sacred College, took possession of the Villa and was dissatisfied with the condition in which the Este agents had left the Villa and gardens.[26] It was decided, however, that the Barcho at Tivoli was not covered by the Cardinal's will, and on December 15, 1587, the Estes ceded the Barcho back to the commune of Tivoli.[27]

The interregnum, that is, the period when the Villa and gardens at Tivoli were controlled not by the Estes but by the Dean of the Cardinals, was a period of neglect and decay for this property. It was only natural that the various Deans of the Sacred College would not invest much money or attention in the betterment of the Villa when the election of a new Este cardinal might dispossess them.

The misfortunes of the Estes came to a climax with the death of Duke Alfonso II in 1597. As the Duke had no direct heir, the Duchy of Ferrara reverted to the control of the Papacy, leaving the Estes only the Imperial fiefs of Modena and Reggio. In recompense for this Papal action Pope Clement VIII gave a Cardinal's hat to Alessandro d'Este in 1599, and in 1605 appointed Cardinal Alessandro to be governor of Tivoli, following the example of the two earlier Este cardinals. It is from this time that the Cardinal began to devote a great deal of attention and money to his ancestral Villa at Tivoli but, owing to the neglect that had befallen the Villa during the interregnum under the Deans of the College of Cardinals, the Cardinal's role was more that of a renovator than an innovator.

---

[24] E. Rossi, *op.cit.*, pp. 133-134.

[25] The will is published in F. S. Seni, *op.cit.*, pp. 244-250.

[26] The Urbinate *avvisi* which describe the sequestration of the Villa are published in E. Rossi, *op.cit.*, pp. 385-387, and republished in *Bollettino di studi storici ed archeologici di Tivoli e regione*, no. 54 (April 1932), pp. 1987-

1989.

[27] ASM, Fab. e Vill., Busta 70, Pte. 9, fasc. 1. See also F. S. Seni, *op.cit.*, p. 103 n. 1 and G. Presutti, "Alcuni documenti a proposito delle questioni tra il Cardinale Ippolito d'Este giuniore ed i Tiburtini," *Atti e memorie della società tiburtina di storia e d'arte*, 1 (1921), pp. 49-57.

One account book at Modena, dated from 1606 through 1614, is entitled the "Account of the Expenses for Building Executed at Tivoli for Restoring the Palace, Fountains and Garden."[28] In this account alone, more than eleven thousand *scudi* were expended for restoration and some new work. Since even the architectural parts of the Villa had to be renewed, from 1607 through 1609 there were purchased numerous quantities of brick in part "for bricklaying of the loggias of the Palace." The architect in charge, at least until 1610, was Gaspare Guerra, who was born at Modena and was active at this time building some churches in Rome. In 1615 more work was necessary to restore the loggias of the Villa, as an account of 1616 reveals that over two hundred and fifty *scudi* were spent for the purchase and transportation of bricks for restoring the loggias.[29]

The fountains, also, needed refurbishing, especially the renewal of stucco and shell decoration, and one account for restoring the Fountain of the Emperors gives the name of the *fontaniere* as Orazio Olivieri. Revisions were also made in the extant fountains. In 1609 the eagle now surmounting the Organ was dragged into position, and in 1612 Francesco Fulcari was paid for inscribing the coat of arms of the Cardinal on a brass plate for the Organ. The inscription on this metal plate commemorating the work executed at the Water Organ by the *fontaniere* Curzio Donati is preserved

[28] ASM, Fab. e Vill., Busta 71, Pte. 1. Many of the individual accounts were published in F. S. Seni, *op.cit.*, p. 118 n. 2. The accounts which Seni did not reproduce and are referred to in this work are as follows: f. 4r: "E adi 27 d'ottob [1607] ▽ 5 dim^ta pag^ti a messer Gasparo Guerra Architetto per sua mercede d'esser statto tre giornate à Tiuoli per seruiz° di quelli Reparamenti"; f. 4v: Nov. 18, 33.55 *scudi* for "9320 mattoni datti"; f. 5r: July 6, 1608, 12 *scudi* to "Gasparro e Giouanni Guerra per diuerse giornate e hà lauorato messer Giouanni à Tiuoli et per hauerci condotto aneo messer Gasparo"; f. 6r: July 30, 10.50 *scudi* for "m^ra 3 di mattoni" and 3 *scudi* for "600 mattoni grande"; f. 6v: Aug. 6, "m^ra 2 di mattoni" and on Dec. 20, "m^ra 2 di mattoni"; f. 7v: Dec. 30, 1609, 14 *scudi* for "mra' 4 di mattoni"; f. 8r: Dec. 30, 44 *scudi* "per migliara otto di mattoni . . . per mattonar le loggie del Palazzo di Tiuoli."

It should be noted that the accounts of payment to Francesco Naldini, Perin, and Rinaldo Lombardo Veronese, published by Seni as of the year 1616 are actually of the year 1614 in the accounts and that Rinaldo's payment was on Aug. 16, 1614, not Aug. 6, 1616. The sculpture for which Naldini and Perin were paid only in 1614 was completed at least by 1610 as they are described in A. del Re, *Dell' Antichità tiburtine capitolo V*, Rome, 1611, p. 55.

[29] ASM, Registri del Card. Alessandro d'Este,

Pacco 11, Ristretto de Conti della Casa di Roma dell'Illmo et R^mo Sig.^re n'ro Il sig.^r Card^le d'Este di tutto l'anno primo 1616, f. 34r: "Ressidui delle Spese di fabriche fatte à Tiuoli per tutto Giugno 1615, saldati e pagati nell'anno 1616."

f. 35r: "Spese di fabriche à Tiuole per ristaurare et mattonare le loggie del Palazzo."

Mar. 23, 7.20 *scudi*, "per mig^ra dua di mattoni."

April 12, 12.40 *scudi*, "per condutura à Tiuoli di n° 3100 mattoni."

April 29, 69.30 *scudi*, "per tagliatura et arroiai^na (?) di mattoni n° 12,800."

May 6, 50 *scudi*, "p il prezzo di undici mig.^ra di mattoni et . . . per cond.^ra di mattoni."

May 6, 8 *scudi*, "per portatura di 20 some di mattoni."

May 31, 2.80 *scudi*, "per resto di cond^ra di mattoni da Roma a Tiuoli."

June 28, 17.20 *scudi*, "per condutura da Roma à Tiuoli di 4300 mattoni."

Aug. 6, 14 *scudi*, "amro Giouanni Gentile murat^re à Tiuoli phauer rifatto a tutta sua robba un pezzo di uolta nell' andito che paua dal Cortile alle scale di Cucina ch'era cascata."

f. 35v:

Dec. 22, 3 *scudi*, "per n° 390 mattoni grandi."

Dec. 30, 76.85 *scudi*, "per il costo e condutura di pesi nouantanoue di calce."

in Lolli's eighteenth century diary.[30] It is probably at this same time that other additions to the Water Organ were made. The statues of Apollo and Orpheus which now stand in the side niches (Figs. 11 and 12) must date during this restoration but after 1610, since they are not mentioned in Del Re's description written in 1610. This is true likewise of the reliefs depicting Apollo and Orpheus above the side niches and probably the two Victories in the spandrels of the central niche. The four snake-limbed caryatids in the attic above the herms belong to this same work. There is at least negative evidence for this in the fact that they are mentioned neither in the sixteenth century accounts for the fountain nor in the early descriptions. Finally the central statue of the Goddess of Nature was removed and set in its own rustic fountain against the entrance wall at the north of the gardens where it is now (Fig. 10), while the present *tempietto* (Fig. 13) was erected to protect the organ.

The small fountain now standing at the left of the Water Organ undoubtedly dates from the same period as that of the refurbishing of the Water Organ. Del Re's description, written in 1610, relates only that a small square garden was created there "a few months previously," but before 1618 Maggi depicts the side fountain (Fig. 106), which still exists, although now without statues.[31] This may be, therefore, the "very beautiful fountain" which Giustiniani claims that Cardinal Alessandro added to the gardens.[32] Maggi's engraving portrays a rectangular frontispiece framed by Ionic pilasters supporting a straight lintel top. Beside the pilasters project engaged Ionic columns, entwined with spiraling vine decoration, over which the entablature breaks out *en ressaut*. Within the recessed niche of the fountain a nude Venus reclines against a water jug from which the water falls into a semicircular basin. On the inner sides of the niche are smaller niches containing statues.

In the Ashmolean Museum at Oxford are four drawings which may be preliminary designs or projects for this fountain.[33] All these drawings have the Este crowned eagle as a decorative element on the fountain and two are surmounted by a Cardinal's hat. The projects seem to fall into two groups. Perhaps the earliest designs (Figs. 107 and 108) are the two with segmental pediments borne by rusticated, banded pilasters. The

[30] "Tivoli dal 1595 al 1744 nella storia di F. A. Lolli," *Atti e memorie della società tiburtina di storia e d'arte*, VII (1927), p. 62. V. Pacifici ("Il Bernini a Tivoli," *Atti e memorie della società tiburtina di storia e d'arte*, III, 1923, pp. 123-126) attributes the central *tempietto*, which replaced the statue of the Ephesian Diana, to Bernini's activity in 1661, but his only evidence is the lack of mention of the *tempietto* in Croce's poem of about 1644. The style of the architecture and sculptural decoration of the *tempietto* all suggest an earlier date, probably between 1610 and 1612 when the statues of Apollo and Orpheus were added. I believe that an argument *ex silentio* is not as

convincing as the artistic style and the fact of other earlier changes to the Water Organ.

[31] A. del Re, *op.cit.*, p. 69 and [G. G. Rossi], *Nvova racolta di fontane che si vedano nel alma città di Roma, Tivoli, e Frascati*, Rome, n.d.

Rossi reissued the plates made by Giovanni Maggi, whose death in 1618 furnishes a date *ante quem* for these depictions.

[32] M. Giustiniani, *De Vescovi e de' governatori di Tivoli*, Rome, 1665, p. 190.

[33] K. T. Parker, *Catalogue of the Collection of Drawings in the Ashmolean Museum, II. Italian Schools*, Oxford, 1956, pp. 409-410, nos. 772-775.

shallow niche of these designs contains a large shell from which the water flows into a series of basins suspended above one another. In front of the pilasters are sketched attenuated statues. One of the statues (Fig. 107), a nude male (Hercules?), is almost a reversal in pose in proportions similar to the nude Apollo added at this time in the left niche of the Water Organ (Fig. 11). The other drawing has an architectural scale which, if the measurements are in Roman *palmi*, suggests a width of about seventeen and one half feet for the fountain, agreeing approximately with the measurements of the present fountain.

The other two drawings (Figs. 109 and 110) resemble the executed fountain with a straight entablature supported by pilasters or, in one alternate, by a herm. Down the face of the pilasters and herm hang garlands of golden apples, the chief symbol of the Tiburtine gardens, as used earlier on fountains such as that of the Owl, the little fountain in the Salotto, or in the Grotto of Diana. The central niche has splayed sides in which are small niches with statues and busts. In the main niche a nude Venus is placed above a series of shell basins. One drawing, which has a coffered barrel vault apparently meant to be in perspective, is accompanied by the plan of the fountain and its principal basin.

By 1611 Curzio Donati was in charge of the working and repair of the fountains, probably succeeding Orazio Olivieri. Donati's activity was at first concerned with the refurbishing of the Water Organ to which he added new musical notes as well as the sculpture discussed above, but he remained in charge of all the work until at least 1619.[34] At about the same time the question of the water rights and expenses arose. In 1610 the city of Tivoli desired to build new conduits and a new reservoir for the Rivellese water. An accord was finally prepared in 1614 by which the city was to receive two-thirds of the water and the Cardinal's garden one-third. It was agreed on the advice of three architects, Guerra, Carlo Lambardi, and Carlo Maderna, that the new reservoir was to be attached to the façade of the Capuchin monastery near Santa Croce, and the work was finally undertaken in 1618.[35]

The condition of the Villa and gardens during the early part of the ownership of Cardinal Alessandro is fully described in Antonio del Re's *Dell'Antichità Tiburtine Capitolo V* published in 1611 (the imprimatur is dated October 18, 1610). In fact it furnishes a much fuller and more accurate description of the gardens than any that we have for the period of the Cardinal of Ferrara. This, as well as some building accounts, proves that Cardinal Alessandro made several new additions to the fountains and gardens. The principal innovations were made at the Fountain of Rome. In September 1607 G. B. Albergati was reimbursed "for two drawings for making the

[34] F. S. Seni, *op.cit.*, p. 118, note 2 on p. 122. Add to these published records of Donati's work: ASM, Registri del Card. Alessandro d'Este, Pacco 11, Ristretto de Conti della Casa di Roma dell'Illmo et R^mo Sig^re n'ro Il sig.^r Card^le d'Este di tutto l'anno primo 1616, f. 34r: Aug.

17, 1616, 30.20 *scudi*, "per diuerse robbe datte sotto li 20 di Giugno 1612 a Curtio Donari fontaniero . . . per la fattura dell'organo."

[35] G. Presutti, in *Atti e memorie della società tiburtina di storia e d'arte*, II (1922), pp. 41-58.

horse at the [Fountain of] Rome."[36] This was the statue of a horse attacked by a lion which Del Re relates was to symbolize the struggle between Tivoli and Rome.[37] The statue is visible in Venturini's engraving of the Fountain (Fig. 23), although it no longer exists. On the small grassy plot at the left of the Fountain of Rome was placed a rustic group of shepherds and goatherds with their animals, carved by Francesco Naldini and one Perin,[38] but this tableau did not survive long as the Venturini print of the Fountain (Fig. 21) dating from the late seventeenth century reveals no evidence of it.

Some painting was necessary. In the Villa the painter Rinaldo Lombardo worked for sixteen days in the "apartment above"; whether this was retouching or new work and where specifically in the upper apartment it was done is not indicated.[39] In the garden from 1609 through 1612 Giulio Calderoni painted most of the fountains with decorative friezes, foliage, or coats of arms, but in this case his decoration is very specifically described as to type and location in a plea which Calderoni addressed to Cardinal Alessandro requesting payment for the work.[40]

As has been noted, after the death of Cardinal Luigi all the movable sculpture in the gardens and Villa was taken away by the Este agents. Cardinal Alessandro, however, replaced almost all the statues,[41] but during the restoration some changes in location occurred, which had consequences for the original iconography of the gardens. Del Re notes the existence of a seated figure of Jupiter, holding a thunderbolt, in the niche behind the Fountain of the Dragon (Fig. 16), where the Parisian copy of the original project called for a statue of Hercules; and Calderoni decorated the piazza of the Fountain of the Dragon with stories of Jupiter.[42] The statue of Jupiter is undoubtedly the one that the inventory of 1572 and Zappi in 1576 describe as being at the entrance of the garden.[43] This introduction of Jupiter with the thunderbolt behind the Fountain of the Dragon and, as it were, between the Dragon and the statue of Hercules above, begins to confuse the sixteenth century iconographical relation between Hercules and the Dragon. At the base of the Fountain of the Dragon, according to Del Re,[44] were set four nude youths, which are seen in place in Venturini's engraving.

An even greater dismemberment of the sixteenth century idea occurred at the Grotto of Venus next to the Oval Fountain. Zappi's description, the Dupérac engrav-

[36] F. S. Seni, *op.cit.*, p. 118 n. 2.

[37] A. del Re, *op.cit.*, p. 59. This group is based upon the ancient Roman sculpture, now in the Palazzo dei Conservatori, which stood in the sixteenth century on the Campidoglio, see H. S. Jones, *The Sculptures of the Palazzo dei Conservatori*, Oxford, 1926, pp. 249-250, illus. pl. 96, no. 100, which quotes Vacca as relating that the ancient group was known as the Storia dei Tivolesi.

[38] F. S. Seni, *op.cit.*, p. 118 n. 2, and note 28 above.

[39] *Idem.*

[40] ASM, Fab. e Vill., Busta 70, Pte. 10. Published in F. S. Seni, *op.cit.*, pp. 254-260.

[41] A. del Re, *op.cit.*, p. 40.

[42] *Ibid.*, p. 65, and Calderoni in F. S. Seni, *op.cit.*, p. 259.

[43] G. M. Zappi, *op.cit.*, p. 56 and inventory of 1572 in T. Ashby, *op.cit.*, p. 242. The inventory indicates that the hands of the statue were missing, so that it must have been restored with the thunderbolt before Del Re's description.

[44] A. del Re, *op.cit.*, p. 64.

ing (Fig. 1, no. 17), and the anonymous Parisian description of the original project all specify the grotto that opens off the piazza in front of the Oval Fountain as the Grotto of Venus, and imply, as has been noted in Chapter Five, the idea of the Choice of Hercules and the conversion of Ino into Leucothea or the Tiburtine Sibyl. By the time of Del Re the Grotto of Venus was changed into a grotto dedicated to Bacchus, presumably as a result of the replacement of the statues by Cardinal Alessandro. The statue of the modest Venus, mentioned by Zappi and the inventory of 1572 as in the Grotto of Venus, disappeared after the death of Cardinal Luigi and a statue of Bacchus was substituted (Fig. 38). The four statues of nude *putti* holding vases which accompanied Venus in the Grotto were put back into place, but two of the *putti* riding geese, or swans as Del Re describes them, were used in combination with a reclining statue of Venus to create a new fountain, the Fountain of the Swans, at the lower western corner of the gardens. The original appearance of this Fountain can be seen in Venturini's engraving (Fig. 111), as now only the architectural form of the Fountain is preserved without any of the ancient statues (Fig. 112). However, this change in the nomenclature and decoration of the original Grotto of Venus destroyed the basic iconography of the Choice of Hercules which was so fundamental in the initial layout of the garden. The title of the new fountain as given on Venturini's engraving, "The Fountain of the Swans with the Statue of a Nymph Sleeping at the Level of the Garden," suggests, as does the pose of the female figure resting her head on one hand with a flowing water jug behind her head, that this is another late example of the favorite Renaissance fountain of the Sleeping Nymph.[45]

The sixteenth century cross-pergola at the center of the lower gardens is not described in Del Re's very detailed account of the gardens, nor does it appear in any of the later views or descriptions of the gardens. Presumably the pergola was removed sometime before 1610, but the circle of large cypresses which are now at the location of the cross-pergola was not planted until, at least, after 1610.

In 1619 a new *fontaniere* Vincenzo Vincenzi appeared to be in charge of the fountains at Tivoli. He soon submitted to the Cardinal an account of the condition of the fountains in which he especially noted difficulties in the two hydraulic marvels of the Water Organ, which received insufficient water, and the Fountain of the Owl, which he claimed should be almost completely remade because of the damage it had suffered.[46] More interesting in Vincenzi's memorial is a detailed and lengthy description of a group of "inventions" for new hydraulic fountains at the Villa. At the lower entrance to the gardens he proposed the addition of two arquebusiers, one in each of the rustic side niches. These marksmen, aiming their weapons at the entrance, could be made to turn and follow any visitor and to shoot a jet of water at him as he retreated. Leading across the lower garden Vincenzi suggested the creation of a long pergola of water springing up from each side of the walk and arching over the spectator without

[45] O. Kurz, "Huius Nympha Loci," *Journal of the Warburg and Courtauld Institutes*, XVI (1953), pp. 171-177.

[46] See below Appendix D, no. 2.

touching him. He considered too naïve to fool any visitor the surprise jet of water actuated by the opening of the gate on the bridge leading to the Fountain of Rome, and he had plans to redesign more deceptive jets. He also wished to create within the Villa several tricks, combining air and water, such as a ball supported by alternating jets of water and air to puzzle the spectator, who would see no support for the ball when levitated by air. In the Grotto of Diana were to be trees, flowers, and singing birds activated by water and air. In the two empty grottoes above each end of the Hundred Fountains (Fig. 1, nos. 11 and 12) Vincenzi wished to place two hydraulic statues, one a satyr with a reed pipe, the other a shepherd with a bagpipe, both of which would play their musical instruments with accompanying movement of hands and eyes.[47] All these hydraulic figures, which were to be of wood to save expense, would be removed from the fountains and kept in storage during the winter. Although Vincenzi's plans were very specific and his estimate of cost was not high, there seems to be no evidence that any of these "inventions" were created at Tivoli.

The restoration and refurbishing of the fountains was a constant problem. In 1622 the main restoration was centered on the stuccoes of the Alley of the Hundred Fountains.[48] The small stucco boats were refashioned and painted a bronze color, presumably to give the illusion of metallic sculpture. It may have been at this time that eagles were added between the fleur-de-lis, the vases, and the boats. At least a letter of June 18 relates: "The small boats and little fountains are finished and now they expect to make the lilies, the eagles, and vases." Since the eagles are not mentioned in Del Re's description written in 1610 but can be seen in a drawing by Israel Silvestre of about 1643-1644,[49] they must have been created between these dates and probably during the 1622 restoration. The reliefs depicting Ovid's *Metamorphoses* were likewise restored at this time.

The problem of the inheritance of the Tiburtine Villa worried the Estes throughout this whole period. In 1615 it was suggested that an arrangement might be made with Pope Paul V whereby, if the Pope were given freely the garden on Monte Cavallo in Rome, which the Cardinal of Ferrara created but which was enjoyed by the Popes since the time of Gregory XIII, Pope Paul V might be willing to change the will in favor of the Este family.[50] Late in 1620 and early 1621 the negotiations with the Pope

[47] The idea of these two hydraulic fountains may have been inspired by Scamozzi's architectural treatise, which had appeared four years previously (V. Scamozzi, *L'Idea della architettura universale*, Venice, 1615, pt. I, p. 344), where Scamozzi suggests as fountains: "Vn Fauno, che sonando con le sette canne, ò con vn Flauto, & anco vn Pastorello con qualche Piua," but such hydraulic figures by this time may be standard in the repertoires of *fontanieri*.

[48] V. Pacifici, "Luigi d'Este e la villa tiburtina," *Atti e memorie della società tiburtina di storia e d'arte*, XX-XXI (1940-1941), p. 144 n. 1.

[49] Drawing in the P. Hofer Collection at Cambridge, Mass. reproduced in the 1940 catalogue of *Master Drawings* shown in the Golden Gate International Exhibition at San Francisco, California, p. 24, no. 97, illus. p. 65.

[50] ASM, Fab. e Vill., Busta 73, letter from Francesco Forcieroli at Rome to the Cavaliere Giovanni Barazoni at Modena, dated Aug. 22, 1615: "Non è mai stato messo in consideratione, che sia bene di donare o di offerire liberam.te al Papa il giardino di Monte Cauallo per hauere la commutatione del testamento del

had proceeded favorably almost to completion, but the death of Paul V on January 28, 1621, delayed the publishing of a Papal Brief which would permit the Este Duke of Modena and Reggio to possess *pro tempore* the Villa at Tivoli when there was no Este cardinal. On June 18, 1621, this Brief was finally issued by Gregory XV.[51] Thus the annoying condition in the Cardinal of Ferrara's will was eliminated in favor of the Este family, although five years later there was a momentary danger of a revocation of this Papal Brief.

While the Villa was becoming the property of the Estes, the Cardinal began to build a large new stable for horses and a small one for mules at Tivoli near the Barchetto on the street leading from the city gate to the Rocca. There is preserved at Modena a site plan (Fig. 113) for the stable by the architect Francesco Peperelli, dated November 15, 1621, as well as several letters regarding the progress of the work in 1621 and 1622.[52] By the middle of 1623 the Este agent Giovanni Arquier could write to the Cardinal: "At the end of June the stable will be entirely covered and, I believe, will also be finished."[53]

Cardinal Alessandro made little use of the new stables for he died on May 13, 1624, and his death created again the dreaded problem of succession. Duke Cesare d'Este of Modena immediately took possession of the Villa in accordance with the Papal Brief of Gregory XV, but the Estes were very insecure in their position as Pope Gregory had died in 1623 and the new Pope, Urban VIII, was not friendly to the Este family. In fact the Dean of the Sacred College, Cardinal Del Monte, was soon urging the new Pope to issue a Papal Bull annulling the Brief of his predecessor and renewing the original conditions of the will of the Cardinal of Ferrara. By 1626 the crisis was very acute with a barrage of letters between Rome and Modena indicating the imminent publication of such a Bull,[54] but the emergency was surmounted through careful diplomacy and it never tormented the Estes again.

Vincenzo Vincenzi remained as *fontaniere* under Duke Cesare, but in November 1624, after claiming that he had restored many of the fountains "so that they could be used," Vincenzi complained bitterly against the *residente* Carandini, who had accused him of doing nothing.[55] Apparently the *residente* won the argument for in January 1625 Vincenzi wrote the Duke again requesting twenty-seven *scudi* to settle his accounts. Vincenzi's letter mentioning the repairs necessary for the fountains is merely one minor example of the problem constantly facing the owner of the Villa

---

Card.ᶫᵉ di Ferrara per il Palazzo di Tiuoli e per siti delle case di Roma, . . ."

[51] The copy of this Brief in ASM, Fab. e Vill., Busta 70, Pte. 10, fasc. 17 is published in F. S. Seni, *op.cit.*, pp. 251-254. See also pp. 122-130.

[52] ASM, Fab. e Vill., Busta 70, Pte. 10, fasc. 18 and 19, see Appendix D, nos. 3 and 4; drawing is on f. 3 of fasc. 18. See also Lolli's diary in *Atti e memorie della società tiburtina di storia e d'arte*, VII (1927), p. 70; V. Pacifici, in *ibid.*,

XX-XXI (1940-1941), p. 144 n. 1; and F. S. Seni, *op.cit.*, p. 215.

[53] ASM, Fab. e Vill., Busta 70, Pte. 10, fasc. 21: Letter dated May 26, 1623, from Giovanni Arquier to the Cardinal Alessandro d'Este, f. 3v: "Alla fine di Giugno la stalla sarà coperta tutta et credo de sarà anche finito. . . ."

[54] F. S. Seni, *op.cit.*, pp. 131-147.

[55] ASM, Fab. e Vill., Busta 71, Pte. 4, fasc. 1.

d'Este, that is, that the hydraulic devices of the fountains and their stucco and shell decoration required perpetual repair and refurbishing. In fact, this was one of the most convincing arguments Cardinal Alessandro d'Este had presented to the Pope in support of the contention that the Dean of the College of Cardinals should not possess the Villa. The Cardinal could point to the state of disrepair into which the Villa had fallen during the interregnum before his ownership. The responsibility of personal attention and interest created only by family ownership had to be supported by Ducal wealth in order to keep the Villa and its gardens in an attractive, functioning condition. For example, Duke Alfonso III had to expend over five hundred *scudi* for masonry repair in a four-month period in late 1628 and early 1629. There is preserved at Modena an evaluation for this work by the mason Matteo Gorotii, approved by Francesco Peperelli who was still serving as the architect for the Villa. This evaluation reveals that most of the masonry was for the restoration of the Fountain of Rome and the "loggia of the Lords Cardinal," which is the Dining Loggia at the western end of the Villa.[56]

[56] ASM, Fab. e Vill., Busta 71, Pte. 5, ff. 1-3:
"Adi 14 sett^e 1628 sino alli 14 gennaro 1629 Misura, e stima delli lauori di muro, et altri fatti di tutta robba da M'ro Matteo Goroti muratore in restaurare la Roma, loggia de SS.^{ri} Cardinali, et altro nel giardino di Tiuoli dell'A. Ser.^{mo} di Modena mesurati, e stimati da me Fran.^{co} Peperelli Archit.^{o} di S. A. per ambe le parti.

Piano sopra la Roma

Astrico di coccie piste . . . ∇ 28.32
Per hauer tagliato l'astrico uecchio doue si e fatto il nuouo per darli il derliuo accio scoli ∇ 1.50

Piazza al pian della Roma

. . . hauer disfatto et tagliato il uecchio monta ∇ 52:19
Per hauer p^{so} la pagha e fieno alla stalla e portate per coprir tutto il sod^o astrico per amor del sole ∇ 1:— (f. 1r)

Astrico fatto nella fiancata della Roma

. . . doue è la Naue . . .
. . . sotto il Ponte lastrico . . . ∇ 25.94
Muro del fondam^o del p^o Arco remurato sotto la Roma inc^o al ritorno dell'acqua . . . ∇ 10.50
Muro d'un pezzo rifondato sotto il uecchio . . . —.56
Muro sopra . . . ∇ 10.46
Muro del Pilastro doue sono li condotti da ritorno . . . ∇ 6.52
Muro d'un straccio . . . —.24
Muro del fond^o sotto d^o . . . ∇ 4.20
Muro che cresce e fa la Vasca . . . —.35
Muro che fa la Vasca . . . —.31 (f. 1v)

Per hauer rotto il muro et fatto l'apertura della Porta che passa sopra à d^o Pilastro . . . —.80
Per hauer messo leuato, et rimesso l'inscritt^e alla Roma . . . —.80
Per il costo del fil di ferro . . . per attaccare li condotti di terra grossi, acciò si potesse dare l'acqua mentre faceua psa il muro ∇ 1.65
Per hauer smattonato e rematton^o il tetto s^a il tauolato del gioco di palla . . . et fattura et hauer rimesso n° 27 pianuccie sotto d^o che fanno armatura @ 13.19 ∇ 3.95
Muro del fondam^o sotto il Pilastro fatto ne la cantonata della Roma . . . @ 12.90
Muro del fondamento che seguita . . . @ 6.09
Muro sopra d^o . . . @ 9.68
Per il muro dell'Arco di teuolozzo fatts^a d^o et imposta nella facciata uecchia . . . 15.21
Muro deserra s^a d^o . . . @ —.54 (f. 2r)
Muro del fondam^{to} sotto il Pilastro di mezo . . . @ 7.62
Muro del fond^{to} che seguita . . . @ 2.13
Muro soprad^o e serra con il uecchio . . . @ 11.97
Muro del fondamento fatto sotto l'altro pilastro dell'arco inc^o . . . @ 3.66
Muro sopra dello . . . @ 5.05
Per hauer rimesso in opera le doi tazzette alle statue della ciouetta murate co sue spranghe . . . —.50

Fontanone

Per hauer specionato e fatto l'astrico di coccie piste nel canale che passa dietro la balaustrata di sopra doue è l'Aquila . . . ∇ 5.62.2
Per l'astrico simile fatto al canale dietro doue sono li q^{to} . . . @ 10 ∇ 14—
Per hauer messo una tauolezza in calcie sotto a

Francesco I d'Este succeeded in 1629 to the Duchy of Modena after the abdication of Duke Alfonso III and thereby became owner of the Villa at Tivoli. Again the major work at the Villa is in the nature of restoration. The stuccoes of the Alley of the Hundred Fountains were so worn that a contract was let in 1630 with the stucco-worker Giovanni Vincigli (or Venciglia) from Padua to destroy the "old *termini*" and to remake them at a cost of six *giuli* each.[57] The contract implies that the same thing had happened to the stucco reliefs with stories from Ovid. At the same time the balustrades in front of the Water Organ and above the statue of Hercules had to be renewed.[58] The Roman architect Francesco Peperelli was still in charge of the work at Tivoli. In 1632 he was particularly active, especially with the fish pools. Probably at this time the third fish pool at the northeastern side of the garden, left incomplete by the death of the Cardinal of Ferrara, was finished, as Peperelli was paid for drawings for the fish pools and for a model for the *bollori* there.[59] The work on the fish pools was presumably terminated in this year as there is at Modena a copy of the inscription dated 1632 which commemorated the restoration carried out under

---

parte di d⁰ astrico per alzar dou'era scauato il m⁰ assai q^to p 350 ▽ 2.25 (f. 2v)

Loggia de SS^ri Card^li

Per hauer fatto d'amatt⁰ bag⁰ sopra a d⁰ loggia con suo astrico di coccie piste sotto fatto con mattoni di casa il resto del Mastro ... ▽ 84.80

Per hauer tagliato il massiccio della Volta per dare la pend^a a d⁰ amatt⁰ et remurato un busio, che si sfondò la Volta ▽ 3.—

Per hauer disfatto l'amatt⁰ uecchio, che era in d⁰ luogo con suo astrico sotto scalinato li mattoni con di lig^a q^ali si sono rimessi in opera ▽ 13.56

Per hauer tagliato il muro attorno per incastrarui il mattone acciò l'acqua non penetri tra il muro et mattone e poi incollato ▽ 5.44

Per la colla riu^a ... ▽ —.69

Per hauer leuato et rimesso li doi condotti che scolaro l'acqua di d^a loggia con hauerli abbassati ▽ —.60

Per hauer fatto un pezzo di muro s^a l'arco del risalto uerso Roma ... ▽ 1.8

Per il costo tagliat^a e port^ra di n⁰ 1800 mattoni tag^ti seruiti ad^a loggia computatoui n⁰ 700 che sono auanzati monta ▽ 28.30" (f. 3r).

The evaluation is signed by Peperelli for a total cost of ▽ 569.69.

[57] ASM, Fab. e Vill., Busta 71, Pte. 6, fasc. 2, f. 5r; published in Appendix D, no. 5.

The contract is dated Jan. 7, 1630, and the work must have been begun immediately for on Jan. 19 a *garzone* was paid "per hauer' spiconato li Termini che fa il Padouano" (*ibid.*, fasc. 3, f. 2v).

Giovanni Vincigli is probably identical with the *scultore* Giovanni Venciglia who did some work at Tivoli in 1616 (F. S. Seni, *op.cit.*, p. 118, note 2 on p. 122).

[58] ASM, Fab. e Vill., Busta 71, Pte. 6, fasc. 3, f. 4v: 40 *soldi*, "A Mr⁰ Ant⁰ scarpellino per hauere accomodato li Balaustrate inanzi all'organo, et sopra l'Hercole" (undated, but soon after April 13, 1630).

[59] ASM, Fab. e Vill., Busta 71, Pte. 6, fasc. 5, f. 85r: "Lista de i denari spesi da me Franc^co Mantouani per seruiggio del Giardino, e Palazzo di Tiuoli"; f. 87r: "Adi 6 marzo [1632] diedi al Sig.^r Franc^co Peparelli Architetto della Ser^ma Casa per hauer misurato diuersi Cose che pagano Canoni, et per oltre fattiche fatte al mio tempo ... ▽ 12."

f. 88r: April 27, 1632, "Diede al Sig. Franc^co Peparelli Architetto della Ser^ma Casa per hauer misurato due uolte la cosa del Paganelli ▽ 2.

Al med⁰ per hauer fatto due dissegni delle Peschiere di Tivoli che furono mandati a V. Alt. ▽ 2.

Al med⁰ Per esser' andato due volte à uedere li lauori di Tiuoli [worn] che si faceuano intorno alle Peschiere, era' ordinare quello che bisognaua ▽ 8."

f. 88v: "Al med⁰ per fare un modello de i bollari da mettere alle peschiere."

f. 92r: "Adi 25 Marzo 1633 spese in due pacchi d'oglio di [worn] per accomodare il fontanile, e li bollori delle peschiere, accioche resistino all'acqua ▽ 2."

Duke Francesco I.[60] Meanwhile work was proceeding on the Fountain of Hercules above the Fountain of the Dragon. The Fountain was almost completed except for some mosaic decoration, the marble for which was being sought at Hadrian's Villa, a quarry for the decoration of the Este Villa ever since the time of the Cardinal of Ferrara.[61]

The restoration of the Villa was particularly appreciated by the city of Tivoli, since the Villa was already a great tourist attraction and bestowed "splendor on our city" as a letter of the city officials remarked in November 1632.[62] The letter especially praises the restoration of the fish pools executed, as we have seen, after the designs of Peperelli. The city fathers urged the Duke "to continue your favor to the site and to recommend it to your Ministers, so that the beauties of that garden, perhaps the best of every other site, may continue and may increase." Duke Francesco followed the spirit of this petition for during the next year one of his letters to his *residente* at Tivoli rebuked the latter for permitting "the garden at Tivoli to be cultivated as a kitchen garden."[63] However, for almost the next decade there are no accounts preserved indicating work or maintenance at Tivoli.

The scarcity of documents and the lack of an accurate description after Del Re's of 1611 prevents a precise dating of some of the elements of the Tiburtine gardens. The famous circle of cypresses situated at the center of the lower garden (Fig. 114) is first mentioned in Croce's poetic description of the gardens, written about 1644 but published only in 1664.[64] Croce also records in the lower garden the four fountains of the Mete Sudanti (Fig. 115),[65] modeled on the ancient Meta Sudans which stood in Rome near the Arch of Constantine until 1936. The original project for the gardens preserved in the Parisian manuscript[66] and Dupérac's engraving (Fig. 1, no. 28) show that Mete Sudanti were planned to stand in the middle of the two central fish pools. The Mete were finally created during the first half of the seventeenth century, symmetrically placed about the cypress circle. These changes recorded by Croce must date between Del Re's account of 1611 and Croce's of about 1644.

In December 1641 the Villa returned to the ownership of an Este cardinal when Rinaldo d'Este received the red hat. Remembering the glory of the Villa under the Cardinal of Ferrara and Cardinal Alessandro, the city of Tivoli greeted the election of a new Este cardinal with great rejoicing and fireworks.[67] This happiness was perhaps

---

[60] F. S. Seni, *op.cit.*, p. 149.

[61] ASM, Fab. e Vill., Busta 71, Pte. 6, fasc. 1, letter dated July 6, 1632, from Giovanni Arquier at Tivoli: "Credo che alla fine di questa sara quasi finita la Fontana del Ercole, ci mancaua dlle lastre di marmo bianco per il mosaico che hiersera fui col s. Rampani alla Villa Adriana per trouarne come fece, et questa matt.ª ci sono andato a ott'hore con quattro Bestie et due Christiani per farle portare, . ." (f. 5v). "Trà tanto V. S. procuri dlo Peparelli il

modello per li Bollori accio ui si possa dar principio . . ." (f. 6r).

[62] F. S. Seni, *op.cit.*, pp. 147-148.

[63] *Ibid.*, p. 148.

[64] V. Pacifici, "Luigi d'Este e la Villa tiburtina," *Atti e memorie della società tiburtina di storia e d'arte*, XVII (1937), p. 157 n. 2.

[65] *Ibid.*, p. 160 n. 2.

[66] Appendix A, p. 145, no. 4.

[67] F. S. Seni, *op.cit.*, p. 151.

excessive, for Cardinal Rinaldo I seems to have been more attached to his native city of Modena. However, the Cardinal did make some notable additions to the gardens at Tivoli, which reveal him as following the spirit of the earlier Cardinals rather than that of the Este Dukes, who at best were satisfied merely in maintaining the gardens and fountains in good repair.

The Cardinal's interest in his Villa seems to have been restricted, at least on the basis of the extant documents, to the last two decades of his life. In 1660 and 1661 a new fountain was created in the garden at Tivoli as some brief records of expense disclose.[68] This is undoubtedly the Fountain called the Bicchierone (Fig. 116) which is on the main axis of the garden below the Villa. It was originally behind the central statue of Hercules, but the latter is, of course, no longer in place. The basin of the Fountain is a huge conch-shell, within which a large foliated sphere or pine cone holds a tall serrated chalice. One tall jet of water, accompanied by smaller ones, shoots up from the chalice and, falling back into it, flows down into the shell. The design for the Fountain was created by the leading sculptor of the century, Gian Lorenzo Bernini. Although the expense accounts do not mention Bernini's name in connection with the new Fountain, Giustiniani's history of the governors of Tivoli remarks in 1665 on a fountain done "with the design of the famous architect Cavalier Gio: Lorenzo Bernini,"[69] and there are records of Bernini being consulted on the waterworks at Tivoli in 1661.[70] This Fountain was completed by May 1661 and turned on in honor of several notable guests, while on June 13 Bernini himself inspected his creation and made several suggestions for its improvement.[71] At this same time the Water Organ that Cardinal Alessandro had embellished (Fig. 117) received a very important addition when Bernini designed the famous cascade of water (Fig. 118) that plunges down from the Fountain to the fish pools below.[72]

An undated memorial reciting a long list of necessary repairs in the Villa and gardens must date from this period as it notes that "the wall which supports the principal high alley threatens ruin as Signor Bernini observed the last time that he was here."[73] This survey is particularly concerned with the disrepair of the masonry

[68] ASM, Registri del Card. Rinaldo I, Pacco 175, Tivoli 1603-1666 (loose sheets and registers), fasc. 34: After an account dated June 13, 1660, "Altri simili fatti tegare in Tiuoli per la fabrica della fontana noua. . . ." *Ibid.*, Pacco 185 (loose sheets): "Ristretto de mandati fatti il mese di Agosto 1660: Tiuoli. A Gio: Palazzi manouale per 10 giornate lauorate per fontana nuoua ▽ 3.50." *Ibid.*, Pacco 173, Conti diversi 1651 al 1674 (loose sheets): "1661. Ristretto de mandati fatti dalli 28 a 30 luglio. Spesa di Tiuoli. Al stagnaro per condoto di Bandone per il Palazzo di Tiuoli Piastra di Piombo per le fontane e Giornate lauorate cola ▽ 51." "1661. Ristretto de Mandi fatti

dalli 7 atutto li 9 luglio. A spesa di Tiuoli. Al s^e Bonifatio Darti per pesi 36 Calce data in Tiuoli dalli 27 Gen° a 5 feb° per la fontana noua ad adli 6 il peso ▽ 21:60." "A 31 Ott. 1661. A spesa di Tiuoli scudi 1 b 90 spesi . . . per le fontane ▽ 1.90."

[69] M. Giustiniani, *op.cit.*, p. 156.

[70] S. Fraschetti, *Il Bernini*, Milan, 1900, p. 228.

[71] *Ibid.*, pp. 228-229.

[72] F. Imparato, "Documenti relativi al Bernini e a suoi contemporanei," *Archivio storico dell'arte*, III (1890), pp. 137-139.

[73] ASM, Fab. e Vill., Busta 71, Pte. 6, fasc. 4, f. 3r: "La muraglia che sostiene il uialone prin-

in "the chief wall of the secret garden toward the Piazza di San Francesco,"[74] the water supply of the fountains, and damage in the stables where thirty horse stalls were destroyed. Several building accounts soon reveal activity at Tivoli to help carry out some of the recommendations of the survey. A rather detailed account in 1662 lists a great deal of new woodwork, such as doors and windows.[75] The architect of the Villa at this time was Giovan Antonio de' Rossi, a pupil of Peperelli, the former architect at Tivoli; at least, G. A. de' Rossi submitted an estimate for about nine hundred *scudi*, dated November 12, 1664, for rebuilding the cistern and conduit which controlled the Rivellese water furnished to the city and Villa.[76] Soon, thereafter, a great deal of masonry repair was undertaken in the Villa itself, some of it, such as the buttressing of the wall in the Secret Garden, is obviously in answer to the undated memorial which suggested buttresses in the Secret Garden along the wall toward the Piazza di San Francesco.[77]

---

cipale alto, minacia ruina come osseruiò il S. Bernini l'ultima uolta ui fu, sendo crepata, e pende fuori de suoi Piombi, pare che alcune catene fossero sufficienti per reparare." The entire memorial is on ff. 1r-6r.

This memorial is filed in the Archives at Modena with accounts during the reign of Duke Francesco I d'Este, but the above reference indicates that it must be much later in date.

[74] *Ibid.*, f. 2v: "Giardino: La muraglia maestra del giardino secreto uerso la Piazza di S. Francesco che sta puntalata minaccia ruina dice il s. Costantino che S. A. pensaua di ripararla con Piloni che corispondessero alla fontana del Leon Corno che sta nell Angolo a destra di d.ta muraglia."

[75] ASM, Registri del Card. Rinaldo I, Pacco 175, Tivoli 1603-1666 (loose sheets and registers), fasc. 34 (undated but accompanied by a "confeso" of Andrea Sforza dated Oct. 10, 1662):

"Tauoloni di Tiuoli si di Albuccio come dj olme et altro.

Nota di tutte le taule et tauicelli come di albuccio et di castagnia et olmo che ha messo in ci iera (?) Andrea Sforsa falegniame nell palazzo di S. A. S. in Tiuoli.

In primis fatta una fenestra sotto al logia dell Cortile uerso il Giardinetto e ci sono andate taule tra il fasto et guarnitione taule di olmo leuate nell bottecha. . . .

Et piu fatta una porta al Giardino doue stanno li merangoli. . . .

Et più fatta una porta noua all ultima camera dell pian tereno doue sta la fontana. . . .

Et piu fatta una porta noua all partamento nobile nell coritoro incontro all portone di S. francesco. . . .

Et piu fatta una finestra all apartamento nobile doue sta l'aparato uerde ueso il Giardinetto. . . .

Et piu fatta una porta noua alla cammera delli corami, che risponde all Cortile. . . ."

[76] ASM, Fab. e Vill., Busta 71, Pte. 9, fasc. 1, ff. 62r-65r: "Relazione dell'Architetto Giouan Antonio Rossi intorno al rifarcimento della botte e del condotto dell'acqua di Rivoli, per il quale veniva introdotta nella citta di Tivoli."

[77] ASM, Fab. e Vill., Busta 71, Pte. 9, fasc. 1:

"14 Marzo 1668

Lauori di Muro fatti nel Palazzo del A. S.ma del sig.e Cardinal d'Este in Tiuoli dalli Mri Giacomo et Antonio Longhi, e Giacomo Mattia murat.ri

· · · · · · · · ·

Nelli Camerini

P.o pilastro del cantone del Camerino	4 b 16	
2.o pilastro nel Corr.e	2 b 98	
3.o pilastro nel Corr.e	3 b 95	
Volta del d.o Cor.o	12 b 80	
Volta del Camerino	3 b 72	
Muro sopra terra nel fianco uerso li frati	8 b 66	(f. 87r)
Volta a schifo di d.o Camerino sotto il tetto	11 b 10	
Porta che ua in credenza		
Volta del corritore sotto il tetto	12 b 24	
Doi fenestre in d.o		

More creative activity at the Villa commenced in 1670, when Mattia de' Rossi appeared as architect. By February 1670, at least, De' Rossi was in the service of the Cardinal with the salary of ten *scudi* a month.[78] As Bernini's chief assistant Mattia de' Rossi had returned in 1667 from France where he had been sent to attempt to carry out the ill-fated design for the Louvre. At Tivoli De' Rossi was first concerned with the service rooms of the Villa, that is, the kitchens, pantries, and wine cellar. As early as September 1670 there is a record of payment to masons for work in the "new kitchen."[79] There are preserved in the Archives at Modena numerous drawings and descriptive memorials signed by Mattia de' Rossi which help to explain this construction and other work executed, or at least planned, by him. Most of them are dated 1671, and the undated ones probably belong to this year. An account carrying the date February 14, 1671, explains plans to create a pantry and wine cellar below the section called the "little rooms" (*camerini*) next to the kitchen court.[80] This memorial is accompanied by a drawing of the plan of the Villa (Fig. 119a) as it was, with an attached flyleaf indicating the proposed changes (Fig. 119b). The memorandum and plan show a pantry of two rooms below the *camerini* with a side passage to the wine cellar and a stepped ramp (*cordonata*) leading from the small court, around which the service rooms are arranged, down to the kitchen court. In the secret kitchen are drawn six small pieces of masonry, presumably buttresses, which may be the masonry recorded as executed in September 1670. On March 4, 1671, Mattia de' Rossi sent a new memorandum[81] with some changes from his earlier project as revealed in three detailed plans, labeled A, B, and C (Figs. 120-122), of the floors involved. The principal change from the earlier idea was to destroy part of the *cordonata* which joined the small court of the *camerini* to the kitchen court, gaining at a lower level direct communication by two long narrow rooms (Fig. 122) between the kitchen court and the main stairs to the central court of the Villa. The second project was soon found impossible as three undated drawings of a third design reveal (Figs. 123-125).[82] One of the drawings (Fig. 123) explains the necessity for the third project, since "the place where it was thought originally to make the stairs going up

---

Fabrica nel Giardinetto

Primo pilone	3 b 75
2° pilone	6 —
3° pilone	6 —
4° pilone	4 b 40
5° pilone	5 b 55 (f. 87v)
6° pilone	3 b 56" (f. 88r)

Total of ▽ 526 b 22.
For the earlier memorial see above notes 73 and 74.

[78] ASM, Registri del Card. Rinaldo I, Pacco 185 (loose sheets):
"Salariati per il Mese di febraro 1670 Sᵣ Mattia di Rossi ▽ 10."

[79] *Ibid.*: "Il s.ᵉ Carlo Croce da conto di hauer

speso nella fabrica della cucina nuoua in Ti-uoli dalli 30 Agosto a tutto li 6 sett.
    133 some Pozzolana
    muratori . . . ▽ 55.15½
[Dated] 10 sett. 1670."

[80] ASM, Fab. e Vill., Busta 71, Pte. 10, fasc. 11, ff. 1r and v. See Appendix D, no. 6 for this memorial.

[81] *Ibid.*, fasc. 11, ff. 9r-23v. See Appendix D, no. 7. Plans A and C of this project are included incorrectly in the Archives with the earlier project on ff. 4v-7r.

[82] *Ibid.*, ff. 16r-19v. For the explanation accompanying the third drawing see Appendix D, no. 8.

to the pantry could not be used, for it was found that below the earth the lateral wall [was] too thick." A much simpler project was substituted entailing primarily the building of a vaulted passage (Fig. 125) leading from the pantry to the wine cellar below the court of the *camerini* and not disturbing the *cordonata* to the kitchen court. An account of July 22 listing some masonry and supplies for the *camerini* suggests that some work was undertaken immediately.[83]

A plan of Mattia de' Rossi (Fig. 126a) depicts the stables in which the earlier undated memorial had noted much disrepair. On the plan is pasted an overleaf (Fig. 126b) in which De' Rossi shows how the stables can be more than doubled in terms of the stalls so as to provide housing for ninety-two horses, and on the rear of the drawing he estimates that this work will cost about one thousand *scudi*.[84]

An additional concern was the quantity of water which was necessary for supplying the fountains. A cistern was built in the orchard of the Capuchins to furnish water for their monastery and to increase the resources for the fountains of the Villa.[85] It may be for this that there is a payment of May 1672 for conduits "for the new fountain made with Rivellese water."[86]

On July 9, 1671, De' Rossi wrote the Cardinal that he had been at Tivoli to inspect the work accomplished there.[87] He found that the mason Maestro Angelo had "completed the frontispiece (*prospettiva*) of the fountain at the head of the alley of the garden under the palace." As we shall see later, this must be the Fountain of Europa, originally the Fountain of Thetis, standing at the northeastern end of the terrace in front of the Villa opposite the Cardinal's Dining Loggia. De' Rossi also relates that a stepped ramp (*cordonata*) leading from the garden to the gate next to the church of San Pietro was partially finished. Meantime, the mason Angelo had aided another mason, Maestro Carlo, in refurbishing the frontispiece of the Fountain of the Emperors where much of the rustication in stucco had fallen off. De' Rossi adds that the nearby Fountain of the Owl was also in need of repairs but that the small boats and lilies lining the Alley of the Hundred Fountains had been cleaned and restored.

[83] ASM, Registri del Card. Rinaldo I, Pacco 173, Conti diversi 1651 al 1674 (loose sheets): "Il s. Carlo Croci ha dato conto di hauer speso per servizio di S. A. in Tiuoli dati 4 atutto li 17 luglio.

Pagati a 32 opere di Murat. al 25 cias.	▽ 8.—
In Calce pesi x cioe 8 per li Camerini e due per la Vasca noua	▽ 7.50
In Pozzolana some 85 a mezo Paolo	▽ 4.25
In Mattoni 2700 per li camerini à Paoli cinque il cento condoti	▽ 13.50
Ad Andrea Carrarino scalpelino a conto de Trauert.^ni per la uasca	▽ 10.—
In una tauola Albucio per il fondo del [illegible]	▽ —.25
Sapone per la Vasca noua	▽ —.30
Olio per li Camerini	▽ —.10

[Dated] 22 luglio 1671."

[84] ASM, Fab. e Vill., Busta 71, Pte. 10, fasc. 2, ff. 1r-4r. The inscription on the plan and the cost estimate on the rear of the drawing are published in Appendix D, no. 9.

[85] F. S. Seni, *op.cit.*, pp. 153-154.

[86] ASM, Registri del Card. Rinaldo I, Pacco 185 (loose sheets): "Mandati fatti d mese di Maggio 1672 in Roma.
Tiuoli.

Per condota da Roma a Tiuoli di n° 674 condoti Bastardi grossi per la fontana nuoua da farsi del Aqua riuelese a Paoli 12 il cento di cond^ti ▽ 8."

[87] F. S. Seni, *op.cit.*, pp. 154-155.

Finally he mentions that he is sending some drawings and ideas of "more substance" for the Cardinal's approval.

There is also at Modena another memorial with several drawings, likewise dated July 9, which must be the projects of "more substance" to which De' Rossi was referring.[88] In this letter of explanation the architect first proposed an important change in the Fountain of Rome and illustrated the revision with a drawing of the Fountain as it was (Fig. 127a), and an attached flyleaf representing the suggested new appearance (Fig. 127b). De' Rossi wished to create a fountain of water behind the statue of *Roma* which would rise up between the statue and the Pantheon. There would also be a cascade gushing down from in front of the statue of *Roma* into the basin below. De' Rossi said that this change "would make a very lovely sight," because "in this way there will be created a very fine correspondence with the large fountain opposite," that is, the Oval Fountain. It is interesting to note, therefore, that the architect's reason for this revision is purely of a formal, visual nature. If De' Rossi's project had been executed (as, of course, it was not) it would have destroyed the symbolism of the two fountains as representing Tivoli and Rome with the Tiber, or Alley of the Hundred Fountains, running between them across the garden. In fact, this seventeenth century design suggests that much of the symbolism was probably already lost to the second half of this century since the cascade at the Oval Fountain was meant to symbolize the famous natural Cascade at Tivoli and would make no sense from a symbolic point of view when added to the Fountain of Rome.

In the same memorial De' Rossi proposed to open a large window through a small tower that stood in the wall of the garden toward the *campagna* "at the head of the alley which goes alongside of the fish pools." There is the usual drawing[89] of the tower (Fig. 128a) with an attached flyleaf depicting the window as it was to look (Fig. 128b). Actually the architect wished to cut through the mediaeval wall an arched opening surrounded by a classic frame and closed off at the bottom by a balustrade. The purpose of this window was to permit a vista of distant Rome.

An undated memorial with two drawings discloses De' Rossi's ideas for adding a more impressive architectural accent to the front of the Villa on the axis leading up to it.[90] One design shows an obelisk (Fig. 129) supported by a pedestal which stands in the low basin of a fountain. At the four corners of the pedestal streams of water spurt into the basin from the noses of dolphins. At the top of the obelisk the Este lily likewise shoots up a jet of water which at a height just below the cornice of the Villa breaks and falls down onto the obelisk. Since Bernini and his assistants had been concerned several times with the concept of an obelisk as the central feature of a

[88] ASM, Fab. e Vill., Busta 71, Pte. 10, fasc. 13. For the memorial see Appendix D, no. 10.

The drawing for the revision of the Fountain of Rome is included in the above fascicule, but a drawing of the proposed new opening in the wall of the garden which makes up fasci-cule 3 in the same Busta must have originally belonged to this memorial.

[89] ASM, Fab. e Vill., Busta 71, Pte. 10, fasc. 3, f. 1r.

[90] *Ibid.*, fasc. 4. For the memorial see Appendix D, no. 11.

fountain or monument, as for example in the Fountain of the Four Rivers of the Piazza Navona at Rome or the obelisk carried by an elephant in front of Santa Maria sopra Minerva in Rome, the use by a pupil of Bernini of an obelisk as a feature in the gardens of Tivoli is understandable. In fact, the obelisk of Santa Maria sopra Minerva had been erected as recently as 1667 so that the concept must have been still quite vivid to Mattia de' Rossi, although it had a long tradition. The symbolism of the obelisk as a monument was very prevalent in the Baroque age and had been stated in Cesare Ripa's handbook of symbolism for artists. Ripa claims that the obelisk "signifies the illustrious and lofty glory of Princes, who with magnificence erect sumptuous and great buildings which demonstrate their glory."[91] Such a concept was, therefore, very appropriate to the original symbolism developed in the gardens.

The second drawing presents a large fountain centered in front of the Villa. This fountain (Fig. 130) has a large basin from which rise four curved struts forming an openwork support for a round basin. A very tall jet of water rises to the level of the third story windows of the Villa. This stream of water then forms a lily, the Este symbol, as it breaks and falls back into the basin. There are other minor jets of water, one from each of the four struts of the base, and a small one within the center of the openwork base. This second design in its wider base and triangular form, which harmonizes with the staircase of the Villa behind the fountain, is more fitting to its location. The obelisk of the first drawing as a fountain with the water springing from the lily at the top is not very successful; the whole composition is narrow and vertical making very little real use of the jets of water.

There is likewise an undated drawing (Fig. 133) accompanied by an account by Mattia de' Rossi describing a new arrangement for the Secret Garden.[92] This plan probably dates from the same time as these other designs of 1671, and illustrates the proposed new planting. Four compartments are surrounded by low hedges of myrtle with pedestals, intended to support vases, at the corners and openings of the hedges. These compartments are all planted with myrtle, which was not to be allowed to grow higher than three-quarters of a Roman *palmo* (about six and one-half inches), and a small fountain is placed in the center of each. The circle at the center of the garden was to be unchanged, with a cypress hedge forming a circle around four fountains (*scogli*) and the central mosaic pavement, which had been created for the Cardinal of Ferrara.

The most interesting feature of this drawing is that the two compartments near the Villa are composed of large ovals, while the farther ones have circles. Since all four compartments are oblong the difference must exist for an aesthetic, visual purpose.

[91] C. Ripa, *Iconologia*, Siena, 1613, part 1, pp. 296-297. For a complete analysis of the symbolism of the obelisk with relevant bibliography see W. S. Heckscher, "Bernini's Elephant and Obelisk," *Art Bulletin*, XXIX (1947), pp. 155-182.

[92] The drawing is in ASM, Fab. e Vill., Busta 71, Pte. 10, fasc. 1, but the description is to be found in ASM, Fab. e Vill., Busta 72, Pte. 2, f. 10. For the description see Appendix D, no. 12.

The parterres were designed most probably to be viewed from the windows of the *piano nobile* of the Villa. A furniture inventory of 1678 reveals that these windows belonged to the "apartment which, being located on the east, is called the Winter Apartment, since during that time it served His Highness and has served the Lord Cardinal D'Estrees."[93] In winter the Secret Garden with its myrtle parterres would be the principal exterior enjoyment for the Cardinal. As seen in the perspective angle from the Cardinal's winter apartment the circles of the further compartments would tend to become ovals which would harmonize with the actual ovals of the nearer compartments.

The plan of the Secret Garden has three entrances: one at the further end of the garden toward the city of Tivoli, a second at the center of the long wall between the main garden and the Secret Garden and a third leading into the Villa itself. This entrance is located in the western corner of the Secret Garden opening into the Room of Noah, as it does today. The drawing, therefore, suggests that the old entrance from the Secret Garden into the Grotto of Venus was to be closed, but as the inventory of 1678, discussed below, proves, this was not carried out.

Another memorial, dated September 25, 1671, accompanied by a drawing (Fig. 131),[94] describes the work that De' Rossi planned to carry out at the old Fountain of Europa. De' Rossi's letter of July 9 revealed that the mason Angelo had already restored the frontispiece of this Fountain. The September drawing indicates that the Fountain was to be remade to resemble the architecture of the Cardinal's Dining Loggia at the other end of the terrace. The statue in the drawing of a nude youth half reclining above a basin was already in place according to the memorial but the rocky setting was to be renewed. This is another attempt by De' Rossi to unify the fountains of the garden by having the confronting fountains resemble one another, as he had planned to do with the Fountain of Rome and the Oval Fountain.

Despite Mattia de' Rossi's detailed descriptions and drawings for these elaborate additions and revisions to the Villa of Tivoli, very little was executed. His principal accomplishment was the utilitarian revision of the interior of the Villa in the service quarters.

An inventory of the furniture in the Villa dated November 1678 is rather important in describing in part the conditions within the Villa. In this inventory it is noted that the Grotto of Venus which faces out upon the Secret Garden still preserves the original "door and window which issue into the little garden."[95] There remained in the Grotto

---

[93] ASM, Fab. e Vill., Busta 72, Pte. 1, f. 44r: ". . . e serue ad altro apartamento, che per esser posto à Leuante si chiama l'apartam^to d'Inuerno, nel qual tempo seruiua à S. A. et hà seruito al Sig^re Card^e Déstres. . . ."

[94] ASM, Fab. e Vill., Busta 71, Pte. 10, fasc. 12; the drawing is on f. 4r. For the memorial see Appendix D, no. 13.

[95] ASM, Fab. e Vill., Busta 72, Pte. 1, ff. 40r-45v:

"Adi p.° Noue'bre 1678 [f. 40r]
. . . Gioco della Raccheta, mà scoperto, e poco ben in ordine per non dar recapito alla Turba calandouiso per una scala lomaca grande, che arriua al piano superiore [f. 40v].
. . . Nell'altra, et ultima [stanza] di facciata

the sleeping Venus which was recorded by Del Re in 1610, but there was no water in the Grotto nor in the Secret Garden owing to the decay of the conduits. The open tennis court at the other end of the Villa was likewise in disorder.

The neglect of the Villa, which begins to become more and more apparent in the records of this time, is probably a result of the death of Cardinal Rinaldo I on September 30, 1672. At least twice the *fontaniere* Aragoni wrote to Duke Francesco II d'Este specifying numerous repairs to the fountains of the gardens. In September 1681 Aragoni listed almost all the fountains as in need of repair.[96] On the other hand, one fountain, the *Bicchierone* of Bernini, was in excessively good condition. Aragoni complained that the *Bicchierone* "gushes so high as to be unbelievable,"[97] and recommended that its jet be lowered in order to conserve water for the other fountains. Again in 1685 the *fontaniere* observed that the conduits to the Hundred Fountains and the Fountain of the Emperors needed attention in order to furnish those fountains with water. According to the inscription preserved at the northeastern end of the Alley of the Hundred Fountains the Duke is credited with restoring the fountains in 1685.

The last Este cardinal to possess the Tiburtine Villa was Rinaldo II, who was elected to the purple in 1686. As a result there was some projected activity at Tivoli in 1687. In honor of the Cardinal a new bed and bed alcove were designed (Fig. 132). The alcove was to be arched with flanking half columns and pilasters supporting an entablature topped by the Este eagles and the Cardinal's arms. The accompanying note explains that the bed and alcove were to be of carved wood painted and polished to imitate marble, the columns and pilasters green, the walls yellow, and the decorative elements gold.[98] With this project for a bed alcove is a plan of the Villa dated

---

detta la saletta [Room of Noah], la quale guarda con due finestre nel Giardino, e per essere di cantone, guarda con due altre, e con una porta in un Giardinetto secreto, che ui è al pari con diuerse fontane, ò fontanelle, mà senz'acqua per il consumo de condotti [f. 41r]. . . . Nell'altra, et ultima camera con porta, e finestra che esce ne Giardinetto med⁰, infaccia della quale ui è una fontana in forma di prospetiua con una gran nicchia di tartari, nella quale ui è una Venere di marmo corca che dorme con un vaso gra'de di marmo d'auanti in forma di pilo per l'acqua della quale hora ne manca per rispetto de condotti. Dalle parti della med⁰ fontana sono due statue di marmo in piedi ne piedistallo di trauertino [f. 41v]."

The inventory also mentions that in the room on the *piano nobile* beyond the Cardinal's Bedroom, the room now called the Biblioteca, the ceiling was covered with a canvas painted to imitate the sky ("La seconda camera con una suffitta di tela depinta che finge aria" [f. 43r]). On the altar of the Cardinal's Chapel was a canvas of the *Assumption* (f. 43v).

96 F. S. Seni, *op.cit.*, pp. 159-160.

97 ASM, Fab. e Vill., Busta 72, Pte. 2, f. 1v: "Occore alla Fontana Fatta fare dal Cauag.ʳᵉ Bernini, la quale riesce troppo alta che non si può credere, e godere le altre sud.ᵗᵉ, onde bisogna farla abbassare al pari della strada con farli giocchi più picoli atteso l'esser queste acque di conserua."

98 ASM, Fab. e Vill., Busta 72, Pte. 1, f. 55r: "Il Presente disegno dell'Alcoua si puoti fare nelli seguenti modi. Uno sarebbe farlo di legno di Rilieuo, con fingere le colonne, è pilastri di uerde antico, è dargli il lustro nel medemo modo, come si furse di pietra, li fondi trà li pilastri fingerli di giallo Antico, e li capitelli, base, Acquile, Arme, fame, e Cornice di oro.

"L'altro modo dipingere sopra Telari la

1687 (Fig. 40), which speaks of the *camerini* involved in the 1671 projects of Mattia de' Rossi as the "new small vaulted rooms."[99] This plan is much less accurate in its delineation of the shapes and proportions of the rooms of the Villa than the 1671 plan (Fig. 119a). However, it describes the Gallery of the *piano nobile* as the "saletta with the plain vault [whose walls are] decorated with azure damask," proving that the present hunting landscapes painted on the walls of the Gallery are later than 1687 in date.

Despite this evidence of interest in the Villa little attention was actually devoted to the building and gardens at Tivoli. Before a decade had elapsed Rinaldo II gave up his Cardinal's hat and retired from the Sacred College in 1695 in order to assume secular power as the Duke of Modena. More than a century previously the Estes of Ferrara had attempted to secure retirement for Cardinal Luigi d'Este when there seemed to be no hope that his brother, Duke Alfonso II, would have an heir. At that time the impact of the reforms of the Council of Trent was too recent and the Papacy too unfriendly to the Estes to permit such action, but by the end of the seventeenth century the Pope and Sacred College consented to this abdication so that Rinaldo might marry and have offspring to carry on the Este dynasty of Modena and Reggio. The new Duke, former Cardinal, immediately married Carlotta Felicita of the House of Brunswick, thus reuniting two branches of the Estes that had been parted since the Middle Ages. The many children of this marriage solved the problem of dynastic inheritance, but external political events harassed Duke Rinaldo. Twice he was temporarily deposed by French troops. It was only inevitable under such conditions that the distant Villa at Tivoli was neglected. Even before Rinaldo resigned from his cardinalate the Villa was suffering from lack of attention. Misson reports in 1688 in his description of the Villa that "the greatest Part of the Water-Pipes are unfortunately stopp'd, and the Machins out of Order. The whole House appears at present in so forlorn and neglected a Condition, that 'tis impossible to behold the Remainders of its Beauty without a Pleasure mix'd with Grief."[100]

The history of the Villa and gardens in the eighteenth century and first half of the nineteenth century, a very sad one of neglect, disarray, and disrepair, is fully narrated by Seni.[101] The Este dukes considered the Villa primarily a liability. The maintenance expense of a Villa and gardens, which the Dukes could rarely enjoy, seemed excessive to them. At least from 1743 the Villa was being offered for sale,[102] and from 1751 on there were numerous negotiations for the sale or lease of the Villa or its furnishings. None of the offers for the purchase or lease of the Villa were at all adequate for consideration despite the fervent desire of the Dukes to divest themselves

---

med:ᵃ Alcoua nel med:º modo descritto ò pure di altre pietre. È quelli reportarli adosso il Muro doue sarà l'Apertura dell'Arco."

[99] *Ibid.*, ff. 58r-59v.

[100] [F. M. Misson], *A New Voyage to Italy,*

4th ed., London, 1714, II, p. 65. Misson's letter (no. XXVI) is dated, from Rome, April 11, 1688.

[101] F. S. Seni, *op.cit.*, especially pp. 161-187.

[102] T. Ashby, *op.cit.*, p. 234 n. e.

of this encumbrance. The difficulty in all these negotiations was the obvious great expense necessary to rehabilitate the Villa and to maintain it. Both Pope Pius VI in 1780 and the Marchese di Squillace in 1782 raised this factor as a consideration.

Unfortunately for the beauty of the present Villa the negotiations for the sale of some of the furnishings of the Villa were successful. One of the greatest attractions in the Villa at Tivoli were the numerous ancient statues which the Cardinal of Ferrara had purchased or excavated to decorate his Villa and gardens. When it was known that the eighteenth century Este Dukes no longer had any real interest in the Villa, the collectors of antiques began to bid against each other for the sculpture. In 1752 the King of Naples offered to purchase ninety-four marble statues, but in the following year Pope Benedict XIV, through Cardinal Valenti, was willing to buy only fourteen pieces for almost the same price. Naturally the latter offer was accepted, since it would leave the Villa with most of its original decoration and would, therefore, cause little harm to any later considerations for selling or renting the entire Villa. Most of these fourteen statues are consequently now preserved in the Capitoline Museum at Rome. Other collectors, such as Winckelmann on behalf of Cardinal Albani, acquired other works until the Villa and gardens were almost completely despoiled of their ancient statues.[103]

At the turn of the century the Estes finally parted with the Tiburtine Villa, not by sale but by the extinction of the Este dynasty itself. Duke Ercole III d'Este, deposed by the French in 1796, left all his property to his only child Maria Beatrice, the Archduchess of Austria, so that at Ercole's death in 1803 the Villa d'Este came into the hands of the Hapsburgs of Austria. Unlike their sixteenth century ancestor the Emperor Maximilian II, who had manifested great interest in the Villa, the nineteenth century Hapsburgs had no concern for the Villa even as their own possession. The neglect which began gradually to appear in the late seventeenth century and which became more acute during the second half of the eighteenth century reached its acme throughout the first half of the nineteenth century. For example, most of the Fountain of Rome fell to its destruction in April 1850 as the buttressing wall beneath it gave way, probably owing to the century of neglect.[104]

At the middle of the century a young German priest of noble family, Gustav Adolf von Hohenlohe, became enchanted with Tivoli and the Villa d'Este. In 1850 he signed a contract with the Duke of Modena in which Monsignor von Hohenlohe was permitted to possess for life the Villa d'Este in return only for his maintenance and restoration of the Villa and gardens. Gustav von Hohenlohe had a rapid and notable career in the Church, being appointed Almoner to Pope Pius IX in 1857 and elected Cardinal in 1866. The new Cardinal attempted quite successfully to emulate his earlier Cardinal predecessors of the Este family by making the Villa a center of culture

[103] The history and identification of most of the statues have been thoroughly studied by T. Ashby, *op.cit.*

[104] V. Pacifici, in *Atti e memorie della società tiburtina di storia e d'arte*, XX-XXI (1940-1941), p. 144 n. 1.

and of political activity. The healthy climate of Tivoli and the reinvigorating qualities of the nearby Acque Albule were two of the features which attracted the German Cardinal to Tivoli, as previously they had attracted the Cardinal of Ferrara. In an endeavor to follow the example of the Este cardinal as a patron of the arts, Cardinal von Hohenlohe invited several artists to reside in the Villa at Tivoli, but his protégés were rarely of the caliber of those who frequented the court of the Cardinal of Ferrara. The most eminent nineteenth century artist accustomed to visit or to reside at the Villa d'Este was the musician Franz Liszt, who was there from 1870 until 1884, usually arriving on September 8 and remaining until early December.[105] Another artist who had an apartment in the Villa was the American sculptor Moses Ezekiel, who even contributed to the decoration of the Villa.

The Cardinal devoted great attention to restoring the Villa and its gardens, but the spirit of his restoration was quite foreign to that which had inspired the Cardinal of Ferrara. The religiosity of the nineteenth century could never understand nor permit the classical, pagan elements which the sixteenth century fused with the Christian spirit. This is shown by the statues with which Cardinal von Hohenlohe filled many of the niches in the gardens at Tivoli. The niche of the Fountain of Pandora, the source of the evil which Hercules conquered, was exorcised by substituting Tadolini's group of the Virgin and Child. In the niche of the Fountain of Leda was placed Christopher Columbus presenting the Cross of Christianity to a kneeling America, and Ezekiel's statue of Sebastian was located in the Fountain of the Unicorn within the Secret Garden. Most typical of this transformation was the remodeling of the old Grotto of Venus within the Villa off the Secret Garden into the sacred Grotto of Lourdes.

The death of Cardinal von Hohenlohe in 1896 left the Villa again to the negligence of the Hapsburgs. It became the property of the unfortunate Archduke Franz Ferdinand, who visited there until his assassination at Sarajevo which precipitated World War I. After the War the Villa and its gardens were given to the Italian government as a result of the peace treaty. Later there were plans to convert the Villa into a museum of Italian ethnography, plans which never fully materialized. The government has maintained the Villa and gardens as a public monument, so that they have now become one of the favorite tourist attractions near Rome. Many restorations were undertaken in an attempt to preserve the original quality of the Villa. For example, the whitewash on the walls of the ground floor Salotto was removed to reveal the remains of the sixteenth century frescoes, and in 1949 these frescoes were completely restored. The second World War caused rather serious damage to the Villa during the terrible aerial bombardments of Tivoli. The gravest injury to the Villa was inflicted by a bomb that fell on the northeastern wing and the Secret Garden. Fortunately only the upper part of the walls collapsed, as can be seen in a

[105] G. Tani, "Filippo Guglielmi: L'uomo e l'artista," and F. Guglielmi, "Ricordi su Liszt," in *Atti e memorie della società tiburtina di storia e d'arte*, xxv (1952), 327ff. and 371ff.

photograph of the restored outer wall (Fig. 7). The untouched lower section preserved the frescoes of the rooms of the ground floor. The destroyed upper section, which belonged on the *piano nobile* to the seventeenth century winter apartment, was not frescoed on the interior. On the court side the upper story was rebuilt from the top of the sixteenth century arcade. The cascade of the Water Organ was likewise damaged by another bomb and diverted from its usual course at the base of the cascade.

The most injurious ravages of war and time have gradually been repaired.[106] Although some of the latter will always remain, they are part of the charm of the Villa to most of the modern visitors, who are still steeped in eighteenth century romanticism. The gardens of today are, of course, not truly the formal gardens enjoyed by the Cardinal of Ferrara nor are they even the lavish waterworks of the late seventeenth century as they were maintained by Cardinal Rinaldo I. The present gardens are an accumulation and synthesis of the ideas of the seventeenth and eighteenth centuries fused to the nucleus and layout of the sixteenth century gardens.

[106] There is, of course, always a certain amount of minor damage occurring at the Villa. For example, sometime soon after the summer of 1952 most of the central panel depicting the allegory of Glory by Zuccaro fell. One of the most lamentable sources of damage to the Villa is the constant defacing by visitors of the frescoed walls.

CHAPTER VII · APPRECIATION AND INFLUENCE OF THE VILLA D'ESTE

APPRECIATION

ON DECEMBER 18, 1568, the Imperial agent at Rome, Niccolò Cusano, wrote to his master, Maximilian II, that the Cardinal of Ferrara had built at Tivoli "a royal palace filled with infinite delights and very choice fountains which costs more than a hundred thousand ducats and, indeed, I have not seen another such in all of Christianity."[1] This very brief appreciation marks the commencement of a public interest in the Villa d'Este and its gardens that has remained constant down to the present tourist enthusiasm. In fact, it was during the next year that the first description of the Villa was written by Uberto Foglietta, while he was enjoying the hospitality of the Cardinal at Tivoli. The description was in the form of a long letter sent to Cardinal Flavio Orsini,[2] who had expressed a desire to hear of its wonders.

The report of Cusano to the Emperor must have aroused interest in Vienna, for late in 1571 the Cardinal mentioned in a personal letter to the Emperor that he had sent to Vienna several statues and "the drawing of my garden at Tivoli."[3] Indeed the archives at Modena record that on September 21, 1571, an artist called variously Sosso de Gasso or Josso de Gasso was paid a little over two *scudi* "for the manufacture of a frame made for the drawing of Tivoli sent to His Imperial Majesty."[4] The gardens at Tivoli must have been considered by the Cardinal completed sufficiently to warrant their depiction at this time for in July 1571, a few months previous to the creation of the Emperor's drawing, another Northern painter called Agnelo d'Ambosia (Abonsia or Ambrosia) began two canvases of the gardens at the rate of ten golden *scudi* each.[5]

---

[1] L. von Pastor, *The History of the Popes*, XVII, London, 1929, p. 406.

[2] See Chapter Two, note 3.

[3] H. von Voltelini, "Urkunden und Regesten aus dem K. u. K. Haus-, Hof- und Staats-Archiv in Wien," *Jahrbuch der kunsthistorischen Sammlungen des allerhöchsten Kaiserhauses*, XIII (1892), p. LXI, no. 8906.

[4] ASM, Registri del Card. Ipp. II, Pacco 122, Protetione di Francia 1571, f. 20v: "A spesa de fabriche de Tiuoli ▽ doi, e b doi pagati a Sosso de Gasso Pittore per fattura d'una quinta fatta al desegno di Tiuoli mand.to alla M.ta Ces.a . . . ▽ 2.2" (the same account in ASM, Registri del Card. Ipp. II, Pacco 122, unlabeled register of 1571, f. 95v calls the artist "Josso de gasso").

[5] ASM, Registri del Card. Ipp. II, Pacco 122, Protetione di Francia, f. 16: July 1, 1571, "A m.ro Agnelo de Abonsia Pittore Fiamengo ▽ quattro, e b sessantaquattro à lui ctj à conto de depingere dui quadri della prospettiua de Tiuoli, app.e m.to sig.to n° 120, ▽ 4.64"; f. 17r: July 16, "A maestro Agnelo Ambrosia Fiamengo ▽ cinque, e b ottanta à lui ctj à conto di fare due prospettiue à Tiuoli app.e m.to n.o 135, ▽ 5.80"; f. 19r: Aug. 28, "A m.ro Agnelo d'Ambosia Pittore Fiamengo ▽ uno, e, b sedeci à lui ctj per resto de ▽ 10 d'oro in oro per la prospettiua che ha fatta di Tiuoli app.e m.to sig.to n.o 169, ▽ 1.16"; ASM, Registri del Card. Ipp. II, Pacco 122, unlabeled register of 1571, f. 95r: Aug. 28, 1571, "E adi 28 detto scudi vndec. di m.ta et b sessanti per SS Ill.ma a m.ro Angelo d'Ambosia pittore per fattura d'vna prospetiua di pittura sopra la tela del giardino et palazzo di Tiuli . . . ▽ 11.60."

One of these depictions of the Villa may

The paintings for the Cardinal and the drawing prepared for the Emperor seem no longer to be preserved, but we have an excellent idea of what the Imperial drawing was like in Dupérac's engraving of 1573 (Fig. 1), which immediately became very popular.[6] In 1575 Mario Cartaro published a version of this engraving, while in 1581 Claude Duchet brought out still another version with minor changes, and this republishing or reprinting continued into the seventeenth century.[7] Even a majolica plate made at Urbino in 1575 appeared with a view of the Villa d'Este based upon Dupérac's engraving.[8] As a result of the demand for his engraved birds-eye view of the gardens, Dupérac prepared in 1575 another engraving of the Villa d'Este, this time depicting only the Oval Fountain (Fig. 134).

While these depictions spread the fame of the Villa and its gardens throughout Italy and Europe, literary encomia, the first ones private letters or manuscripts, began to appear. Some of the finest were the Latin poems written by the Cardinal's humanist friend Marc-Antoine Muret, who spent the summers with the Cardinal at Tivoli.[9] Two poems of some length were composed by Muret in 1571 describing some of the fountains and marvels of the gardens, which he claims "bear the name of Hippolytus to the stars." Muret also created four short poems which are likewise concerned with the Villa. Two of these short poems are dedications of the Tiburtine gardens and are extremely important, as has been noted earlier, for interpreting the symbolism of the gardens. The other two poems are dedicated to the rustic fountains of Bacchus opposite the great Oval Fountain.

The local notary Giovanni Maria Zappi has left in manuscript form his annals of the city of Tivoli composed principally of the historical events occurring at Tivoli during his lifetime which spanned most of the sixteenth century. He also included the descriptions of several ancient villas at Tivoli and an extensive description of the Villa d'Este, dated 1576.[10] Such a description, not published until the twentieth century, of course had no effect on the reputation of the Villa, but it is very useful now in furnishing a picture of the gardens soon after the death of the Cardinal of Ferrara.

---

have remained as decoration of the Palace throughout the lifetime of Cardinal Luigi d'Este, as one is listed in three of his inventories. ASM, Registri del Card. Luigi d'Este, Pacco 153, Libro dare e hauere delle Robe di Guarda Roba di Tiuoli . . . da di 20 Marzo 1573 per tt° di 13 Agto 1582, listed twice under the dates 1573 and August 13, 1582, and *ibid.*, Pacco 162, Inuentaria generale . . . della Guardarobba 1579, f. 173v: "Il retratto di Tiuolli in Tella cioe del Palazzo et Giardino n.° 1."

[6] See Introduction to Appendix A.

[7] T. Ashby, "The Villa d'Este at Tivoli and the Collection of Classical Sculptures which it contained," *Archaeologia*, LXI, pt. 1 (1908), p. 222 and notes c and d.

[8] G. Ballardini, "Per la mostra del giardino italiano," *Bollettino d'arte*, ser. 3, XXV (1931), pp. 14-17 and fig. 1.

[9] M. A. Muret, *Orationes, epistolae & poemata*, Leipzig, 1672, the poems are in the section entitled "Poemata varia duobis libris distincta," Book I, pp. 45-47, nos. 50-55.

[10] G. M. Zappi, *Annali e memorie di Tivoli di Giovanni Maria Zappi*, ed. by V. Pacifici, Tivoli, 1920, pp. 55-65.

A description by the Fleming Pighius not only represents the interest of foreigners in the gardens but furthered this interest. Pighius, whose real name was Stefan Wijnants, accompanied the youthful Prince of Cleves on his grand tour of 1574-1575. Unfortunately the young Prince died at Rome during the trip, but Pighius commemorated the tour with his book *Hercules Prodicius* which appeared at Antwerp in 1587. Pighius and the Prince had visited the Villa d'Este early in 1575, so the author included a lengthy account of the Villa in his book. The description, however, as Pighius admits, was written on the basis of Duchet's engraved birds-eye view of 1581.[11] This account by Pighius had a long history, for when François Schott wrote his guidebook to Italy (1600), he merely copied the description of Pighius. The Schott guidebook then reappeared in many printings and editions until 1761.[12]

The French, more than any other foreign nation, seem to have been interested in the Villa d'Este, perhaps because the Estes shared French interests. Michel Montaigne has left one of the earliest records of a Frenchman's appreciation of the Villa in the diary of his trip to Italy. During his visit in April 1581 Montaigne noted: "It is a very beautiful piece, but incomplete in several parts, and the work is not being continued by the present Cardinal [Luigi d'Este]."[13] He continues that he would attempt to describe the Villa very completely but that there were already books and "public paintings" on this subject. However, Montaigne does report quite fully the various hydraulic devices such as the Water Organ, the Fountain of the Owl, and the Fountain of the Dragon. It has been the quantity of water at Tivoli which has charmed visitors of all periods, and Montaigne, as he reveals in his comparison of the Villa d'Este with the Medici Villa at Pratolino, is no exception:

In richness and beauty of grottoes, Florence [i.e. Pratolino] excels infinitely; in abundance of water Ferrara [i.e. Tivoli]; . . . in the disposition and arrangement of the total layout of the location, Ferrara surpasses; in ancient statues and in palace Florence. In site, beauty of vista, Ferrara infinitely excels.[14]

Montaigne, however, laments the condition of the water at Tivoli. "If it were clear water, good to drink, as it is on the contrary muddy and unsightly, this place would be incomparable."

[11] D. R. Coffin, "John Evelyn at Tivoli," *Journal of the Warburg and Courtauld Institutes*, XIX (1956), p. 157.

[12] E. S. de Beer, "François Schott's *Itinerario d'Italia*," *The Library, Transactions of the Bibliographical Society*, ser. 4, XXIII (1942-1943), pp. 57-83.

[13] M. de Montaigne, *Journal du voyage du Michel de Montaigne en Italie*, ed. by A. d'Ancona, new ed., Città di Castello, 1895, p. 323.

[14] M. de Montaigne, *Journal de voyage en Italie*, new ed. by P. Faure, n.p., 1948, p. 146.

In this quotation I have followed the punctuation of the more recent edition by Faure rather than the more scholarly edition by D'Ancona. Montaigne's description is only preserved in a manuscript copy with very little punctuation. The different punctuations suggested in the two editions create two entirely different meanings in this passage, but it seems to me that in this case Faure's punctuation comes closer to Montaigne's intent on the basis of what we know regarding the two villas.

The great renovation of the Villa d'Este under Cardinal Alessandro had its expositor in Antonio del Re, who included a very detailed description of the Villa in his account of the antiquities of Tivoli. Since only chapter five of Del Re's work was published in 1611[15]—the chapter containing in one part the portrait of the Villa d'Este and in the other the ancient Roman villas in and near Tivoli—the book as published is principally concerned with the Este Villa. It was, therefore, very important in spreading the fame of the Villa in Italy, but another book printed at about the same time carried its influence to other countries. The French hydraulic engineer and architect, Salomon de Caus, studied closely the gardens at Tivoli, Pratolino, and Frascati. In his book *Les raisons des forces mouvantes*, published first in 1615, De Caus described many of the hydraulic devices in the Italian gardens. Two of them are found in the Villa d'Este, that is, the Fountain of the Owl and the Water Organ.[16] As we shall see later, it was by means of the book of De Caus and his own garden work that the influence of the fountains of the Villa d'Este was carried into many countries of Europe outside of Italy.

For the seventeenth century the particular appeal of the Villa d'Este was in the fountains and especially the hydraulic tricks in the gardens. The poet Gabriele Ginani dedicated in 1627 two of his sonnets to the same fountains which De Caus had analyzed, the Water Organ and the Fountain of the Owl.[17] A few years later the German architect Furttenbach depicted the Oval Fountain in his book on architecture. In another plate he then indicated how this fountain could be used as an accent in a garden of his own design.[18] Indeed, artists and art lovers from most of the European countries came to study or observe the Tiburtine gardens. About 1643 or 1644 the French artist Israel Silvestre made sketches in the gardens,[19] which were followed in 1646 by a set of engravings. The latter, however, were not accurate transcriptions of what Silvestre had seen at Tivoli. As with many of his Italian engravings Silvestre made minor changes or transpositions in his views of the Villa d'Este. At the same time the English amateur, John Evelyn, visited Tivoli and left a description of the Villa d'Este in his *Diary*, but most of it is derived from printed sources which ultimately are based on Duchet's engraving of the original project and not on what actually existed.[20] Later the German Böckler repeated the interest of his countryman

[15] A. del Re, *Dell'Antichità tiburtine capitolo V*, Rome, 1611.

[16] S. de Caus, *Les raisons des forces mouvantes avec diuerses Machines*, Frankfort, 1615, ff. 29v-30v and 39v-43r. Ultimately these hydraulic contrivances come from the writings of the ancient Greek Hero of Alexandria, and Hero's book was published several times before De Caus' work, but De Caus drew in part upon his study of the Italian gardens as well as upon Hero's account.

[17] G. Ginani, *Rime diverse di Gabriele Zinano*, Venice, 1627, p. 12, no. 322, and p. 14, no. 325.

[18] J. Furttenbach, *Architectura universalis*, Ulm, 1635, pt. III, p. 81, pls. 24 and 28.

[19] H. Granville Fell, "Drawings by Israel Silvestre, 1621-1691," *Connoisseur*, XCVII (1936), p. 22, fig. VI, and San Francisco, California: Golden Gate International Exhibition, *Master Drawings*, 1940, p. 24, no. 97, illus. p. 65.

[20] J. Evelyn, *The Diary of John Evelyn*, ed. by E. S. de Beer, II, Oxford, 1955, pp. 394-396, and D. R. Coffin, *op.cit.*, pp. 157-158.

Furttenbach by including several of the fountains in his book on garden architecture.[21]

This interest in the Villa d'Este especially by foreigners was remarked on twice in 1665 by the Italians Marzi and Giustiniani. The latter, quoting the former Bishop of Tivoli, noted how the beauty of the Villa d'Este "allures a great number of visitors, and particularly those from beyond the mountains, who come daily to Tivoli to see it."[22] Indeed, in the sixties the gardens had attained under the patronage of Cardinal Rinaldo I another peak of eminence, reflected in the travel accounts of Skippon and Lassels.[23] The latter was so lavish in his praise that at the end he could only add that the wonders of the Villa "are rather to be seen, then described: and my traueler will wrong himself much, if hee staye not here three or four dayes to view *munitamente* these wonders of arts." It is this appearance of the gardens at Tivoli which must be pictured in the engravings of Venturini published about 1685.

This period of the sixties was about the last moment that the fountains of the Villa d'Este would reign unchallenged in the eyes of foreign visitors, for at this moment King Louis XIV and André Le Nôtre were creating at Versailles in France gardens and waterworks which would outrival Tivoli. However, it must also be noted that after the seventies the gardens and fountains at Tivoli began to fall into decay as a result of neglect. The description by Misson in 1688 reflects this.[24] He admits that the waterworks at Tivoli may excel all those of Italy, in fact, he notes that they "far exceed those at *Frescati*," but Misson immediately comments on "these small things here," and concludes "that *Versailles* has incomparable Beauties; that the Water-works of that place exceed a thousand times those that are at *Tivoli*; and that the very Lead of the Canals at *Versailles* cost ten times more than all *Tivoli*." By this time local legend had overwhelmed historical truth at Tivoli for Misson believed: "The greatest Rarities that it can boast of, are three Chambers painted in *Fresco*, by *Raphael*."

For the remainder of the seventeenth century the Villa d'Este had little interest for foreign visitors, both because of its increasing decay and the creation of marvels elsewhere. The eighteenth century, however, brought a growing revival of interest in the Villa d'Este, but for new reasons, and again it was the French who particularly admired the gardens. Poerson, the Director of the French Academy at Rome, considered the Villa d'Este in 1721 as "the most beautiful palace and the most beautiful waterworks of Italy."[25] In fact, at about this time the painter Vleughels took his pupils in painting at the Academy to Tivoli to study presumably not the Villa d'Este but

[21] G. A. Böckler, *Architectura Curiosa Nova: Amaenitates Hydragogicae*, Nuremburg, [1664], figs. 21, 29, and 67.

[22] F. Marzi, *Historia ampliata di Tivoli*, Rome, 1665, p. 3, and M. Giustiniani, *op.cit.*, p. 155.

[23] P. Skippon, "An Account of a Journey Made thro' Part of the Low-Countries, Germany, Italy, and France," dated Dec. 26, 1665, in [A. Churchill], *A Collection of Voyages and Travels*, VI, London, 1732, p. 674, and R. Lassels, *The Voyage of Italy*, Paris, 1670, II, pp. 314-316.

[24] [F. M. Misson], *A New Voyage to Italy*, 4th ed., London, 1714, II, pp. 65-66.

[25] A. de Montaiglon and J. Guiffrey, *Correspondance des directeurs de l'académie de France à Rome*, VI, Paris, 1896, pp. 107-108, no. 2395.

the antiquities and landscape or, as Vleughels relates, "the fantasy of nature, the marvelous sites, the disposition of the buildings, all that will unfold their genius and will teach them to compose in an ingenious and new manner."[26] Soon, however, it will be this "fantasy of nature" which will bring the visitors of the eighteenth century to appreciate anew the gardens at Tivoli.

Toward the middle of the century President Charles de Brosses admired the quantity of water expended at Tivoli very much in the manner of his fellow countryman Montaigne more than a century and a half previously. "If they [the gardens] were not so badly tended, they would excel all those of Frascati in grandeur and in magnificence, and by the abundance of water." However, Montaigne's objection to the condition of the water was solved by the eighteenth century. At least De Brosses, while praising the gardens of Versailles in comparison to all of Italy, remarks: "One must confess, nonetheless, that the waters of Tibur [i.e. Tivoli] and of Frascati are clear and limpid, and that those of Versailles are very imperfect in this regard, which makes an enormous difference."[27] The neglect and disarray that De Brosses noticed at Tivoli were soon to acquire a value of their own.

In 1749 a very important group of travelers left France for Italy. These travelers—an engraver, Cochin, an architect, Soufflot, an amateur and critic of the arts, the Abbé Le Blanc, and a young nobleman, the Marquis de Marigny—were sent to Italy by Mme. de Pompadour, the sister of the Marquis, to train her brother for his future position as the Director of Royal Buildings for the King of France. Charles-Nicolas Cochin soon wrote an account of this grand tour giving his opinions on the architecture and art of Italy.[28] Cochin's feelings toward the Villa d'Este were mixed. He admitted that "the garden is very beautiful, although almost abandoned," but he criticized many parts. For Cochin the decoration of the Water Organ was "very heavy" and the "whole quite poorly executed, and makes a bad effect." The small scale of the buildings of the Fountain of Rome "make an effect more ridiculous than pleasing." However, the most interesting comment of Cochin is on the Oval Fountain: "The whole, nevertheless, has a very picturesque aspect, enriched by the grasses which grow everywhere, and by the trees which crown the crags." It is this picturesque effect of the Villa d'Este created by the overgrowth of nature in the untended and decaying gardens which soon inspired the most charming of all evidences of admiration of the gardens at Tivoli, the drawings of Fragonard and Hubert Robert.

On August 27, 1760, Natoire, the Director of the French Academy at Rome, wrote to the Marquis de Marigny: "M. l'abbé de Saint Non has been at Tivoli for a month and a half with the *pensionnaire* Fragonard, the painter. This amateur is extremely busy and applies himself a great deal. Our young artist is creating some very lovely

[26] *Ibid.*, VII, Paris, 1897, pp. 84-85, no. 2818, and p. 86, no. 2820.

[27] C. de Brosses, *Lettres familières sur l'Italie*, ed. by Y. Bezard, Paris, 1931, II, pp. 304 and 306.

[28] C. N. Cochin, *Voyage d'Italie*, Paris, 1758, I, pp. 109-113. The first edition is dated 1751.

studies which can only be very useful to him and bring him much honor. He has a very lively fancy for this type of landscape where he introduces rustic subjects which are very successful with him."[29] It was early in July 1760 that the wealthy amateur the Abbé de Saint-Non obtained permission from the Este ambassador to live at the Villa d'Este for the summer. The Abbé went there immediately with the young painter Jean-Honoré Fragonard from the French Academy, and they were soon joined by another young French artist, Hubert Robert. Saint-Non reported that "Fragonard is all on fire; his drawings are very numerous; one cannot wait for another; they enchant me. I find in them some sort of sorcery."[30] Many of these exquisite drawings are preserved, most of them in the Museum at Besançon.[31] Executed usually in sanguine, Fragonard's feathery touch presents a superb contrast of the sharp accent of dark shadows and glancing lights against the swelling softness of nature (Fig. 136). The nature is the free one of Romanticism, climbing to the sky unhampered by the pruning-knife or spreading over the architectural walls and statuary. Large patches of stucco have fallen from the walls; broken branches and stones clutter the walks. The drawings present in a striking fashion the picturesque element that Cochin admired at Tivoli, the picturesque which was a product both of the Estes' neglect of the gardens and of eighteenth century Romanticism.

The experience of the Villa d'Este gardens was a rich one for Fragonard. Under the guidance of the Abbé de Saint-Non the painter began to experiment with the etching needle and produced the print entitled *Le Petit Parc*, based on a drawing depicting the Fountain of the Dragon at Tivoli.[32] A charming painting by Fragonard in the Wallace Collection at London then reproduced the same scene (Fig. 137). In 1765 the Abbé likewise issued a series of prints after drawings by Fragonard and Hubert Robert which included several views of the Villa d'Este.[33] Only a few drawings in sanguine or bistre are attributed to Hubert Robert, and some of these may be by Fragonard.[34]

The remembrance of these excitingly creative days at Tivoli remained long with Fragonard, and it is not surprising that when he returned to Italy in 1774 with his patron, the financier Bergeret de Grancourt, they visited the Villa d'Este. Bergeret wrote a journal of this trip to Italy. As usual the Frenchman compared the Tiburtine gardens with those of his native land. In general Bergeret was rather favorable toward

[29] A. de Montaiglon and J. Guiffrey, *op.cit.*, XI, Paris, 1901, p. 354, no. 5459.

[30] L. Guimbaud, *Saint-Non et Fragonard*, Paris, 1928, p. 98.

[31] See especially *Les dessins d'Honoré Fragonard et de Hubert Robert des Bibliothèque et Musée de Besançon*, Paris, 1926, nos. 31-35; Paris, J. Seligmann and Sons, *Exposition de dessins de Fragonard*, 1931, nos. 79-82 and 84; F. Fosca, *Les dessins de Fragonard*, Paris, 1954, pp. 52-53, no. 8, pp. 55-56, no. 13, p. 60, no. 24

(probably not the Villa d'Este), and p. 64, no. 35, and L. Reau, *Fragonard, sa vie et son œuvre*, Brussels, 1956, p. 222.

[32] G. Wildenstein, *Fragonard aquafortiste*, Paris, 1956, especially pp. 2 and 8-10.

[33] L. Guimbaud, *op.cit.*, p. 193.

[34] For example, in the catalogue of the *Exposition Hubert Robert* at the Musée de l'Orangerie at Paris in 1933, p. 88, no. 122 and p. 89, no. 126.

the gardens of the Villa d'Este, commenting as all critics did on the quantity of water. He considered the water displays small in scale but so numerous that they produced "a general effect which creates a sensation."[35] Bergeret adds that the gardens were "praised and admired by painters who find there a choice of very varied and stimulating views. For a long time past, painters have never left Rome without making numerous drawings in the gardens of the Villa d'Este." Undoubtedly this information was given to Bergeret by Fragonard on the basis of his own early experience.

An extensive description of the Villa was made by another Frenchman, Lalande, in the account of his visit to Italy in 1765 and 1766. Not only is Lalande's report on the Tiburtine Villa quite lengthy for such a travel book, but it is an impartial and accurate account, although there is one slip. Lalande lists as the most remarkable fountains "those of the Unicorn, of Thetis, of Arethusa, of Pandora, of Flora, of Pegasus, of Bacchus, of Aesculapius, of the Anio and the Nymphs, of Diana, of Pallas, of Venus, of Neptune, and that of Apollo or of Nature."[36] Of these fountains Arethusa and Flora were never completed and existed for the most part only in Dupérac's engraving of 1573; the architectural grottoes for the fountains of Arethusa and Flora were built, but no statuary or representational elements were ever placed in them to support their nomenclature in Dupérac, and the Fountain of Neptune was, of course, never created.

Although Lalande fell into error in this respect, he did not make Misson's error of attributing the interior frescoes to Raphael. He notes that they are by Zuccaro and, although he dislikes them—referring to the "mauvais plafonds"—Lalande is the first to note that the fresco of the Feast of the Gods is derived from Raphael's fresco in the Farnesina. His criticism resembles much of the French criticism of the late seventeenth and eighteenth centuries and particularly that of Cochin. He says of the Oval Fountain: "All this decoration is little and niggardly,"[37] and of the Fountain of Rome that the "little buildings are bad, and their small size make them unsuitable to the decoration."[38] The French could never forget the monumentality of the conception and details of their own Versailles. Lalande, however, continues: "Finally the water, which is very abundant on this mountain, as one can judge by the cascade of Tivoli, has been distributed in these gardens with a great deal of charm, and there is scarcely any place in the world where there is such a beautiful view below it." As usual it is the quantity of water and the beauty of the natural site which overwhelm a French critic.

At least one other important artist of the eighteenth century depicted the Villa d'Este. The Italian etcher Giovanni Battista Piranesi included a view of the Villa and its gardens in his series of the *Vedute di Roma*.[39] Created in 1773, when Piranesi was

[35] P. J. O. Bergeret de Grancourt, *Voyage d'Italie, 1773-1774*, Paris, 1948, p. 97.

[36] [J. J. L. F. de Lalande], *Voyage d'un français en Italie, fait dans les années 1765 & 1766*, new ed., Yverdon, 1769, v, p. 164.

[37] *Ibid.*, p. 165.   [38] *Ibid.*, p. 166.

[39] A. M. Hind, *Giovanni Battista Piranesi*, London, 1922, p. 66, no. 105, pl. LVI.

busy measuring, drawing, and etching the antiquities of Tivoli, the etching of the Este Villa (Fig. 135) was taken from a viewpoint rather similar to one of Fragonard's sanguine drawings (Fig. 136), but the results are very dissimilar. Both representations depict the great central alley down the middle of the gardens with the Villa rising above. Fragonard, however, stepped back far enough to have as his principal feature the great rotunda of cypresses climbing like clouds of smoke up to the heavens. Piranesi moved into the center of the cypress circle but then omitted the cypresses entirely. There are a few verticals of cypresses and umbrella pines in the middle distance, but the prime vertical accent is the series of grottoes, fountains, and loggias which mount up to the Villa dominating the whole. It is a fairly accurate portrait of the Villa, but there is a distortion of scale, as is usual in Piranesi's prints. In the foreground small human figures work or wander in the gardens close to the fountains and statues of the Liberal Arts which encircle the central rotunda where the great cypresses should be, but the statues are over twice life-size and set a Baroque scale which then seems to pervade the complete vista. Except for the exaggeration in scale, Piranesi's etching is perhaps closer to the original conception of the gardens than most depictions. Fragonard's drawing, on the other hand, is a very accurate delineation of what he saw and what one sees today at Tivoli, but it is Romanticism with nature overwhelming man and his handiwork. Piranesi's conception is Baroque—man is small, not in nature but before man's creation of statuary and architecture.

INFLUENCE

The interest that visitors and artists displayed in the gardens of the Villa d'Este through the centuries had its counterpart in the influence which the Tiburtine gardens and fountains exerted on many later gardens. It is rare to find the total composition or layout of the gardens reflected in other gardens, but the motifs of several fountains seen first at Tivoli turn up frequently later. The idea of a stone boat as a fountain shooting jets of water, as in the Fountain of Rome and the Hundred Fountains, soon appeared in the gardens of the Villa Lante at Bagnaia, where Montaigne saw four of them in 1581.[40] Montaigne noted that the gardener at Bagnaia had worked at Tivoli: "The same Messer Tomaso da Siena, who managed the work at Tivoli, or the principal work, is likewise the manager of this [garden] which is not yet completed." These stone boats still exist at Bagnaia planted with flowering bushes, but they originally were provided with arquebusiers who shot at the pyramid set in the center of the four boats.

In the seventeenth century the boat fountain appears several times in Italy, for example, the Fontana della Barca of the Villa Aldobrandini at Frascati, Bernini's Barcaccia in the Piazza di Spagna at Rome, and the very realistic boat in the Fontana del Vascello of the Vatican. It is possible that the idea of a boat used as a fountain may

[40] M. de Montaigne, *Journal de voyage du Michel de Montaigne en Italie,* ed. by A. d'An- cona, new ed., Città di Castello, 1895, p. 527.

be in part derived from the so-called Navicella set in front of Santa Maria in Domnica at Rome, where it was rebuilt by Pope Leo X after a damaged antique one.[41] At least the boat fountains in villa gardens, such as those of Bagnaia and Frascati, are more likely derived from those of Tivoli, not only since they are all garden fountains but also because of the probability that the *fontanieri* of these gardens had worked at Tivoli.

Another fountain subject prominent at Tivoli recurs later in the gardens of other Italian villas. Both the Villa Lante at Bagnaia and the Villa Aldobrandini at Frascati had fountains dedicated to Pegasus like the one above the Oval Fountain. The Greek legend related by Pausanias (IX, xxxi, 3)—that a fountain was created on Mount Helicon or Parnassus in the hoof prints of the winged horse Pegasus—was, of course, most appealing as the theme of a fountain, which at Frascati was expanded to show Apollo and the Muses also on the mountain. At Bagnaia the form of the Pegasus Fountain, as well as the subject matter, came from Tivoli. The oval fountain of Pegasus with a semi-oval back wall decorated with nine female busts spouting water, probably the Muses, and topped by a balustrade is very like the Oval Fountain at Tivoli.

The composition of the Oval Fountain at Tivoli likewise may have influenced the Water Theater of the Villa Aldobrandini, for the latter's semicircular arcaded screen and the cascade of water plunging down from above to spray out over the figure of Atlas has some resemblance to the fountain at Tivoli. In addition, there was at the Villa Aldobrandini a Fountain of the Girandola which Lassels tells us "imitateth perfectly *Thunder, Hale, Rayne* and *Mist*."[42] This description of the changing character of the water recalls Del Re's account[43] of the water effects of the Fountain of the Dragon at Tivoli, called also the Girandola, and suggests that the Tiburtine fountain may have been influential at Frascati.

It is natural that the Cardinal's native city, Ferrara, should reflect an interest in the wonders of his Villa at Tivoli. There was a long tradition of extravagant gardens and pleasure houses at Ferrara, which probably contributed ideas to the Cardinal's own gardens and villas at Tivoli and on Monte Cavallo in Rome. The Cardinal's nephew Alfonso II d'Este, the Duke of Ferrara, had visited the Tiburtine Villa at least once, during his trip to Rome in 1573 soon after his uncle's death.[44] In 1590 the Ducal architect, Giovanni Battista Aleotti, planned for the gardens near the Castello at Ferrara a series of fountains and waterworks. These gardens and fountains, of course, no longer exist, but documents preserve some account of them.[45] A letter of Aleotti

[41] F. Mastrigli, *Acque, acquedotti e fontane di Roma*, II, Rome, n.d., pp. 201-202.

[42] R. Lassels, *op.cit.*, II, p. 309.

[43] A. del Re, *op.cit.*, p. 65.

[44] A. Solerti, *Vita di Torquato Tasso*, Turin and Rome, 1895, I, p. 180 and note 4.

[45] L. N. Cittadella, *Notizie amministrative,* *storiche, artistiche relative a Ferrara*, I, Ferrara, 1868, pp. 231-232, and A. Zanoletti, "Un importante documento Aleottiano," *Atti e memorie della R. deputazione di storia patria per l'Emilia e la Romagna: Sezione di Ferrara*, I (1942), pp. 195-205.

to the Duke explains some of the water effects which he planned for the gardens, and he specifically refers to Tivoli in the letter. Aleotti planned a fountain of singing birds with an eagle which silenced them, as he noted, "in the manner of the owl of Tivoli."[46] Other fountains would have mirrors from which water would suddenly shoot into the faces of innocent spectators, figures of Hercules with the Nemean Lion and with Antaeus, and water organs. Of these at least the Fountain of the Birds was created. Although Aleotti was undoubtedly influenced by the fame of the fountains at Tivoli, as he himself admits, he also went directly to the ancient source for his knowledge, since in 1589 he had published the first Italian translation of Hero of Alexandria's *Pneumatica*.[47] Aleotti had probably been a protégé of Pirro Ligorio during the latter's later life in Ferrara, at least Aleotti owned some of his writings,[48] and it may have been Ligorio who introduced Aleotti to Hero's treatise on hydraulics.

The Villa d'Este also exerted an influence on gardens outside of Italy. The interest of the Emperor Maximilian II, which resulted in the drawing of the Villa sent to him by the Cardinal of Ferrara, had a practical reason. The Emperor was building near Vienna at that time the Neugebäude with very lavish gardens, which unfortunately no longer remain in any really recognizable condition, but an engraving in a book by Fischer von Erlach the Younger preserves some idea of this layout. The building director was Pietro Ferrabosco, but Pirro Ligorio's former assistant architect in the Vatican, Sallustio Peruzzi, may have created the basic design.[49] Along with the drawing of the Tiburtine Villa the Cardinal of Ferrara had sent to the Emperor several ancient statues, which the Emperor used to decorate his new gardens. In fact, since late 1568 Maximilian had commissioned Count Arco at Rome to acquire antique statues for his gardens, and it has been suggested that this idea of embellishing his gardens with antiques may have been inspired by the Villa d'Este.[50] Fischer's engraving of the Viennese garden, however, reveals very little, if any, dependence upon the Italian gardens at Tivoli. There is a series of terraced gardens and walks leading up from a large pool at the base to the casino above. Then at the upper level behind the casino was another enclosed garden, but there is no central axis as at Tivoli. Indeed the general layout of the Neugebäude is slightly more reminiscent of Vignola's Farnese gardens on the Palatine at Rome.

In France beginning in 1599 Henry IV refashioned the gardens of Saint-Germain-en-Laye into a series of terraces from the casino down to the river. The layout is so suggestive of that of the Villa d'Este that the latter is probably its source, and the designer may be Etienne Dupérac, who made the 1573 engraving of the Tiburtine

[46] A. Zanoletti, *op.cit.*, p. 203.

[47] G. B. Aleotti, *Gli artifitiosi et cvriosi moti spiritali di Herrone*, Ferrara, 1589.

[48] For example, some drawings and notes of Ligorio are interleaved in Aleotti's copy of Vignola's *Regola delli cinque ordini d'architettura*, see G. Antonelli, *Indice dei manoscritti*

della civica biblioteca di Ferrara, Ferrara, 1884, pp. 126-127, no. 217.

[49] J. Schmidt, *Wien*, 7th ed., Vienna, 1949, p. 56.

[50] A. Lhotsky, *Die Geschichte der Sammlungen*, Vienna, 1941-1945, p. 159.

gardens.[51] In addition, some of the waterworks at Saint-Germain are descendants of those at Tivoli. There was a Grotto of the Dragon in which a dragon beat his wings and spewed water, surrounded by singing birds. Another grotto contained a mechanical female figurine playing a water organ, all controlled by the flow of water.

In particular the waterworks at Tivoli, such as the Water Organ, the Fountain of the Owl, or the Fountain of the Dragon, exerted a powerful influence upon later gardens. From at least 1615 on, most of these hydraulic devices became the common knowledge of European landscape architects and fountain designers through the publication of Salomon de Caus' book, noted earlier. De Caus, who had studied the gardens and fountains of the Villa d'Este, as well as those of Pratolino and Frascati, designed gardens at Brussels, Greenwich, and Richmond, and the Castle Gardens of Heidelberg.[52] These gardens built by De Caus either no longer exist or are radically changed, the fate of so many sixteenth and seventeenth century gardens when the fad of the English garden swept Europe in the late eighteenth and nineteenth centuries. However, the gardens at Heidelberg were built on a hillside with leveled terraces supported by a great retaining wall reminiscent of Tivoli.[53]

It is possible that one of the greatest examples of Italian eighteenth century gardening, that of the Royal Palace at Caserta, was laid out under the influence of the Villa d'Este. Pacifici claims that Luigi Vanvitelli was required by Carlo III to stay at Tivoli to study the gardens there before planning Caserta.[54] The arrangement at Caserta of four long pools ending in a cascade rushing down the small mountain at the end of the garden is somewhat like the cross-axis at Tivoli of the four fish pools with the great artificial cascade under the Water Organ.

Even the name of the Villa d'Este had its effect. When Caroline of Brunswick bought the Villa Garrovo at Cernobbia in 1815, she renamed it the Nuova Villa d'Este. Her reason for the new name was the fact that the House of Brunswick was descended from the Estes,[55] but there must have been in her mind also the idea of possessing a summer resort emulating the more famous one at Tivoli. Likewise in 1843 when Georg Carstensen designed an amusement park at Copenhagen in Denmark, he named it the Tivoli and Vauxhall Gardens after the two most renowned sites associated with pleasure, entertainment, and relaxation. As the Vauxhall Gardens of England disappeared so did their name from the Danish gardens, but the Tivoli

[51] L. de la Tourrasse, "Le Château-neuf de Saint-Germain-en-Laye: Ses terrasses et ses grottes," *Gazette des beaux-arts*, LXVI (1924), pp. 68-95; A. Mousset, *Les Francine*, Paris, 1930, pp. 35-41; A. Blunt, *Art and Architecture in France, 1500-1700*, Melbourne, London, and Baltimore, 1953, p. 113, note 2 on p. 131; and A. Marie, *Jardins français créés à la renaissance*, Paris, 1955, pp. 30-33.

[52] C. S. Maks, *Salomon de Caus, 1576-1626*, Paris, 1935, pp. 92-101.

[53] M. L. Gothein, *A History of Garden Art*, London and Toronto, 1928, II, pp. 38-43, illus. fig. 383.

[54] V. Pacifici, "Luigi d'Este e la villa tiburtina," *Atti e memorie della società tiburtina di storia e d'arte*, XXII-XXIII (1942-1943), p. 100 and note 1. I have not been able to trace Pacifici's source for this.

[55] N. Podenzani, *Villa d'Este*, Milan, n.d., pp. 55-56.

Gardens at Copenhagen remain perhaps the most charming amusement center in the world. Even the United States was affected. During the twenties and early thirties of this century many of the motion picture theater buildings in the United States were named the Tivoli, probably in deference to the reputation of the Danish gardens as a center of entertainment.

The fame of the small mountain town of Tivoli, which was a favorite summer retreat for the ancient Romans and the Renaissance Italians, therefore, lives on as a name signifying pleasure. It was then and remains now the pleasure of cooling water in quiet reflecting pools and splashing fountains, water which inundates all the senses giving relief from the oppressive heat and turmoil of the city.

APPENDICES

APPENDIX A

PARISIAN DESCRIPTION OF THE GARDENS

Paris, Bibliothèque Nationale, cod. Ital. 1179, ff. 247r-266v.

Bibliography:

- A. Marsand, *I manoscritti italiani della regia biblioteca parigina*, II, Paris, 1838, pp. 111-112, no. 788 (formerly Saint-Germain 1466).
- G. Mazzatinti, *Inventario dei manoscritti italiani delle biblioteche di Francia*, I, Rome, 1886, p. 204, no. 1179.

Introduction:

Although Dupérac's engraving of 1573 is dedicated to the French queen Catherine de' Medici, Dupérac claims in the legend below the engraving that it was prepared from the drawing which he made for the Emperor Maximilian II. In the funeral oration which Ercole Cato gave at the burial of the Cardinal of Ferrara in December 1572 (E. Cato, *Oratione fatta dal Cavaliere Hercole Cato nelle essequie dell'Illustriss. et Reuerendiss. Sig. D. Hippolito d'Este Card. di Ferrara, celebrate nelle Città di Tiuoli*, Ferrara, 1587, p. 11), he recalls that both the Emperor Maximilian and the Queen of France were so "enamoured by the fame of the beauty and fascination [of the gardens at Tivoli] that they wished to have them depicted." There is other evidence preserved of the interest of these rulers. In libraries at Paris (Bibliothèque Nationale, cod. Ital. 1179, ff. 247r-266v) and Vienna (Nationalbibliothek, cod. 6750, ff. 449r-461v) are identical manuscript copies, made at a later date, of an anonymous description of the Tiburtine gardens. There is also a fragment of this same description in the Biblioteca Estense at Modena (Campori MS γ.G.2.3), beginning with no. 20 in the description and ending with no. 63 (see L. Lodi, ed., *Catalogo dei codici e degli autografi posseduti dal Marchese Giuseppe Campori*, pt. III, Modena, n.d., p. 233, no. 457). The Parisian and Viennese manuscripts must be copies of descriptions sent to the courts of Paris and Vienna to explain the drawings picturing the gardens. In fact, the description at least twice affirms that it is to accompany a depiction of the gardens. In the introduction it is mentioned that the alphabetical and numerical designations under which the fountains and points of interest in the gardens are listed are used to "show their position in the present depiction" (see below, p. 143). Also when the two rustic fountains of Bacchus in front of the Oval Fountain are described, the manuscripts state that "the painting has not been able to represent" these fountains (see below p. 147), and this is true in the Dupérac engraving, since the Bacchic fountains are hidden by the wall around the Oval Fountain. That these descriptions were written to accompany the drawings made for the foreign rulers is further indicated in the introduction which specifies that Tivoli is fifteen *Italian* miles from Rome, a qualification of the type of measurement which would not be necessary for an Italian reader.

The original descriptions, therefore, must have been written about 1571, and this date agrees in general with the remark in the descriptions that the Water Organ was still incomplete owing to the death of its inventor (see below p. 145). In the accounts of payment for the Water Organ the French fountain expert, called in the records "Lucha Clericho," was paid for work through November 1568, when his name disappeared from the accounts, probably because of his death. However, the history of these manuscripts is not quite so simple. The descriptions depict the gardens and fountains as totally completed with the above exception of the Water Organ, but this does not agree at all with later descriptions and the building accounts. As in Dupérac's engraving, many of the features of the gardens, such as the four fish pools and the Fountain of Neptune, which have never been created, are described as if extant. Therefore, these descriptions represent in part a project or plan of how the gardens and fountains were to look. There is likewise one small, puzzling detail in the description of the statue of Rome seated in the center of the Fountain of Rome. Both manuscripts claim that this personification has a statuette of "winged victory in her hand" (see below p. 148), yet the present statue of Rome has a lance in her right hand. The contract which the sculptor Pierre de la Motte signed in August 1568 relates that he will carve the statue in accordance with a drawing by Pirro Ligorio "save that in place of that statuette which said Rome has in her hand in accordance with the drawing, I intend to make a sword or lance" (F. S. Seni, *La Villa d'Este in Tivoli*, Rome, 1902, p. 66, note 1 on p. 69). Thus, the manuscript sent to the foreign courts still contained a detail of the original project for the gardens which was changed in actuality, presumably sometime before the manuscripts were written. This suggests very strongly that there must have been another earlier account of the gardens composed as a project or plan for the gardens and written before August 1568. If such a written project ever existed, it is possible that its author was Pirro Ligorio. M. Giustiniani (*De Vescovi e de' governatori di Tivoli*, Rome, 1665, p. 154 and note 210) lists as descriptions of the Villa d'Este, in addition to those by Foglietta and Del Re, one by Pirro Ligorio which was then extant as a manuscript, volume 254, in the Barberini Library. Giustiniani seems tantalizingly explicit in listing such a description with those of Foglietta and Del Re, but he may have been misled by an old catalogue of the Barberini Collection. The seventeenth century catalogue by Carlo Morone (MS Barb. Lat. 3159, Vatican Library) claims on fol. 268r that Barberini MS 2959 was in part a "Descrittione della Villa Tiburtina Estense di Pyrro Ligorio." This is repeated in Manzi's manuscript catalogue of 1817-1820 (MS Barb. Lat. 3107, Vatican Library). The old Barberini MS 2959, which is now Barb. Lat. 4310, no longer contains any writing by Ligorio, but, according to a note in front of the manuscript, it was rebound in 1832, presumably leaving out Ligorio's writing. The missing portion is probably in the present MS Barb. Lat. 5219, ff. 127-147, entitled "Descrittione della superba et magnificentissima Villa Tiburtina Hadriana di M Pirro Ligorio dicata all'Ill.mo et R.mo Sig.re Hippolito Card.le di Ferrara."

Text:

Descrittione di Tiuoli, et del Giardino dell'Ill.mo Cardinal di Ferrara, con le dichiar.ni delle statue antiche et moderne, et d'altri belli, et marauigliosi artificij, che ui sono, con l'ordine come si trouano disposti.

Tiuoli antichissima città del Latio già gratissimo ridotto degli antichi Imperatori, é posta nei primi Colli, che da man destra uerso Leuante chiudono le pianure dell' Territorio Romano, è celebratissima per la bontà dell'aere, il quale oltre che per la lontananza dalle palude et per la rileuatura del sito é netto d'ogni cattiuo [f. 247r] uapore é anco continuamente purgato dai venti di settentrione et di Ponente; ha il paese fertilissimo et molto ricco d'oliui, et de viti, che uestono con quasi perpetua uerdura le piaggie del colle, et gran parte della uicina pianura, riceue dentro il famoso Aniene, il quale entrando per le cauerne del Monte, con diuersi rami si scuopre poi all'improuiso i canali et i fonti in diuersi luoghi della città à commodo, et diletto degli habitatori. Hà un prospetto bellissimo uerso la Città di Roma la quale guarda nel basso quasi à dritta linea per Ponente garbino lungi xv miglia Italiane con molti Castelli, che sono sparsi per quelle [f. 247v] campagne. È illustre per infinite uestigie di nobilissimi antichi edificij; Et benche per l'ingiuria del tempo, et per le continue calamità d'Italia habbia perduto l'antica faccia, et magnificenza, è non dimeno assai commoda d'habitatione. Ha di circuito piú di due miglia et mezo, cominciando con un braccio per la salita del Colle, allarga il suo corpo su la schiene di quella. Tra questo braccio et le muraglie della Città uerso Roma, si rinchiude un gran uacuo, il quale pochi a'ni sono era pieno di dirupe di sassi, et di macchie, ma hora dadue lati contigui é rileuato talmente, che fà una dolcissima collina, alle radice [f. 248r] della quale s'allarga unpiano in quadro di grandezza di piú di . . . [sic] passi per diametro ridotta in questa forma per ordine dell Ill.mo et Rmo sig.r Don Hippolito da Este Cardinal di Ferrara, il quale hauendo fatto stirpare le macchie, romper' i gran sassi, et agguagliar' i dirupi, et condottoui un grosso ramo del fiume hauendo fatto forare con grand.ma fatica et spesa il Monte passando sotto la Città hà fabricato le sua famosissima villa, et Giardino Estense con rarissima, et singolare magnificenza, i compartimenti le fabriche, i cenacoli, le statue, et altre infenite marauiglie, lequali sono notate ad alfabeto, et numeri, che mostrano [f. 248v] il lor sito nel presente ritratto.

A. Porta principale del giardino ornata di quattro colonne con statue antiche, et con le arme del Cardinal sostenuta da due fanciulli.

B. Cerchiata coperta di bellissime uerdure, la quale serue come per uestibolo fuor del riquadramento del giardino lungo circa 60 passi.

C. Muraglia che chiude tutta la larghezza del giardino, il qual muro è tutto coperto d'una spalliera di Cedri.

D. Viale di mezzo intersecato da xiij viali, che attrauersano tutto il giardino; da una muraglia all'altra é accompagnato da otto altri viali per la med.ma dirittura di quel di mezzo, i quali tutti hanno i suoi rincontri [f. 249r], ò di fonte, ò di statue, ò di altra simil cosa, che rappresenta bellissima uista.

E. Crociata di Pergole coperte di uerdura con li suoi portoni.

F. Cuppola, ó Padiglione di cerchiate coperte di uerdura, nella cima del quale si ueggono tre Aquile, che tengono un giglio.

G. Partimento di xij quadri ben destinto con arbori fruttiferi circundati di spalliere di uerdura.

H. Laberinthi fatti di legname, et piantati per ogni cantone di uarie sorti d'Arbori, il primo de Haranci con spalliere di Mortella; il secondo di cerase marine con spalliere di Madre selua; il terzo di Pini con le spalliere [f. 249v] di Lentaggine; il quarto d'Abbeti con le spalliere di fior fiorella.

I. Boschi, che occupano sino alle muraglie l'uno della Terra, l'altro del Giardino.

K. Luoghi sotterranei, ò vogliamo dir Grotte dedicate alle sibille per honorar massimamente la Sibilla Tiburtina; il n.ro delle grotte sono ix, con le statue antiche delle sibille per ciascuna grotta ornata di uarie Pitture, et cose Marine.

L. Sesto viale trasuersale, il quale finisce tutto il piano del Giardino, et da principio al resto, ch'è in spiaggia.

M. Boschi di uarie sorti d'Alberi posti in spiaggia, tra l'una scala et l'altra.

N. Settimo viale chiamato della fontana della Ciuetta più lungo et più largo de tutti gli altri, et dal quale si puo [f. 250r] uscire del Giardino nella terra.

O. Ottauo viale, che interseca le scale per mezzo con alcun' altre uie trasuersali, che fanno la spiaggia più commoda à caminarui sopra, et seruono àueder piú distintamente ogni cosa.

P. Nono viale, piú ricco, piú bello, et piú grato di tutti gli altri per la gratissima uista che rendono innumerabili capi d'acqua che ui sono, et per esser tra le due piú belle et ricche cioé principali fontane del Giardino.

Q. Bosco de lauri direto al Monte dell' fontana di Tiuoli ben compartito, che serue per uestibolo del riquadramento del Giardino.

R. Alcune uie sotterranee, et fresche [f. 250v] non percosse mai dal sole, che conducono dal fonte al Caual Pegaseo, et sono tanto commode et spatiose, che capeno un' huomo à Cauallo.

S. Piazza della fontana di Tiuoli circondata di muro, nella quale sono piantati dieci Platani.

T. Muro che circonda la piazza ornato tutto di spalliere d'Haranci, et di Cedri.

V. Grotta che fà facciata di fuori con un bel portone con colonne et finestre per allumar due Camere, che sono al pari, questa é dedicata al piacer uoluttuoso et é ornata insieme con le due stanze congiunte oltre alla fonte, delle quali si fà mentione al suo luogo di molte statue antiche di Pitture é tauole di marmo commesse [f. 251r] di uarie sorti di pietre con alcuni lettisterni d'estate per riposaruisi il giorno.

X. Decimo viale soprastante alli tre Acquedotti.

Y. Vie trasuersali per render la spiaggia piú commoda à salire et scendere, le quali sono diuise dall'undecimo viale.

Z. Duodecimo viale, che per esser piú lunghi et piú coperti di boscaglia, et di spalliere et per rispetto dell'altezza del muro, et altri ornamenti, che ui sono, é anco il piú frequentato, et percio è chiamato il viale del Cardinale, et é tanto lungo quanto è largo il Giardino, che sono circa 300 passi [f. 251v].

a. Muro tutto coperto di spalliere di Melagranate.

b. Piantata d'Albori Olmi per render tuttauia più il viale difeso dal sole.

c. Grotta che per mezo de grossi Pilastri con le sue uolte sostiene il terreno dell'ultimo uiale sotto il Palazzo assai grande, et fresche sebene non tanto come quella della Venere per essere il luogo più alto et più scoperto et come quella é dedicata all'appetito, et al piacere uoluttuoso, cosi questa é dedicata al piacer honesto et alla Castità.

d. Scale di Treuertino con quattro nicchi due grandi, et due piccoli per salire all'ultimo uiale.

e. Terzodecimo uiale sotto il Palazzo [f. 252r] grande tanto che ui si potrebbe giostrare.

[f.] Parapetto del terzodecimo uiale pieno de uasi di uerdura.

g. Scala del Palazzo tutta di Pietra di Treuertino, che fà per di fuori tre loggie due coperte, et una scoperta di rara bellezza.

h. Loggia scoperta, et pauimentata in faccia di tutto il Palazzo, che serue per poggio per guardar nel giardino.

i. Loggia con unportone da riguardar fuori del giardino risponde al cenacolo uerso Roma.

k. Giardino secreto al primo piano delle stanze sopra la scala tutto circondato di muro con spalliere di cedri granati e rododafani, et è fatto appartamenti [f. 252v] di semplici.

l. Padiglione ò Cuppula coperta tutta di uerdura nella cui Cima sono tre Aquile che tengono un giglio.

m. Giuogo di Palla grande et scoperto al modo di Francia.

1. Due fontane di sassi rustichi poste l'una per banda nel mezo del giardino.

2. Quattro fontane nelli quattro canti di questo Padiglione fatte in forma de gigli grandi.

3. Quattro belle et grande Peschiere, due delle quali come si uede sono aperte, l'altre coperte con pauimenti.

4. Mete sudanti lequali gettano acqua dalla Cima al basso.

5. Canali di Poste intorno al muro delle [f. 253r] Peschiere prime come per finimento le quali gettano acqua.

6. Ponte nel mezo delle due Peschiere coperto, artificiosamente fatto, per far cadere nel'acqua senza pericolo.

7. Fontana grande, che rappresenta il Mare come quella che raccoglie in se tutte l'acque del giardino con molti ornamenti di marmo, et di treuertino Nicchi et statue.

8. Statua di Nettunno col tridente su un Carro tirato da quattro Caualli marini i quali gettano acqua.

9. Cascata che fà tutta l'acqua della Fontana del mare, ò di Nettunno fuor della Città per certe spiaggie raccolta ad uso d'alcuni Viuiai da Pesce, et altri animali acquatici [f. 253v].

10. Fontana del diluuio cosi chiamata per infiniti capi d'acqua, che n'escono con mirabile impeto; in essa si doueuano rappresentarele uoci de molti animali et suoni di quasi tutti gl'istrumenti cosi bellici, come musici, ma resta imperfetta per la morte dell'Artifice inuentore.

11. Le statue, che seruono per inuentione, et ornamento della detta fontana sono la Dea della Natura nel mezo, con Apollo, et Diana dalle bande che gettano acqua, et quattro gran termini fuori per colonne et due Fame, che tengono l'arme del Car.^{le} conl'Aquila in cima.

12. Scale per salir piu commodamente la [f. 254r] spiaggia fatte à cordoni di treuertino ample con iparapetti dalle bande et con isuoi vasi, et vaschette, che gettano acqua l'una nell'altra.

13. Altre scale della med.^{ma} bellezza, et inuentione, quanto al gettar dell'acqua ma per la maggior ripidezza fatte agradi, delle quali quella che é posta nel mezo rinchiude in se una bellissima Fontana di forma ouata.

14. Fontana del Dragone cosi detta per che rappresenta il famoso Dragone, che custodiua l'Orto dell'Esperidi; questo Dragone come si fauoleggia dell'antico hà cento teste, et per ciascuna bocca getta acqua dentro à una gran Peschiera [f. 254v].

15. Le statue, che accompagnano la detta Fontana sono prima un'Hercole di forma colossa conlasua mazza in mano, il quale stà in un Nicchio nel mezo come Protettore dell'Aquila, che uccide il Dragone, alludendo cosi all'impresa del Cardinale, la quale è un'Aquila con un ramo del pomo dell'Esperide et il motto dice ab insomni non custodita dracone, doppo l'Hercole nell'entrata sopra due posamenti sono due statue de gladiatori come custodi della fonte, et alli fianchi del nicchio di mezo doue é l'Hercole sono due altre statue di Dei armigeri quasi per dar' animo et aiuto all'Aquila, l'uno d'essi è Marte [f. 255r] l'altro è Perseo.

16. Fontana della Ciuetta cosí chiamata perche inessa, é una Ciuetta con molti vcelli, i quali mentre si uersa l'acqua rappresenta naturaliss.^{te} le uoci de Rosignuoli, Cardellini, Fanelli, et altre sorti d'vcelli, et l'inuentione è tale, che scoprendosi acerti tempi la Ciuetta gli vcelli come per paura tacciono, ma non si tosto la Ciuetta si è dilungata unpoco, che gli vcelli tornano alloro canto; gli vcelli et la Ciuetta sono di rame colorato, et fanno il canto et il moto per la forza dell'acqua mentre si uersa.

17. Le statue della detta Fontana, la quale é tutta fatta di musaico rustico [f. 255v] di uarie sorte di pietre, sono alcuni satiri, che sostengono un vaso, nel quale certi Fauni uersano acqua da un'Otre che tengono nelle mani.

18. Piazza recinta di muraglia, che serue per cenacolo con nicchi intorno, et statue che rappresentano le feste baccanali.

19. Fontana degl'Imperatori cosi detta perche nel suo Cenacolo ornato tutto di Nicchi et sedili di marmo sono quattro statue d'Imperatori antichi cioé Cesare Aug.^{to} Traiano et Adriano, ciascuno de quali fabricó superbissime Ville nel Territorio Tiburtino, si come appare dalle uestigie, che ue nesono fin'al di d'hoggi.

20. Le statue di dentro sono un'Aretusa [f. 256r] getta acqua nel mezo del fonte, et dalle bande due Ninfe, che gettano acqua anch'esse in un gran uaso, la Fonte dentro é rustica composta di tartari, ma gli ornamenti di fuori sono di musaico et stucco, et in anzi ad essa sono quattro gran colonne di musaico gentile ritorte come q^elle del Tempio di Salamone.

21. Due scale di teuortino per montare, et scendere essendo fabricata la fonte nel mezo della spiaggia.

22. Fontana di Tiuoli principalissima di tutte le fontane di questo giardino, et forse di tutta Italia, cosí chiamata per che rappresenta il monte et ifiumi del Paese di Tiuoli; per far questa Fontana é conuenuto [f. 256v] forare una Montagna intiera da un Capo all'altro della Città, et per uia d'un acquedotto largo sei, et alto 20. palmi s'è tirato un ramo del Fiume Aniene, che passa dall'altra parte dentro nel Giardino, il qual ramo arriuato ai piedi del Monte si diuide intre parti alseruitio di questa fontana nel modo, che si potra comprendere da ciascuna parte, che s'andera discriuendo.

23. Monte fatto detartari naturalissimo é molto alto tutto coperto di uarie sorte dipiante di uerdura, che secondo itempi rende gratissima uista, et son mantenute le statue dall'acque, che di continuo piouono dalla montagna med.^{ma} [f. 257r].

24. Grotte ò Cauerne nel Monte ciascuna delle quali hà una statua di Teuertino moderna grande come colosso, che rappresentano itre fiumi del Territorio Tiburtino, cioé l'Aniene hoggi detto Teuerone Albuneo, et Erculaneo, stando l'Albunea come quella, ch'é stimata la sibilla di Tiuoli nel mezo àsedere et gli altri due dalle bande à giacere.

25. Vasi grandi nei quali l'acqua già detta diuisa in treparti fa la prima cascata uscendo come mandata da quelli tre Fiumi.

26. Corritore scoperto, che circonda tutta la Montagna difuori, et uiene à fare unbellissimo Teatro, dal quale si uede commodissimamente la Mo'tagna [f. 257v], i Fiumi le cascate, che fa tutta l'acqua il cui mezo ètutto pieno d'inganni dabagnare per piacere chi su si posa.

27. Canaletto che gira intorno il corritore nel quale si uiene tutta l'acqua che sopra-bondando casca dalli tre vasi delli Fiumi, et s'unisce nel mezo del sudetto corritore dalla banda di fuori doue riempie un'altro vaso del quale si dirà poco appresso.

28. Grotticelle poste alle radici del Monte trà u'fiume et l'altro, doue sono diuersi animali, che gettano acqua con inuentioni bellissime, et rappresentano nelle Pioggie Padiglioni uentagli becchierie, bollori, gigli, et altre simili cose.

29. Parapetto del corritore fatto di balaustri [f. 258r] di Teuertino, et per ogni spatio di tre balaustri é un uaso donde esce unbello bollor d'acqua si come ancora escono per tutti li cantoni delli balaustri d'alcune tazze di marmo.

30. Vaso alto circa palmi 40. et largo di bocca piú di 60. nella circonferenza fatto di musaico, nel quale riducendosi tutte l'acque delli tre Fiumi condotte nel Canaletto, che circonda il corritore esso la sparge poi come un uelo per l'Orificio della bocca, il che riesce marauiglioso alla uista.

[31.] Scoglietto posto nel mezo del detto vaso dal quale sorge unbel bollor d'acqua che con artificio fá un bellissimo giglio proportionato alla grandessa [f. 258v] del vaso, alle cui radici sono due gra Delfini di pietra, iquali essi ancora gettano accqua dalla bocca.

32. Vaso ouato molto grande, nel quale con mirabil caduta si riuersa tutta l'acqua del vaso sopradetto, ornato tutto negli orli del parapetto di teuertino, et nella facciata di quadretti inuetriati di diuersi colori, ne i quali sono desegnati Aquile et gigli.

33. Dieci Pilastri che sostengono il corritor di sopra scoperto dietro alli quali nasce un' altro corritore ò uogliam dire loggia coperta con li suoi Archi, che rispondono nella piazza dei Platani; la qual loggia oltre ch'é fatta come i Pilastri stessi di stucco et musaico, che rappresenta cose [f. 259r] maritime hà la uista di tutta l'acqua che casca dal uaso grande, et ui sono giuochi d'acqua bellissimi, et inganni dabagnar, et pigliarsi piacere.

34. Dieci statue poste in dieci Nicchi tra li gia detti Pilastri, che rappresentano dieci Ninfe quasi di grandezza naturale con li suoi vasi, che tutti gettano acqua in copia nell' ouato.

35. Due scale di teuertino, le quali dai capi del corritore disopra conducono al piano della piazza.

36. Caual Pegaseo posto nel mezo del Boschetto dei lauri dietro la Montagna di Tiuoli, il quale ad imitatione del fauoloso fà scaturir perpetuamente.

37. Due Fontane rustiche nei canti del muro della piazza infaccia dell'ouato [f. 259v], le quali non hà potuto esprimer la pittura, i cui ornamenti sono due bacchi maggiori del naturale, che gettano acqua da due vasi, et nel gettarla fanno due bellissime ueli.

38. Fontana della Grotta ornata, di bellissime statue di marmo antiche, trà le quali é una Venere, per esser la grotta come si disse dedicata al piacere, maggior del naturale, et ai piedi di essa sono due fanciulli, che fanno gettar acqua per bocca da due Cigni sopra li quali siedono, et intorno ui si ueddono quattro Amorini et altre tante Ninfe marine, che tutti gettano acqua in un laghetto in capo alla grotta, che rende grattissima uista [f. 260r].

39. Quattro ordini di muraglia, che fanno tre acquedotti scoperti distinti l'uno dall'altro palmi cinque; et perche si parlerà di ciascuno in particolare, quiui solo basti disapere, ch'essendosi per la fontana di Tiuoli rappresentato il Monte et ifiumi di quelpaese, hora con questi acquedotti si dimostra il camino, che fanno uerso Roma unitamente, doue poi raccolti dal Teuere come nella Fontana della Roma si uedrà se ne uanno di compagnia al Mare figurato perla fontana di Nettunno, di cui s'é detto disopra, doue si raccogliono tutte l'acque del Giardino.

40. Primo acquedotto piú alto degli altri due, hà 23 barchette di pietra, et [f. 260v] ciascuna barchetta hà la sua Anten'a di mezo, della quale esce un grande et bel bollore, lacui acqua casca in dette barchette, et doppó per certi fori ornati di mascare acquatili si spende gentilmente sopra l'orlo del muro disopra nel quale sono posate le barchette in modo che proprio par che nuotino, et dilà finalmente si uersa tutta insieme nel secondo acquedotto piu basso, facendo nel cascare un effetto mirabile, perche ui sono accommodati certi grondali sopra li quali passando l'acqua rappresenta una gagliardissima pioggia quando casca dalli tetti facendo infiniti ueli gorgoli d'acqua che di lettano incredibilmente [f. 261r].

41. Secondo acquedotto, che per uariare getta l'acqua nel terzo acquedotto da molte cannelle, lequali nonsono in cima al muro, ma unpalmo sotto, et fan'o diuerse forme nel gettare l'acqua fuori, perche ciascuna hà il suo ornamento de mascaroni d'animali acquatici di rosoni, et altre simile fantasie.

42. Terzo acquedotto, il quale per esser piú basso degli altri et uicino al Viale nonhà altro, che il suo Fiumicello che corre scoperto, ma ornata nella suafacciata di quadretti inuidriati.

43. Fontana della Roma cosi detta, per che rappresenta Roma nell'antico esser suo, questa come non é men bella cosa é maggiore ò piú larga [f. 261v] infacciata circa 20. passi che in uece del Monte artificioso hà la uista del monte naturale fuori della Città di Tiuoli piantato di spessissimi, et sempre uerdi oliui, é di tutta la campagna che scuopre fino alla uera Roma.

44. Sette parti della Fontana che rappresentano isetti Colli di Roma ciascuno de quali acció che possa essere distintamente conosciuto hà un Tempio sopra il piú celebre, che dagli antichi ui fosse fabricato come per essempio sul monte palatino il Tempio di Apollo, il quale fù celebratissimo dagli antichi, et ciascun Tempio hà la sua statua in anzi di marmo per la quale si uiene in facile cognitione [f. 262r] di chi fusse quel Tempio, et nel resto poi delli colli ui sono rappresentate tutte le maggiori fabriche, et piu notabili di quel tempo come l'Anfiteatro di Vespasiano il Pantheon, il Campidoglio, le colonne Traiane et Antoniane, la Naumacchia i Cerchi gl'Hippodromi, il Corritor di Caligola, le Piramile, il Mausoleo, la Mole d'Adriano, et infinite altre cose.

[45.] Congiungimento d'un Colle con l'altro per il quale si rappresentano le porte gli Archi trionfali, et gli Acquedotti antichi, et questi massime sono rappresentati con tanta arte, che ad mitatione degli acquedotti di Claudio per esser ipiú famosi seruono quasi à tutta la Roma doue sono parimenti [f. 262v] i suoi Castelli d'acqua et per ogni castello Fontane, che gettano perpetuam.^{te}

46. Piazza bella et spatiosa, che serue per cenacolo della fonte, nella quale in certi luoghi, che non impediscono sono alcune Fontane famose come il Lago Curtio, l'Ippodromo di Domitiano et alcune Mete sudanti, che gettano acqua in anzi l'Anfiteatro, la Naumachia di Nerone, et il fonte.

47. Statua di Roma trionfante nel mezo d^ella Piazza maggiore del naturale che hà sotto ipiedi lespoglie barbare et i trofei di tante uittorie riceuute conla uittoria alata in mano et la ghirlanda da coronare i uincitori.

[48.] Statua colossa, che rappresenta il Teuere famosiss.° Fiume di Roma la cui acqua [f. 263r] ad imitatione del uero Teuere uà irrigando leradici del Colle, et scorrendo q^asi per tutta Roma come quello ch'entra per la flaminia, et esce per la porta trigemina.

49. Isola, che si uede nel mezo del Teuere trale sudette due Porte, chiamato hoggi di San Bart.° con due Ponti per passare ilfiume, et due altri ipiú famosi appresso cioé il trionfale et l'Elio uolgarm.^{te} detto di Sant'Angelo.

50. Muraglia fatta ad uso d'un belliss.° corritore drieto la Roma, onde si rappresenta il pomerio, ch'era lospatio trale mura della Città, et iterreni departicolari.

51. Nicchio grande corrispondente alla fontana del Dragone dabasso, nel q^ale é posto un'Hercole d'età senile à giacere di forma golossa di marmo antico et molto bello, et questo si posa sopra tutte le spoglie et trofe; et [f. 263v] há la sua Claua et pelle del leone sotto il capo, il nicchio poi ètutto depinto di cose che rappresentano le forze del med.^{mo} Hercole.

52. Due fontane n^elli due capi del uiale di materia rustica gli ornamenti delle quali sono due statue colosse, che gettano acqua.

53. Tre gran nicchi senza frontespicio co' tre statue antiche maggiori del naturale et molto b^elle, due delle quali sono di pietra nera, l'altra é di marmo bianchiss.° et stan'o tutte tre àsedere con decoro conueniente à tal imagini, essendo l'una, cioé q^ella di mezo del sapentiss.° filosofo Socrate, l'altra Solone, et la terza licurgo due grand.^{mi} legislatori.

54. Pie distallo grande, sopra il q^ale è collocata una statua colossa antica di marmo che rappresenta il med.^{mo} Hercole, et hà unfanciullo in braccio auuolto nella pelle del lione et una [f. 264r] ceruia appresso in'anzi ai piedi, et perche alcuni fauoleggiano che q^el fanci-

ullo fusse Achille nodrito delatte della Cerua, et fattato per esser' stato inuolto nella pelle del leone per questo esse'dosi di mostrato con le due prime statue la fatica doue uccide il dracone, et il riposo doue giace sopra le sue spoglie, quiui si dimostra l'im'ortalità per ragione della quale fú adorato dagli huomini per Dio.

55. In questa grotta, la q^ale s'é detto esser dedicata al piacer honesto et alla castità fatta di tre Nicchi gra'di uno in faccia, et due dalle bande, benche q^ello, che riguarda uerso Roma sia sfo'dato per dar aria alla grotta sono due fontane una dedicata a Diana Dea d^ella castitá l'altra a Hippolito giouane castiss°; il q^ale uolse piú presto patir la morte, che co'sentire al furor di Fedra sua madrigna; nello spatio, che resta [f. 264v] tra li due nicchi d^elli fianchi all'entrata del Portone sono due altre statue sopra due posamenti, l'una di Pantasilea Regina dell Amazone, l'altra di Lucretia Romana tutte quattro statue antiche belliss.^e maggiori del naturale per di dentro cosi le fontane come lauolta et tutte le parti col pauime'to é lastricata d'un musaico minutiss.° di petre finiss.^e come profidi, serpe'tini alabastri et marmi.

56. Loggetta di Pilastri co' parapetto et balaustri di teuertino dipianta tutta di musaico, et stucco messa à oro, nella q^ale de'tro a'un sfondato, che fà un nicchio grande infaccia con dui piccoli alle bande è una bella fontana di musaico minuto di prete finiss.^e et quiui é posta la statua d'una Pa'dora maggior del naturale antica et molto bella, che possa sopra un scoglio, et tiene in mano un uaso, dal q^al'esce un bel becchier d'acqua, sotto lo scoglio é un Dracone che dalla bocca getta acqua in u' gran uaso, et fa u' belliss° uelo, due altri belli bollori sorgono dadue uasi [f. 265r] fatti informa di fiorini quiui posti sopra due gran finestre, nelli due nicchi piccoli che sono dalle ba'de della Pandora sono due statue di Pallade antiche assai belle dal naturale.

57. Due nicchi grandi, et due piccoli posti al pié d^elle scale, nelli gra'di sono due statue colosse à giacere, l'una d'huomo l'altra di don'a, che gettan' acqua in dui belli uasi di marmo, nelli piccioli sono due altre statue minori cioé una Eternità et una Cibile.

58. Due fo'tane ne capi del uiale con due statue colosse d'Esculapio et d'Igia sua figliuola.

59. Canacolo di muraglia conli conci di Teuertino co' due nicchi per di fuori, et due fauni di naturale.

60. Fontana il cui ornam^to sono tre Monstri marini, che gettano acqua in un bel uaso di marmo antico.

61. Fontana d^ella Leda posta disotto la p.^a loggia coperta dalla scala, cosi chiamata perche la sua statua principale è una leda col Cigno che getta acqua per un uaso, nella detta sono quattro altre statue in 4 nicchi, due dentro, edue difuori [f. 265v] le prime sono Helena et Clitenestra, le seconde Castor et Polluce, tutte quattro figliuoli di Gioue et di Leda.

62. Pie di stalli grandi di quà et di là al montar d^ella scala, sopra li q^ali sono le statue d'Hercole, et d'Acchille antiche mag.^ri del naturale, che serueno come per custodia del Palazzo.

63. Seconda loggia co'punta ornata di stucco pitture et oro co' unbel uaso di mischio configurine, che gettano acqua, da questa loggia s'entra in una sala della q^ale come che non sia intione diparlar del Palazzo s'é peró giudicato bene dirare alcuna mentione perhauer' essa ancora due Fontane belliss.^e l'una in faccia della sala, l'altra in un corritor di rimpetto à una finestra, cherisponde all loggia già detta; la p.^a è tutta composta di musaico minutiss.° di pietre finiss.^e con molte co'chiglie radici di coralli, et altre cose marine, et hà la statua d'un fauno antica belliss.^a, il q^ale dauna zampogna ò fistola getta acqua per sette can'elle, l'altra é fatta parim.^ti di musaico gentiliss.° con la statua d'una Ninfa, che getta acqua daun uaso; et [f. 266r] appresso questa pur nel med.^mo corritore ui è un'altra fo'tana

quasi del med.ᵐᵒ lauoro si come a'co nel Cortil maggiore del Palazzo sene uede una assai gra'de di stucco indorata con una Venere mag.ʳ del naturale, che dorme et getta acqua per un uaso.

64. Fontana nel giardino secreto tutta rustica il cui ornam.ᵗᵒ è una Venere che dorme sopra unscoglio et getta acqua, il qᵃl è cauernoso, et pieno di grotte, doue sono animali, che sono andati àber di quelle acque cioé un capriolo un lebre, un orso et una Capra seluatica.

65. Per ogni canto di questo Padiglione é una Fontana picciola àguisa di scoglio di cose marine uaghiss.ᵉ nella uista, et nel mezo un'inganno d'acqua, et uno ue n'hà parimenti per ciascun partim.ᵗᵒ del Giardino [f. 266v].

APPENDIX B

TEXT OF THE LIGORIO MANUSCRIPT, MORGAN LIBRARY

New York City, Pierpont Morgan Library, MS M.A. 542: White paper, 19 folios, 325 x 222 mm.

Owned previously by Francesco Villamena, as indicated by the later title page, and much later by G. Cavalieri of Ferrara (sales catalogue, Florence, 1908).

On folios 10 through 18 is damage consisting of a hole worn through the lower center of each folio, which is now repaired.

Bibliography:

Ricci, S. de and Wilson, W. J., *Census of Medieval and Renaissance Manuscripts in the United States and Canada*, II, New York, 1937, p. 1436, No. 376.

Copies:

1. France, Paris, Bibliothèque de l'Arsenal, MS Ital. 8529: White paper, 20 folios, 301 x 213 mm.

Seventeenth century copy of the New York manuscript. This is proven by the fact that the title page added to the New York manuscript, which relates that the manuscript was in the collection of Francesco Villamena, is written in the same hand which copied all the rest of the manuscript. The drawings in the Paris copy are very close to the New York original but are on separate pieces of paper pasted into the Paris version. At the end of the Parisian manuscript is also included a copy of Ligorio's manuscript on the Villa Adriana at Tivoli.

This manuscript formerly belonged to the Gaignat (no. 2349) and De Pauling Collections.

Bibliography:

Mariette, P. J., *Abecedario de P. J. Mariette*, ed. by P. de Chennevières and A. de Montaiglon, III, Paris, 1854-1856, pp. 201-202.

Marsand, A., *I manoscritti italiani della regia biblioteca Parigina*, II, Paris, 1838, pp. 270-272, no. 24.

Martin, H., *Catalogue des manuscrits de la bibliothèque de l'Arsenal*, VI, Paris, 1892, pp. 476-477, no. 8529.

Mazzatinti, G., *Inventario dei manoscritti italiani delle biblioteche di Francia*, III, Rome, 1888, p. 133, no. 24.

Métral, D., *Blaise de Vigenère*, Paris, 1939, p. 197 n. 2.

Nolhac, P. de, "Notes sur Pirro Ligorio," *Mélanges Renier* (Bibliothèque de l'école des hautes études 73), Paris, 1887, p. 325 n. 1.

Pacifici, V., *Ippolito II d'Este*, Tivoli, [1920], p. 395.

Venturi, A., *Storia dell'arte italiana*, IX, pt. 5, Milan, 1932, p. 781 n. 1.

2. Italy, Modena, Biblioteca Estense, Campori γ.S.4.48: White paper, 19 folios, 328 x 224 mm.

Another copy of the New York manuscript probably executed in the seventeenth century. Like the Parisian copy the title page which says the manuscript belonged to the collection of Francesco Villamena is in the same hand as all the manuscript itself. Unlike the Parisian copy this version has no illustrations but simply gaps left in the text intended for the later addition of drawings.

A note written on the verso of the flyleaf says that this manuscript was acquired at the sale of the collection of books of art of F. V[illot] at Paris in 1870.

Bibliography:

Vandini, R., *Appendice seconda al catalogo dei codici e manoscritti posseduti dal Marchese Giuseppe Campori*, Modena, 1894, p. 641, no. 2200.

The title page reproduced below is not autographic but added later in what is probably a seventeenth century hand:

Vita di Virbio
detto altrimente
Hippolito figlio di Theseo
Descritta e dissegnata
Con immitatione del'Antico
In sedici historie
Da Pirro Ligorio Antiquario famoso
Di sua propria mano
Per seruitio del Card. d'Este Il Vecchio
Che voleua farne fare vna tapezzeria d'Arazzi

S'hebbe dallo studio delle cose vecchie
che haueua raccolto in Roma
Francesco Villamena.

The text which follows is in Ligorio's own hand:

Illmo et R:^{mo} S:^{or} et Padrone mio oss:^{mo}

Se hò tardato à mandarle il schizzo dela uita di Hippolyto, figliuolo di Theseo, quella mi perdoni, per ció che nel uero, éstato parte per la debolezza dela mano, parte per cercare le cose che di lui si scriuono; et per poterne fare il giuditio secondo le materie che dicono, Pausania, Ouidio, seneca, et glialtri ne la tragedia di Phedra: et parte anchora per altri diuersi fatti, per altri conti, di sua Eccellenza; che iddio uoglia che si mettino cotali disegni in opera. Ora per breue compendio sua signoria Illma si degnerà uedere, la bontà infinita di un giouane ueramente fatto immortale per la sua uita celibe, et come meritamente l'hanno chiamato Virbio et casto, ciò è due uolte huomo et pudico. La onde la piu parte di poeti, Virbio l'appellano da duoi proprij nomi che egli hebbe, per che pria fu detto Virbio et poi Hippolyto et di nuouo Virbio, alcuni deriuano il nome di Hippolyto da Hippolita sua Amazone, altri dal domar' di caualli: ma sia come si uoglia, egli da principio, et nel fine fu detto Virbio, come l'appella Ouidio nel quindecimo dela Metamorphose, et cosi lo dicono i Latini: ma ui agiungono Hippolyto, cognome datagli da Greci

TVM MIHI NE PRAESENS AVGEREM MVNERIS HVIVS
INVIDIAM DENSAS OBIECIT CYNTHIA NVBES:
VTQVE FOREM* TVTVS, POSSEMQVE IMPVNE VIDERI,

* Originally Ligorio wrote "florem" and then cancelled the "l."

ADDEDIT AETATEM: NEC COGNOSCENDA RELIQVIT
ORA MIHI: CRETEMQVE DIV DVBITAVIT HABENDAM
TRADERET AN DELON, DELO, CRETAQVE RELICTIS.
HIC POSVIT: NOMENQVE SIMVL, QVOD POSSIT EQVORVM
ADMONVISSE, IVBET DEPONERE, QVIQVE FVISTI.
HIPPOLYTVS DIXIT NVNC IDEM VIRBIVS ESTO.

Nacque Virbio di Theseo figliuolo di Aegeo, et di Hippolyta Regina dele Amazzone; acquistata da Hercole et da Theseo: Hercole ne hebbe il Baltheo per portarlo ad' Euristheo per sadisfare alla persecutione di Iunone sua madregna; et Hippolyta per moglie prese Theseo innamorato dela nobiltà et ualor' di lei, et per far' all'usanza antica, che con l'armi et co' lo ualore s'acquistauano le moglieri. Cosidunque sendó dilei generato Virbio, accrebbe nelli buoni et honoreuoli essercitij, si diletto domar caualli, come fecero i Lapithi Centauri di Thessaglia, onde ne acquisto il cognome di Hippolyto cioé, domitore di corsieri. Essendo, poi, doppo la morte di sua madre per inuidia amorosa calumniato da Phedra sua crudelissima madregna; fu' ciecamente cacciato del stato da suo Padre. Onde passô in Creti, et poscia in Delo, oue l'oracolo lo mandò in Italia, et quiui uenuto doppo che Neptuno il mandasse il Terrore et spauento per mare, et sendo fauorito da Cynthia chiamata Diana é Aricia, campo da una grauissima rouina; per che cadendo dal carro quando il mostro del mare l'assalto tutto infranse et quasi al fin dela uita per opera di Diana fu risuscitato da morte à uita; fu di nuouo chiamato Virbio, et lasciato quello di Hippolyto come entrano in un altra età Heroica è immortale, a guisa di uno Iddio fu adorato, et riceue Tempij et altari à suo honore. Dicono che quantunque egli potesse tornare nel stato paterno, non curo cosa alcuna, non uolendo ritornare in Troezene ne nell'Attica, hauendosi eletta Italia è il paese Latina per albergo, sedici [f. 2r] miglia discosto doue fû poi Roma edificata da Romolo nella selua che egli consecrò à Diana Aricia, resto il suo nome per uno Iddio latiale; oue perla miseratione hauuta, di lui quella dea, primieramente à suo honore gli fabricò la città è la denomino dala sua Aricia denomino il lago Aricino è la selua attorno, che hora si dice Lago di Nemo, che sudetto speculum Diane. Feceui il Tempio alla medesimo, et fu chiamata Diana Vesta Nemorense; oue Oreste nel' tempo dela guerra Troiana dedico il simulacro dela Diana Aulydense Fascelite, come si dirrá poi nelli quadri partiti dell'attioni di gesti di Hippolyto. Fece in Aricia il Tempio di Aesculapio, che lo guari: et quiui dimorando per li luoghi seluaggi è reposti nela caccia si trastullaua: quando poi essendo uscito dal consortio degli huomini, comparue à Troiani: che queste contrade Arecine passarono, apparue ad' Aegeria Nympha doppo la morte di Numa pompilio Re di Romani et consolando quella Nympha che già era fatta di lacrime un fonte, fu estimato uno iddio amatore é custode dela pulchritudine, et uirginita dele Donzelle: gli fu fatto il Tempio presso quello dela Diana, doue le Vergini consegrauano i primi capelli de la loro coma. Quiui ogni anno i serui ueniuano à lottare dentro del septu ò uogliamo dire rinchiuso ch'era fatto dauante al tempio ouè non poteuano entrar animali et tutti quegli che lottauano è rimaniuano uincitori erano spogliati dall'habito seruilo è liberati da la seruitu et fatti sacerdoti di Hippolyto Virbio è custodi del Tempio di Diana. Sculpiuano qualche uolta Virbio con Diana insieme, l'uno uestito militarmente con una bianca tunica et mantello bianco coronato di Agno Casto et con uno Giglio in mano, come portauano le Vergini in Eleusina, per esser egli initiato nelle sacre cerimonie ch'erano in Eleusi, oue si initiauano gli casti et fortissimi Heroi. Dicono che Hippolyto hauea i capelli longhi et flaui, ó uogliamo dire biondi aurigni. Diana etiandio con uestimenti corti, è succinti, con l'arco e la pharetra et suoi Artemydi cioè stilaletti fatti di pelle d'anima [destroyed] seluaggio. Vogliono alcuni

153

che Aricia Diana fusse mogliere di esso Virbio e [destroyed] che essa scoperse la calumnia di phedra à Theseo, et retirô Hippolyto alla uita c [destroyed] be (celibe) nei luoghi solitarij è ascesi, et nelli de porti dela caccia si essercitauano. Il resto come le cose passassero, hauemo fatto che nelle sue partitioni in sedici quadri si dichiarano et cosi uerremo à raccontare del primo quadro. [f. 2v]

DELA VITA DI HIPPOLITO DETTO VIRBIO

Partite le Amazone da Themiscyra loro Regia, sendo signore dela Ionia di Caria et diquanto è tra il fiume Alys et il Thermodonte, et passate nela Thessaglia nela Beotia, entrarano nell'Attica doue fecero di gran battaglie, et hauendo ridutta Athene à graue pericolo, et gli Atheniesi per adolcir' lo loro aspro furore del combattere si armarono à guisa di donne uagamente tutta la giouentù et glialtri di età

Drawing: Fig. 90

cosi combattendosi sotto di Athene, nel campo, che fu' da loro detto Amazonico, fatte timide dell'uccisione, ui furono rotte et dissippate da Theseo figliuolo di Aegeo Re del Attica, il quale Theseo fatto acquisto del Baltheo di Hippolita et di essa Regina dele Amazone; parte perla uirtù parte perla formosa bellezza et parte per la nobiltà di quella, la fece degna del suo congiungale matrimonio; dala quale generò Hippolito, che fu educato al casto Epitheo, che per la sua celibe uita meritó esser posto tra gli huomini immortali. Dicono che inquesta battaglia si trouò Hercole [f. 3r] il quale fece l'acquisto del Baltheo cintura di Hippolyta ma lo concedette a Theseo con Hippolyta sendo Theseo il Re. [f. 3v; rest of folio blank]

Hippolita Amazona con Theseo si congiungono in matrimonio, giurando presente il sacerdote di Minerua su la Aegide Mineruale osseruantia reciproca nel loro connubio, oue Hymeneo iddio dele Nozze si uede finto all'usanza antica, uestito del Flammeo di color di croco, con due Facelle accese; l'una per lo maritò, l'altra per la moglie: accio che Ioue et Iunone Iugali recassero felice ligamento, sicome l'aere et il Regimento Celeste sono congiunti insieme. Ci è parso mettere questo atto per dimostrare come Hippolita sendo nella battaglia presa da Hercole et conceduta à Theseo si uedesse: per che

Drawing: Fig. 91

Hercole che mostra esser di presente significa l'aiuto che egli fece per hauere il Baltheo di Hippolyta, per portarlo ad'Euristheo Re del Pelopenneso secondo gliera stato imposto. Con queste nozze si mostra il ualore di Hippolyta, la formosità et la bellezza et nobiltà sua, come donna inespugnabile, poscia uisi mostra anchora illeggitimo matrimonio, lo quale prima mostra Cecrope ali popoli dell'Attica, che pria à uso di fiere seluatiche communemente usuauano [f. 4r] non più s'obligauano ad' una che à un altra come dice Dionysio ma più omeno ò communemente sollazauansi: il che dispiaciuto alla bonta di Cecropè, fece la legge che ciascuno singolarmente hauesse la sua moglie legata et acquistata per forza, come fù Hippolyta: et uolle che la Aegis di Minerua come dea dele uirtù et dell'armi ui fusse portata significante l'immortale et prudente legamento. Vi inuocauano Himeneo per che questo giouanetto saluô molte vergini prese da corsali, celerese caste et pure, ali loro padri, et fù degno dele nozze de la piu bella; come fù presso di Romani il nome di Thalasso che nel ratto dele sabine tolse la più bella che fù Ersilia moglie di Romolo donna prudentissima cosi etiandio Hippolyta per la sua prudentia et uirtù fu fatta degna del gran Theseo, da cui nacque Hippolyto huomo due uolte immortale; et fu essa degna per forza d'armi essere acquistata come cosa più cara et più desiderata. [f. 4v; rest of folio blank]

NATIVITA DI HIPPOLITO

Drawing: Fig. 92

È cosa necessaria seguitare l'ordine di porre la natiuità di Hippolyto: oue si uegga Lucina cio è Diana che dale fascie l'amo essendo propitia ale Donne partorenti, et alla casta giouentù. Laquale prese come in tutela Hippolyto, et da fanciullo infino all'ultimo con la Deita l'accompagno et seco stette. Essa fù quella che lo trasse dal pericolo dela morte con lo aiuto di Aesculapio: essa le tolse dala Calumnia di Phedra amante terribile et maligna che presso Theseo lhauea posto indisgratia et dal stato di Troizene cacciato, essa fatto assapere à Theseo come al caso era successo, come Hippolyto non hauea uoluto consentire al furore dela matregna era stato accusato perlo oppito; cosi Phedra scoperta la cosa s'uccise. Diana dunque lo seguitò in Italia et Hippolito a sua gloria edifico un Tempio et una città come si e detto piu oltre. [f. 5r; f. 5v blank]

AMMAESTRAMENTO DATO AD HYPPOLITO DA PYTHEO

Essendo passata ad questa uita Hippolita, et il figliuolo di lei rimasto giouanetto, fu dato ad educare ad casto Pytheo ò uero Epytheo nel tempo che Theseo andò in Creti isolii ad espugnare il minutauro nel laburyntho di Gnoso Città opera di Dedalo fatta fare dal Re Minoe; doue Theseo sendo uincitore et tolto il tributo degli Atheniesi lo condusse seco et menato uia Ariadna et Phedra figliuo—

Drawing: Fig. 93

le del Re Minoe ambedue innamorate di Theseo. Ma Ariadna fu lasciata a Baccho; et Phedra presa per moglie da Theseo per che era la più bella agli occhi di Theseo: costei poi si innamoro di Hippolyto suo figliastro con troppo sinscerato amore et con troppo ardore si pose a seguitarlo tanto che impi la corte regale di estremo odio et finalmente pericolo lei et pago la pena del [f. 6r] dishonesto appetito. Ordunque il presente quadro mostra come Pytheo dichiaro che cosa sia la imagine di Pallade et di Diana: et l'aperse, come la uirtù le arti liberali sono quelle che grandemente giouano alhuomo: et massimamente quando sono accompagnate con le cose Dia Diana che sono la caccia et la castità et la honesta fama la quale fu a Hippolyto di supremo giouamento, et questa è la somma dela moralita dela pittura. Percio che haueuano gli antichi per costume tenire et riguardare le imagini uirtuose che sono memoria lotale: come riguardo Cesare la imagine del grande Alexandro cosi giouenetto posto nel Tempio di Hercole come' huomo forte, sospiro in uederla figura giouenile, che già fusse annumerata in quella eta tra le cose Heroiche. [f. 6v; rest of folio blank; f. 7r contains just the following drawing; f. 7v is blank]

Drawing: Fig. 94

Hippolyto, essercitandosi con altri giouanetti, per lo giuocho Olympico dele carrette; per cioche cotale giuocho ogni quattro anni si faceua la olympia Festa ad'honorar di Ioue Olympo in Helide, per che un tale giorno Ioue uinse i suoi nimici chiamati Giganti dela Titana stirpe. Da tutte le parti molti principi in concorreuano, ò in mandauano, per hauer la corona di oliuastro supremo et dignissi—

Drawing: Fig. 95

mo premio. Hippolyto dunque sendo uno di quelli che desideraua acquistarla con industriosa marauiglia, uinceua glialtri della sua eta. La onde Phedra sua Neuerca la doue si

155

essercitaua si pose tuttauia a remmirarlo, col suo smisurato amore desiderandolo di cogliere dal suo campo un fiore per suo gusto: tuttauia risguardandolo, da una parte alta ingiu, pregaua Venere chel suo uago disire penetrasse nel cuore di Hippolito: facendo uoto se quello hauea à sua possanza edificarle un Tempio: ma quantunque la cosa non succedessi: gli pareua mille anni di mettere una tale [f. 8r] memoria in campo fece nanzi il uoto che fusso essaudito parere in opera, edificando il Tempio, lo quale dal guardar da sù ingiú il cognomino di Venere Cathascopia et doppò fatto questo come hauesse sadiffatto à Venere gli pareua che ogni cosa bene succedere gli potesse non lascio mai di seguitarlo ouunque il giouanetto andasse sempre lo segui focosamente. Questo quadro dunque rappresenta il degno et Heroico essercitio dela buona educatione di Hippolyto, et l'error' graue di Phedra che lo seguitasse dal qualo appetito alfine impi il mondo dela fama di sua istessa tragedia dise istessa omicidiale. [f. 8v; rest of folio blank]

Essendo Hippolito partito da Troizene città del Peloponneso, et andato in Eleusi à prender l'ordine dela Casta Eleusina; cio è di Cerere, per cio che era di oppenione, che chiunche inquell'ordine fosse initiato, non potessi morire. Anzi, fauolauano, che poteua andar'uiuo all'inferno è ritornare tra gli huomini uiui glorioso. Il che allegoricamente significa la fama immortale dele buone opre. Come furono quelle di Theseo, di Hercole, di Perithoo, et di Orpheo, et degli altri famosi huomini, che con la fama dela buona fatica uinsero la morte tra mortali. Cosi dunque menne apre

Drawing: Fig. 96

dell'altare di Eleusina con altri giouani si uedeua Hippolyto initiare è coronare di Agno casto; Phedra tuttauia gli éra di presente, a uagheggiare la sua bellezza, che in talhora sendo uestito di bianco, la sua faccia accesa di rose campeggiaua in maggior desiderio attorno al cuore di quella che senza misura l'amaua; et lo seguiua per non ne fare perdita alcuna. Veniuano gli initiati uestiti tutti di Bianco col Giglio bianco in mano et la corona di [f. 9r] Agno casto che ha la fronde simile al salice d'un uerde non molto accesa, come si puote uedere hoggidi et Araceli inquella parte del monasterio che riguarda Macel di corbi, nell'andito per uenire nel palazzo delli pontefici. [f. 9v; rest of folio blank]

Hauendo Phedra uisto Hippolyto initiato nelle cose Sacre di Cerere Eleusina, un maggior stimulo d'amor gli trapasso il cuore: come una fuor di ogni senso ragioneuole, si deliberò ò per forza ò per buona uoglia farlo piegare al suo talento, ò pur condurlo à pericolo di farle corre la uita armandosi di disperatione, tosto che di Eleusi furono tornati in Troizene.

Drawing: Fig. 97

Focosamente chiamo in camera Hippolyto: et lo pregó humilissimamente, che uolessi seguire l'amor di lei promettendogli uiuere e morire perlui, et farle uenire ogni suo stato prestamente nella sua possanza. Delche adirato Hippolito, presa la uia di andarsene fuor di camera Lei lo prese gridando et dimostra andogli di uolerlo con la spada di Theseo in mano farlo parere homicida et traditore: tuttauia ad alta noce si fesentire tutta furiosa come Hippolyto lhauea [f. 10r] uoluto ucciderla et uiolarle la sua pudicitia; et con tal uoce piena d'ira et di disdegno ai familiare dela corte si fe sentire: oltre scrisse à Theseo in Athene come il figliuol in camera d'accoso sendo entrato lhaua cerca del suo honore; et sendo lei difesa, egli lhauea uoluta uccidere conla paterna spada. [f. 10v; rest of folio blank]

Theseo hauendo inteso lhauiso da Phedra; come essa era stata quasi che sforzata da Hippolyto, et creduta la cosa per uera, senza pensamento, che potessi esser' calumnia, come era, uenuto in Troizene, con la

Drawing: Fig. 98

ira et con la spada in mano fatto impito contra del figliuolo: il quale si trouaua sul carro, et non potendo dar luogo alla ragione dela cosa per scamparla uita; sene parti uia, et lasciato Theseo suo padre nella sua iracundia et cecita dela mente affuscata dale parole scritte falsamente dela scelerata madregna. [f. 11r; f. 11v blank]

Diana hauendo intesa la calumnia data al suo Casto Hippolyto; et esser mandato quello in essilio, et uisto Theseo ingannato, et hauere chiamato Aegeo suo padre fatto iddio del mare, che uolessi mandar tal cosa contra Hippolyto che le fusse terrore et morte. Scoperse la fraude di phedra come lei hauea uoluto sforzar' Hippolyto sendo di quel giouanetto inuaghità: in questo atto dunque phedra s'uccise Theseo rimase lamentantesi dela sua trista sorte: per che hauessi mandato il figliuolo in esiglio, et pria che hauessi fatta la uendetta Phedra si fusse

Drawing: Fig. 99

uccisa: la quale per cuoprire le metristitio che già si scuopriuano hauea scritte le sue false scuse. Nelle cui mani cosi morta furono trouate scritte. [f. 12r; f. 12v blank]

Seguita come Aegeo sendo inuocato da Theseo che mandassi il terrore contra del figliuolo et suo nepote: alla cui uolunta Aegeo non poteua mancare, hauendo gia promesso col giuramento stygio, ilqualunque domanda. Sendo giunto Hippolyto allitto sovonico mentre fuggeua l'ira del padre incontenente, un mostro uscendo dal mare segli fece incontro con tanto spauento entrato sotto il carro, che pose in rouina Hippolyto i caualli, et ogni cosa ruppe et infranse, et tirato quello atterra se' spezzo et si condusse all'estremo passo dela uita, oue concorse all'

Drawing: Fig. 100

horrendo spettacolo la sua Diana, la qual poi operô tanto che ritorno il giouane morto in uita. [f. 13r; f. 13v blank]

Doppo la sudetta disgratia dela caduta di Hippolyto: Diana Arecina che di buon cuore lo amaua, et di lui teniua meriteuole conto: non uolle che all'hora morisse si fatta bonta de facendolo immortale, col mezzo di Aesculapio figliuolo di Apollo et di Coroni, il quale operando la uirtù dell'herbe il fece resuscitare; et cosi ritornata da morte à uita, lo seguito sempre sotto dela sua protetione lo guardo. Cosi dunque in questo quadro si rappresenta la resurrettione dele uirtù di Hippolito, et per esser stato due uolte in questa humana uita fatto huomo uiuo, fu appellato Hippolyto Virbio, et hauuto poi dele paterne ricchezze fece città et Tempij, mantenendo la sua gloria sopra à gli huomini immortale.

Drawing: Fig. 101
[f. 14r; f. 14v blank]

Quantunque Hippolyto doppo lhauer superate tutte le sue disgratie, potesse hauere il stato paterno, si tolse dala signoria dela Grecia, stimando quelle niente. Onde passato prima in Creti Isola, ui dimoro alquanto, doppo nela Trinacria, ciò é nela Sicilia isola, che fu poi chiamata da Sicani Sicilia, et quiui fabricato il Tempio di Diana, come quell'altro che fece in Creti; et d'indi seguitando la sorte del Mare uenuto in Italia, hebbe dall'Aborigini popoli latini una parte del Territorio, oue egli edificò Aricia città col Tempio di Aesculapio, et unaltro Tempio ala sua Diana, a cui consecro una selua. Quidunque in questa pittura si mostrano gli errori et andata per mare di Hippolyto, et come per fortuna di mare trasporrato allitto del mare Tyrrheno tra i latini, si elesse quel luogo per perpetuo albergo, oue finalmente fu adorato come per uno iddio.

Drawing: Fig. 102
[f. 15r; f. 15v blank]

Hauendo hauuto Hippolyto ricetto presso gli Aborigini populi latini di potere edificare una Città à suo modo egli cinse un colle alto ne monti Aruncini, posto hoggidi nella Via Appia oltre ad'Albano circa due mila passi, oue egli attorno tirô il solco, et nella sommità fece la Rocca, et il Tempio di Aesculapio in memoria del suo medico che lhauea data la uita, consecro il fonte ala sanità, et la citta denomino dala Diana Arecina Aricia, per questo dunque, inquesta quadro si dichiara il modo, che Hippolito tenne all'usanza latina in designare la citta, presso la quale consecro una selua et il lago à Diana Nemorense.

Drawing: Fig. 103
[f. 16r; f. 16v blank]

Hippolyto, hauendo già edificato il Tempio di Diana Nemorense Aricina, altrimente detta Vesta, Thaurica Fascelite, et Agrotera, fece ancho unaltro tempio nel medesimo luogo: consecrò il bosco. Fu la Diana cosi chiamata per causa di diuersi significati, da uarie accadentie. Arecina fu detta dal proprio nome di Aricia che fu fauoreuole ad esso Hippolyto. Fu appellata Vesta per esser proposta al suo regimento, come nel cielo: Thaurica et Fascelite, dala statua dela Thaurica Diana che quiui Horeste ui porto dela Diana Artemyde Aulydense, per cio che hauendo quella tolta da Aulide, la ascose et la infascio et la condusse

Drawing: Fig. 104
[f. 17r]

nela Thaurica Regione et d'indi in Italia, et messa nel Tempio di Hippolyto, quando quello non era più nel consorto degli huomini, ma degli iddj, et Genij del Latio, ala cui diuinita et à Diana erano stati eretti Templi et altari, et dicono che nel Tempio di Diana era la imagine di Hippolyto Virbio, et attorno ad'esso Tempio un ristretto di un rinchiuso accio che i caualli et gli altri animali non ui potesseno entrare. Fu questo Tempio sopra del Lago, che hodiernamente si dice di Nemo: doue credeuano, che Diana et Hippolyto nei riposti luoghi dimorauano et per la selua cacciauano le fiere seluaggie con le saette, et con li cani, et nei loro deporti sene stauano tranquilli et contenti. Per questo dunque hauemo fatti il Tempio dell'uno et dell'altro, il lago et la selua, dedicati à Diana et à Hippolyto Virbio per la Verginitá loro, quiui le fanciulle coronate di Agno casto uirginelle à diuotion di Hippolyto difensore dela Verginità, ala sua castimonia offeriuano una certa parte di lor capelli nanzi che uenissero all'atto Nuptiale del matrimonio. [f. 17v; rest of folio blank]

Nel giorno dela festiuità di Hippolyto Virbio et di Diana, non era niuno padrone che potessi retenere alcuni di suoi serui, che hauessero uoluto andare alla festa à far proua dela sua sorte. Doue andati bastandogli l'animo e le forze di lottare, se rimaneuano uincitori, da i sacerdoti di Virbio erano fatti liberi, et initiati nel sacerdotio istesso: et li perditori rimaneuano serui come prima da padroni ritornauano. Queste sono le cose dela reuerenza, che gli antichi portauano ala deità di Virbio, questo è quanto di lui è stato scritti da diuersi auttori i quali hanno toccata la sua uita celibe, et massime sene troua scritto nella tragedia di Phedra crudelissima nouerca, ò madregna come la uogliamo chiamare. Ordunque non hauendo altro che dire sendo di mestiero nela dipintura altri reimpimenti, si possono fare dele caccie conla sua Diana, sotto la

Drawing: Fig. 105
[f. 18r]

quale uissono coloro che la uita di cacciatori pigliarono, seguitando i boschi et le latebre et li riposti luoghi dele caste Nymphe, sendo reuerenti di Diana et di Virbio à cui la caccia non dispiacque mai, et redattero che esso nele selue Aruncine, dei monti oltre al Tusculano in terra latina dimorasse castissimamente et poi al secolo di Numa pompilio Re di Romani fauolano quiui si uedessi: et uogliono che Aegeria perla morte di Numa inqueste parti Nemorense entrasse piangendo con amarissime lacrime; onde uinta dal dolore, in un fonte uiuo si cangio presente Diana et Virbio, con questo facendo fine humuissimamente mele raccomando et iddio la conserui felice. Di Ferrara il di   di Nouembre del M:DLXIX.

Di vostra Illma et R^{ma} S^{ria}
Hu^{mo} S.^{re}
Pyrrho Ligorio Romano meisopogniero
[f. 18v]

The last folio of the manuscript has been added to Ligorio's original document probably in the early seventeenth century and is printed in the same hand as that of the added title page:

Inscrittione trouata a Nemi Castello de Signori Frangipani sopra il lago detto di Nemi antichamente Speculum Dianae nel Giardino di detti Signori, doue era il Tempio di Diana Nemorese nelle retroscritte historie da Pirro Ligorio descritto

DIANAE
NEMORESI VESTAE
SACRVM DICT
IMP. NERVA TRAIANO AVG.
GERMANICO III COS. PRAEF.
EIVS T. VOLTEDIO M. AEMILIANO
QVAESTORIB.
L. CAECILIO VRSO. II. M. LVCRETIO
SABINO. II AEDILIB. Q. VIBENNA QVIETO
ET CLAVDIO MAGNO
P. CORNELIVS TROPHIMVS PISTOR
ROMANIENSIS EX REG. XIIII IDEM CVR.
VICI QVADRATI. LANIA ETHIONOE CONIVG.
EIVS VOTVM LIBENS SOLVERVNT
[f. 19r]

APPENDIX C

PERSONIFICATIONS OF THE VIRTUES IN THE
CARDINAL'S APARTMENT

The personifications of the Virtues in the three rooms on the *piano nobile* which comprise the Cardinal's Apartment are listed here with their attendant symbols:

I. SALON

1. *Hilaritas* holds palmfrond in her right hand; her left hand supports a cornucopia resting on the ground.
2. *Fiducia sui* wears a veil attached to headdress and holds in her lap jewelry and baubles.
3. *Cupiditas vitae* holds upright in her left hand a cornucopia filled with money and jewelry, in her right hand a phoenix.
4. *Maiestas* wears a small jeweled diadem in her hair and holds in her right hand a scepter topped by a pelican; at its base is a four-legged animal (dog?).
5. *Industria intensio bona* holds a globe in her lap on which she measures with a compass.
6. *Tutela sui* with head wrapped in a turban or nurse's cap, sits with right breast bared, a clothed female child at her left side and a nude boy standing at her right.
7. *Patientia* holds in upraised left hand a wheel on which is supported a balance; her bare right foot is planted on thorn branches.
8. *Parentum indulgentia* with head wrapped in a turban or nurse's cap and right breast bared, sits with nude child in her lap and another nude child kneeling at her right side.
9. *Sapientia* wears Minerva's helmet on her head and holds a shield (?) in her left hand.
10. *Sublimitas ex humili* with veiled headdress and left breast bared, holds on her right knee a round temple with two windows and in her left hand a scepter, her right foot resting on a globe.
11. *Verecundia* wears helmet on her head, carries scepter in her right hand and holds upright between her left arm and side a cornucopia of fruit.
12. *Iucunditas* wears an elegant headdress with a slight veil, earrings on her ears and, nude to the waist, is clad in a diaphanous garment. She holds a caduceus in her right hand and rests her left hand on the top of a basket of fruit.
13. *Benignitas*, modestly dressed, holds upright in her right arm a cornucopia filled with jewelry and money and in her left hand a patera.
14. *Inocentia* holds a small pipe organ in her lap.
15. *Continentia* holds a staff in her right hand and has a sheathed sword by her left side.
16. *Valetudo* holds in both hands a snake which is partially wrapped around her right arm; the ends of a priest's stole hang down from her girdle.
17. *Temperantia* (see Fig. 42), modestly dressed, pours water from a patera in her right hand into a large vase at her left.
18. *Religio* (see Fig. 42) supporting against her right arm tablets entwined with a chain and inscribed: *Liber generationis Iesu Christi,* holds with her left hand folds of the end of her garment under her left breast. Her left foot is raised on a squared block surrounded by religious objects, a book, ewer, censer, and paten. In the left background is a glimpse of an octagonal domed temple.

19. *Eloquentia*, a veil attached to her headdress, holds a caduceus in her right hand and a short staff in her left hand, while her left foot is raised on a carved block or footstool.

20. *Tellus stabilis* holds a cornucopia filled with foliage in her right hand; supports a plow with her left hand.

II. ANTECHAMBER

21. *Regalitas* wears a crown on her head and holds in her left hand a scepter topped by a pelican.

22. *Gloria* holds upright in her left hand a cornucopia of fruit and in her right hand a statue of Truth (in accordance with C. Ripa, *Iconologia*, Siena, 1613, I, p. 300).

23. *Opulentia* holds in her right hand jewelry and baubles, and on her left arm sits a nude child with satyr ears and a large satyr mask in his left hand.

24. *Constantia* wearing a helmet on her head leans on a staff.

25. *Senectus* (Ruined in part, title given by A. del Re, *Dell'Antichità tiburtine, capitolo V*, Rome, 1611, p. 14.) An elderly woman.

26. *Religio*, clad in a nun's habit, holds a cross in her right hand and a book in her left hand against her left thigh.

27. *Modestia* (Ruined for most part, title in Del Re, *op.cit.*, p. 14.) Apparently had scepter in left hand.

28. *Iucunditas* (Almost completely ruined, title in Del Re, *op.cit.*, p. 14.)

29. *Pudicitia* holds at one end a veil which is attached to her headdress and partially covers her forehead. She holds an ermine (see C. Ripa, *op.cit.*, II, p. 169) on her right forearm and hand.

30. *Amicitia* holds a chain in her two hands over the head of nude child, who looks into a mirror held in his left hand.

31. *Concordia* supports upright with her two hands a double horned cornucopia containing fruit.

32. *Immortalitas* crowned with foliage (perhaps flowering amaranth after C. Ripa, *op.cit.*, I, p. 365), she holds a phoenix in her left hand and her right hand is covered by a fold of her garment.

33. *Tranquilitas* (see Fig. 46) with a crown of roses in her hair, holds a cornucopia in her right hand and a fold of her skirt in her left hand. At her left is an anchor and in the right background the prow of a ship.

34. *Providentia* (see Fig. 46) holds a globe in her right hand and a scepter or short staff in her left hand.

35. *Caritas*, with her left arm, holds a child who is drinking from a cup; in her right hand holds fruit over the head of another child embracing her right knee.

36. *Humanitas* has flowers at the neck of her dress and holds in her right hand several bejeweled chains.

III. BEDROOM

37. *Virtutes* (The generic title is used here and is inscribed under the two Virtues in the northern corner of the Bedroom, see no. 52.) This Virtue has both hands veiled in diaphanous garments.

38. *Spes* holds a small floral bouquet in her right hand.

39. *Letitiae* holds a ship's rudder in her right hand and a floral crown in her left.

40. *Salus* holds in her right hand a chalice covered with a paten.

41. *Veritas* holds a cornucopia filled with fruit balanced on her left shoulder and in her right hand a purse.

42. *Iustitia*, crowned, holds a scepter upright in her right hand and with her left hand a fasces head downward.

43. *Abundantia* holds with her right hand the stem of a cornucopia filled with fruit and flowers.

44. *Pietas* bears a chalice covered with a paten in her right hand. A small child stands on either side of her and she holds the arm of one with her left hand.

45. *Fortitudo* (see Fig. 48), seated on the back of a small lion whose head and paw are visible, holds a ship's rudder with her right hand.

46. *Pax* (see Fig. 48) holds an olive branch in her left hand and probably the stem of a cornucopia with her right hand; her right foot rests on an object difficult to identify, perhaps a vase on its side.

47. *Aequitas* holds a staff with her right hand and a balance with her left.

48. *Felicitas*, crowned with a diadem, holds a caduceus in her right hand and a cornucopia of fruit in her left hand against her left shoulder.

49. *Lex* holds a fasces upright with her right hand and in her left hand an open book and inkwell.

50. *Fides* holds a pair of tibia with veiled hands. A dog is by her right side.

51. *Nobilitas*, wearing helmet of Minerva on her head, holds a long staff with her right hand and in her left hand a small standing statue of Minerva similarly garbed.

52. *Virtutes* (see no. 37), wearing helmet on her head, she holds a staff with her right hand and a sheathed sword with her left.

APPENDIX D

UNPUBLISHED DOCUMENTS

1. *Contract dated May 18, 1568, for the Fountain in the salotto*: ASM, Fab. e Vill., Busta 70, Pte. 3, ff. 7r-8r.

Io m.ro Pauolo Calandrino da Bologna fontanieri per la pr'nte confesso et dichiaro di hauer preso dall'Ill.mo Car.e di Ferrara ò suoi Agenti a finire la fontanina della sala nel palazzo di SS. Ill.ma in Tiuoli principiata da Curtio co' li infrascritti capitoli, patti, et conditioni.

Et p.a mi obligo finire detta fontana del modo et forma che e cominciata in termine di doi mesi dal di d'hoggi, cioe dalla cornice in giu et prometto, che il lauoro che io faro sara cosi minute et cosi ben fatto come detta cornice et meglio et non il facedo mi contento, che s.s. Ill.ma lo possa far rifare da altri a mie spese ò uero mi obligo di rifarlo io, et prometto di non pigliare altra opera, et di lauorare continou.te in detta fontana, sino che sia racconcia, et finita—et perche piu distintam.te si sappia quello che mi obligo di fare nominaro particular.te alcune parti et membri di detta fontana et in che modo l'ho da fare, uolendo pero esser tenuto à quelle parti che io non ne facesse mentione uolendo io essere obligato a finirla tutta: Perta.to mi obligo a coprire di smalti et altre pietre che vi andassero li doi puttini di stucco, che sono sop.a la cornice, et di fare l'Agla chi posa sop.a li rami de cotogni, et coprirla di smalti minuti, et simil.te finire li rami co' li suoi pomi di tutto quello chi ui andassi à quella bellezza, et qualita, sicome, è cominciata, et maggiore.

Item mi obligo finire la cornice di quello ui mancasse, ta.to di festoni, come rosette, o coptura di smalti à quella bellezza et qualita come è cominciata.

Item mi obligo di fare li doi termini di fora delle cornice di detta fontana co' festoni et altre cose che ui andassero, si come si puol uedere dalla abbozatura di essi, et simil.te coprirli di smalti minuti come la cornice, et finirli bene secondo laqualita che ricercano essi termini.

Item mi obligo di fare ò finire li doi stipiti, ò cornice dalla banda di fora di essa fonte sino in terra, co' uestire di smalti minuti le queste di fiori secondo chi ricerca il natur.le di esse fiori, quale sono abbozate in esse cornice, et pmetto di sarano ben fatte alla bellezza et qualita di essa cornice gia fatta.

Item mi obligo finire le doi facciate di dentro dalle bande con uestire di smalti minuti li rami di edera, che sono abbozati, et prometto che saran'o ben fatte, et finite, alla bellezza, et qualita della cornice sop.a nominata;

Item mi obligo fare la facciata di mezzo dentro la fontana in forma di paese, et prometto di uestirla di pietre minute, et smalti come la cornice di sop.a con farui dentro di belle fantasie di uerdure, animali, et uccelli, et prometto che saran'o ben fatte, et finite alla bellezza, et qualita di detta cornice. [f. 7r]

Item mi obligo di fare un belliss.o scoglio sotto la statua di marmo, che ua dentro la detta fontana, con uestirlo di smalti minuti, et altre pietre, come la cornice, et ornarlo di molte fantasie, et cose marittime, et prometto che stara bene, al paragone della sop.a detta cornice.

Item mi obligo di coprire il uaso che al presente è abbozzato sotto detta fontana di smalti et altre pietre che ui andevano, et prometto che dette pietre saranno apportione della cornice, et che il lauoro di detto uaso, sara cosi bello, et ben fatto e le non difformen al resto della Fontana.

Item mi obligo fare doi tartenule o altri animali marittimi sotto detto Vasa in cambio di basa ò posam.^{to} et prometto di coprire detti animali simil.^{te} di smalti minuti et altre pietre alla bellezza della cornice fatta,

Item mi obligo fare il letto sotto detto uaso in forma di pauim.^{te} il quale prometto che sara di pietre minute, conforme alla qualita del resto della fontana, con farui dentro di uarie sorti di pesci, che para che uadino scherzando nelle Aegina che caschera dal Vaso.

Item mi obligo di coprire il parapetto che ua attorno à detto letto in forma di scoglio con uestirlo di uarie sorte di pietre coralli, et altre fantasie marittime, et prometto che il lauoro sara minuto, conforme al resto della fontana; Le quali tutte cose prometto farle per prezzo di ▽^{ti} sessanta d'oro in oro, da pagarmisi in questo modo, cioe ogni stimana scudi otto di mo.^{ta} et io prometto lauorarui di continuo, con quella qualita d'homini che ricerca il lauoro con opera, et non lauorare ne pigliare altre opere sino che so' sia finita; Con questo ch'il Car.^{le} o suoi Agenti siano obligati à darmi tutta la materia de andera in detta fontana, ta^{to} di smalti come ogni altra cosa, et io sia tenuto di mandare sempre tre giorni auanti qual si uogli cosa mi bisognasse accio habbino tempo à prouederle, et in altre uoglio stare tenuto del mio à pagare coloro che romperano le pietre ò smalti et farano ogni ala cosa o li si appartengli à fattura et opera di detta fonte, et mi contento stare al giuditio di maestro Gio. Alberto Galuano, se in alcuna cosa ò in tutto mancagne di quanto ho pmesso, et mi sono obligato et prometto di esseguire quato lui giadilmo (?) et stare al suo detto et per osseruatione di tutte le cose per dette ho fatto scriuere la presente, quali uogli habbi forza di obligo in forma camera con tutto sue che et censura et cosi mi obligo et iuro, et in fede ho fatto scriuere la presente, quale sara ap^p—per sottoscrittione di mia propria mano presente gli infra^{tti} testimonij. Questo di xviii di Maggio 1568 a Roma in Monte Cauallo.

Io Paulo cholandria ho fatto scrivere. [f. 7v]

[Subscribed to by Vincenzo Stampa among others on f. 8r.]

2. *Memorandum of 1619 on fountains by the* fontaniere *Vincenzo Vincenzi*: ASM, Fab. e Vill., Busta 71, Pte. 3, ff. 5r-11r.

Prima Informatione della Villa di Tiuoli di Vincenzo
Vincenzi fontanaro.

È difficile il discorrere dello stato et dell'occorrenze della Villa di Tiuoli se non si uede il luogho nondimeno perche se ne tratta con chi n'hà perfetta notitia anco di lontano si renderà capace del bisogno a luogho per luogho Però se ne dirrà con quell'ord.^e che è stato commandato cioè

P.° Si proporrà quanto il fontaniero hà potuto fare nello spatio di soli 4 mesi da serue che se bene è poco alla quantità del luogho è pero ali.^a cosa rispetto alpoco tempo di seru.° et ciò sarà col foglio congionto segnato A.

2.° Se narreranno alcuni pensieri del fontanieri che sono picciola parte al molto che si potria fare nella Villa sud.^a per continuarli l'antico nome e splendore anzi per condurla ad' essere un miraculo in questo genere che tanto si può pretendere quanto alla Villa in se stessa con la rara commodita della copia immensa d'acque che ui è cosa non conceduta à qualuq altra Villa intorno a Roma et si può dire in Italia col foglio segnato C.

Perfondamente presente di quanto si hà da rinouare et conseruare et decrescere sappiasi che conuiene di prouedere alla facilità del dar l'acqua à tante fontane che ui sono et che l'acqua sia chiara et pulita hora l'acqua si da per uia di tappi o sugheri da luoghi m.^{to} lontani alle fontanze et m.^{to} scommodi onde perche tal uolta conuiene in 'aspettare che l'acqua giongha uno due o tre miserere di cagiona ne Prencipi et personaggi che ui capitano marauiglia et poca sodisfat.^e la merauiglia per l'indugio, la poca sodisfat.^e rispetto alli effetti che ne seguono come al bagnarsi ad alcuni Inganni poiche non potendo il fontaniero dar regula ali.^a all'inganno et tal uolta auaduto che alcun personaggio se n'è piciato contro delli fontanieri et hanno corse di brutte busasche et pericoli; il remedio sarebbe adambedoi l'incouenienti di mettere l'inuentioni alle fontane mediante lequali il fontaniero potrebbe subito dar l'acqua et nell'inganni ualersene con discreta modestia, la spesa di queste inuentioni non sarà eccessiua ma circa trenta scudi per che il più lo lauorara' il medesimo fontaniero et sarà con molto [f. 5r] auantaggio di spesa lose bene al fontaniero sarà accrescimento di fatiga non però lo stima per ben seruire conform' all'obligo et alla uolonta che bene

Quella che il fontaniero desidera per somma gratia et per poter piu quieto et commòdo attender al seruitio è che si fornisca il Casino per cio cominciato, che hauendo già fabricate le muraglie principali et tetto resta solo il diuidere le stanze far solari porte et finestre in che si è fatto conto poteruisi spendere cento scudi che sarà molto auantaggio delle occorrenze della Villa onentre il fontaniero ui farà di continuo sua stanza et non hauerà occasione d'allontaner sene per l'habitat.^e

Tanto didq uuole il fontaniero hauer proposto in generale per zelo del buon seru.^o al quale egli è tenuto remettendosi nel resto a' quanto uerra auennato per prontam.^{te} douesto escegire.

Tutte le fontani hanno li moti dell'acque molte disordinati ne altro modo ui è per ben concertarli che metter alle fontane spiragli fatti à uite di piombo e stagno li spiragli li farà il fontaniero hauendone le forme di quattro ò cinque sorti le quali anco fonderà il fontaniero da serbesso già che anco di getto di metallo ha tanta pratica che li puo bastare. Questi spiragli a uite seruono non solo per ben ordinare i moti dell'acqua ma par che leuandosi et ponendosi danno commodità di ben ripurgarli. Et perche di questi spiragli a' tante fontane andaranno à centinaia et migliaia la spesa pero' sarebbe molto grande io il fontaniero non lauorasse di sua mano come fara il getto et il resto.

3.º Si narreranno le resolutioni, che fece ultimam.^{te} il Sig.^r Card.^{le} R^{mo} di gloriosa mem. a parte per parte col foglio segnato. B. [f. 5v]

Foglio A. Di quello che nella Villa si è fatto fin'hora

P.^o Si è purgato l'Acquedotto pnte che uiene dal fiume che è di palmi 3⅓ di larghezza palm. 6. di altezza è canne 300. di longhezza era ripieno di terra portataui dal fiume torbido; si credeua spesa eccessiua ma col modo proposto dal fontaniero si ridusse a 30 scudi inc.^a Quest'Acquedotto hà di bisogno di remedio si perche in breue non si riempia come per non hauer del continuo acqua torbida che riempie l'altri Acquedotti il remedio è al folio B. n.^o p.^o

2.º L'Organo era affatto perduto non hauendo acqua per oprarlo almeno abastanza et perche nel resto era fracassato in tutto si è ripurgato il suo Acquedotto con la spesa sud.^{ta} et si è riordinato in modo che hoggi può oprarsi comodamente potrebbe perfettionarsi con due altri Registri come al foglio B. n.º 2.º

3.º Alli scogli del fontanone saliua anticam.^{te} l'acqua per bagnarli et era l'acqua detta di Reuelese quest'acqua era perduta affatto et si è ricondotta fino alla Conserua resta di farla risalire alli scogli come al foglio B. n.º 3.º

4.° La fontana della Ciuetta e cominciata a resarcire anzi si può dire a t° rifare di nouo tanto era in Rouina sono quasi compiti per mano delfontaniero gl'Alberi che ui uanno le foglie et i frutti il resto si contiene nel folio B. n.° 4.

5.° Alla scalinata detta de Bollori che la più bella uista d'acqua che sia alla uilla si era cominciato ad applicare l'animo tutt.ª non ui si è fatto cosa di momento perche si era risoluto quello che contiene il foglio B. n.° 5.°

La Breuità del tempo che hà seruito il fontaniero e gli accidenti occorsi hanno impedito che altro non si possa esceguire ne in g.ᵉ parti ne meno nel restasse delle fontane. [f. 6r]

Foglio B. Ordini dati dal s.ʳ Cardinale Ill.ᵐᵒ non potuti compire

P.° Vide' il s.ʳ Card.ˡᵉ Ill.ᵐᵒ di gloriosa mem.ª che l'Acquedotto pn'le alla bocca come dal fiume si prende l'acqua, hà cattiua Cataratta, e perció riceue l'acqua torbida, e ui penetra ogni sorte di riempitura, che scorrendo poi per l'acquedotti li riempie, e danneggia le fontane. Rimedio è, e fù accettato di fare alla bocca sudetta un uolto con una Cataratta buona, e con una ferrata, che impedisca legni, e materie grosse.

L'acqua che si piglia da questa bocca scorre torbida, come è fino al fontanone, doue hoggi per opera del fontaniero l'acqua può lasciarsi salire alle fontane, ò permettere, che scorra alle peschiare; In questo luogo del fontanone fù risoluto di mettere un'altra cataratta, laquale stia sempre alzata, acciò l'acqua scorra uerso le Peschere, e non salisca alle fontane, come il fontaniero uorrà l'acqua alle fontane calarà la Cataratta del fontanone, che farà salire l'acqua alle fontane in quella maniera, che si uede à sostegni frà Bologna, e ferrara, e ne succederanno due benefitij, l'uno, che l'acqua ascenderà chiara; e senze arena, mentre l'alzarà, media'te il sostegno, e Cataratta, che farà rimanere l'arena in fondo; l'altro che tornandosi àd alzare la cataratta quando dall'acqua nonui è più bisogno alle fontane scorgando ueloce uerso le Pischiere, portara' seco l'arena iui condotta, etterra' l'acquedotto pn'le sempre purgato, in modo, che non ui bisognara' più la manifattura che poco fà hà bisognato per ripurgarlo. La spesa per tutto questo sarebbe da 40. scudi inc.ª

Erasi anco risoluto di fare delle reti in diuersi luoghi dell'acquedotti per ritenere particolarm.ᵗᵉ le foglie, e le bacche del lauro, che cascando danneggiano li acquedotti; Queste reti uogliono essere di filo di rame sopra uerglitte di ferro minute secondo il bisogno, che recercaranno spesa di 15. scudi incirca. [f. 8r]

2.° L'organo, come è può seruire, mà é ordin.° e sazieuole si pensó di accrescerli due Registri d'un trombone, e d'una Piua, et accrescarli una sonata, che fusse boscareccia. La spesa sarebbe di 50 s.ᵈⁱ ò circa.

3.° Li tratto' di far salire l'acqua alli scogli per bagnarli, come prima, ui li spenderebbe l'uno à diece scudi

Per questo ui é necessità d'una chiaue di dar l'acqua, che pigliandoli da una conserua, ricerca d'esserne tenuto buon conto, non ui entra spesa, essendouenetre ò quattro, In guardarobba di Tiuoli, che si possono mettere in opera.

4.° Per compire la fontana della ciuetta, fù mostrato al s. Card.ˡᵉ Ill.ᵐᵒ che bisognaua di redurre il pauemento, e le Nicchie in termine, che potesse operarli il bagnatino senza hauerli à dar l'acqua di tanto lontano, quanto hora si fà, che conducendo uento in copia, lostia, e fá tanto strepito, che è cosa ridicola, spropositata, e scommoda. Per tutto questo la spesa non sarà più di 15. s.ᵈⁱ ò circa, e si fara cosa di garbo, è degnadel nome di q.ª fontana, haueua già mass.ᵉ presto gli oltramontani, et fontaniero, che il più del lauoro farà di sua mano, la migliorarà assai sopra quello, ch'era per prima

5.º La scalinata de' Bellori, uuole qualche manifattura, e la machina lo comporta potendosi ridurre à perfettione isquisita. Vidono Pilastri alle bande della scalinata con un bollore per ciasced.º, e da pilastri cade l'acqua in una conca, piu sotto del pilastro, e cosi procede fino della scala, i bollori hoggi sono piccoliss.ⁱ e guasti tutti, e la machina affetto inutile. Si era risoluto di restituirli l'acqua, come prima, et era opra di qualche spesa, perche conuiene di scomporre tutta la scalinata, solo per rimetter l'acqua altermine di prima, che pero' non riuscirebbe di gusto, essendo l'acqua pochiss.ᵐᵃ di quantità rispetto del luogo et à quello, che si potrebbe, e douerebbe fare.

Pero per ridurre cosi nobil machina à perfettione due cosi ui bisognano. [f. 8v]

P.º che i bollori siano bollori, e non squilli, come erano per p.ᵐᵃ 2.º si puó con la med.ᵃ spesa fare un uolto d'acqua, che sopra tutta la scalinata incrociandosi, e senza impedire l'ascendere, ò il descendere per essa si camini sotto l'aqua, che come cosa insolita, e finqui altroue non ueduta, sarebbe di quel gusto, che altri puo' rapresentarsi, ne' come s'è detto la spesa perció s'accrescie; laq.ᵃle sarebbe di cento scudi, e meno, si replica solo, che la med.ᵃ spesa uuole il restituirui solo i bollori.

Il s. Card.ˡᵉ Illᵐᵒ uolendo il più delle fontane consumate in quelle parti, che haueuano compartimenti di stucchi, e di graffiti; propose di riscercirle; Il fontaniero disse, che il rimanerui graffiti, e stucchi, era un mantenere la spesa, perche inquei luoghi ben presto si consumano, epropose di farui compartimenti rustichi di tartari, e di spucogli, che uagliano mediocre spesa, epiù lung.ᶻᵉ durano. La spesa di discorse potere ascendere à 300 scudi.

Alle 3. peschiere haueua risoluto S.S.ʳⁱᵃ Illᵐᵃ di fare due muraglie cadute poggioli, e scarricarle, consultò col S.ʳ Architetto, e dissero entraui di spesa fino à 500. scudi.

Vide il S.ʳ Card.ˡᵉ Illᵐᵃ; che ui é continuo bisogno di un muratore, quale continuamente ui é stato, occorendo ogni giorno di ualersene in cose, che il fontaniero non può farle, e se fare le potesse, conuerrebbe di lasciare altri lauori di sua mano, che molto più importano.

Di più si pensò di risarcire la Roma, e si conobbe, che rechiedeua eccessiua spesa, massime per mantenerla, poiche di tanto intanto si guasta come esporta all'Ingiurie del tempo. E però forse meglio sarebbe di conuertir quella spesa in altro di più maesta, egusto. [f. 9r]

C. Inuentioni del fontaniero per la Villa de Tiuoli

1.º Al portone della Prospettiua, che è la principale entrata, ela prima parte che si ueda della Villa sono due Nicchie rustiche, ui se possono adattare due statue, come per guardia, che tenghino due archibugi in mano calati in atto di mirare à chi entra. Entrati i forastieri nel viale cominciassero le statue à mouersi, pur in quell'atto di mira, e continuassero cosi fin tanto, che chi è entrato uolti loro le spalle, all'hora, se il fontaniero uorrà, sparevanno una botta d'acqua per ciasc.º Nel ritorni trouando i forastieri le statue nella med.ᵐᵃ positura di mira più si appressaranno alla porta, più le statue uolgendosi le seguitaranno di mira, tanto che aperto il Portone per andarsene, potrà di nuouo il fontaniero farli salutare di altro tiro di acqua. Questo effetto, perche lacqua deue condutti da alta, ricercarebbe un poco di spesa, la quale però non si crede passarebbe 150. scudi, ò circa.

2.º Nel med.º viale cominciando dal Portone sino alla scalinata di Draghi, si puo fare un pergolaro d'acqua, che all' improuiso sorgesse da ambe le parti, dando commodo di passarui sotto senza esser punto bagnato. L'Acqua per questo effetto sara la med:ᵐᵃ che si conducesse perle statue al Portone; onde per il pergolaro non si spenderebbe altro de più, che per i Canali di piombo i quali ualerebbono 50. scudi, ò circa. Ma auertasi, che se le statue al Portone non si uolessero e solo si auertasse questo Pargolaro, tanto solo per questo si douerà

Condurre l'acqua, che senza le statue importarebbe da 100. scudi. In somma una sol acqua serue ad ambedue l'Inuent.ⁿⁱ

3.° Il Cancello per andare alla Roma hà un bagnatorio ridicolo, e da persone cieche per essere il Cancello attaccato un sughero, con uno spogo che nell'aprir si del Cancello si lieua, e bagna, parue al Sor Card.^{le} Illmo un'inganno di polo garbo; propose il fontaniero di farci alcuni spiragli, che senza esser ueduti [f. 10r] all 'aprire del Cancello si aprissero, e nella schiena bagnassero i forastieri, e nel ritorno, perche il Cancello si ritornarebbe ad aprire da med.^{mi} spiragli uenissero bagnati in faccia, e si può in modo adattare il gioco, che bagni, e non bagni sempre, secondo i Personaggi che ui fussero, bagni nell' andare, è nel ritornare à uoglia del fontaniero, e non per forza. La spesa è leggiera di circa tre scudi.

4.° La Villa di Tiuoli è dilittiosiss.^a d'acque, ma non ui è stato mai dilitia di uenti artifiziosi. Anco per queste ui è molta Commodita e due luoghi ui sarebbono a proposito. Il p° alla stanza detta delli specchi, doue è una fontana con una semplice statua. Questa fontana si potrebbe inuaghire, facedoui spiragli, che con l'acqua sostenano in aria una palla, e di tanto, in tanto cessando l'acqua, la palla fusse pur sostenuta in aria dal uento cosi alternatamente succedesse l'acqua, e di nouo il uento à uoglia del fontaniero. Nella med.^a stanza possino mettersi statue, che faccino qualche moto Curioso, da condurre i forastieri à mirarle più da uicino, et auorta'dosi, farli rimaner percossi da ungagliardo soffio di uento in uece d'inganni d'acqua, che si uedono in alcuni di questi giardini di Roma, che percotono in faccia chi guarda uno specchio, ò si accosta al uiso ad una maschera. Il 2° luogo è alla stanza della Diana, che pur' è semplice, qui possono mettersi arbori, fiori, e cose boschereccie, con canti d'uccelli, et altre cose proportionate a Diana, e gl' inganni sarebbono ad arbitrio e d'acqua, e di uenti. La spesa per ciò non si può determinare per l'appunto, la più consisterebbe nelle statue e nelli acquedotti per acqua, euenti, che i fiori, li arbori, egli uccelli, e l'altre cose naturali, il fontaniero le leuorarebbe di sua mano, onde quello, che esso può operare, ricercarebbe solo circa 25 ∇^{di} di spesa. Delle statue non se ne parla, essendo fuori della sua professione. [f. 10v]

Fuori del fontanone è una fontana alla mano manca, et un'altra nel fine alla mano medesima, che sono simplicissime, e quella parte della uilla benche uaga, e bene intesa, non ha cosa che diletti. Si potria ad una di quelle fontane mettere un Satiro con una sirenga, che uersam.^{te} sonasse, ementre suona mouesse occhi, e mani, nell'altra fontana metterui un Pastore con la piua, che pur sonasse, alla pastorale, co'l moto delle mani, e dell' occhi, con abbellimento di piante, e le fiori d'uccelli, e quando gli astanti fussero intenti allouista nello stesso luogo ui potrebbono essere Inganni da bagnarli con garbo, e gentile via. La spesa non passarebbe 150 scudi in tutto.

Vi sarebbono delle Inuenzioni à centenaia, secondo la grandezza, e nobiltà della Villa della quale nel Progresso si darà parte, e tutto con si poca spesa, che fosse parerà incredibile, ma procede perche il fontaniero presuppone di potere auantaggiare molto, lauorando il più di sua mano, che porta sparmio di robba e di moneta da non poterlo considerare, senon da chi sperimenta la maniera, ele strauaganti per tenzioni, ne' pagamenti delli Artefici di Roma—

Le statue nominate douerebbono essere di legno, e non di pietra, e così non ualerebbono eccessiuo prezzo, e si pensa di legno per la commodità delli snodam^{ti} e moti, come anco per poterle leuare, e mettere giache nell'Inuerno non seruono, e così anco più si conseruarebbono. [f. 11r]

3. *Letter of October 31, 1621 to Cardinal Ludovisi*: ASM, Fab. e Vill., Busta 70, Pte. 10, fasc. 18, f. 1.

Illmo et R.^{mo} Sig.^{re}

Il Card.^{le} d Este hà bisogno di fabricare a Tiuoli una stalla per seruitio della sua Casa, e pensarebbe di farla in un sito uerso la porta dell'oliueto la mag.^e parte delquale è suo prop.^o ma perche d.^{ta} stalla sia capace di mag.^e num.^o di Caualli, gli conuerrebbe passare sop.^a un'altro poco di sito, ch'é della Cam.^{ra} da che po' secondo il disegno fatto non restarebbe impedita la strada ne il passò: ma perche ciò non può farsi senza licenza di Il S.^{re} supplica il med.^o Card.^{le} V.S. Illma à degnarsi d'impetrarglie: la, ch'oltre che da ciò ne risultarà ornam.^{to} alla Citta, e com'odo a forrestieri, s'obliga l'istesso Card.^{le} à risarcire, e rifare quella poca parte di muro, che pertal causa occorresse gittar a Riua. E tutto si riciescerà per gratia sing.^{ma} dalla benig^{ta} di SS.^{ta} et di V.S. Illma   Qual Deus

All'Ill:^{mo} et R.^{mo} S.^{re} Il s^{rl}

    Card^{le} Ludouisio

4. *Letter dated August 3, 1622, of Francesco Peperelli to Cardinal Alessandro d'Este*: ASM, Fab. e Vill., Busta 70, Pte. 10, fasc. 19, f. 7r.

Ill:^{mo} et R:^{mo} sig: et Pron mio Coll:^{mo}

Domenica prossima passata andai à Tiuoli con il Muratore à uedere la fabbrica della stalla per uedere se gli gran Catoi poteua patire et anco per uedere ua che termine irà, ho trouato che è abbasa tutta sino sopra al'imposta della uoltà et se anco armato un terzo di d.^{ta} uolta et riescie un bellissimo uaso è spero che sarra di gusto à V. S. Ill:^{ma} hò fatto tralasciare il Murate per rispetto delli grandiss^{mi} Catoi qual credo che alli prime acque d'Agosto siare per cessare et subbito farrò remetter mano con ogni solicitudine et V. S. Ill:^{ma} si arriua che si lauorà con ogni deligenzia ho d.^{to} anco à Maestro Gio: Garda robba che fussia dismettere al fontanile perche tutto quello che si fà per questi Catei ua ogni cosa à male et intanto ci attend^o à fare una bona monitione di robbà per poter poi requistare il tempo perso con che fine facendo a V. S. Illma humiliss.^{ma} Reuernzia e retificandomeli obblig^{mo} seru.^{re} la pieghe à uolermi Conseruare quel laogho di seruitu che sin hora mi ha dimostrar con fauirimi de suoi Comandamenti che piegho dal Cielo ogni desiderato bene di Roma li 3 d'Agosto 1622

D. S. S. Il^{ma} et R^{ma}

                                    humiliss:^{mo} et obblig.^{mo} ser^e

                                          Francesco Peperelli

5. *Contract dated January 7, 1630, for repairs to the Fontanelle*: ASM, Fab. e Vill., Busta 71, Pte. 6, fasc. 2, f. 5:

Adi 7 Genaro 1630 in Roma

L'Illmo Sig.^r Co: Camillo molza Cons.^{re} di stato del Ser^{mo} Sig.^r Duca di Modona come Gou.^{re} del Giardino di Tiuoli, dà, et concede al Sig.^r Giouanni Vincigli Padouano stuccatore, à fare li termini del Fontanile del d.^o Giardino, che deuono rinouarsi per compimento dell'opera, con gle in'fre conditioni.

P.^a Ch'il Sig.^r Co: sia obligato di prouederele à spese del luogho della calce, chiodi, et altre cose che bisognaranno per lauorare.

2.^a Ch'il Sig.^r Co: sia tenuto di far guastare li termini uecchi si come si è fatto dell' historie.

3.^a Ch'al Sig.^r Giouanni se le diano le solite stanze con le solite commodità sino che lauorarà per il luogho.

4.ª Che per ciaschedun termine che farà se le deua dare giulij sei.

5.ª Il detto Sig.ʳ Giouanni promette, e si obliga che li termini che farà, saranno della qualità, e conditione de i primi, e piu'tosto più belli degli altri rinouati, che inferiori.

6.ª Ch'il Sig.ʳ Co: non sia obligate di pagar' il prezzo se non al fine del mese di Aprile [illegible]iache possa chiarirsi [f. 5r] che li termini fatti non habbiano patito la gelata, ne in altra maniera; perche quando hauessero patito anche in minima parte, dourà il Sig.ʳ Giouanni rifarli à tutte sue spese, ne potrà mai pretendere il pagamento se non doppo' che sarà perfetionata tutta l'opera, e che saranno leuati tutti li potimenti, e corrette gle imperfetioni.

7.ª Che per patto espresso il Sig.ʳ Giouanni non possa fare li detti termini per quest' Inuerno, e durante il freddo caso che si habbiano da scoprire le historie già fatte da lui, et che hora sono coperte con li storini, perche il Sig.ʳ Co: non uuole in niuna maniera che possano patire il freddo, la brina, e l'acqua: mà dourà aspettare che passi il rigore dell' Inuernate, e farle all'hora.

E così promettono di osseruare inuiolabilm.ᵗᵉ le parti, e uogliono che la pn'te polize habbia forza d'instro giurato coll'obligo in forma Camera questo di, et anno sud.°

Cam. Molza

jo Giouanni Vencilia afermo che prometo quam disopra. [f. 5v]

6. *Memorandum regarding service rooms dated February 14, 1671, from Mattia de' Rossi*: ASM, Fab. e Vill., Busta 71, Pte. 10, fasc. 11, f. 1.

Ser:ᵐᵃ Altezza

Si manda Il disegnio nel modo che si pensa di fare la credenza, è buttiglieria. È acciò V:ª Alt:ᶻᶻᵃ S:ᵐᵃ possi con più facilità uedere alla prima, è riconosciere Il sito de' Camerini sotto li quali uà la d:ª Credenza si manda la pianta di tutto il Palazzo di Tiuoli si è pensato tuttele uolte che uerrà aprouato da V:ª Al:ᶻᵃ fare sotto d:ª Credenza un passo che dal repiano delle scale grande doue si deue fare la porta che entrerà nella d:ª Credenza, farui una scaletta, che cali a basso, è uadi ind:° passo per comunicare con Il Cortile delle Cocine è d:ª scala grande. Il modo come potrebbe uenire li dimostra il desegnio In profilo fatto sop:ª la medema pianta colorito di Rosso, nel quale si uede, che dal repiano della scala doue è segniata la porta che si douerebbe fare in sono disegniate tanto nel profilo come nella pianta due scalette una sallirebbe alla credenza, restando più alto Il piano di d.ª che Il repiano della scala doue sarebbe la porta, è l'altra scienderebbe nel passo che sarebbe sotto d:ª et anderebbe à comunicare con Il Cortile delle Cocine ind.ª scala, è pare che riuscirebbe molto comodo ad ogniuno. [f. 1r]

La Bottiglieria deue andare al piano della d:ª credenza sottoli camerini uecchij come impianta si uede. È pare che non sarebbe male comunicarle assieme con un passo sotto Il Cortile de Camerinj come si uede segniato acciò uolendo uno andare nell'altro possi andarui senza uscire fuori allo scoperto come dimostra il n:° 9.

Si era pensato anco fare un passo ad uso di bassola sotto Il Cortile de frati di S: Fran:ᶜᵒ che dal tinello potessi entrare nella stanza dietro la Cocina nuoua per ogni buon comodo. Il modo come uerebbe lo dimostra Impianta doue è Il Colorito di giallo el n:° 14—Tutti li sud:ᵉ lauori si eseguiranno con ogni puntualità tutte le uolte che saranno aprouati per buoni e bene distribaiti da V:ª Alte:ᶻᵃ Ser.ᵐᵃ al quale Dia orand. fo hu.ᵐᵃ riu.ª di Roma q.° di 14—Feb.ʳᵒ 1671.

D. V:ª Alt:ᶻᵃ Se.ᵐᵃ

D.ᵐᵒ hu.ᵐᵒ et oblig.ᵐᵒ Se.ʳᵉ
Matthia de Rossi [f. 1v]

7. *Memorandum regarding service rooms dated March 4, 1671, from Mattia de' Rossi:* ASM, Fab. e Vill., Busta 71, Pte. 11, ff. 9 and 23.

S.ma Altezza

Li tre disegni Inclusi dimostrano il sito doue si pensa fare la Credenza, bottiglieria, legniara, stanza per Il Carbone, Cantina, grotta, è stanza per la biada; uno di questi disegni segniato A è la pianta del piano de Camerinj, doue destintamente dimostra cosa per cosa. L'Altro disegnio segniato B dimostra Il piano della Credenza, con bottiglieria, passo, che comunica l'una e l'altra con scala libera che salli ad:ᵃ bottiglieria, è stanza per la biada.

Si è pensato per ogni buon comodo leuare quella scala a cordoni che dal Cortile de Camerinj cala al Cortile delle Cocine, et abassare quel sito é farui una stanza per la biada come nel disegnio al n:º 14 si uede, è sarà alta dal piano del Cortile delle Cocine p:ᵐⁱ 8, é per poterui andare fare una scaletta per di fuori nel Cortile come dimostra il n:º 15; accanto d.ᵃ stanza farui un passo per potere comunicare la Credenza è buttiglieria, et abassare quel passo doue è lad.ᵃ Cordonata al pari della d.ᵃ Credenza per quanto è largho d:º passo, è farui il suo muro con una porta nel mezzo dell'uano per potere tutte le uolte che si uole andare dalli Camerinj alle sud:ᵉ Credenza, e bottiglieria senza passare [f. 9r] per altre parti, con lassare tutta quella cordonata che al presente risponde nel Cortile de Camerini; sop:ᵃ la sud:ᵃ porta si lasserà una feritoia per Il trauerso acciò possi alluminare d:º passo.

Questa scala che si pensa leuare si crede non possi riuscire male perche al presente quel sito è tutto perso, che allhora doppo fattoui quello si è detto di sop:ᵃ seruirebbe per utile è comodo, è tutta quella quantità che anderebbe leuata lo dimostra Il desegnio segniato C per quanto si uede colorito di uerde al n:º 11, è quelli medemi scalini à cordoni potrebbono seruire per li uiali che salleno nel giardino doue sono l'Arbori sotto Il uialone grande, li quali hanno necessità di metteruene.

Il disegnio segniato C dimostra Il passo da farsi sotto la Credenza per andare à dirittura dalle scale alle Cocine doue ui si farà una scala infaccia à quella che ui è al presente con n:º 8 scalini che sarà giusto al piano del Cortile delle Cocine. La stanza per Il Carbone è quella del n:º 8 è Il sito per mettere le legm'e è quello doue al presente si passa, Il quale doppo fatto Il sud.º passo sotto la Credenza pu le seruire benissimo per legm'e, con fare una porta di legnio [f. 9v] dalla parte doppo scienta la scala da poterla leuare è dall'altro parte' uerso il Cortile delle Cocine farui un cancello dà poterlo medemamente leuare.

Vi sono due Cantine segniate in d:º disegnio n:º 10 una delle quale confina con Il muro della loggia del Cortile, è l'altra arriua sino sotto Il Corritore della scala segniata n:º 5. È questa ultima si crede che cauandola potrebbe seruire per grotta, è cosi si hauerebbe cantina è grotta unita assieme, benche di grotta pare non uenesia necessità mentre ui nè un' oliua sotto li frati di ogni grande Capacità come in altri desegni mandati si uede. Le due Cantine sud:ᵉ sono senza lume affatto, è uolendogline dare si è pensato fare due ferritore sotto due scalini che sono della scala che dal piano del Cortile salleno alle loggie di sop.ᵃ

La Camera segniata n:º 8 doue si è desinato mettere Il Carbone si troua tanto alta Inuolta che si è pensato farui un solaro al piano di quella della Credenza è darla per comodo della med.ᵃ Credenza come nel disegnio si uede.

A capo Il sito doue fà buttato la terra del Giardinetto per la parte di fuori accanto Il uialone doue pote restare coperta è dal muro è dall'arbori, et Insito dà non offendere, ne essere offesa. Li si potrebbe fare la giaccicia uolendo simile cose stare allo scoperto con farui le sue di fere di coperto [f. 23r] solito è necessarie.

V.ª Altezza S:ᵐᵃ trouarà da questi disegni à quell'altri Inuiatoli qualche mutatione, Il tutto è cagionato perche sop.ᵃ Il fatto si è esaminato con diligenza, è agiustatosi in modo che pare che in quest ultima determinatione possi passare, questo è quanto si puote dire intorno alle fabriche di Tiuoli—fò hu:ᵐᵃ riu.ᶻᵃ à V.ª Altezza Se:ᵐᵃ di Roma Il di 4 Marzo 1671

D V.ª Al.ᶻᵃ S.ᵐᵃ

Dᵐᵒ hu.ᵐᵒ et oblig.ᵐᵒ
Matthia de Rossi   [f. 23v]

8. *Explanation to drawing of third project for credenza*: ASM, Fab. e Vill., Busta 71, Pte. 11, f. 20r.

Il Camerino segniato A destinato per la credenza uà inpiano con Il Camerino segniato B et altra stanza segniata C si è stabilito Il piano come Il profilo dimostra è si è abassato più di quello si era già destinato perche doppo hauere leuato tutta la terra, è in tempo che si uoleua stabilire Il piano, si e trouatola uolta del Camerino segniato B tre p:ᵐⁱ più bassa di quella del Camerino segniato A nella parte di sotto come dal profilo si uede, é per renderlo più sfogato si è abassato il piano della Credenza, è doue prima si faceua una scaletta per sallire dal repiano della scala segniato D; hora non ui si farà solo che due scalini, come il medemo profilo dimostra:

Il Camerino sud:º segniato A la sua uolta è fatta à schifo, è per mantenimento di quella si uolterà un'arco come nel profilo si uede In lettera E è similmente impianta colorito di giallo, questo arco seruirà per mantenere questa uolta è non farà conosciere la uolta che resta più bassa del Camerino segniato B restando decotta da d:º Arco.

Dal piano del Cortile delle Cocine al piano delli camerini terreni si sallirà uno scalino di mezzo palmo d'altezza come Il profilo dimostra

A. Camerino destinato per la credenza
B. Altro camerino destinato per la mede'ma credenza
C. Altro camerino destinato per la me'dema credenza
D. Repiano apiedi la scala che scende dal cortile del palazzo
E. Arco che serue per mantenere la uolta à schifo del Camerino A
F. Stanza incomune, che uà alla credenza è buttiglieria
G. Passo che conduce alla buttiglieria con tre scalini nella grossezza del muro
H. Buttiglieria
I. Luogho doue è la scala à cordoni [f. 20r]

9. *Inscription and cost estimate on plan of stable*: ASM, Fab. e Vill., Busta 71, Pte. 10, fasc. 2, ff. 3r and 4r.

Il Colorito di negro sotto la Carta reportata dimostra le stalle nel modo che si ritrouano di presente, le quale sono eleuate con muri bassi è coperte con tetto con le pendenze uerso li Cortili.

Il Colorito di giallo nella Carta reportata dimostra le stalle che si pensa fare di nuouo, le quale sono capace di n:º 80 Cauallj è nell'altra stalluta inuerso il Cortile grande dietro la Fontana sotto la loggia scoperta ui potranno stare n:º 12 altri Caualli che as:ᵉ dette stalle saranno capace di n:º 92 Caualli. [f. 3r]

Per far le stalle nel Palazzetto secondo il disegno mandato di Roma, l'Architetto figura, ch ui forse andare di spesa intorno à mille scudi.

Per risarcir poi tutto il Palazzo, e farui quello, che occorre, perche non sia così mal'andato, come si ritruoua, fanno conto, che con due milla scudi si ridurrà in qualche migliore stato, e più decente. [f. 4r]

10. *Memorandum regarding Fountain of Rome dated July 9, 1672, from Mattia de' Rossi:* ASM, Fab. e Vill., Busta 71, Pte. 10, fasc. 13, ff. 1r-2r.

Ser:ᵐᵃ Altezza

Si è considerato che nel sia doue è la fontana della Roma resta assai pouero d'acqua, è non hà corispondenza alcuna alfontanone incontro adiritutiera dell'Viale delle fontanelle, è perche si chiede farebbe bene in d:º luogho una grande apparenza d'acqua senza hauere à guastare nè demolire punto di quello è fatto è sarebbe in fare nel modo che si uede disegniato, il quale dimostra come sta di presente, è la Carta reportata Sop.ᵃ dimostra come si pensarebbe fare quando da S:ᵃ Alezza uenisse approuato, è sarebbe nel modo che segue, cioè tra la uasca della Roma, è il uestibuolo del panteon ui sono p:ᵐⁱ otto di distanza si pensa deuare una fontana dietro d.ᵃ Roma in modo che quando non ui sia acqua non si uedi, nè leui la uista al medemo panteon uedendosi altro che la tazza la quale arriuerà giusto all'altezza delle spalle della figura della medema [f. 1r] Roma, la quale quando butterà farà la mostra che si uede nel disegnio, è uerà à cadere dentro la uasca sottola Roma et il ritorno della medema uerà nel piano sotto il piedistallo della Roma, è farà la Cascata nel fiume doue è la barchetta con la guglia; facendo in questo modo farà bonissima corispondenza alfontanone incontro, et In fare d.ᵃ fontana sarà di pochissima spesa, che il più sarà il condurre l'acqua dalla Cascata, che è di già per fianco della medema Roma sino ad:ᵃ fontana doue deue fare la prima cascata, il resto della spesa consisterebbe in puoco è farebbe bellissima uista.

Nel giardino intesta il Viale che è per fianco delle peschiere ui è un torrione, doue e la scala che cale all'arboreto sarebbe bene aprirui unfenestrone nel modo che si uede disegniato con adornamento corispontende all'altro della uiale doue [f. 1v] è la spaliera de cedri, dal qual fenestrone si uederebbe Roma è farebbe effetto bellissimo uenendo dal d:º Viale; Il disegnio che si manda del torrione si uede nel modo che è di presente è la carta repatata sop.ᵃ dimostra nel modo che sarebbe quando il d.º fenestrone fusse fatto, è questo si douerà fare quando uerà approuato da S.ᵃ Altezza.

Agiungendo inquanto la fontana dà farsi dietro la Roma come dimostra il desegnio si puote accrescere l'acqua che cade per fianco come si è detto di sop:ᵃ senza leuarne niente della medema, bastondone tanta che seruirebbe per darne à una e l'altra il che e facilissimo fohᵐᵒ rid.ⁱ all'Altezza V.ᵃ S.ᵐᵃ di Roma Il di 9 lgº 1672.

D. V.ᵃ Altezza S.ᵐᵃ

L'Adornamento di metallo che si
fà per il quadro dell'Altare si
tira auanti con celerità epende
di già fatto il gettito della
Cera con apparenza di bona riuscita.

Dᵐᵒ Suʳᵉ et Obj Le
Matthia de Rossi

[f. 2r]

11. *Memorandum regarding fountain to be in front of Villa:* ASM, Fab. e Vill., Busta 71, Pte. 10, fasc. 4, ff. 1r-5r.

Relatione in ordine il disegnio della fontana dà farsi di
nuouo à Tiuoli nell'Vialone del Giardino sotto il Palazzo

Per fare che questa fontana facci la sua mostra secondo si desidera, che dall'entrata del portone del giardino si ueda superare di gran lungo il tetto del Palazzo, è che la medema apparischi una gran montagnia d'acqua; si è pensato fare un disegnio nel modo che si uede delineato in grande, con una portione della facciata del Palazzo che dimostra dietro d:º fontana.

Questa fontana sarà formata ad uso di Pirimide per potere tirare l'acqua in alto è coperta più che si puote, acciò doppo uscita possi fare quella mostra desiderabile. Questa piramide sarà formata con tre resalti doue uscirà con forsa l'acqua, è farà tre cascate per d:º piramide, è poi uerrà à schersare abasso gli scogli che faranno piedistallo è posam:ᵉ à d:ᵃ, è caderà nella tazza che posera al piano dell'uiale. Il bullore di mezzo che dall'entrata della porta del giardino si uederà superare il tetto del Palazzo per l'altezza di p.ᵐⁱ quindici incirca come dal disegnio in grande si uede, sarà di quantità d'acqua per una uolta è mezza di quella del bicchierone [f. 1r] l'altra partira per le tre cascate sud:ᵉ di d: piramide, che accompagniata con la medema del sud:ᵉ bullore farà l'effetto che dimostra il disegnio, li altri due bullori che escono dalli scogli che sono nel posamento di d: Piramide che uanno in alto si crede possino fare bellissimo effetto stante che la ueduta farà credere che crescino dalle bande dell'acqua del bicchierone, é uerrà ad allargare, è apparirà essere magior quantità d'acqua di quella che ui e al presente à d:ᵉ bicchierone.

Il Retorno di questa fontana si prensa farla uenire à cadere auanti la fontana dell'Ercole acciò facci una gran cascata sotto il bicchierone come dimostra il desegnio della ueduta di tutto il giardino à stare doppo l'entrata del portone al primo teatro de' Cipressi che è il piano doue sono le peschiere delli uiali grandi del Giardino sotto l'organo; poi sotto detta cascata si uedrà la fontana della girandola la quale è gran copia d'acqua; si che quando sarà data l'acqua à tuttele sud: fontane si crederà un fiume in aria, che unita la uista à tutta l'acqua, non si conoscierà di doue scaturischi, è si uede possi rendere amiratione à riguardanti [f. 1v] é perche doppo fatta la mostra l'acqua della nuoua fontana da farsi, che terminerà il suo effetto sotto la fontana dell'Ercole; hà bisognio di retorno, si crede potersi fare una uasca grande nel boschetto che è sotto il uiale delle fontenelle, che uà alla Roma dà una parte, è dall'altra alfontanone per d: ritorno, è dà quella portarne una parte alli due parapetti della scala che cala incontrola fontana della girandola doue sonole catene che portano l'acqua per li medemj parapetti, è nel mezzo di detti fare alzare gran zampiglionj dalle parti di d: scala, come dimostra il disegnio, et un'altra portione portare auanti le peschiere che sono ne uiali grandi al pari del' teatro de Cipressi, è li medemamente fare alzare gran zampiglionj, che seguitino per tuttala lunghezza sino al' medemo teatro di Cipressi, [in margin: accantole palliere] due altre parti portarne una à fare un gran bagniatore nel medemo teatro de Cipressi, che mentre i riguardanti stanno in d: teatro mirando una marauiglia simile d'acque possino essere bagniati in modo che dificilmente si possino saluare, è l'altra portione portarla alla porta principale che entra nel giardino acciò quando escono li forastieri possino essere accompagniati dall'acqua per la parte di dietro. [f. 2r]

L'Effetto, è l'amiratione che douerà rendere tutto il giardino alla prima uista doppo che si sarà entrato nella porta, è si uerrà uerso il teatro è peschiere lò dimostra il disegnio che per l'apparenza d'acque si crede possi essere singulare:

La medesima acqua che douerà seruire per la fontana nuoua sud: potrebbe anco seruire alla fontana che si resarciscie incontro il uialone sotto il Palazzo che riescie ortimamente bene in quanto al prospetto, quando si uolesse ornare di fontana più propria, et seruire anco alla fontana delli scogli ingiunta della sua propria di conserua auanti li frati, é per fare anco di gran giuochi sotto l'organo doue è la fontana principiata, stante che doppo si sarà fatta la mostra, che appariscie nel disegnio si leuerà l'acqua è quella medema con una Chiaue mandarla nelli luoghi sud:, et altro sicondoche si uorrà per hauerla dà per tutto ad'arbitrio.

Nel disegnio che mostra tutto il prospetto del giardino non ui si sono disegniati l'arbori di pigni come che deformano per la confusione è per l'altezza che ua crescendo fuori della semitria del giardino mentre non sono dall'altra parte, è quella medema [f. 2v] resterà confusa mentre si lasciono cresciere tutti indiferentemente senza ordine alcuno. [f. 3r]

———

Per la nuoua fontana che si deue fare à Tiuoli nell'Vialone del giardino sotto Il Palazzo si è pensato che Inuece di fare adornamento di fontana, non farebbe male effetto il Piantare una Guglia, che all'entrata del Giardino si fusse ueduta auanti il Palazzo come Il disegnio dimostra, et hauerbbe fatto fenimento sopra tutte le altre fontane, è doppo dato l'acqua al bicchierone si sarebbe uista scaturire l'acqua dalla cima della Guglia, è dalle parte di essa alzare le fontane che escono dal naso de' delfinj, è quando fussero cessate le fontane si uederebbe la guglia senza acqua, è renderebbe maestà é magnificenza al Palazzo; è inquesto modo sarebbe una fontana che giungerebbe all'Improuiso à riguardanti. [f. 5r]

12. *Explanation of layout of Secret Garden*: ASM, Fab. e Vill., Busta 72, Pte. 2, f. 10.

Relazione per Il desegnio del Giardinetto che si deue
agiustare à Tiuoli, posto nel fianco del Palazzo uerso
la Piazza di S: Fran.ᶜᵒ

A. Colorito di giallo tanto li due tondi, come li due ouati sono le quattro fontanelle che si pensa tassare nel mezzo delli quattro spartimenti del Giardinetto.

B. Sono le quattro fontanelle detti li scogli che ui sono al presente, è queste non si mouono.

C. Sono le spalliere di mortelle che reserrano li quadri del d:º Giardinetto da un piedistallo all'altro.

D. Sito che recorre con la spalliera, mà è piantato di cipressi, li quali restano, come si trouano di presente.

E. Piazzetta ad uso di Theatro nel mezzo del giardinetto, laquale resta medemamente come stà di presente con il suo pauimento fatto di musaico.

Tutto Il Colorito di giallo sono li piedistalli che si pensa di fare nelle testate delle spalliere, sopra li quali si doueranno metterui de uasi per adornamento del Giardinetto. [f. 10r]

Tutti li spartimenti tinti di uerde che sono li due ouati grandi, è li due tondi con requadri attorno si deuono fare piantati di mortelle, mà che non si faccino cresciere niente più di tre quarti di p.ᵐᵒ Romano, è mantenerle senpre à quella medema altezza. [f. 10v]

13. *Memorandum regarding the Fountain of Europa dated September 25, 1671*: ASM, Fab. e Vill., Busta 71, Pte. 10, fasc. 12, ff. 1-4r.

Il di 25 7mbre 1671
Relatione per il Resarcimento dà farsi alla fontana Intesta il uialone del Giardino sotto il Palazzo à Tiuoli

Questa fontana è fabricata con due ordini d'Architettura, cioè primo ordine Dorico, è 2:º ordine Ionico come dimostra il disegnio che si manda, et è corispondente all'adornamento incontro che entra nella loggia de Cardinali; ne hè fatto di d:º Adornamento tutto il primo ordine dorico, è del secondo ordine nè hè fatto dà una parte sino sop.ᵃ li capitelli, è dall'Altra parte sino l'altezza dell'Ametà delli pilastri come Il tutto dimostra il delineato di giallo in d:º disegnio è dal giallo in sù non ui è niente di fabrica, ò perche d:ª fabrica sia rouinata, ò perche sia remasta imperfetta.

Per perfettionare d.ª fabrica si crede non potessi essere male di seguitare il mede'mo ordine d'Architettura sino sop.ª la Cornice senza guastare il fatto; è ben uero, che in uece di fare sop.ª li capitelli l'Architraue, fregio, e cornice, si potrebbe fare un fenimento d'una cornice Architrauata come dimostra il disegnio con agiungerui un fenimento nel mezzo con la sua Arme come dal d:º disegnio si puote uedere & l'Altro adornamento Incontro doue è la loggia de Cardinali corispondente alsud:º il suo fenimento. [f. 1r]

Sop.ª è d'Architraue, fregio, e Cornice con balaustrata come dal ultimo disegnio già mandato si potrà uedere, mà perche questo prospetto non si uede nel medesimo tempo che si uede l'Altro per la lontananza della fontana, si crede possi essere bastante et anco di buona proportione Il fare la Cornice Architrauata sop.ª nominata con quel fenimento nel mezzo Il quale si crede non possi fare male. [f. 1v]
[In another hand]

Quanto poi alla prospettiua della facciata io mi sono inteso, che habbia da cominciare dal fondo fondo [sic], e coprire tutta la scala unendo un fiocco d'acqua con l'altro, in modo che semtri tuttj uno masso d'acqua uolanto sino all'ultima fontana demonti dissegnata ultimam.te principiando dà basso con fiocchi larghi e pieni, et andando di mano in mano degradando sinche si formi una liquida Piramide, e tutto lo studio hà dà mettersi à riempire ogni uacuo che la potesse deformare.

Per Intendere il sud:e Capitolo è necessario mandare à Roma una copia del disegnio della prospettiua del Giardino che si mando costà et in quella segniare con numeri, ò altro segnio il luogho doue si desidera fare uedere l'acqua nel modo che si accenna; in altro modo non si puote fare studio sop:ª di ciò, che non hauendo il desegnio contraregniato si potrebbe fare errore. Quando non si uolesse copiare tutto il disegnio, basterebbe il pezzo di mezzo doue sonole scale, è uedute delle fontane et in quello contraregniareli si si [sic] che [f. 2r] che sibiamano, per potere por' sopra di questo fare studio particolare.

Il disegnio del Palazzo di Reggio é à buon porto, e facilmente questi altra settimana si potrà mandare.

Sarebbe bene mandare un profilo ò spaccato del Palazzo del Vescouato è farlo nel sito delli Cameronj fatti di nuouo, con metterui l'altezze che saro dà un piano di mattonato all'altro cominciando dal piano terreno sino al tetto. Questo si domanda perche si uole fare un disegnio della facciata principale del Palazzo, acciò si uede in che modo si potrebbe fare. [f. 2v]

Disegnio nel modo che sarebbe la fontana nell'Vialone sotto il Palazzo, quando fusse resarcita, conlasciarui la statua che ui si troua di presente nel modo che stà, con un rustico di sassi da faruisi di nuouo sotto doue è l'arco, accio l'acque scersino; et Inquanto all'Architettura che fà adornamento à d:º fontana per di fuori, uiene acompagniare l'Altra Architettura incontro della loggia detta de Cardinale per si era però pensato di lassare adietro la Balaustrata quando non ui si uolesse fare, ancorche nel giardino si potrebbono trouare di molti balaustri fuori d'opera da posessene ualere. [f. 4r]

INDEX

Aaron, rod of, 59
Abbate, Niccolo dell', 62
Abundantia, 163
Accademia degli Agevoli, 95
Achilles, 72, 80, 82, 85 n. 16, 89, 99
Actaeon, 35
Active Life, 91
Aequitas, 43 n. 4, 163
Aesculapius, 70, 74, 75
Agamemnon, 82
Agnelo d'Ambosia (Ambonsia or Ambrosia), 125
Agresti, Livio, 5, 41, 42, 43, 45, 46, 67, 69, 77
Albani, Cardinal, 122
Albergati, G. B., 27, 105
Alberti, Durante, 65, 66
Alberto da Caselano, 100 n. 17, 101 n. 23
Albio, 61, 86
Albunea, 31, 32, 63, 64, 86
Albuneo, river, 85, 87
Aleotti, Giovanni Battista, 134-35
Alexander IV, Pope, 6
Alexander VI, Pope, 3
Alfonsi, Aluigi, 41 n. 2
amaranth, flowering, 162
Amazonomachy, 70, 71 n. 5, 85, 88, 90 n. 29
Amici, Ascanio and Guido, 7 n. 13
Amicitia, see Friendship
anchor, 162
Andrea, pittore, 55
Andrea da Reggio, 46 n. 18
Andrea Romano, fontaniere, 22 n. 24, 55
Andreon, maestro, 18 n. 10
Andromeda, 35
Angelo, 116, 119
Anio, King, 63, 86
Anio, river, 24, 32, 63, 85, 86, 87
Annunciation, 50
Antiope, 71
Antonio, scarpellino, 111 n. 58
Antonio da Cagli, 62 n. 70
Antonio da Pesaro, 46 n. 18
Antonio Francesco Fiorentino, 37
Antwerp, 45 n. 13
Apennines, 24
Apollo, 19, 35, 51, 60, 63, 86
Apollodorus, 56
apples, golden, see Apples of the Hesperides
Apples of the Hesperides, 22, 35, 47, 52, 57, 65, 78-79, 80, 81, 88, 90, 95, 105
Aragoni, fontaniere, 120
Ararat, mount, 66
Arco, Count, 135
Arethusa, 23
Ariccia, founding of, 74, 76; sanctuary of Diana, 75-76; Temple of Aesculapius, 75, 76; Temple of

Diana Nemorense, 75; Temple of Hippolytus-Virbius, 75, 76; Temple of Vesta, 75, 76
Ariosto, 5
Aristeo, 8 n. 15
Arno, river, 91
Arquier, Giovanni, 109, 112 n. 61
Asinaio, mount, 91
Assumption of the Virgin, 120 n. 95
Athamas, insanity of, 56, 60, 63, 86
Atlas, 84, 134
Atreus, house of, 81
Augustus, 89; denarius of, 74 n. 10

Bacchus, 33, 34, 36, 50, 51, 60, 86-87, 107
Bagnaia, Villa Lante, 6, 14, 39, 133, 134
balance, 58, 161, 163
Balbo, 99 n. 8
Banquet of the Gods, 56
Barazoni, Giovanni, Cavaliere, 108 n. 50
Baroccio, Federigo, 67
Baroque, 39, 133
basket of fruit, 161
Bassi Bolognese, 28 n. 41
Battista da Lugnano, 10 n. 21
Baviera, 8 n. 15
Belgio, see Bergio
Bembo, Pietro, medal of, 33 n. 54
Benedetto Fiorentino, 46 n. 18
Benedict XIV, Pope, 122
Benedictine Order, 6
Benignitas, 161
Bergeret de Grancourt, Pierre Jacques, 131-32
Bergio, 61, 86
Bernardino del Borgo, 62 n. 70
Bernardo, 8 n. 15, 20 n. 16
Bernardo da Chiaravalle, 44
Bernardo da Melia, see Bernardo da Chiaravalle
Bernini, Gian Lorenzo, 104 n. 30, 113, 115, 117, 118, 120, 133
Besançon, Musée, drawings by Fragonard and Robert, 131
Bianchi, Giovanni, 50
Bias, 57
Biasioto, 10, 11 n. 22, 17 n. 8, 23 n. 27, 33 n. 55 and n. 58
Birth of Dionysus, 71
Birth of the Virgin, 49, 71
block, squared, 161
Bocca, Valerio, 62 n. 70
Boccaccio, Giovanni, 17, 56, 71 n. 5
Bochetto, Lorenzo, 46 n. 18, 61 n. 62
Boeckler, Georg Andreas, 128
Bogarde, Cornelis, 44 n. 12
Bologna, 45 n. 13
Bologna, Pinacoteca, *Vigilance* by Calvaert, 45 n. 13
Bolognini family, 45 n. 13
book, 58, 63, 161, 162, 163

Borgia, Lucrezia, 3, 71
Borgia family, 4
Borgo San Sepulcro, 44
Boulanger, Flaminio, 41 n. 2
bouquet, 162
Bramante, stuccatore, 43 n. 6, 45 n. 14
Bramante, Donato, 14, 39
bridle, 58
Briganti, 8 n. 15
Brosses, Charles de, 130
Brussels, 136
Buonarroti, Michelangelo, the Younger, *Il Natal d'Ercole*, 85 n. 16

Caccacuore, 8 n. 15
caduceus, 161, 162, 163
Caffi, Giuseppe, 7 n. 13
Calandrino, Paolo, 31, 35, 52, 54, 165, 166
Calcagnini, Lelio, 95
Calcica, Spica, 8 n. 15
Calderoni, Giulio, 106
Caligula, 26
Callisto, 35
Calvaert, Denis, 44
Cambio, Marc Antonio, 65 n. 74, 93 n. 43
Cambridge, Mass., P. Hofer collection, drawing by I. Silvestre, 108 n. 49
Camera Apostolica, 6
Camillo, pittore, 65 n. 74
Caprarola, Palazzo Farnese, 6, 14, 39, 44, 67, 91, 92; Sala dell' Ercole, 54, 67, 91
Capriani, Francesco, 98, 99
Carandini, residente, 109
Cardinal d'Este, see Este, Luigi d', Cardinal
Cardinal of Ferrara, see Este, Ippolito II d', Cardinal
Cardinals, College of, 4; Dean of, 13, 98, 102, 109, 110
Careggi, Villa Medici, 14
Caritas, see Charity
Carlo, 116
Carlo III, King of the Two Sicilies, 136
Caro, Annibal, 43 n. 4, 91
Caroline of Brunswick, 136
Carrarino, Andrea, 116 n. 83
Carstensen, Georg, 136
Cartaro, Mario, 126
Caserta, Royal Palace, gardens, 136
Castello, Medici gardens, 6, 39, 91, 92, 96 n. 55
Castor, 36, 81, 82
Catani, Giacomo, 46 n. 18
Catillus, 60, 86
Cato, Ercole, 72, 95 n. 51, 141
Caus, Salomon de, 136; *Les raisons des forces movvants*, 128, 136

179

ILLUSTRATIONS

Since the legend of the Dupérac engraving proved illegible in reduction it was eliminated, and the numbered identifications that appear in it are translated below and keyed to the illustrations in this book. The numbers on the engraving were illegible also and the surprinting corrects the position of No. 18, misplaced in the Fountain of Rome on the engraving. Projects marked with an asterisk either were not executed or were not completed with the symbolism originally planned.

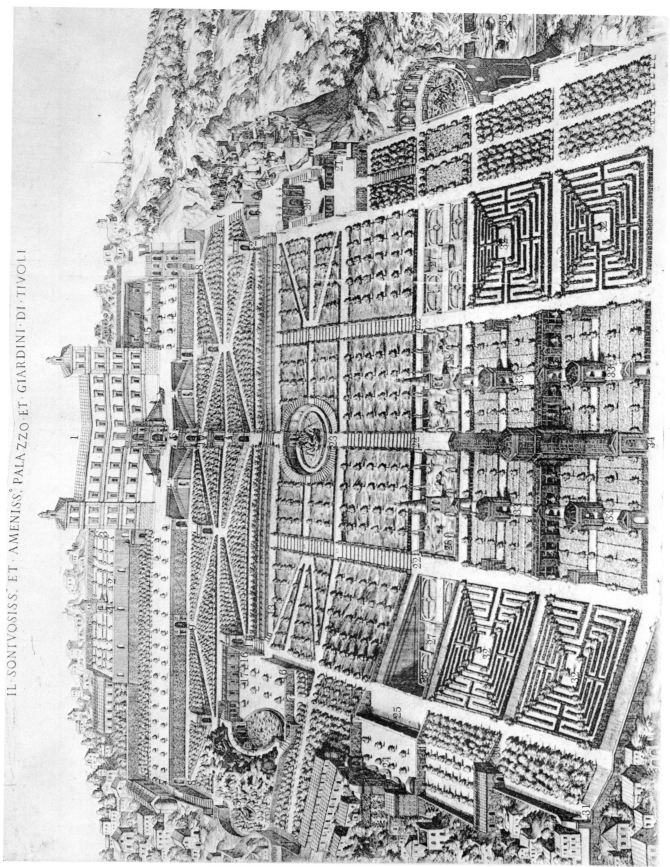

IL·SONTVOSISS.·ET·AMENISS.·PALAZZO·ET·GIARDINI·DI·TIVOLI

1. E. Dupérac, *Engraving of the Villa d'Este*

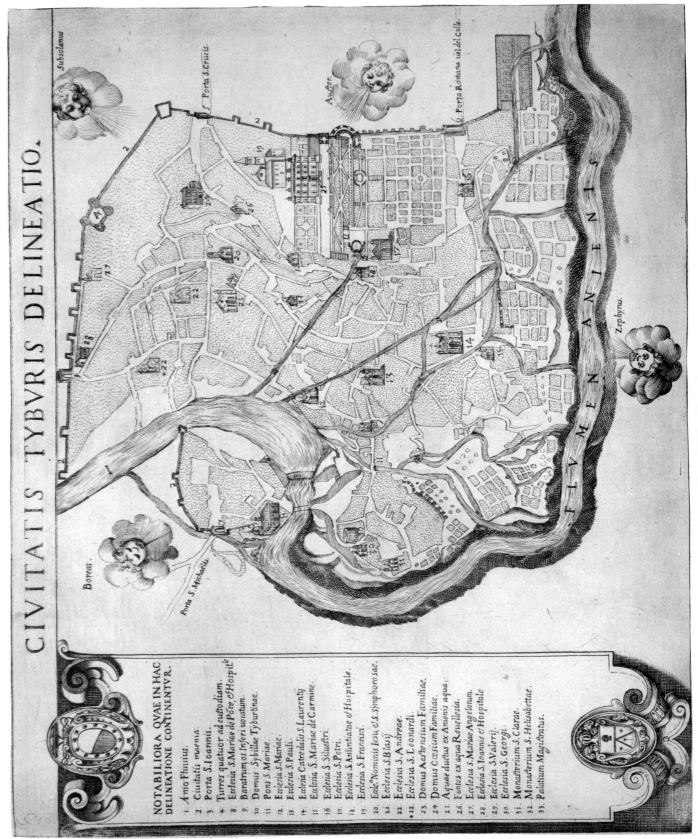

2. Map of Tivoli, 17th century

3. Courtyard

4. Courtyard with Fountain of Venus

5. Entrance Loggia

6. Dining Loggia

7. Northeastern Façade

8. SALOTTO. Fresco of the Villa d'Este

9. Water Organ

10. Statue of Mother Nature

11. WATER ORGAN. Statue of Apollo

12. WATER ORGAN. Statue of Orpheus

13. WATER ORGAN. Tempietto

14. Venturini, Engraving of the Fish Pools

15. Venturini, Engraving of the Stairs of the Bubbling Fountains

16. Venturini, Engraving of the Fountain of the Dragon

17. Fountain of the Dragon

18. Venturini, Engraving of the Fountain of the Owl

19. Fountain of the Emperors, now Proserpina

20. FOUNTAIN OF ROME. Full View

21. FOUNTAIN OF ROME. Venturini, Engraving of the Cascade

22. FOUNTAIN OF ROME. Boat

23. FOUNTAIN OF ROME. Venturini, Engraving

24. FOUNTAIN OF ROME. Ruins of Buildings

25. FOUNTAIN OF ROME. Statue of Roma

26. FOUNTAIN OF ROME. Statue of Wolf with Twins

27. ALLEY OF THE HUNDRED FOUNTAINS
Present State

28. ALLEY OF THE HUNDRED FOUNTAINS
Reliefs

29. ALLEY OF THE HUNDRED FOUNTAINS
Venturini, Engraving

30. OVAL FOUNTAIN. Full View

31. OVAL FOUNTAIN. Detail of the Nymphs

32. OVAL FOUNTAIN. Tiburtine Sibyl

33. OVAL FOUNTAIN. Erculaneo

34. OVAL FOUNTAIN. Pegasus

36. OVAL FOUNTAIN. Orpheus (?)

35. OVAL FOUNTAIN. Bacchus

37. Maggi, Engraving of the Fountain of the Swans

38. Venturini, Engraving of the Grotto of Bacchus

39. Grotto of Diana

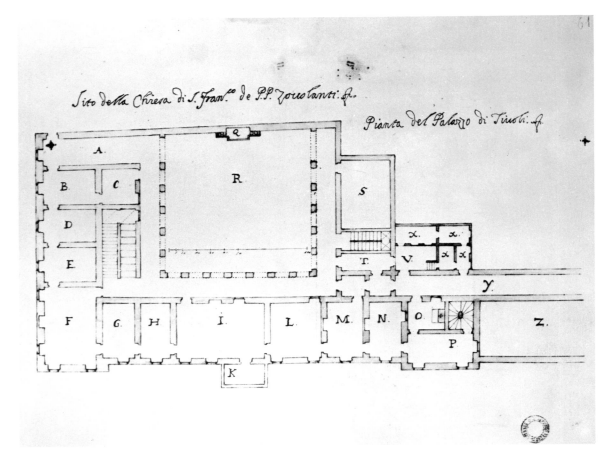

40. Plan of the Villa d'Este, 1687

41. SALONE. Full View

42. SALONE. Virtues: Temperantia and Religio

43. SALONE. End Cove

44. SALONE. Landscape with the Temple of the Sibyl

45. SALONE. Landscape with the Temple of Hercules

46. ANTECHAMBER. Virtues: Tranquilitas and Providentia

47. ANTECHAMBER. Corner of Room

48. BEDROOM. Virtues: Fortitudo and Pax

49. BEDROOM. Corner Showing Frieze

50. CHAPEL. Sanctuary

51. CHAPEL. Fresco of Prophet

52. CHAPEL. End Wall

53. SALOTTO. Full View

54. SALOTTO. Cove with Fresco of Jupiter and Juno

55. SALOTTO. Cove with Fresco of Mercury and Minerva

56. SALOTTO. Cove with Fresco of Mars and Venus

57. SALOTTO. Cove with Fresco of Bacchus and Ceres

58. SALOTTO. Fresco of Feast of the Gods

59. SALOTTO. End Cove

60. SALOTTO. Small Rustic Fountain

61. SALOTTO. Fresco of the Water Organ

62. SALOTTO. End Wall with Rustic Fountain

63. ROOM OF HERCULES. Corner of Cove

64. ROOM OF HERCULES. Detail Showing Illusionistic Painting

65. ROOM OF HERCULES. Long Cove

66. ROOM OF HERCULES. Fresco of the Council of the Gods

67. ROOM OF NOBILITY. Southwest Wall

68. ROOM OF NOBILITY. Opposite Wall

69. ROOM OF NOBILITY. Fresco of Personification of Nobility

70. ROOM OF NOBILITY. Corner of Cove with Cardinal's *Impresa*

71. ROOM OF GLORY. Detail Showing Illusionistic Painting

72. ROOM OF GLORY. Ceiling and Cove

73. ROOM OF GLORY. Fresco of Allegory of Tempus

74. ROOM OF GLORY. Fresco of Allegory of Fortuna

75. ROOM OF GLORY. Fresco of Allegory of Religio

76. FIRST TIBURTINE ROOM. Fresco of Landing of Catillus

77. FIRST TIBURTINE ROOM. Detail Showing Illusionistic Painting

78. FIRST TIBURTINE ROOM. Fresco of Founding of Tivoli

79. FIRST TIBURTINE ROOM. Fresco of Hercules Saxanus

80. SECOND TIBURTINE ROOM. Fresco of Apollo the Sun-god

81. SECOND TIBURTINE ROOM. Northeast Wall Showing Illusionistic Painting

82. SECOND TIBURTINE ROOM. Fresco of the
Madness of Athamas

83. SECOND TIBURTINE ROOM. Fresco of the
Drowning of King Anio

84. SECOND TIBURTINE ROOM. Fresco of Venus

85. SECOND TIBURTINE ROOM. Fresco of the
Worship of the Tiburtine Sibyl

86. ROOM OF NOAH. Fresco of the Sacrifice of Noah

87. ROOM OF NOAH. Corner with Antique Landscape Frescoes

88. ROOM OF MOSES. Fresco of Landscape

89. ROOM OF MOSES. Fresco of Moses Striking the Rock

90. Ligorio, Battle of the Greeks and Amazons

91. Ligorio, Marriage of Theseus and Hippolita

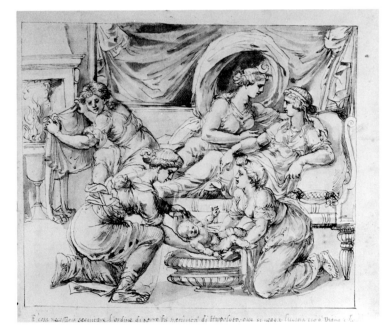

92. Ligorio, Birth of Hippolytus

93. Ligorio, Education of Hippolytus

94. Ligorio, Hippolytus the Horsetamer

95. Ligorio, Phaedra Spying on Hippolytus

96. Ligorio, Hippolytus Initiated into the
Eleusinian Mysteries

97. Ligorio, The Attempted Seduction of
Hippolytus

98. Ligorio, The Curse of Theseus

99. Ligorio, The Suicide of Phaedra

100. Ligorio, The Death of Hippolytus

101. Ligorio, The Revival of Hippolytus as Virbius

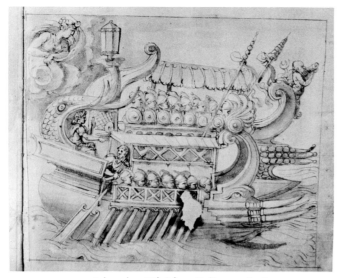

102. Ligorio, Virbius Sails to Italy

103. Ligorio, The Founding of Ariccia

104. Ligorio, The Sanctuary of Nemi

105. Ligorio, The Battle of the Slaves at Nemi

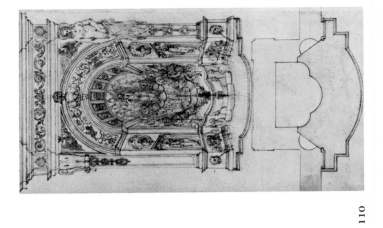

108

110

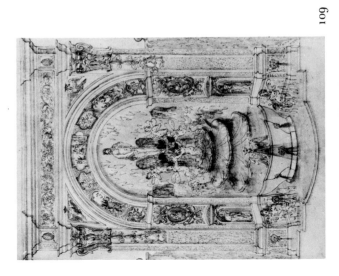

109

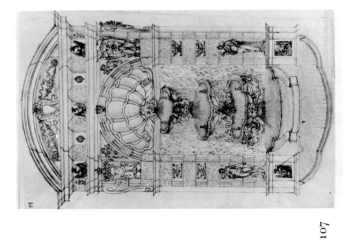

107

106. Maggi, Engraving of the
Fountain of Venus

107-110. DESIGNS FOR THE FOUNTAIN OF VENUS

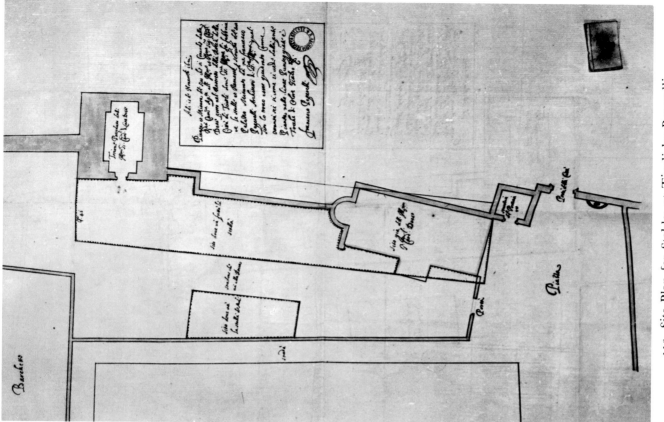

113. Site Plan for Stables at Tivoli by Peperelli

111. Venturini, Engraving of the Fountain of the Swans

112. Fountain of the Swans

114. Cyprus Circle

115. Venturini, Engraving of the Mete Sudanti

116. Fountain of the Bicchierone

117. Venturini, Engraving of the Water Organ

118. Venturini, Engraving of the Cascade of the Water Organ

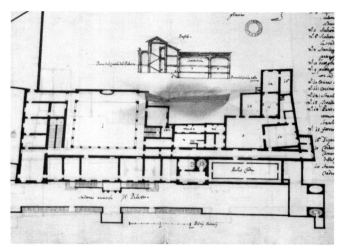

119a. Mattia de' Rossi, Plan of
the Villa d'Este, 1671

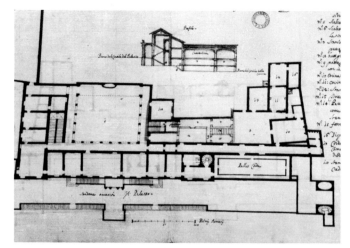

119b. Mattia de' Rossi, Plan of the Villa d'Este
with Added Leaf Showing New Service Rooms, 1671

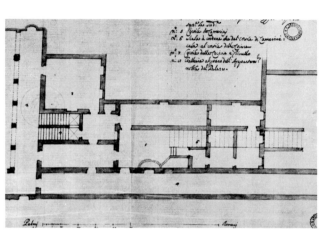

120. Mattia de' Rossi, Plan of the *Camerini*,
Second Project

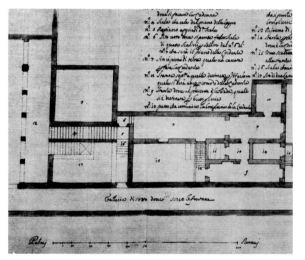

121. Mattia de' Rossi, Plan of the New
Service Rooms

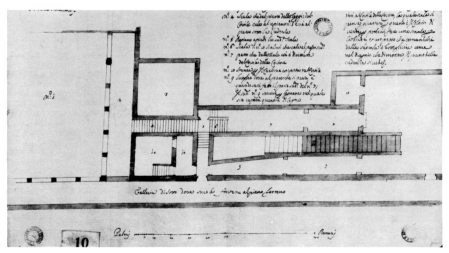

122. Mattia de' Rossi, Plan of Floor Below the New Service Rooms

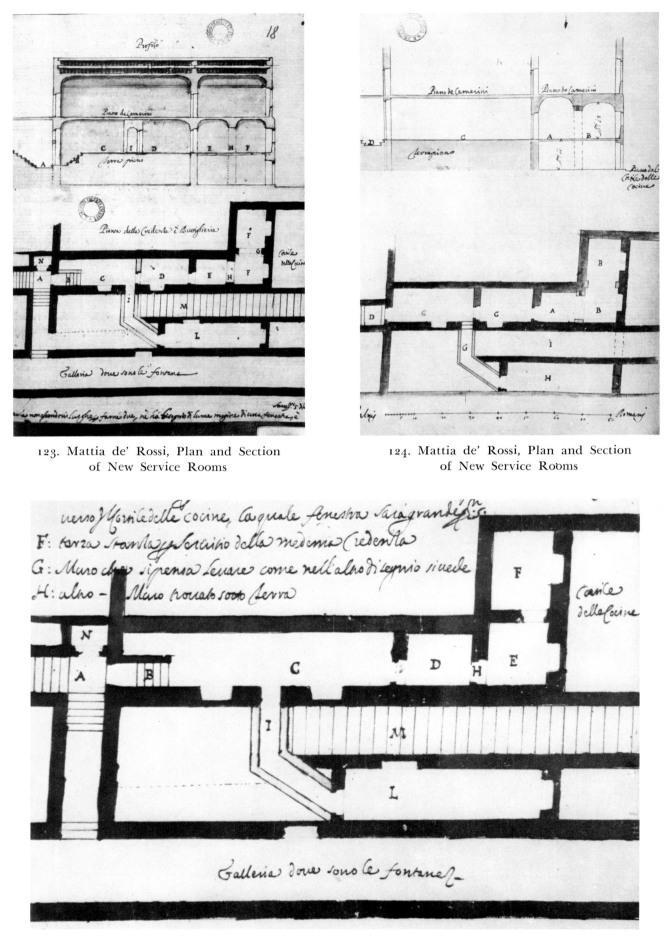

123. Mattia de' Rossi, Plan and Section
of New Service Rooms

124. Mattia de' Rossi, Plan and Section
of New Service Rooms

125. Mattia de' Rossi, Plan of New Service Rooms, Third Project

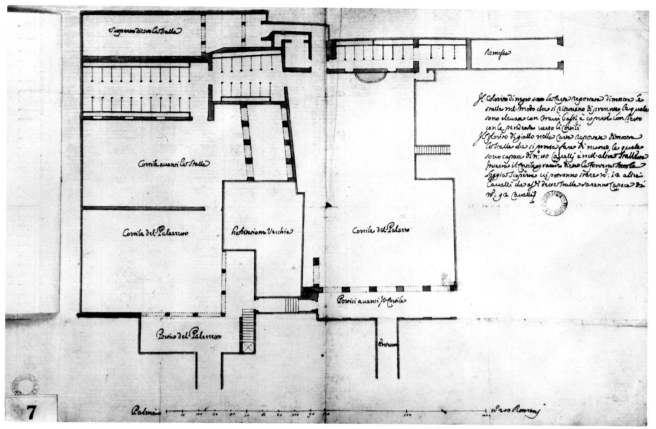

126a. Plan of Stables

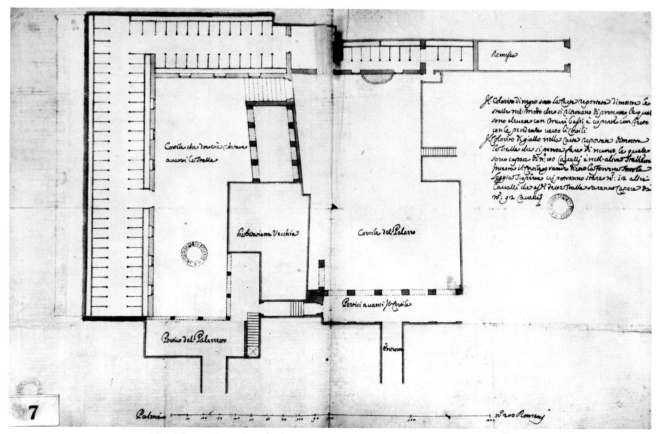

126b. Plan of Stables with Added Leaf Showing New Facilities

127a. Mattia de' Rossi, Drawing of the
Fountain of Rome

127b. Mattia de' Rossi, Drawing of the Fountain of
Rome with Added Leaf Showing Proposed Changes

128a. Mattia de' Rossi, Drawing of Tower
in Garden

128b. Mattia de' Rossi, Drawing of Tower with
Added Leaf Showing Proposed Change

129. Mattia de' Rossi, Drawing of Proposed Obelisk Fountain in Front of Villa

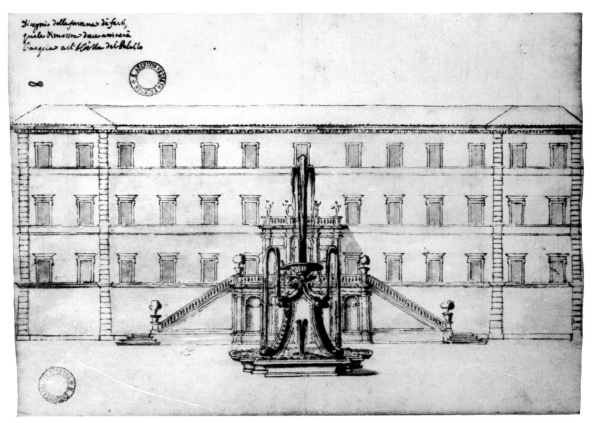

130. Mattia de' Rossi, Drawing of Proposed Fountain in Front of Villa

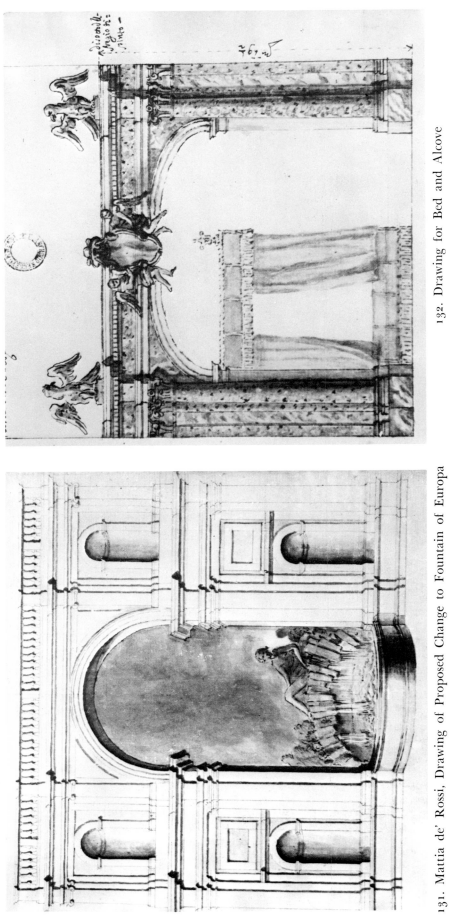

131. Mattia de' Rossi, Drawing of Proposed Change to Fountain of Europa

132. Drawing for Bed and Alcove

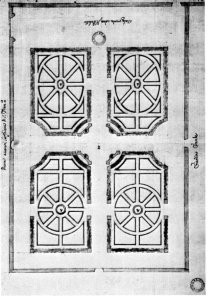

133. Mattia de' Rossi, Plan of Secret Garden

134. Dupérac, Engraving of Oval Fountain

135. Piranesi, Etching of the Villa d'Este

136. Fragonard, Drawing of the Villa d'Este

137. Fragonard, *Le Petit Parc*, based on a drawing depicting the Fountain of the Dragon